THE
SHOWMAN

THE
SHOWMAN

INSIDE THE INVASION THAT SHOOK THE WORLD
AND MADE A LEADER OF VOLODYMYR ZELENSKY

SIMON SHUSTER

wm

WILLIAM MORROW
An Imprint of HarperCollins*Publishers*

HarperCollins books may be purchased for educational, business, or sales promotional use. For information, please email the Special Markets Department at SPsales@harpercollins.com.

FIRST EDITION

Designed by Elina Cohen
Maps by Lon Tweeten

Library of Congress Cataloging-in-Publication Data has been applied for.

ISBN 978-0-06-330742-1

23 24 25 26 27 LBC 5 4 3 2 1

| TO NINA AND MARIE |

| CONTENTS |

Part IV

April 1, 2022

UKRAINE AFTER RUSSIA'S INITIAL ADVANCE

December 1, 2022

AFTER REPELLING RUSSIAN FORCES AND RECLAIMING TERRITORY

RUSSIAN CONTROL AND ADVANCES   UKRANIAN OFFENSIVES

THE
SHOWMAN

ON THE NIGHT WE FIRST MET, BACKSTAGE AT HIS COMEDY SHOW IN THE SPRING OF 2019, Volodymyr Zelensky looked more scared than I would see him for a while. It wasn't only stage fright, which often made him jittery before a performance. He looked half mute with fear that night, his lip clenched in his teeth, his eyes fixed on the floor as he paced around in his tuxedo, oblivious to the noise and the people around him. His bid to become the president of Ukraine was about three months old at the time, and the premiere of his new variety show was set to begin in less than an hour. Zelensky would play the lead role, the ringmaster in his peculiar brand of vaudeville, and millions of people would watch the broadcast on television, his medium of choice.

For the live event inside the Palace of Ukraine, the biggest concert hall in Kyiv, the good seats sold for more than the average Ukrainian earns in a month, and the entrance was mobbed when I arrived. It wasn't only Kyiv's high society waiting at the metal detectors to get inside. There were plenty of retirees, hipsters and office workers, young couples on expensive dates, the full range of the middle class that had formed in Ukraine since the collapse of the Soviet Union. They were all Zelensky's fans. Soon they would become his voters.

At the front of the crowd, one of his media advisers, Olha Rudenko, who would ride Zelensky's coattails into parliament that summer, pulled me through the door and showed me the way to get backstage, where the performers were already in costume. A few looked familiar from their movies, though it was hard to recognize anyone among the mass of producers and backup dancers, the actors jostling near the entrance to the stage, the makeup artists and the lighting techs, the choir of girls with crimped hair and white dresses. The older members of the troupe knew not to bother the star before showtime. "Give him a minute," Rudenko said when she saw me sidling up to Zelensky. "I'll introduce you when it's over."

He had a lot on his mind, much more than the night's performance. Earlier that day, someone had called in a bomb threat at the theater. The anonymous voice on the line said the building was rigged with explosives that would detonate in the middle of the show. It sounded like a hoax, and Zelensky told his troupe not to panic. Most likely, he figured, it was an overzealous supporter of one of the other candidates in the presidential race trying to sabotage his big premiere. Even so, the law required the theater to take precautions, and a few police officers had come with a canine unit to sniff around the coat check and concession stands. They found nothing suspicious, but the cops still advised the theater to call off the show. That afternoon, Zelensky conferred with the venue's management, and they decided to carry on. They didn't even inform the concertgoers of the danger. More than three thousand of them were in the hall by the time I got backstage, enough to start a stampede if Zelensky told them of the bomb threat. So he pretended everything was fine and allowed his audience to enjoy the act in ignorance.

Even the performers were not all aware of the danger. Backstage during the show, they sat around on costume trunks between their sketches, eating takeout and raising toasts. A handful of them had been performing with Zelensky for decades, and this would be his last big show before the elections pulled him through the looking glass from satire into politics. They knew he might never return, and they wondered whether he would take them along to the office of the president. "It's not that I want any job in particular," one of the comedians, Oleksandr Pikalov, said after pouring me a shot of whiskey in a plastic cup. "But I think I'd make a pretty good defense minister."

In his opening monologue, Zelensky leaned into the absurdity of his campaign, admitting that the jokes had not been easy for him to write. Lawyers had studied the script for violations of election law. There were limits to what he could say on television as the frontrunner in the race. He could not openly "agitate" for his viewers to vote a certain way, though the legal lines were blurry when it came to the use of irony and humor. "No campaigning," Zelensky told the audience with a wink and a laugh. "It's just a concert. Fair and square. Besides, you guys paid money for it." Before pausing for a breath to let the weirdness of it all sink in, he added, "The world has never seen such a thing."

The crowd found that hysterical. Comedian or candidate, it didn't matter. They seemed to love him in either role. When the show was over, Zelensky spent nearly an hour with his fans, taking photos with them and accepting their bouquets. He looked tired but happy, the anxiety having lifted from his features by the time one of his aides introduced us. His friends would later tell me about his addiction to the applause, the adulation. He had just received another dose of it, and it showed in the ease of his smile and the slope of his shoulders. "Going onstage gives me two emotions," he once said of these moments. "First comes the fear, and only when you overcome the fear, the pleasure kicks in. That's what always drew me back out there." For all his life he had been chasing that feeling, ever since he started doing comedy as a teenager, and it struck me as strange that he would now abandon everything he'd built.

Politics might have its moments, but the response Zelensky was accustomed to getting from the crowds at his performances, from the soldiers he went to entertain at the front, from the journalists who invited him onto their morning shows to talk about his movies—none of that would follow him into the presidency. His life was about to get a lot less fun and a lot more complicated. He would no longer be a movie star. No matter how much he might try to resist the metamorphosis, the job would turn him sooner or later into the thing he claimed to despise: a politician.

For a start, the media would question him, then turn on him. There would be gaffes and scandals, budgets to balance and weapons to procure. Worst of all, there'd be a war to fight. By the start of 2019, when Zelensky launched his campaign for the presidency, Ukraine had been at war with Russia for five years over control of its eastern regions. Dead soldiers came back in caskets from the fighting almost every week. More than 10,000 people had already been killed by the time Zelensky entered politics. Did he really want that job? Was he even vaguely ready for it? Even if he was, why would he give up his life as an actor and drift further from the people he loved—his wife, his friends, the business they had built together? Was it the power he wanted? Was he bored?

Zelensky had no clever or convincing answers to such questions when we went back to his dressing room to talk that night after the show. Standing there, he glanced at his own reflection in the Hollywood mirror. To his left the costume rack was laden with pressed tuxedoes that took up most of the space, leaving us nowhere to sit. So he leaned his weight on the makeup table and answered my question with a question. "They're all snobs, or what?" he said, referring to the leaders of the world. "None of them are any fun?"

It sounded like a joke, but he insisted he was serious. He would only meet with the fun ones, and he would send "professionals" to deal with the rest. "I don't want to change my life," he said. "I don't want to become politically correct. That's not my thing." Maybe it was hubris, or maybe he was ignorant of what the job would take. But he seemed to believe that leadership would not require him to change. His life as a showman had taught him what he needed to play the role of president, and he was intent on remaining the person his experience had forged. "If you lose yourself," he said, "you'll sink into the swamp."

It was getting late. He looked spent, and his friends were waiting for him at the after party. Before we said goodbye, I asked him about the bomb threat. What did he make of it? "Well there's the answer to your first question," he said, meaning the one about his motives in running for office. The political class in Kyiv had devolved into a bunch of pranksters and hooligans, he said. They were on track to blow up the economy within a few years. The senseless war in eastern Ukraine was bleeding the country dry. He carried on for a while, with jokes and metaphors, about the need to save Ukraine from its current leaders, describing them as a threat to everything he had spent his life creating. "If I didn't run for office, all of this might be gone soon," he said, waving at the mirror and the costume rack. "Just like that," he said. "Gone."

❖

That night, and in the months that followed, it never occurred to me that I might one day write a book about Zelensky. Now it seems obvious that our meeting at the Palace of Ukraine opened the door for me to write this one. It was the moment when Zelensky's team first allowed me backstage and into his entourage. After he won the elections later that spring, I continued to cover his administration for *Time*. I followed him as he struggled to govern, to manage relations with Donald Trump's White House, and to negotiate a lasting peace with Russia under Vladimir Putin. I followed him as his talks with Putin broke down and the Russians prepared a full-scale invasion, and I stayed as close as possible once that invasion began.

Throughout that period of several years, when I would come home from a reporting trip to Kyiv, people would often ask me, What's he like? My answers evolved over time, as did his character. On the campaign trail he struck me as a naive charmer preparing to enter a world of cynics, oligarchs, and thugs who took him for an easy mark, and not without reason. By the time we met again in the presidential compound in the fall of 2019, he had absorbed some of the poison from that world and burned off a lot of his innocence. But the experience of power hadn't hardened him, at least not yet, and not nearly enough to prepare him for confronting Putin face to face.

The greatest changes in Zelensky, the ones that became a central focus of this book, took place in the first few months of the Russian invasion of Ukraine, when he turned into a wartime president unique to our age of instant information. Stubborn, confident, vengeful, impolitic, brave to the point of recklessness, resistant to pressure, and unsparing toward those who stood in his way, he channeled the anger and resilience of his people and expressed it with clarity and purpose to the world, becoming a symbol of the kind of fortitude all leaders hope they can muster when called. But it was the showmanship he honed over more than twenty years as an actor on the stage and a producer in the movie business that made Zelensky so effective in fighting this war—a war that required Ukraine not only to hold the world's attention but to win the sympathy of people and their governments across the globe. Technology gave him the means to do that job. In public his friends and staffers said Zelensky always had the qualities to do it well. Privately they would admit to feeling shocked by his new self. Most Ukrainians did not believe he had it in him. Neither did I.

His success as a leader in the first hours of the invasion relied on the fact that courage is contagious. It spread through Ukraine's political ranks as everyone realized the president had stuck around. The other officials responsible for keeping the state together mostly fell in line behind him after that. Instead of running for their lives, many Ukrainians grabbed whatever weapons they could find and ran to defend their towns and cities against an invading force armed with tanks and fighter jets.

How much credit does Zelensky deserve for that defense? He was informed at the start of the invasion that the Russians aimed to capture Kyiv and unseat his government, and he gave orders to stop them by any means available. But the Armed Forces of Ukraine did not need his dispensation to defend the capital. The machinery of their resistance was already in motion, and Zelensky was not at the wheel. He had spent months downplaying the risk of a full-scale war, even as U.S. intelligence agencies warned that it was imminent. When it started, he gave the military brass the freedom to lead on the battlefield, while he focused on the dimension of the war where he could be most effective: keeping Ukraine in the headlines, and persuading the world to help.

These aims would drive him through the early months of the invasion, and they shaped the way he responded to my plan for writing this book. He was ambivalent about it. In the middle of a war, Zelensky needed his message to reach the world in seconds, and social media gave him that power. So did television. Books take far too long, and he made clear to me on more than one occasion that mine seemed a little premature. Three years into his presidency and barely halfway through his forties, he felt he had not lived or achieved enough to be the focus of a biography. "I'm not that old yet," he once told me with a smile. As long as the war in Ukraine continued, he also found it hard to see how a book about the war might end. When we first talked about it in his office in Kyiv in the spring of 2022, on the fifty-fifth day of the Russian invasion, he asked when I would plan to finish the book, and I told him my aim would be to capture roughly the first year of the war and then publish. His face fell when he heard me say that. "You think the war will not be over in a year?"

In the end it took well over a year to finish the book, and still the war raged on. By the one-year mark it had claimed hundreds of thousands of lives, uprooted millions in Ukraine, and shattered the world's illusions about the permanence of peace in Europe three decades after the end of the Cold War. Even though Zelensky and I both hoped this war would end in a decisive victory for Ukrainians, and that Russia's attempt to subjugate or annihilate its neighbor would result in justice for the war criminals in Moscow, Zelensky knew as well as anyone that the balance of forces was not in his favor. In any case, he let me carry on with my reporting.

If the epicenter of this war had a physical location, a set of coordinates, they would probably lead to Zelensky's offices in the government quarter of Kyiv, to the presidential compound at 11 Bankova Street, through its barricaded gates and into its dim and outdated rooms. The president and his team agreed to let me spend much of my time there during the first year of the invasion, observing the way they worked and interviewing them about the state of affairs at the front, the tensions inside their administration, about their hopes, plans, fears and memories. After a while the place began to feel familiar, at times almost normal despite the air-raid sirens, and the staffers got used to seeing me around. We cracked jokes, drank coffee, waited for meetings to start or end, and we relied on the soldiers, our ever-present chaperones, to warn us of threats and guide us around, shining flashlights down dark corridors, past the rooms where they slept on the floor.

Some of Zelensky's aides, in particular the ones responsible for his security, did not always appreciate the access the president gave me, especially on the days when he invited me to travel with him to the front. He never explained his reasons for doing that. His staff only said that he trusted me to write an honest account. By then he knew my work, and he understood that I would not be coming at this project from afar. I've been reporting in Kyiv, on and off, since 2009, practically my entire career as a journalist, and the city has become a second home. Half my family is Ukrainian. The other half is Russian. My father grew up in central Ukraine, not far from Zelensky's hometown. He met my mother in a suburb of Moscow, where we lived for the first six years of my life before fleeing to the United States in 1989, two years before the collapse of the Soviet Union. At home in San Francisco, I grew up speaking Russian, which gave me a language in common with Zelensky.

On Bankova Street, the central aims of my reporting were to record the history of the war as it unfolded, to understand the events that led up to the Russian invasion, and to chronicle the way Zelensky and his team experienced it. To my frustration, they did not keep diaries or careful records of these events, at least none that they agreed to share with me, while the text messages and photos they showed me on their phones captured little of their emotions, their exhaustion, and fear. The president had a habit of responding to their texts with a thumbs-up emoji, which his aides had trouble interpreting. When the topic turned to his inner world, he could be vague and taciturn, inclined to reassuring banter or deflections that obscured the way the war had changed him.

Over time he revealed a lot about himself, but our interviews would not be enough for me to write this book, not without the accounts of his friends and enemies, his advisers, ministers, members of his staff and, perhaps most of all, his wife, First Lady Olena Zelenska. She did more than anyone else to clarify the record and, on plenty of occasions, correct her husband's recollection of events. Taken together, the stories I heard from all these sources, all these witnesses, revealed much more about Zelensky's wartime leadership than he ever could. Sometimes, in the middle of a story, he would call his bodyguard or one of his aides to check the details. They often remembered things differently.

Memories are like that. They tend to deceive us, and some of those deceptions have probably made it into this book despite my best efforts to weed them out. Some of the mistakes will be mine, because I misunderstood someone or recorded the details wrong. Sometimes the memories of the participants will prove inaccurate, including those of the president. I would not blame them for it. As one of his close advisers told me of the invasion in its early weeks, "Every new day completely erased the one that came before—where you were, what was happening." It seems to be a common reflex in a time of mortal danger. The mind devotes its power to surviving, not recording.

Although I witnessed many of the events described in this book, many others were recounted to me by the people involved. Some of them spoke to me during these events or very soon afterward, when the memories were still fresh, and before their stories settled into an accepted narrative of what had happened. I did my best to verify their accounts with multiple sources, and to include the accounts that are most revealing and important to the public understanding of the war. To the best of my knowledge, they are all true.

What they reveal about Zelensky is not always flattering. Sometimes his laudable qualities, such as his bravery, put him in greater danger than seemed necessary for his cause. Sometimes, while following him around, I wished he felt more of the fear I had seen in his face that night at the Palace of Ukraine. Fear can protect us. It can also make us run away, and the president's ability to manage it, to conquer it, has a lot to do with the way Ukraine survived this threat to its existence. Maybe a different path in life would have prepared him better to lead his country through the war. But now, looking back, I'm not so sure.

Part I

CHAPTER 1

DAYBREAK

VOLODYMYR ZELENSKY FELT NO DEEP ATTACHMENT TO THE HOME HE LEFT BEHIND when the invasion started. For a year and a half it served as a convenient place for him and his family to live, with a separate house on the grounds for their bodyguards and a few acres of land to run the dogs till they were tired. On a normal day, his trip home from work would take less than thirty minutes from the center of Kyiv, just far enough to escape the noise of the city and breathe clean air before going to bed. But the house itself—with a neoclassical facade of yellow stone, situated on lot number 29 in the gated community of Koncha-Zaspa—seemed overly grand to the former comedian, bordering on ostentatious. It felt, in a word, too presidential for Zelensky.

It also made him seem like a hypocrite. When he took office in the spring of 2019, at the age of forty-one, the president made a promise not to live in the properties reserved for government officials in Ukraine, especially not the one in Koncha-Zaspa, among the most palatial of the bunch. Its floor plan featured a billiard room, a home theater, and a separate wing with an indoor pool beneath an elegant glass dome. Previous heads of state had used the villa and filled it with gaudy furniture. Zelensky, in his career as a comedian, mocked them for it. "Guys, how about we let some kids live in these residences," he said while running for president. "It's like when you travel around Europe on those tours and you see the old residences of some big kings," he said. "What is that now? It's all for touring." Yet here he was, not touring these rooms but living in them, coming home each day through an entrance where a pair of lions sat carved in stone, life-sized, their color matching the columns of the portico. Here he was greeting his kids beneath the soaring entryway and climbing the marble staircase to his bedroom.

For a man who had spent his entire life as an actor, capable of switching roles as quickly as his stagehands could change the scenery for his next sketch, Zelensky chafed at the big and kingly role of president. It grated against the persona he had spent decades cultivating on the screen and stage, the grinning gagman, the tireless charmer, the backslapping believer that all would be right with the world in the end. Standing around five and a half feet tall, with glinting eyes that bulged a little beneath his dark, expressive eyebrows, Zelensky knew that his success in both comedy and politics relied on his ability to play that role, to seem relatable, normal, like one of the guys. Millions of people in Ukraine had watched that figure mature over the years into his generation's greatest satirist, one whose wit had a way of winning any audience by nailing politicians to the wall. When it came to preserving that image, the residence at Koncha-Zaspa did Zelensky no favors. It had been built for politicians, not political comedians, and the president had trouble calling it his home. "For me it's like a hotel, otherwise I wouldn't use it," he said, making excuses, after his family moved there in the summer of 2020.

The press never forgave him for it. Right up until the day when he became a wartime president, virtually immune from criticism, reporters loved to remind Zelensky of the most famous lines he ever delivered in his career on television. In the defining scene of his most popular sitcom, the one that served as his path to the presidency, Zelensky's character, a high school history teacher, goes on a rant about the greed of the political elites and, in particular, their lavish homes:

THESE MOTHERFUCKERS COME TO POWER, AND ALL THEY DO IS STEAL AND TALK SHIT, TALK SHIT AND STEAL. IT'S THE SAME SHIT EVERY TIME, AND NO-BODY GIVES A FUCK! YOU DON'T GIVE A FUCK. I DON'T GIVE A FUCK. NONE OF US GIVES A FUCK, NOT EVEN A LITTLE TINY BIT OF A FUCK. BUT IF I HAD JUST ONE WEEK IN OFFICE, JUST ONE WEEK, I'D SHOW THEM ALL. FUCK THE MOTORCADES! FUCK THE PERKS! FUCK THE FUCKING CHALETS! FUCK ALL YOU MOTHERFUCKERS! FOR ONCE, LET'S HAVE A SIMPLE TEACHER LIVE LIKE A PRESI-DENT, AND LET THE FUCKING PRESIDENT LIVE LIKE A TEACHER.

That speech, which first aired in Ukraine in 2015, was the birth cry of Zelensky's career as a politician. It propelled him into office and haunted him afterward, and it helps explain why he was not a popular leader during the third winter of his presidency, when Russian troops surrounded Ukraine from the north, east, and south. He was a frustrated leader who had promised peace and failed to deliver it. He was an upstart who'd thought he could govern a nation of forty-four million people the way he had run his movie studio. He was a reformer who'd promised to evict the politicians from their mansions. Yet on that awful night, when the sound of Russian bombs woke the residents of Koncha-Zaspa, there was Zelensky in his mansion, bathed in soft light from the chandelier.

❖

Upstairs, the house was quiet when the bombing started. The first ones to make much fuss about it were the animals. The German shepherd stirred and began to pace around. So did the family parrot, a nervous bird named Kesha, who lived at a window near the kitchen downstairs. Around four thirty a.m. on the morning of February 24, 2022, the disquiet of the pets reached up to the president's bedroom, where the First Lady, Olena Zelenska, was still asleep. It took a few moments for her to register the low booms coming through the windows. They sounded like fireworks at first. Then her eyes flipped open and, reaching over in the dark, she found that her husband's side of the bed was empty. The president stood in the adjoining room, preparing to go to work, already dressed in a dark gray suit. When she found him there, the look of confusion on her face made Zelensky utter one word to her in Russian, the language they most often spoke at home. "*Nachalos*," he said. *It's started.*

She understood what he meant. The news in Ukraine had been warning for months of an impending war. Talk shows had been debating which officials and lawmakers were most likely to flee. One program offered advice on what to pack in an emergency suitcase before setting out as a refugee. Some of the most severe predictions came from Ukraine's Western allies, especially the U.S. intelligence services, which had concluded that Russia planned to invade from three directions, and was likely to overrun the capital in a matter of days. The Russian aim, they said, was to seize most of the country and remove Zelensky's government from power.

To many Ukrainians, these predictions had sounded absurd. The attack, if it came, was not expected to go beyond the border regions in the east. For about eight years, Ukraine and Russia had been fighting a protracted war over two separatist regions in eastern Ukraine. Few in Kyiv believed the latest escalation would spill too far beyond those regions. Even fewer believed it would ever reach their homes. Until the final hours, Zelensky did not believe it, either. He did not warn his wife to prepare. Only on the eve of the invasion, the First Lady made a note to pack a suitcase or at least collect the family's passports and other documents. But she never got around to it. The day had passed too quickly, as it often did, in a rush of routines and errands. She did chores and homework with the kids. They had dinner and watched TV.

The president came home well after midnight, and he said nothing to make his wife believe they were in danger. He felt pretty sure their home would be safe, and it had never been his style to worry her. More often he veiled his concerns behind jokes and smiles, then made excuses when she learned what he was hiding. That night they went to bed without making any wartime plans, and they slept for just a few hours before the bombing started. Now, from the look in his eyes, the First Lady understood that things were far worse than she had imagined.

"Emotionally," she later said, "he was like the string on a guitar," his nerves stretched to the point of snapping. But she does not remember any confusion or fear on his face. "He was completely together, focused." So focused, it seems, that he missed his chance to wake his children and say goodbye to them. He only asked his wife to tell them what had happened, and he promised to call her later with instructions for what to do next. "We were still processing," she said. "We never thought something like this could happen, because all the talk about war had just been talk." The sound of the explosions outside had jolted them into a new reality, and they both needed more than a brief moment at the top of the stairs to adjust to it. "He had nothing else to say," she later told me of this exchange, one of the last they would have in private for months. "And I didn't know what to ask."

❖

Outside, the president hopped the few steps to the driveway and got into his waiting motorcade. The metal gate slid open, and his driver eased onto the tree-lined road through Koncha-Zaspa, heading north. Only a few cars made their way into the city that early, but in the other direction the traffic had started to thicken. Many of those with the luck and foresight to have their bags packed and a tank full of gas tried to leave Kyiv as soon as the explosions started. By noon there would be gridlock on every road out of town.

For now, Zelensky passed the usual scenery of his drive to work along the E40 highway, the soccer field on his right, a chapel with its golden domes to the left, the billboards hawking condominiums at every exit. It was the last time in many months that he would see these things in their peaceful state, all the bridges intact, free of military checkpoints, the roads not littered with tank traps and twisted metal. Within a day or two, Kyiv would again resemble a fortress, returning to the state of siege that had formed so much of its history. For a millennium and a half, the empires of Europe have fought over this ancient city on the banks of the Dnipro River. The Vikings, Ottomans, Mongols, Lithuanians, and Poles had all laid claim to Kyiv, its centers of trade and scholarship, its monasteries and cathedrals. The Russians first sacked the city in the twelfth century. Now they were making another attempt.

In the back of the car, Zelensky was quiet, his gaze fixed on his phone. A flood of calls and messages poured in as the motorcade raced through the darkness. One of the first calls came that morning from his friend Denys Monastyrsky, the minister in charge of the national police and the border guard service. He was a couple years younger than Zelensky but looked older and tougher, with the carriage of a prizefighter. For the last three days, Monastyrsky had been sleeping in his office at the Ministry of Internal Affairs, waiting for signs of the Russian assault, and it now fell to him to inform the president that it had started.

Zelensky asked him where exactly, what direction of attack the Kremlin had chosen.

"All of them," said Monastyrsky.

All along the eastern and northern borders, enemy forces pounded Ukrainian positions with artillery, multiple-rocket launchers, and aerial bombs. Russian fighter jets swooped down over the major cities, aiming to take out Ukraine's air defenses and dominate the skies. There was a silence on the line. The president needed a moment to process the information. Then he uttered a phrase that Monastyrsky would long remember: "Beat them back."

That kind of confidence, even in the face of very long odds, had always been one of Zelensky's strong suits. But in that moment it seemed misplaced, verging on the delusional. He knew Ukraine lacked the means to beat the Russians back. At best it could hold them off for a few days, hopefully long enough for the military and political leadership to get their bearings, mobilize resources, and salvage the parts of the country that would not be overrun in the first wave of the attack. Through his actions before the invasion, Zelensky bore at least some of the blame for the flimsy state of the nation's defenses. He had spent weeks playing down the risk of a full-scale invasion and assuring his people that all would be fine. He had refused the advice of his military commanders to call up all available reserves and use them to fortify the border. Apart from the calamity of the invasion itself, the president would need to face his own failure to foresee it. But that would come later. For the moment, he would need to contend with what lay ahead, with the Russian tanks and warplanes, the missiles flying over Ukrainian cities, colliding with the homes of his citizens, leaving them buried under the rubble.

He would recall those first minutes of the war as a series of disjointed sounds and images, many of them faint or unreliable. Fragments, Zelensky called them: "Some things come back to me in a fragmentary way." He was never at the wheel of the car that morning, but it felt to him like he was driving at such high speed that the world blurred at the edges of his vision. He forced himself to ignore it. "It's a question of focus," he later told me. "If you get distracted by someone running in front of your windshield, shining lights, screaming, waving their hands, or loud music or a jingle playing on the radio, if you let all that distract you, then your chances of getting where you need to go—to your interim goal, let's call it that—they are low. Not quite zero, but they are very low."

The goal in that moment was to reach his office on Bankova Street, though it was not the safest place for him to be. The presidential compound sits at the center of a tightly packed neighborhood, surrounded by apartment buildings, busy cafes, and cobblestone alleys lined with boutiques. The nearest flats were close enough to Zelensky's office for someone to lob a grenade through the window. When he arrived at around five a.m., the streets seemed busy for that hour. People were preparing to escape, bringing down their suitcases and pets, clicking their kids into car seats. Zelensky's bodyguards had no idea whether one of the cars parked at the curb could have been loaded with explosives by Russian saboteurs. Around his residence in Koncha-Zaspa, there was at least a security perimeter and a metal gate. The presidential compound in the center of Kyiv had no such safeguards, but Zelensky insisted on going there first. It is the seat of presidential power, and his message was the same for the senior aides and ministers who called or texted him that morning: GO TO THE OFFICE. I'LL MEET YOU THERE.

❖

Oleksiy Danilov, the secretary of the National Security and Defense Council, did not need the president to tell him where to go. He was among the few officials in Zelensky's circle who believed the warnings of an imminent invasion. At times the prospect seemed to excite Danilov at least as much as it terrified him. He believed in his gut that Ukrainians would mount a ferocious defense, and he wanted to be at its forefront. A sullen figure, with a broad paunch and a pair of glasses set at the end of his nose, Danilov, at fifty-nine, was well over a decade older and much more experienced in affairs of state than most of Zelensky's senior advisers, who often rolled their eyes at Danilov's advice the way one might do behind the back of a bloviating uncle. It was hard to blame them. Though he held no military rank, Danilov liked to carry himself like an aging guerrilla commander, even wearing a self-styled uniform, all in black, with a patch on his breast that bore his surname.

On the morning of the invasion, he was already dressed when the first Russian missile struck an air base near his home on the outskirts of Kyiv, close enough to rattle his windows. The strike, as he later recalled it, gave him an unexpected feeling of relief. His wife and son had already left the city in anticipation of the war, and Danilov found it agonizing to live alone with the expectation that an attack could begin at any time. Now the wait was over, and he knew what to do, what mechanisms of defense to set in motion. The weather in Kyiv had been fair that week, far outside the norm for the end of winter in Ukraine. But as Danilov drove to the presidential compound in his armored Land Cruiser, the mist gave way to rain, and he flicked on the windshield wipers with a smile. Ukrainians often say rainy weather brings good luck.

When he pulled up to Bankova Street, Danilov took note of the time—5:11 a.m.—and stomped up the stairs toward Zelensky's office. It surprised him to see the president dressed in a fresh white shirt. The choice seemed out of place and somewhat out of character. Zelensky had been known to come to work in his lucky green-and-black sweater, which resembled something from a *Star Trek* convention. But on this day, of all days, he decided not to keep it casual. He was dressed as though he were about to go onstage. The other surprise was Zelensky's demeanor. He was calm, his voice steady, the lids low over his eyes. The first wartime remark he made to Danilov was the same he had made to his wife about an hour earlier: "It's started." Then he asked a pro-fane question that is difficult to translate from the Russian. Roughly, it means: "Let's kick some ass?"*

Just then, the Russians were doing most of the ass-kicking. The open-ing phase of their invasion involved around seventy thousand troops and seven thousand armored vehicles advancing toward Kyiv from the north, along both sides of the Dnipro River, which runs through the city. It appeared to be a blitzkrieg, similar to the assaults the Kremlin had deployed over the years to devastating effect. During Operation Whirl-wind, Soviet forces took less than four days in 1956 to occupy the capital of Hungary and overthrow its government, whose leader was then ar-rested, tortured, found guilty of treason in a secret trial, and, two years later, executed on the gallows. The Soviet invasion of Czechoslovakia in 1968 took two days to overrun the country and capture Prague, while Soviet special forces needed just a few hours on the evening of December 27, 1979, to storm a heavily fortified palace in Kabul and assassinate the leader of Afghanistan.

Danilov, an avid reader of military history, kept such precedents in mind as he tried to envision the Kremlin's plan for the conquest of Ukraine. He did not believe the Russians could seize and hold the entire country. It was too big, its territory nearly twice the size of Germany, and the will of its people to resist would not allow for a swift occupation. What worried Danilov was the Kabul scenario, a lightning raid on the presidential compound to capture or kill the head of state. For days be-fore the invasion started, Ukraine's intelligence services had been track-ing three groups of assassins tasked with killing Zelensky. All of them

---

* In the original, he asked, "будем хуячиться?"—a standard phrase in a street brawler's lexicon.

came from the region of Chechnya, in southern Russia, home to some of Putin's most ruthless and loyal commandos. "We'd been watching them for a while," Danilov later told me. "And we had specific information that they had been assigned to liquidate our president." The daily intelligence brief Danilov received on February 22, two days before the invasion, included detailed warnings about the plot, and Danilov had taken the top secret document to Zelensky's office that evening to inform him of the danger. But the president brushed it off. He refused to believe that in the twenty-first century, three decades after the end of the Cold War, hit men would try to hunt down a sitting European head of state. Nor could he imagine that Putin would start a full-scale war, a land invasion on a scale that Europe had not seen in generations.

"At the time we thought these were threats," Zelensky later told the BBC. "We talked to the intelligence agencies, with our own and those of our partners. Everyone saw the risks differently." Some of his allies in Europe, including the leaders of France and Germany, assured him that the American predictions of an invasion were overblown. "They called back and told me, 'We talked to Putin. Putin will not invade.'"

They were wrong. At exactly five a.m., Kyiv time, the Kremlin released a video on its website announcing the start of the invasion. The footage showed Vladimir Putin seated in a wood-paneled office, his eyes red and mouth dry, both hands holding the edge of his desk as though he needed to steady himself. The list of enemies and grievances he listed to justify the war went back decades, and he never uttered the name "Zelensky" in that speech. Nor did Putin set Ukraine as his ultimate target. In the first twenty minutes of his declaration of war, he focused instead on the United States, the wars it had waged in Yugoslavia, Libya, and Iraq, and the "fundamental threats" he said it posed to Russia.

Ever since the fall of the Soviet Union, he said, the U.S. had welcomed more and more European nations into the NATO alliance, expanding what Putin described as an "empire of lies" ever closer to Russia's borders. NATO military bases now dotted the parts of Europe that Putin saw as his rightful dominion, and he would not allow Ukraine to follow that path and achieve its goal of joining the alliance. "On our historical territory," he said, referring to the territory of Ukraine, the U.S. and its allies had created "a hostile anti-Russia." Sooner or later, they would use Ukraine to launch a war against Russia itself, and it would be "irresponsible," he said, for the Russian military not to strike first and neutralize the threat.

The speech, like many of Putin's rants against the West over the years, dripped with falsehoods and paranoia. In reality, the U.S. and its European allies had long refused to offer Ukraine a clear path to joining their alliance. NATO leaders had spent a decade and a half stalling Ukraine's requests for membership, and their fears of antagonizing Putin kept them from arming Ukraine with the weapons it needed to defend itself. Some of those fears were no doubt justified. If Zelensky's path to power in 2019 relied on his fame as a comedian, Putin's rise two decades earlier had relied on his victory in a war against Chechnya, a breakaway statelet in southern Russia whose cities he bombed into oblivion in 1999 and 2000, killing tens of thousands of civilians in the process. That vicious subjugation of the people of Chechnya, along with the assassination of their leaders, set the tone for much of Putin's reign, and it foreshadowed his attempt to do the same in Ukraine. While Western leaders wrung their hands and weighed the risk of escalation, Putin made up his mind to strike at Kyiv, leaving no room in his speech for the world to question his intentions. The leadership in Ukraine, he said, were a bunch of genocidal neo-Nazis, and he aimed to overthrow their government, to "demilitarize and de-Nazify" their country. For any foreign nation that tried to stand in his way, Putin issued a veiled warning to respond with nuclear weapons. "Whoever tries to hinder us," he said, "or threaten our country or our people, should know that Russia's response will be immediate and will lead you to consequences that you have never faced in your history. We are ready for any turn of events. All necessary decisions in this regard have been made. I hope that I will be heard."

No one could tell in those first hours of the invasion whether Zelensky and his team would stick around. The military and intelligence services spent months gaming out scenarios for the invasion, but their projections could never resolve that question. Would the president panic? Would the fear of death scramble his ability to lead? "It's the one factor you can never calculate," Danilov later told me. "Before you find yourself in that situation, there is no way to tell how you will react."

Historical precedent favored the pessimists. Only six months before the invasion of Ukraine, the president of Afghanistan, Ashraf Ghani—a much more experienced leader than Zelensky—abandoned his capital as Taliban fighters approached. One of Zelensky's predecessors, Viktor Yanukovych, ran away from Kyiv as protestors closed in on his office during the revolution of 2014. Early in the Second World War, the leaders of Albania, Belgium, Czechoslovakia, Greece, Poland, the Netherlands, Norway, and Yugoslavia, among others, fled the advance of the German Wehrmacht and lived out the war in exile. Even Ivan the Terrible, the first Russian ruler to call himself a tsar, ran away from Moscow when the Ottomans and their regional allies attacked the city in 1571.

Little if anything about Zelensky's biography suggested he might do otherwise. He had never served in the military or shown much interest in its affairs. His professional instincts derived from a lifetime as an actor on the stage, a specialist in improv comedy, and a producer in the TV and movie business. His experience as a statesman added up to about two years and nine months, less than the time it takes to earn a bachelor's degree in international affairs. For just about anyone in his position, the urge to flee would seem as natural as the urge to live. A few Russian bombs of the sort raining down on Ukrainian military bases that morning would be enough to destroy much of the government quarter, demolishing the houses of parliament and the Cabinet of Ministers, both of which stand just down the street from the presidential compound. This part of town, sometimes called the Triangle, has never been easy to defend. The protestors who chased Yanukovych from power in 2014 managed to seize parts of it with little more than shields and sticks. Now the authorities were facing the prospect of Russian tanks rolling through town. When Danilov started calling around to government officials, it did not surprise him to learn that some had turned off their phones, packed up their cars, and headed toward the western border as soon as the bombing started. "A lot of them started to panic," he said.

The worst defections affected Ukraine's main intelligence agency, known as the SBU. "Especially in the upper and middle ranks, there were a lot of problems," another one of Zelensky's top security advisers told me. "A lot of people from the security structures were like, 'Let's get out of here. Resistance is futile. The Russians will beat us.'" Their exodus gutted the agency's ranks. Dozens of its officers went over to the

side of the invaders, effectively handing over the keys to parts of southern Ukraine. But the leadership in Kyiv, for the most part, stood firm,
and Danilov had no trouble gathering a quorum of the security council
within an hour of his arrival on Bankova Street.

One of the first officials he managed to reach was the speaker of the
parliament, Ruslan Stefanchuk, who would play a critical role in those
early hours. If Zelensky were to be killed, Stefanchuk was next in line
to take command. He was also in charge of convening the national legislature, the Verkhovna Rada, home of the democracy that Russia had
set out to destroy. A tall and heavyset man, weighing well over three
hundred pounds, Stefanchuk was out of breath by the time he made it
from his home to Bankova Street. He had known the president longer
than almost anyone in his administration. On the comedy circuit in
the 1990s, Stefanchuk performed as part of a troupe called The Three
Fat Guys, which played the same stages as Zelensky. When they greeted
each other in the president's office, Stefanchuk was struck by the look on
his old friend's face, like a mirror reflection of his own. "It wasn't fear,"
he later told me. "It was a question, 'How could this be?'" The speaker
and the president both recognized that an all-out war had started, but
neither of them could grasp the totality of what it meant. "Maybe these
words sound vague or pompous," Stefanchuk said, "but we sensed the
order of the world collapsing."

Around six a.m., the security council convened inside Zelensky's office
on the fourth floor of the compound, with the president seated at the
head of the conference table, facing the door. A brief report from the
military commanders provided a sense of the invasion's scale. Its main
target appeared to be Kyiv, where missiles had struck a military command post, an ammunition depot, a garrison of the National Guard,
and other targets. Of all the possible scenarios for the invasion, Russia
had chosen the most aggressive, and Zelensky felt he had no choice but
to impose martial law across the country. The security council quickly
agreed. No one raised any objections. Under the circumstances, it felt
like a formality, but the decision would carry enormous consequences
in the months ahead. The terms of martial law, as laid out in Ukraine's
Constitution, grant the president vast powers to rule by decree, suspend-

ing elections and other democratic rights and freedoms of Ukrainians for the duration of the war. Curfews could be imposed, and every man of fighting age, between eighteen and sixty, would be subject to conscription and forbidden from leaving the country. The normal functions of parliament would be put on hold, while the assets of state companies and all private property would be subject to requisition in the interest of national defense.

Once Zelensky approved these measures, Stefanchuk rushed down the street to enact them during an emergency session of parliament. He had considered several places for the legislators to gather that morning. The parliament building, with its iconic glass dome, seemed particularly vulnerable to a Russian attack from the air. Among the alternative venues was an auditorium beneath the Motherland Monument, a hulking statue from the Soviet era that stood over a hundred meters tall and could at least absorb the impact of a missile. But Stefanchuk decided to scrap that idea. He did not want to create the impression that the lawmakers had left their posts, so he told them all to gather in the plenary hall, the same place where they would normally debate budget bills and education policy.

Some of them had already skipped town. Others had trouble reaching the parliament building by car. Around the government district, soldiers and volunteers had begun erecting barricades, blocking some roads with dump trucks and public buses. Long lines formed outside banks and gas stations throughout the city, and the central train station was swarmed with people trying to flee. All flights in and out of Ukraine had been canceled. All passengers and airline staff were told to evacuate Kyiv's main airport. Panic was spreading, and Zelensky understood that it could overtake the capital far more quickly than the Russian tanks. He needed to reassure people that it was safe to stay home, and he made his first attempt at around six thirty a.m.

Seated at his desk, he positioned his phone in front of him and hit record. The message, sixty-six seconds long, showed little of the confidence Zelensky would later command in his wartime videos. Reading too quickly from a set of prepared remarks, he informed the nation that Putin's forces had invaded, that explosions had been heard across the country, and Ukraine's foreign allies were already preparing an international response. Then his voice slowed and traces of a smile appeared on his face. "What's needed from you today is calm, from each and every one of you," he said into the camera. "I'll be in touch again soon. Don't panic. We're strong. We're ready for anything."

The scripted part of his speech was truthful; the rest was not. Zelensky knew better than to suggest, as he did in the video, that people should feel safe remaining in their homes. Some of his aides had already sent their families out of the city, saying goodbye to them as though for the last time. Andriy Sybiha, the president's chief foreign policy adviser, held his wife's hand that morning and explained that they may lose contact once she and their three children left the city. "We looked at each other and said: 'Well, this is it. We have our kids, we had good times.' Those were the notes we ended on."

Zelensky's own parents, both in their early seventies, would soon need to be evacuated as well. Their hometown in southeastern Ukraine stood in the path of the Russian forces advancing northward from the region of Crimea. In their first phone call that morning, Zelensky tried to reassure his mother, or perhaps himself, that everything would be fine. "You're the president's mom," he said, according to an aide who witnessed the conversation. "Nothing can happen to you."

After the declaration of martial law, most members of the security council, including the heads of the military and the intelligence services, left the presidential compound and went to take up command at their respective headquarters. They had clear remits to monitor the battlefield, gather intelligence, and lead the troops. The president's role was less clearly defined. Although his position as supreme commander in chief gave him ultimate authority over the armed forces, he had neither the experience nor the inclination to lead them. He trusted the generals to do the fighting, and he focused instead on the task of diplomacy, the need to rally the leaders of the world. The first number he dialed while pacing around his office that morning was that of Boris Johnson, the British prime minister. It was still dark in London at the time, around 4:40 a.m., but Johnson picked up and greeted Zelensky as a friend. The two had grown close in the months leading up to the war; Johnson tried harder than most of his peers to reassure the Ukrainians and pledge his support. His government had also sent one of the largest consignments of weapons, including anti-tank rockets, in the weeks before the invasion. "We will fight, Boris! We are not going to give up," Zelensky shouted into the speakerphone. A few steps away, Danilov found the scene so moving that he recorded a video of it on his phone.

As dawn broke in Western Europe, other foreign leaders began reaching out to Zelensky from Washington, Paris, Berlin, Ankara, Vienna, Stockholm, Warsaw, Brussels, and elsewhere, their calls lighting up the secure-line phone on his desk every ten or twenty minutes. None of them sounded as encouraging as Johnson, and some offered veiled ultimatums to impress on Zelensky the danger he faced. "There were threats to the president that first day," said Sybiha, the foreign policy adviser, who drafted talking points for these calls and leaned over the president's desk to listen in. "The crux of it was: accept Russia's demands, or you and your family are dead," Sybiha told me. Several of the foreign leaders offered to act as mediators for Ukraine to negotiate the terms of its surrender. "There were offers to this effect: Take the terms! Look what you're up against!"

The Russian military, estimated to have around nine hundred thousand active-duty troops, was at least four times larger than that of Ukraine. The Russians had five times as many armored fighting vehicles and ten times as many aircraft. Ukraine's defense budget, at around $4.5 billion, was about a tenth of what Russia spent on its military every year.

Zelensky's allies all understood the balance of forces and what it meant. So they kept asking him, at the start of almost every phone call, whether he planned to leave Kyiv for his own safety and how they could help. The presidential guards had a menu of safer places for him to go. Bunkers stood ready on the outskirts of the capital. Farther to the west, near the border with Poland, various government facilities would give the president the freedom to lead without the imminent threat of assassination or encirclement by Russian forces. Several European leaders offered to help him escape along with his family and his staff. Among the safest options would be to lead the defense of Ukraine from a facility in eastern Poland, under the nuclear umbrella of the NATO alliance. U.S. officials, including President Joe Biden, were eager to help Ukraine set up a temporary government in exile.

Zelensky appreciated such invitations but also found them a bit offensive, as though his allies had written him off. "I was tired of this," he later said of the offers to escape, which, in his words, "were flying in from all sides." He tried to steer each conversation back to what Ukraine needed to defend itself—weapons in great supply, the closing of its air space—and he grew irritated when, in response, he heard more offers to help him flee. "Excuse me," he said, "it's just poor manners."

The frustration showed when he spoke that morning to Emmanuel Macron, the president of France, who put their call on speakerphone so that his aides could hear Zelensky describe the start of the invasion. "It's total war," Macron said. "Yes," came the answer. "Total war." Zelensky took a breath. If the Russians intended to capture Kyiv in a matter of days, he could not rely on an influx of weapons to arrive quickly enough from the West to improve his odds of surviving. He also understood that the U.S. and Europe would not risk a nuclear war with Russia by sending their own troops to save Ukraine. Western leaders, including President Biden, had made that clear to the Ukrainians. Zelensky felt his only hope, however delusional, was for the West to convince the Kremlin to call off the attack and withdraw its forces. "It's very important, Emmanuel, for you to speak with Putin," he said to Macron. "We are sure that European leaders and Biden can connect. If they call him and say stop, he will stop. He will listen."

❖

Back at his home in Koncha-Zaspa, the president's family waited for his call. His children were already awake when Olena went to get them ready. She was unsure how to break the news of an invasion to a nine-year-old and a seventeen-year-old, and Zelensky had not given her any advice in that regard. "He never said to be honest or dishonest with the children," she said of their last conversation at home. "He just said that I should explain it all to them." Neither of the kids asked many questions. Kyrylo, a playful, sensitive boy who could be easily distracted, obeyed his mother with a quiet intensity, stuffing a few of his things into a little rucksack: some markers, a puzzle book, pieces of a partially assembled Lego set. Oleksandra, whom the family calls Sasha, stayed in touch with her friends through social media, trying to get a better sense of what was happening outside. From the news feeds and TV broadcasts, it was difficult to ascertain the scale of the danger. The headlines focused on immediate facts—the impact of a rocket, the sighting of a tank—and left people to guess at the larger questions, such as their country's chances of holding on.

Through the windows of their home, Zelensky's family could hear the booms of anti-aircraft batteries as they tried to shoot down Russian missiles, planes, and helicopters. At one point, as the First Lady stood near a window, a fighter jet tore through the sky, flying low enough for her to feel the sound inside her rib cage. Her bodyguard told her they needed to take the children down to the basement. There was a risk the Russians would bomb them from the air.* The smaller of their dogs, a miniature schnauzer, had a morbid fear of fireworks and thunder, and he was now approaching a state of shock from the sound of the explosions. Olena picked him up in her arms and carried him downstairs. They would repeat these steps several times that morning, waiting in the basement until the guards said it was safe to emerge, then going back upstairs and putting on a kettle of tea, which would come to a boil just as the next air-raid alert forced them back into the basement. Even then, Olena did not want to run away from Koncha-Zaspa. When the president finally called, she told him she felt safer at home than in some undisclosed location, and they did not want to leave their pets behind. (Apart from the parrot and their two dogs, there was a guinea pig in the house and a tomcat named Lyova, who mostly lived in Sasha's room.) "We tried to argue, but he told us it was pointless." Their home address had long ago been published in the press, and they needed to assume the Russians had Koncha-Zaspa circled on their maps.

With no idea of where they would be going, or for how long, Olena gathered the family documents and packed one roller suitcase for herself and the children. All the pets were left in the care of the maid and security guards, some of whom remained at the estate. By the time they drove out, the city and its suburbs were in a full-blown panic. Traffic had spilled from the highways onto country roads. Huge lines had formed at gas stations, and they could see the first barricades being assembled near the city center in anticipation of the Russian tanks. At Bankova Street, the guards led them upstairs to the executive suite, where the scene was tense but not chaotic. No one yelled or showed much emotion. The loudest noise came from the metal detector on the fourth-floor landing,

---

* In early March, on the second week of the invasion, parts of a missile were found on the grounds of the presidential residence at Koncha-Zaspa. Zelensky posted a photo of it on social media. Next to it, he wrote: "You missed."

which squealed each time a soldier hurried through with an assault rifle. Otherwise, the tone was hushed. Staffers huddled near a pair of ferns by the window or stared intently at the screens of their laptops or phones, writing speeches, sending messages, monitoring the news.

Reports of the onslaught were pouring in faster than anyone could process them. In western Ukraine, near the border with Poland, several airports were on fire. Scores of soldiers were missing and presumed dead after a missile attack on their base outside Kyiv. Presidential aides tried to triage all this information, bringing news to Zelensky when it needed his immediate attention. But each development seemed more alarming than the last. "It's hard to be ready for that," said Andriy Yermak, the president's chief of staff, who had been by his side since the early morning. "We had only ever seen such things in the movies, read about them in books."

Like many of the president's advisers, Yermak was a creature of the entertainment industry, his face round and unshaven, his wrists adorned with folksy bracelets of leather and wooden beads. As a movie producer, he had credits for a couple of gangster films, both heavy on the stage blood and macho dialogue, which Yermak continued to quote long after the pictures flopped. (A favorite line: "Everything has its time.") Before his friend became the president, Yermak served as a lawyer for Zelensky's production company. Now he was in charge of managing a war, fielding calls from frontline generals and the White House. At one point that morning, Yermak looked down at his ringing cell phone and saw a familiar name flash up on the screen. It was Dmitry Kozak, a senior Kremlin official, whom he knew well from their earlier rounds of peace talks. For weeks they had engaged in a secret dialogue, trying in vain to find a set of concessions that might convince Putin to call off the attack. Those talks had failed. Now Kozak was on the line with a different message, urging the Ukrainians to surrender on Russia's terms. Yermak heard him out, then he cursed at him and hung up the phone.

If he felt any fear in that moment, it was not for his own security, he later recalled. "But for our loved ones, yes." A fifty-year-old bachelor, Yermak had no family to evacuate from Kyiv, and he resigned himself to staying by Zelensky's side no matter what happened. Many of his colleagues could not make that choice as easily. Some arrived at Bankova Street that morning with their families and luggage in their cars outside, expecting an organized evacuation of the presidential staff. Zelensky did not stand in their way. As long as these staffers asked permission to get their loved ones out of the city, they were allowed to go. "We're all human beings," he said. "And some fast decisions had to be made."

The president, for his part, decided that his family needed to run. The risk of bombardment was far too high, and he placed more stringent requirements on their security than his own. Their goodbyes that day were unsentimental. The first family did not even step into a private room to talk. They hugged in the hallway, exchanging a few hurried words as Zelensky rushed from one meeting to the next. His wife does not recall him giving her any assurances. After nearly two decades of marriage, the brevity of their farewell did not surprise Olena. She knew from hard experience that her husband would put his work above all else. Standing there in the hallway, Zelensky did not promise her that all would be fine. "He knows that would only make me start to panic," Olena later told me. The danger still felt abstract to both of them, and the First Lady's response was to feign composure. "We couldn't make it a frantic goodbye," she said. "The kids don't need that." Their performance for the children made the moment feel less grave than it was. "It was like I was going on holiday," she said, "an absolutely normal, calm conversation for the road."

In reality, Olena and the kids were running for their lives. At Kyiv's central station, a train stood ready to take them out of the city, their destination a secret even among the president's closest aides. The state railway service had orders from the presidential guard to keep the locomotive idling, prepared to depart, in case Zelensky decided to leave the capital. Every once in a while a group of security men would come through the cars and inspect them for threats in anticipation of his arrival. But Zelensky never came. His family's train departed without him, clattering out of the station with his wife, their two children, their team of bodyguards, and their one roller suitcase.

CHAPTER 2

THE TARGET

Around 11:20 A.M. ON THE MORNING OF THE INVASION, ZELENSKY AND HIS BODY-guards made their way to the ground floor of the presidential headquarters, where his aides had gathered a group of reporters in a windowless briefing room. The president was still dressed in his business suit and collared shirt, but his message had evolved in these first few hours of the invasion. When he took the podium, Ukrainians no longer saw the strained and somewhat patronizing smile of a leader urging them to stay calm, stay home, and await further instructions. Zelensky now called on his people to stand up and join the fight in whatever ways they could. All veterans were to report to the draft office and enlist immediately. Anyone healthy enough to donate blood must offer it at their local hospital. Anyone who wanted an assault rifle, Zelensky said, could go and get one from the distribution points being set up around the city. "We're already giving out weapons, and we're going to continue giving them to everyone who wants to defend our land."

Even the assembled journalists were not exempt from this call to arms. The flow of Russian propaganda had intensified with the start of the assault, and false reports about the collapse of the government had begun to spread on social media. Zelensky wanted every outlet in Ukraine to help him wage the information war and "mobilize the fighting spirit" of the country. "Spread the word about how bravely our soldiers are fighting," he said from the podium. "They need the support of our citizens."

Minutes later, after the press briefing ended, the air-raid sirens started up again. The first of their wails sounded in Kyiv early that morning, and most of the presidential staff ignored them and continued working. This one was different. Around noon, the presidential guards received warnings of an aerial strike on Bankova Street, and they spread out across the compound to begin an evacuation. Zelensky's bodyguards informed him it was time to head down to the bunker.

The president had taken a tour of the facility a couple of years earlier, near the start of his tenure, and he remembered the door, a massive slab of solid metal insulated with rubber around the edges. It opened onto a system of stairs, corridors, and elevators that led deep underground. The journey down took less than ten minutes, but it felt like much longer during that first descent, their voices and footsteps echoing through tunnels that ran the length of city blocks.

They were headed to a facility that dated to the height of the Cold War, designed and built for use in the event of a nuclear strike on Kyiv. Many cities in the Eastern Bloc were equipped with such burrows. The Soviet Union never managed to produce an automobile that could compete on the global market, but they could build a bunker with the best of them. For Ukraine, this inheritance had advantages and disadvantages. Because the shelter had been built in Soviet times, Ukraine only needed to pay for its upkeep, not its construction. The drawback was the bunker had been planned and designed in Moscow. Somewhere in the archives of the KGB, the Russians most likely had floor plans for it, right down to the placement of the presidential toilet.

When they reached it, some of Zelensky's aides found the place weirdly familiar. Parts of it resembled Kyiv's subway system, which had been built around the same time, mostly using the same technology. Even the paint on the walls had the sheen and texture one might find in the stationmaster's office in the metro. The layout of the place also looked like a giant subway tunnel, divided into two floors and retrofitted in the style of an office building. It could house hundreds of people along an enormous corridor that stretched into the distance. To the left and the right were little rooms for sleeping or working, some small enough to make a standard prison cell seem spacious by comparison. The beds were just narrow mattresses on the floor, similar to what you might find atop a bunk at a children's summer camp. There were communal bathrooms and showers, as well as a cafeteria with enough seats for a few dozen people to eat at a time.

Apart from some basic upgrades and renovations—the flat-screen TV hanging in the mess hall, for instance—little had changed in the bunker since it was built. The yellow glow of old lightbulbs had been replaced with the harsh white light from LEDs or halogen. The old wooden doors to the rooms had been swapped out for new ones, made with cheap plastic panels and poorly insulated. Danilov, as head of the security council, had inspected the place in the months before the invasion, and he made sure the Internet connections had several layers of redundancy. On the question that most concerned the president's staff, his answer was: yes, there is Wi-Fi in the bunker.

Zelensky was impressed. Though it was no Koncha-Zaspa, he had spent enough time in flophouses while on tour over the years to make him less picky about accommodations than the average European head of state, and his quarters in the bunker were fine—certainly more comfortable than those reserved for his staff. His bed was small, no more than a cot. But, on the lower floor, he had his own kitchenette with a coffee machine, his own dining area with a table that could seat six people, eight at a stretch. He had a private bathroom and shower, and the floors in his suite had runner carpets, much like the ones in his office upstairs. Cold brown tiles covered the floors in the rest of the bunker.

Once they had a look around, Zelensky gathered his aides in the conference room and asked them to make a choice. "From tomorrow," he said, "it may be that we don't have a chance to leave." Kyiv could be encircled. Russian troops might surround the presidential compound and block the exits of the bunker. "Everyone has their own life and needs to make a decision for themselves," Zelensky told his aides. "Choose to either stay or go somewhere safer." The president's old friend, Davyd Arakhamia, had trouble getting his mind around the choice Zelensky proposed, and what it would require of those who stayed. He later recalled the conversation feeling like a dream. When it was over, he went to another room and called his wife. "She answered me very clearly, maybe with some humor," Arakhamia later told the *Washington Post*. "She'd rather tell our kids that I was a hero once than a deserter many times."

❖

When they went back upstairs that afternoon, Zelensky and Yermak found the corridors overrun with soldiers in combat gear. No protocols existed for a state of siege inside the presidential compound, so the guards needed to improvise, barricading every entrance with whatever they could find. They brought in sandbags to cover the windows. They parked an old truck near one of the gates and rigged it with mines, set to explode if anyone tried to move it. Some of their fortifications resembled heaps of trash. An entrance to the building from Bankova Street was blocked with a desk, a pair of bicycle racks, and a few metal riot shields, objects that had no real hope of withstanding a bullet or even a determined push. At best they might block an attacker's view into the building. But that was all they had.

Throughout the compound, the security officers opened their gun safes and brought out enough assault rifles for Zelensky and his aides. Most of them had no idea how to handle such weapons. One of the few who did was Oleksiy Arestovych, a presidential spokesman who had once served in Ukraine's military intelligence service. "It was an absolute madhouse," he told me. "Automatics for everyone." Piled up on the floor next to bulletproof vests, the weapons did little to calm the rising panic among the staffers. Dozens of them huddled in offices or rushed around the corridors, trying to get a sense of the fighting outside, how far the Russians had advanced, and whether Ukraine had the means to stop them. The rooms pulsed with rumors plucked from social media, mixed up with scraps of information pouring in from military sources and foreign intelligence agencies. One persistent warning suggested that a wave of Russian paratroopers could land in the heart of the capital at any moment.

In half the city, Arestovych told me, "There were no defenses, not one block of concrete in the streets, not one tank trap. Nothing." As a spokesman for the president on military matters, it fell to him to appear in the briefing room and assure the public that everything remained under control, that the Russians had made a desperate mistake and would soon be repelled and humiliated. "I became like the national sedative," said Arestovych. The role suited him well. For well over a decade he had worked as an actor at the Black Square theater in Kyiv, a company known for its improvisational productions. He also had the looks and swagger of a secret agent, with a soft, soothing voice that soon came to symbolize the sense of calm Zelensky's team attempted to impose over the horrifying events unfolding all around them.

"Here's what you need to understand," Arestovych told the people of Ukraine during one of his press briefings that day. "The two hundred thousand troops Putin has gathered on the borders of Ukraine are not enough to attack, to occupy the country, and so on. All they can count on is panic." Across Kyiv, panic reigned. The mayor would later estimate that half its residents—nearly two million people—fled the city. Those unable or unwilling to run sought shelter in the subway system, in bunkers and basements. In the streets of the government quarter, Ukrainian troops went door to door, searching homes for Russian saboteurs and urging residents to evacuate. If the windows of a car parked near Bankova Street were heavily tinted, security forces broke them to look for explosives or weapons hidden inside.

No matter how confident the president and his spokespeople tried to appear, their team prepared for the worst. One of Zelensky's legal aides, Andriy Smyrnov, told him that Russian forces could hijack Ukraine's judicial system and begin to issue rulings to legitimize their occupation or undermine the president's authority. To prevent this, Smyrnov and an officer of the security forces rushed to a courthouse in central Kyiv, broke through the door, and ripped the wires out of its computer servers—the judicial equivalent of blowing up a bridge to frustrate the advance of enemy tanks. "In terms of separation of powers, that's probably not what you should do," Smyrnov later told me. "But these were extraordinary times."

On orders from the president, the military and police forces in Kyiv began emptying their armories, handing out assault rifles to local residents. They intended to prepare the city for guerrilla warfare. But commanders also feared the stockpiles could fall into enemy hands. "If we did not give out the weapons," said Denys Monastyrsky, the minister of internal affairs, "the Russians would have seized them straightaway." Indeed, one armory in Kyiv's northern suburbs emptied out as the Russian forces approached its perimeter.

Across town, about two miles to the west of Bankova Street, plumes of smoke rose from burn pits in the courtyard of the Ministry of Defense and the General Staff. Orders had come down from senior leadership to start destroying sensitive documents stored in their headquarters, a complex of neoclassical buildings painted in a pastel blue. The only way to get rid of that many files in a matter of hours was to incinerate them. But no plans or equipment had been prepared for the task.

The top brass had not expected the Russians to make a dash straight for Kyiv on the first day of the invasion. It now dawned on them that their offices could be overrun along with their records and archives. Throughout the complex, teams of bureaucrats and soldiers began to empty file cabinets, pile their contents into boxes, and take them down to the courtyard, where the fires were started directly on the ground. For the rest of the day, the smoke seeped through the windows of the ministry and ash swirled around the grounds like autumn leaves, some of the larger pieces still bearing faint lines of secret text.

The minister of defense, Oleksiy Reznikov, was meanwhile racing around the city with his coterie of guards, staying in close touch with the office of the president. "For security reasons, I couldn't stay in one place," he told me. "There were sabotage and reconnaissance groups in Kyiv. We all understood that." These groups were thought to function as enemy sleeper cells, made up of Russian special forces units and their local collaborators. Zelensky and his government believed that many of them had arrived in Kyiv long in advance, casing targets and stashing weapons around the city. "A year ago these people were already renting apartments in many places, renting houses," Zelensky said. "They were in position to start the work of the occupiers."

On the afternoon of the invasion, reports of their handiwork began to reach Zelensky from various sources, and they created the sense that the enemy was already in the capital and closing in. This may have been their goal, said Reznikov. Even if they could not kill or capture Zelensky, the Russian sabotage units could try to make him panic and run. "The Russian tactic was to push the president out of Kyiv," he said. "They were testing our nerves."

At one point, a volley of shots struck the northern facade of the Ministry of Defense headquarters, scattering glass from the windows across the parquet floor. The barrage appeared to come from a condominium development, the Manhattan City towers, a trio of half-built skyscrapers on the other side of the railway lines. The towers were unguarded at the time. Anyone could have walked onto the construction site and climbed the stairs to the upper floors, finding a convenient perch for a sniper or machine gunner with a clear line of sight to the Ministry of Defense. When the shots rang out, staffers inside the building dove for cover behind desks and walls. Several officers grabbed their Kalashnikovs and started firing back in the direction of the towers. "I was yelling at them: at least open the windows first!" recalls one staffer, Lyudmila Dolgonovska, who was concerned about the February wind blowing in through the broken glass. For several minutes, bullets whizzed over the pitch of the ministry's soccer stadium. The nearby headquarters of the Ministry of Infrastructure on Victory Avenue happened to be in the line of fire. It got hit with a few stray rounds, breaking windows on the fourth and fifth floors. No one was hurt. Ukrainian special forces later went to search the Manhattan City towers, and they found no sign of Russian saboteurs or their firing positions. But the incident added to the air of paranoia in Kyiv.

Reports of shoot-outs with Russian operatives near the center of town appeared on social media throughout the day. One report claimed that a lone gunman had opened fire at soldiers outside a subway station. Another claimed that a truck full of saboteurs had been shot to pieces at the edge of the city center. Even though these incidents could not be confirmed, let alone investigated at the time, the presidential guards were not taking any chances. Nor was the military. As dawn broke on the second day of the invasion, the Armed Forces of Ukraine issued an alert on their Facebook page, informing residents of Kyiv that enemy formations were already in the city. "Make Molotov cocktails," the statement commanded. "Neutralize the occupiers!"

By noon, around seven hours into the invasion, Zelensky's initial state of shock subsided, and he got a firmer grasp of what his wartime role would require of him. His brief career as a statesman offered little to prepare him for this moment, but his instincts as an actor came with some advantages. Zelensky was adaptable, trained not to lose his nerve under the glare of a massive audience. Now, he realized, his audience was much of the world, all of Ukraine, everyone he knew or was ever likely to meet. If he gave in to panic and handed his capital over to the Russians, he knew the shame would follow him for the rest of his life, and his fear of that indignity seemed to outweigh the fear of being killed or captured in the act of defending his country. He remembers giving himself a pep talk that would play in his mind throughout the day. "They're watching," he told himself. "You're a symbol. You need to act the way a head of state must act."

As the day wore on, his aides could see Zelensky's posture stiffen. His tone became clipped, and he began to issue a stream of orders from the bunker and from his office on the fourth floor. Most of his decisions had no real basis in experience or planning. Zelensky had neither of these things to guide him at the time, but he didn't seem to mind. His assent to the presidency from the world of comedy would not have been possible without a knack for projecting confidence even when he lacked it. Now that skill went into overdrive, and Zelensky became what one of his aides described as a "decision generator."

"The Russians were unlucky in many ways," said Mykhailo Podolyak, who was with Zelensky throughout the day. "This was one of them." In attacking Ukraine from multiple directions, they seemed to calculate that the command structure in Kyiv would crack, overwhelmed by the volume of threats that needed an immediate response. Any such lapse in authority, even a pause to take stock of the country's options, would leave frontline officials to fend for themselves and, in many cases, to flee. Yet there was never such a period of dead air on the radio, as the office of the president quickly began to issue commands. Some would later backfire in tragic fashion, like the order Zelensky gave to distribute weapons to just about any adult with a Ukrainian passport and a trigger finger. The glut of guns soon turned parts of Kyiv into a shooting gallery.

Still, in those early hours of the war, when Ukraine's survival as a country was at stake, Zelensky had no time to weigh risks and analyze data, and he did not need much prompting to fire off instructions to his staff, routinely flavored with profanities. As a result, says Podolyak, "People throughout the hierarchy did not have time to second-guess themselves." During the first of several calls with regional governors that day, some of them looked numb with fear, unable to answer or even comprehend the questions Zelensky posed about the state of affairs in their regions. It was hard to blame them. The Russian advance threatened to overrun several of those regions within hours, and the governors needed to weigh the chances of being killed unless they fled or agreed to collaborate with the invaders. Seeing this, Zelensky issued firm if somewhat vague directives: remain at your posts, coordinate with the military, and be responsive to the needs of the public. "That calmed people down," says Podolyak. "They stopped thinking and started working."*

Soon after the call, reports began to reach Zelensky of a Russian air assault near the edge of Kyiv, around twenty-five miles northwest of the presidential compound. He recognized the target, a major airport in the town of Hostomel. A few weeks earlier, Zelensky had received a warning about that airport from the CIA, which saw it as one of Ukraine's main vulnerabilities. William Burns, the CIA director, visited Kyiv in the middle of January to deliver the latest U.S. intelligence on Putin's war plans, and he explained that the Russian strategy hinged on the landing of forces at Hostomel, enough of them to capture Kyiv. At the time Zelensky was unconvinced. To him, the Russian plan did not involve enough troops to occupy a city of four million people. Zelensky expected many of his citizens to rise up and resist. Besides, the U.S. intelligence looked inconclusive to him. It appeared to spell out one of Russia's options, perhaps the most aggressive one, but not the likeliest. Putin had himself referred to Kyiv as the "mother of Russian cities," the cradle of the civilization he claimed to be defending. Only madness could inspire him to attack that city, to bomb its churches and subjugate its people. In all their interactions over the years, their phone calls, summits, and peace negotiations, Putin struck Zelensky as cold and calculating, bitter and aggrieved, but not insane, not genocidal. "How can you believe this?" he later asked a reporter. "That they will torture people and that this is their goal? No one believed it would be like this."

But the CIA turned out to be right, at least about Putin's main line of attack. At around eleven a.m., a swarm of at least thirty Russian attack helicopters swept down over the reservoir north of Kyiv, flying close enough to the water to avoid air defenses. The Ukrainians shot one of the helicopters down on its approach to Hostomel. But the others managed to land a force of several hundred Russian troops, enough to take the airport by storm. As the battle unfolded, Zelensky and his aides

---

* At the end of the day, the defections among regional leaders were much more rare than some expected. Only one went over to the Russian side. Some of those with the closest historical ties and sympathies toward Moscow, such as the mayor of Kharkiv, right near the Russian border, turned out to be among the fiercest defenders of Ukraine.

huddled around their laptops and phones and watched the images and updates pour in from Hostomel. The president's response caught some of his aides by surprise. They had never seen him in such a rage. "He gave the harshest possible orders," recalled Podolyak. "'Show no mercy. Use all available weapons to wipe out every Russian thing that's there.'"

But the Ukrainians did not have the forces in place to defend the airport. Despite the warnings from the CIA, the Russian assault on Hostomel caught the military by surprise. Many of the troops stationed in that area had been sent to reinforce the eastern front, where their commanders had expected the invasion to begin. Those who remained at the airport ran out of ammunition within hours, and they had no choice but to withdraw under heavy fire. Once in control of the runways, the Russian commandos prepared for the arrival of reinforcements in giant military transport planes, each one packed with soldiers and armored vehicles. "They land ten of those planes," said Monastyrsky, the minister of internal affairs, "and all of a sudden we'd have five thousand Russian troops marching through the streets of Kyiv."

❖

As the battle for the airport raged that night, Zelensky appeared via video link at an emergency summit of European leaders. Some of them joined via video conference, forming a checkerboard of worried faces on each other's screens. The presidents of Poland and Lithuania had visited Kyiv on the day before the invasion to demonstrate their solidarity with Zelensky. Now, as they tried to rally their peers into action, they found no consensus on what punishment Russia deserved. The worst act of military aggression in Europe since World War II was not enough, on its own, to unite the European Union.

The leaders of Germany, Austria, and Hungary, among others, did not want to cut ties with the Russian banking system, because it would hinder the trade in oil and gas. Olaf Scholz, who was less than three months into his tenure as the German chancellor, went so far as to suggest that before agreeing on any new sanctions, Europe should implement the ones imposed on Russia prior to the invasion. Implicit in this position was the idea that nothing had changed. For a while, their debate went in circles, following the customary rules of order and decorum.

No one could summon the force of conscience the moment seemed to require, at least not until Zelensky dialed into the call. Pale and tired, with the early stubble of his wartime beard just beginning to show on his chin, the president was in his bunker at the time, seated at the small, subterranean table that would soon become the epicenter of his life. He did not have much faith in the ability of foreigners to save him, and the pessimism showed.

"This may be the last time you see me alive," Zelensky told the Europeans. Instead of asking to be rescued, he demanded an answer to the question Ukraine had been posing for decades: Would it ever be allowed to join the European Union? Would it be allowed to join the NATO alliance? None of the other leaders offered a direct response. But his remarks, which lasted only about five minutes, had a greater impact on their resolve than many months, if not years, of debates about Russia in Brussels. Here, in real time, they could see the president of a European democracy, holed up in a bunker, preparing to face his own death and the subjugation of his country, all because of the imperial ambitions of his neighbor to the east. Their endless debates about the threat Russia posed to Europe would never again seem theoretical. They were no longer talking about deterrence and brinkmanship, because the crime of aggression had taken place before their eyes. They could see its victim, appealing for help. They could see that Putin, in the twenty-third year of his reign, had launched the biggest European war in generations. He had sent his troops to kill or capture Zelensky for the simple reason that he refused to yield or flee. Zelensky made that clear to the Europeans. Then the signal cut out and he went back upstairs to deliver another statement to his people from the briefing room. The foreign officials he spoke to that day had not expressed a willingness to stand and fight alongside Ukraine. "We are left alone in the defense of our state," Zelensky said from the podium. But that did not mean the people of Ukraine should cower or surrender. "We are not afraid," he said. "We are not afraid of Russia."

At least in public, they refused to show their fear. But all of them felt it in the hours that followed. Denys Monastyrsky remained aboveground, moving around the government district to coordinate the work of the police and National Guard. On the second day of the invasion, as fighting raged on the outskirts of Kyiv, the minister used his phone to record the first of two farewell messages for his family. He wanted to have them ready to send the moment he realized he was about to be killed. "My rays of sunshine," he said into the camera. "I'll keep this recording short. I've made a decision to remain in the city." If the Russians captured it, his subordinates had orders to leave Kyiv and establish a base of operations in western Ukraine, where his family had already fled. "There is no fear," he continued. "We are working in every way to defend Kyiv. We are ready for all scenarios, even the most tragic ones. We'll fight back." Then his voice caught in his throat as he began to address his two young children. "You must proceed through life," he said, "as your essence guides you. That essence can only be found in the heart, in your own heart. I love you." Before shutting off the camera, he forced himself to smile and added, "I'm ready."

At around the same time on Bankova Street, Zelensky delivered a similar message to all of Ukraine. He decided that night to leave the relative safety of the compound for the first time since the invasion started. His bodyguards lit the way with flashlights as he strode through the darkened corridors, past the improvised barricades at the door and into the courtyard. The security men, wearing helmets and carrying assault rifles, formed a loose circle around him, scanning the windows and rooftops. One of his aides experienced a dreadful feeling of exposure to the Russian bombers in the sky, he later told me, "as though we were standing there naked." Their breath rose as vapor under the streetlamps, which cast an orange light on their faces. With his left hand, Zelensky held his phone away from his body and hit record. Four of his closest aides stood behind him, filling the frame. The president name-checked all of them before delivering a line that would ricochet around the world that night. "We're all here," he said. "Defending our independence, our country. That's the way it's going to be."

CHAPTER 3

CITY OF BANDITS

THE FIRST DAYS OF THE INVASION DID NOT LEAVE OLENA ZELENSKA MUCH TIME TO DEspair. It was all too surreal and disorienting. She maintained a look of poise and cheerfulness, partly as a reflex, partly for the children. But the anxiety showed around her eyes, and the muscles in her face began to ache from the smile she forced herself to wear. Sometimes the strangeness of those days on the run with the children made her feel detached from reality, she later said, as though she were trapped in a video game, her movements under the control of some external force. Other moments reminded her of a line from *Through the Looking-Glass*, one of her favorite children's books: "It takes all the running you can do, to keep in the same place."

Their escape from Kyiv began by getting off the grid. The presidential guards insisted on taking away their smartphones, which the Russians could use to track them. Olena and her daughter sent out a few goodbyes to friends and family before handing the devices over, writing that they would be out of touch for a while and not to worry. The First Lady also logged into her Facebook account and posted a final message at 5:13 p.m. on the first day of the invasion. She addressed it to the people of Ukraine, though parts of it read like a plea to herself. "Today I will not panic and cry. I will be calm and confident," she wrote. "My kids are watching."

That night, as the evacuation train rolled out of Kyiv, Olena did not know its destination. Several European governments had offered to host the president for the duration of the war, and the invitations, of course, extended to his family. But Olena and the children were not spirited out of the country. Nor were they locked inside a bunker underground. They stayed in Ukraine, moving around to stay ahead of security threats. The precautions with the family of the president were more severe than for state officials, and the stakes were far higher. If the Russians had managed to locate and abduct Olena and the children, the resulting hostage crisis could have changed the course of the war, and the First Lady had this risk well in mind. She did not want to put her husband in the position of needing to choose between protecting their children and submitting to Russian demands. To avoid that scenario, she knew she would need to accept the security protocols, even if she found many of them suffocating.

For Olena Zelenska, the presence of bodyguards had been a problem since long before her husband took office. She had always cherished her privacy, and her natural state before the war, before politics, had been a kind of serene detachment. It could come off as cool and distant to strangers, even a little snobby, were it not for the jokes Olena liked to deliver, dry and deadpan, usually directed at herself. That sense of humor served as a shield and a crutch throughout her life, at least until the strictures of her role within the presidency forced her to temper her sarcasm and accept the slow erosion of her freedom. The need to plot out her movements, to have armed men drive her around, sit near her at restaurants, pick her children up from school—these aspects of her husband's high profile had always bothered her. They sapped the ease and spontaneity she remembered from their life and their group of friends in the late 1990s, when they all started writing and performing comedy together after high school. Zelensky, the star and leader of their troupe, had always been in the spotlight, posing for pictures with fans and signing autographs. Olena had the beauty and the wit to star alongside him in his romantic comedies, but she preferred to work as one of the writers on his team. She invented the jokes and sketches and developed scripts for his movies, and the role suited her character well. It allowed her to remain behind the scenes, and she prized the ability to retreat, to disappear in a crowded place, unafraid of being recognized.

Her first taste of life under professional protection came in 2014, when someone firebombed her husband's car. The incident seemed more bizarre than terrifying to Olena, even in the context of all the violence Ukraine lived through that year. On the news and in the streets, she and her husband had watched a revolution play out in Kyiv that winter, its central square transformed into a battleground between demonstrators and police. None of their friends were among the scores of protestors who wound up dead during the uprising, most of them gunned down by government snipers. But the violence left them shaken. So did the Russian response. Within days of the revolution, once the leaders of the old regime fled, Putin ordered his troops to occupy the region of Crimea, Ukraine's territorial jewel in the south. Zelensky and his wife owned a summer home on that peninsula. All of a sudden it was under Russian occupation, the first of several regions that Russia would try to steal from Ukraine in the spring and summer of 2014. But back then, at the start of the story, in the early days of the war that would ultimately sweep across Ukraine, Olena tried to keep a distance from politics. She and her husband stuck to the world of comedy and show business. Even if their jokes were often political and patriotic, why would someone want to firebomb their car?

It happened in the middle of Kyiv that December, during Zelensky's act at the city's biggest concert hall, the Palace of Ukraine. His Range Rover stood parked outside, near the service entrance, when a bottle full of burning liquid shattered on top of it. No one was hurt, and Olena could not believe it was an attempt to kill him. He was in the middle of his performance when the car went up in flames. She was also skeptical about the motive. That fall, Zelensky had offended a Russian official named Ramzan Kadyrov, the leader of Chechnya, a region in Russia's south, who styled himself as one of Putin's most loyal enforcers and protégés. Zelensky's joke, to be fair, was not in the best of taste: it poked fun of Kadyrov for crying at his father's funeral. The outrage in Chechnya shocked Zelensky. The death threats continued even after he issued a public apology. In the Russian parliament, one of Chechnya's representatives told the comedian to prepare for his own funeral. Investigators in Ukraine never found the person who lobbed the bomb at Zelensky's car two months later. They just told him the incident was probably related to his joke about Kadyrov. "They were trying to convince us of this," Olena told me. "But we didn't know what really happened. It could have been anything. They carried out an investigation and didn't catch anyone. It's strange, this idea that someone would light the car on fire during his concert. Obviously he was inside at that time, and not sitting in his car outside the staff entrance. So you can't even call that a real assassination attempt."

She saw no need after the attack to make dramatic changes in their lifestyle. She definitely did not want brawny men with earpieces following her into the grocery store. "But everybody got nervous," she said. Friends and colleagues told her: "The kids are small. We've got to do something." The nagging wore her down, and she agreed to try out the services of a private security firm. The arrangement didn't last. "I put up with it for a couple of months, and then I told them to leave me alone."

Eight years later, as she rode a secret evacuation train with her children and a team of armed guards, Olena could no longer ask to be left alone. She was stuck. At least during the first couple of years of Zelensky's tenure she got used to her main bodyguard, Yaroslav, the one who shadowed her everywhere, sometimes even waiting outside the bathroom. A cold and watchful giant of a man, he looked like the mythical god of Scandinavian bouncers. But he had a baby face beneath his grimace, and he was gentle around the children. They called him Yarik for short. On the eve of the invasion, February 23, they had even celebrated Yarik's birthday together at the house in Koncha-Zaspa, like it was some kind of family tradition. None of them imagined they would all be on the run together the next day, Yarik standing in for the father-protector, who decided to stay in his bunker and send them away.

It all felt so sudden. "A black swan event," as one of Zelensky's advisers put it. But it was also part of a continuum that had started years before. The nation of Ukraine, like the Zelensky family, had begun to lose its sense of security in 2014, and now the process was culminating. It was no longer possible to turn inward and ignore the danger. When the guards told Olena there was an air-raid alert, she had to take the kids down to the basement. When they said to turn off all the lights, it meant sitting in the dark. When they said it was time to flee, they had to pack up their stuff and get ready to go to the next safe house.

She cannot recall the danger ever feeling immediate; the Russians never appeared to be on their heels. "Nobody chased me around with a pistol," Olena said with a smile when I asked her about this. But the fear never faded from her mind. During the first days of the invasion, they moved so often that Olena was unsure where they would spend the night on any given day. They quickly learned to make the most of the amenities at every hideout, because it was impossible to know whether the next one would have a decent shower.

Throughout each day in hiding, Olena did her best to keep the children occupied. Sometimes the bodyguards entertained Kyrylo, and one safe house had dogs for him to play with. The boy also spent hours drawing pictures that made his mother nervous. Instead of the usual sketches of Batman and Spider-Man, he depicted scenes of war and destruction. His older sister, Oleksandra, met the strangeness of the moment with a profound maturity. "I think children are not as naive as we would like," her mother told me. "They understand everything." Oleksandra helped cook the family's meals while they were in hiding and, when Kyrylo was out of earshot, she and Olena had candid conversations about the war. The ban on using social media did not prove as difficult for the seventeen-year-old as her mother had expected. "It was all right," Olena said. "It turns out her phone addiction was not all that strong."

One of the president's advisers told me that Zelensky visited his family while they were in hiding, leaving his phone behind in the compound to make sure the Russians could not use the signal to find them. But no one else would confirm whether these visits took place. Olena insisted they were not even allowed to communicate with the president on video calls. Secure phone lines, which had to be arranged in advance, served as their only means of communication for weeks. Throughout the day, the first family would tune in to the president's briefings and his nightly addresses to the nation, which proved to be a comfort to the children, Olena told me. "They could see that Dad was at work and looked all right." In some ways the arrangement felt familiar. It had long been a running joke in the family that his children mostly saw his face on television.

❖

Zelensky was already a celebrity when their first child was born in 2003. In those years, Olena would sit and watch her husband perform on TV, cradling their infant daughter in her arms. They often lived apart back then. He was in Kyiv. She stayed with her parents in their hometown of Kryvyi Rih, the city that Zelensky would later credit for forging his character. "My big soul, my big heart," he once called it. "Everything I have I got from there." The name of the town translates as "Crooked Horn," and in conversation Zelensky and his wife tend to refer to it in Russian as Krivoy—"the crooked place," where both of them were born in the winter of 1978, about two weeks apart from each other.

Few if any places in Ukraine had a worse reputation in those years for violence and urban decay. The main employer in the city was the Lenin Metallurgical Plant, whose gargantuan blast furnaces churned out more hot steel than any other facility in the Soviet Union. During World War II, the plant was leveled by the Luftwaffe as the Nazis began their occupation of Ukraine. It was rebuilt in the 1950s and '60s, and many thousands of veterans went to work there. So did convicts released from Soviet labor camps. Most of them settled into blocks of industrial housing, hives of reinforced concrete that offered almost nothing in the way of leisure, culture, or self-development. There were not nearly enough theaters, gyms, or sports facilities to occupy the local kids. By the late 1980s, when the population peaked at over 750,000, the city devolved into what Zelensky would later describe as a "*banditsky gorod*"—a city of bandits.

Olena remembers it more fondly than that. "It wasn't full of bandits in my eyes," she told me. "Maybe boys and girls run in different circles when they're growing up. But yes, it's true. There was a period in the '90s when there was a lot of crime, especially among young people. There were gangs." The boys who joined these gangs, mostly teenagers, were known as *beguny*—literally, "runners"—because groups of them would run through the streets, beating and stabbing their rivals, flipping over cars, and smashing windows. Some of the gangs were known for using homemade explosives and improvised firearms, which they learned to fashion out of metal pipes stuffed with gunpowder and fishhooks. "Some of them got killed," Olena said. According to local news reports, the death toll reached into the dozens by the mid-1990s. Many more runners were maimed, beaten with clubs, or blinded with shrapnel from their homemade bombs. "Every neighborhood was in on it," the First Lady said. "When kids of a certain age wandered into the wrong neighborhood, they could run up against a question: What part of town you from? And then the problems could start." It was nearly impossible, she said, for teenage boys to avoid joining one of the gangs. "You could even be walking home in your own part of town, and they'd come up and ask what gang you're with, what are you doing here. Just being on your own was scary. It wasn't done."

The gangs had their heyday in the late 1980s, when there were dozens of them around the city, with thousands of runners in all. Many of those who survived into the 1990s graduated into organized crime, which flourished in Kryvyi Rih during the sudden transition to capitalism around that time. Parts of the city turned into wastelands of racketeers and alcoholics. But Zelensky, thanks in large part to his family, avoided the pull of the streets.

His paternal grandfather, Semyon Zelensky, served as a senior officer in the city's police force, investigating organized crime or, as his grandson later put it, "catching bad guys." Stories of his service in the Second World War made a profound impression on the young Zelensky, as did the traumas of the Holocaust. Both sides of his family are Jewish, and they lost many of their own during the war. His mother's side of the family survived in large part because they were evacuated to Central Asia as the German occupation began in 1941. The following year, when he was still a teenager, Semyon Zelensky went to fight in the Red Army and wound up in command of a mortar platoon. All three of his brothers fought in the war, and none of them survived. Neither did their parents, Zelensky's great-grandparents, who were shot during the Nazi occupation of Ukraine, along with over a million other Ukrainian Jews, in what became known as the "Holocaust by Bullets."

Around their kitchen table, Zelensky's relatives often brought up these tragedies and the crimes of the German occupiers. But little was ever said about the torments that Joseph Stalin inflicted on Ukraine. As a child, Zelensky remembers his grandmothers talking in vague terms about the years when Soviet soldiers came to confiscate the food grown in Ukraine, its vast harvests of grain and wheat all carted away at gunpoint. It was part of Stalin's attempt in the early 1930s to remake Soviet society, and it led to a catastrophic famine known as the Holodomor—"murder by hunger"—that killed at least three million people in Ukraine. In Soviet schools, the topic was taboo, including the schools where both of Zelensky's grandmothers worked as teachers; one taught the Ukrainian language, the other taught Russian. When it came to the famine, Zelensky said, "They talked about it very carefully, that there was this period when the state took away everything, all the food."

If they harbored any ill will toward Soviet authorities, Zelensky's family knew better than to voice it in public. But his father, Oleksandr, a stocky man of stubborn principles, refused throughout his life to join the Communist Party of the Soviet Union. "He was categorically against it," Zelensky told me, "even though that definitely hurt his career." As a professor of cybernetics, Oleksandr Zelensky worked most of his life in the fields of mining and geology. Zelensky's mother, Rymma, an engineer by training, was closer to their only son and gentler toward him, doting on the boy much more often than she punished him.

In 1982, when Zelensky was four years old, his father accepted a prestigious job at a mining development in northern Mongolia, and the family moved to the town of Erdenet, which had been founded only eight years earlier to exploit one of the world's largest deposits of copper. (The name of the town in Mongolian means "with treasure.") The job was well paid by Soviet standards, but it forced the family to endure the pollution around the mines and the hardships of life in a frontier town. The food was bland and unfamiliar. Fermented horse milk was a local staple, and the family's diet was heavy on mutton, with the occasional summer watermelon for which Zelensky and his mother had to stand in line for hours.

Rymma, who was slender and frail, with a long nose and beautiful features, found her health deteriorating in the harsh climate, and she soon decided to move back to Ukraine. Zelensky was a first grader in a Mongolian school, just beginning to pick up the local language, when they traveled home in 1987. His father stayed behind, and for the next fifteen years—virtually all of Zelensky's childhood—he split his time between Erdenet, where he continued to develop his automated system for managing the mines, and Kryvyi Rih, where he taught computer science at a local university. Zelensky's parents were often separated in those years by five time zones and around six thousand kilometers. Even at that distance, his father continued to be a dominant presence in Zelensky's life.

"My parents gave me no free time," he later said. "They were always signing me up for something." His father enrolled Zelensky in one of his math courses at the university and began to prime the boy for a career in computer science. His mother sent him to piano lessons, ballroom dance classes, and gymnastics. To make sure he could hold his own against the local toughs, Zelensky's parents also got him into a class for Greco-Roman wrestling. None of these activities were really his choice, but he went along with them out of a sense of duty to his parents. "They were always quick with the discipline," he said. The approach his father took to education was particularly severe. Zelensky called it "maximalist." But it was typical of Jewish families in the Soviet Union, who often felt that overachievement was the only way to get a fair shake in a system rigged against them. "You have to be better than everyone else," Zelensky said in summarizing his parents' approach to education. "Then there might be a space for you left among the best."

Many institutions in the Soviet Union, including universities and state-run firms, set limits on the number of Jews allowed to hold top positions. It did not matter that most Soviet Jews were secular. The Zelensky family did not observe the sabbath or repent on Yom Kippur. They ate pork. But their Soviet passports still bore the infamous "fifth line," which noted a person's nationality below the name and date of birth. That line in the Zelensky family's passports said the word *evrey*—"Jew"—which exposed them to the biases of any bureaucrat who checked their papers. Zelensky's father, through hard work, managed to overcome these obstacles as he reached the heights of his own profession, and he intended to help his son do the same. Above all he wanted the boy to excel at math and pursue a career related to that field, but it was hard going. "He had issues with arithmetic," Zelensky's father later said of his son. "Once in my life, I beat him up a little bit, after which he solved all the equations in three or four days." But the elder Zelensky regretted raising his hand against the boy. It would do nothing to change his ambitions.

❖

Zelensky was the product of an era of change. He was too young to experience the Soviet Union as the stagnant, repressive gerontocracy his parents had known. He was only eight years old when he returned to Soviet Ukraine with his mother in 1987. By then the stage was set for the empire's collapse only four years later. Moscow was broke. Its grand experiment in socialism had failed. Mikhail Gorbachev, the reluctant reformer with the soft southern accent, was two years into his term as the general secretary of the Communist Party, and his attempts to open up the system without breaking it apart were in full swing. Even for someone Zelensky's age, these changes were hard to miss. He could see them in the empty grocery shelves, the endless lines for basic goods, like sausage and toilet paper. And he saw them, clear as day, on television.

In the late 1980s, the censors on Soviet TV became a lot more permissive, reflecting the wider push under Gorbachev to relax the state's control over the media. One of the most popular TV shows of the era was known as *KVN*, which stands for "The Club of the Funny and Inventive." It was a comedy show, but not the kind that most people in the U.S. and Europe would associate with that term. This was not the stand-up of Richard Pryor and Eddie Murphy. There was no minimalism here, no lonely cynic at the microphone, breaking taboos.

KVN was more like a sports league for young comedians. It involved competing troupes of performers, often made up of college students, doing sketch acts and improv in front of a panel of judges, who decide at the end of the show which team is the funniest. By the mid-1990s, the average university and many high schools in the Russian-speaking world had at least one KVN team. Many big cities had a dozen or more, all facing off in local competitions and vying for a place in the championship league. The material was mostly wooden, with a lot of knee-slappers and humdingers. The teams were also expected to sing and dance. Still, in its own hokey way, KVN could be fun to watch. For Zelensky and his friends, it was an obsession.

Most of them went to School No. 95, about a block from the central bazaar in Kryvyi Rih and not far from the university where Zelensky's father worked as a professor. Between classes and after school, they rehearsed sketches and comedy routines, riffing off the ones they saw in the professional league on TV. "We loved it all, the KVN, the humor, and we just did it for the soul, for the fun of it," said Vadym Pereverzev, who met Zelensky in their seventh-grade English class. The top KVN competitions in Moscow also offered a ticket to stardom that seemed a lot more accessible to them than Hollywood, and a lot more fun than the careers available to kids in a dead-end town like theirs. "It was a rough, working-class place, and you just wanted to escape," Pereverzev told me. "I think that was one of our main motivations."

Their amateur shows in the school auditorium soon got the attention of a local comedy troupe that performed at a theater for college students. One of them, Oleksandr Pikalov, a handsome kid with an infectious, dimply smile, came down to School No. 95 to scout the talent. He happened upon a rehearsal in which Zelensky played a fried egg, with something stuffed under his shirt to represent the yolk. The act impressed Pikalov, and they soon began performing together. Two years older and already in college, Pikalov introduced Zelensky to a few of the movers and shakers from the local comedy scene, including the Shefir brothers, Boris and Serhiy, who were both around thirty years old at the time. They saw Zelensky's potential, and they became his lifelong friends, mentors, producers, and, eventually, political advisers.

Around their neighborhood in the 1990s, Zelensky's crew stood out from the start. Instead of the track pants and leather jackets that hoodlums and runners wore to school, their look was a kind of '50s retro: plaid blazers and polka-dot ties, slacks with suspenders, pressed white shirts, long hair slicked back with too much gel. Zelensky wore a ring in his ear. At a time when Nirvana was on the radio, he and his friends sang Beatles songs and listened to old-timey rock and roll. To them this felt like a form of rebellion, mostly because it was their own. Nobody acted like that in their city, and it didn't always go over well.

Once, in his late teens, Zelensky wanted to try busking in an underpass with his guitar. He had seen people do it in the movies. It looked romantic. But this was still Kryvyi Rih, and Pikalov warned him that he wouldn't make it past the second song before somebody came over to kick his ass. "Sure enough, half an hour goes by," Pikalov told me. "Somebody comes over and busts the guitar." But Zelensky was laughing. He had won the bet. "He said he made it through the third song."

Even then, the performing arts did not seem like a plausible career to Zelensky. His parents pushed him to study something practical and stay close to home. When he won a grant to travel to Israel, his father forbid him from going on the trip, resulting in another argument, during which shoes were thrown around their apartment. For a while Zelensky left home and lived with friends from the KVN scene. The rebellion didn't last. He admired his father but had no intention of following his path in life, and he finally got that across to him one night over drinks and a cigarette: "We had a couple shots, and I said, 'Papa, you have to understand me. I want to be number one in my profession. Looking at you, I will never do better than you can. And being worse than you in your profession is not what I want. You understand? I want to be number one.' That made Papa sad. You know, men are stingy with their tears. But then he let me go, like a fish from his hands."

After finishing high school, Zelensky accepted a compromise brokered by his mother: he agreed to enroll in law school at a university in Kryvyi Rih, with vague ideas of becoming a diplomat involved in high-stakes international negotiations. Pereverzev, his friend and classmate, decided to study the same topic. But their dreams didn't change. In their first year of college, they teamed up with others in their class to start their own KVN team and began performing in the local league.

Around that time, his performances caught the attention of his future wife. He and Olena had crossed paths in the hallways of School No. 95. But their homeroom classes were rivals—"like the Montagues and the Capulets," she once said—and it was only after graduation, when Zelensky was on his way to becoming a local celebrity, that they took a liking to each other. Olena was also involved in the KVN scene. To make the connection, Pikalov, their mutual friend, borrowed a video-cassette from her, a copy of *Basic Instinct*, and Zelensky used it as an excuse to visit her at home and return the tape. "Then we became more than friends," she later told me. "We were also creative colleagues." Their routines started winning competitions around Kryvyi Rih and in other parts of Ukraine. "We were together all the time," Olena said. "And everything sort of developed in parallel."

Their big break came at the end of 1997, when they performed at an international KVN contest in Moscow. More than two hundred teams took part from around the former Soviet Union, and Zelensky's team, then called Transit, tied for first place with a rival team from Armenia. It was a remarkable debut for Zelensky, but he felt robbed. A video survives of him in that period, a teenage heartthrob with a raspy voice, wiping his palms against his knees as he explains his anger to the camera. The showrunner had cheated, he said, by refusing to let the judges break the tie. Though he catalogued such gripes with an endearing smile, Zelensky was clearly unwilling to share the crown with anyone. He needed to win. Years later, when he recalled these competitions from his childhood, Zelensky admitted that, for him, "Losing is worse than death."

❖

Though the championship in Moscow was not an outright victory for Zelensky, it put him within reach of stardom. One of his team members, Olena Kravets, said they could hardly imagine getting that kind of opportunity. To young comedians from a place like Kryvyi Rih, she said,

the major league of KVN "was not just the foot of Mount Parnassus"—
the home of the muses in Greek mythology—"this was Parnassus itself."
Its summit stood in the north of Moscow, in the studios and greenrooms
around the Ostankino television tower, home to the biggest broadcasters
in the Russian-speaking world. The major league of KVN had its main
production headquarters there, and Zelensky soon made it inside.

The year after their breakout performance in Moscow, they com-
peted for the first time under the name Kvartal 95—or District 95, a nod
to the neighborhood where they grew up. Along with the Shefir brothers, who served as the team's lead writers and producers, Zelensky soon
rented an apartment in the north of Moscow and devoted himself to
becoming the champion. For all KVN teams, that required winning the
favor of the league's perennial master of ceremonies, Alexander Maslyakov. A dapper old man with a Cheshire smile, Maslyakov owned the
rights to the KVN brand and hosted all the biggest competitions. His
nickname among the performers was "The Baron," and he and his wife,
The Baroness, ran the league like a family business. "KVN was their
empire," Pereverzev told me. "It was their show."

At first, the Baron took a liking to Zelensky and his crew, granting them admission to the biggest stage in Moscow and the touches of
fame that it brought. But there were hundreds of other teams vying for
his attention, and the competition among them was vicious. "Everyone
there lived with this constant emotional tension," Olena Zelenska told
me. "You were always told to know your place. The whole time we were
performing in Moscow, they always told us: 'Remember where you came
from. Learn to hold a microphone. This is Central Television. You should
feel lucky.' And that's how all the teams lived, though not so much the
lucky ones from Moscow. They were loved."

In the major league of KVN, Zelensky came face-to-face with a
brand of Russian chauvinism that would, in far uglier form, manifest
itself about two decades later in the Russian invasion of Ukraine. As
Olena put it when we talked about the KVN league: "Those who were
not from Moscow were always treated like slaves."* The informal hier-

---

* The term she used—"*kholopy*"—has a painful history in Ukraine. It refers to the
slave-like status that Russian rulers imposed on some of their subjects in the Middle

archy, she said, corresponded to Moscow's vision of itself as an imperial capital. "Teams from Ukraine were of course even farther down the ladder than all the Russian cities. They could, for instance, put up with Ryazan"—a city in western Russia—"but a place like Kryvyi Rih was something else. They'd never even seen it on a map. So we always needed to prove ourselves."

The unwritten rules within the league reflected the role KVN played in the Russian-speaking world. Amid the ruins of the Soviet Union, it stood out as a rare institution of culture that still bound Moscow to its former vassal states. It gave kids a reason to stay within Russia's cultural matrix rather than gravitating westward, toward Hollywood. The league had outposts in every corner of the former empire, from Moldova to Tajikistan, and all of them performed in the Russian language. Even teams from the Baltic states, the first countries to break away from Moscow's rule in 1990 and 1991, took part in the KVN league; its biggest annual gathering was held in Latvia, on the shores of the Baltic Sea. Viewed in a generous light, these contests could be seen as a vehicle for Russian soft power in much the same way that American movies defined what good guys and bad guys are supposed to look like for viewers around the world. To be less generous, the league could be construed as a Kremlin-backed program of cultural colonialism. In either case, the center of gravity for KVN was always Moscow, and nostalgia for the Soviet Union was a touchstone for every team that hoped to win. Zelensky's team was no exception, especially since their best shot at victory in the early 2000s coincided with a change of power in the Kremlin. With the election of Vladimir Putin in 2000, the Russian state embraced the symbols and icons of its imperial past, and it encouraged its people to stop being ashamed of the Soviet Union. One of Putin's first acts in office was to change the melody of the Russian national anthem back to the Soviet one.

When it came to KVN, Putin was always an ardent supporter. He

---

Ages, including in the area of Kyiv. For several centuries, a kholop was a person who could be bought or sold by his master, forced to work, and used to repay debts. Modern Ukrainian has reclaimed this term and divorced it from its oppressive history. Today, the word "*kholpets*," or "little kholop," is an informal way to refer to a person, especially a man, usually in a friendly or joking way.

often attended KVN championships, and he liked to take the stage and offer pep talks to the performers. In return, they made him the occasional subject of jokes, though none were ever very pointed. One of the first, when he was still the prime minister in 1999, made fun of his soaring poll numbers after the Russian bombing campaign of Chechnya began that summer: "His popularity has already outpaced that of Mickey Mouse," said the performer, "and is approaching that of Beavis and Butt-Head." Seated in the hall next to his bodyguard, Putin snickered and slumped in his chair. Less than a year later, he made clear that sharper jokes in his direction would not be tolerated. In February 2000, during Putin's first presidential campaign, a satirical TV show called *Kukly*, or *Puppets*, depicted him as a gnome whose evil spell makes people believe he is a beautiful princess. Several of Putin's campaign surrogates called for the Russian authors of the sketch to be imprisoned. The show soon got canceled, and the network that aired it was taken over by a state-run firm.

Zelensky, living and working in Moscow at the time, watched the turn toward authoritarianism in Russia with the same concern as all his peers in show business, and, like everyone else, he adapted. To stay on top, his team understood it would not be wise to make fun of Russia's new leader. During one sketch in 2001, Zelensky's character appealed to Putin as the decider "not only of my fate, but that of all Ukraine." A year later, in a performance that brimmed with nostalgia for the Soviet Union, a member of Zelensky's team said Putin "turned out to be a decent guy." But such direct references to the Russian president were rare in Zelensky's early comedy. More often he joked about the fraught relationship between Ukraine and Russia, as in his most famous sketch from 2001, performed during the Ukrainian KVN championships.

Titled "Man Born to Dance," it cast Zelensky in the role of a Russian who can't stop dancing as he tells a Ukrainian about his life. The script is bland and the humor juvenile. Zelensky grabs his crotch like Michael Jackson and borrows the mime-in-a-box routine from Bip the Clown. At the end of the scene, the Russian and the Ukrainian take turns humping each other from behind. "Ukraine is always screwing Russia," says Zelensky. "And Russia always screws Ukraine." The punch line did not come close to the kind of satire Putin's Russia needed and deserved. But as a piece of physical comedy, the sketch is memorable, even brilliant.

Zelensky's movements, much more than his words, seem to infect the audience with a kind of wide-mouthed glee as he shimmies and high-kicks his way through the lines in a pair of skintight leather pants. The most magnetic thing about the sketch is him, the grin on his face, the obvious pleasure he gets from every second on the stage. The judges loved it, and that night, before a TV audience of millions, Zelensky's team became the undisputed champions of the league in their native Ukraine. But, on the biggest stages in Moscow, victory would continue to elude them.

CHAPTER 4

MR. GREEN

Zelensky did not last long in the major leagues of KVN. After competing and losing in the international championships three years in a row, he gathered his troupe and left Moscow in 2003. Members of his team agree their departure was far from amicable, though they all seem to remember it a little differently. One of them told me the breaking point with KVN was an anti-Semitic slur. During a rehearsal, a Russian producer stood on the stage and said loudly, in reference to Zelensky, "Where's that little yid?" In Zelensky's version of the story, the management in Moscow offered him a job as a producer and writer on Russian television. It would require him to disband his troupe and send them back to Ukraine without him. Zelensky refused, and they all went home together.

Halfway through their twenties, they were now successful showmen and celebrities across Ukraine. But it was still difficult for Zelensky's parents to accept comedy as his career. "Without a doubt," his father said years later, "we advised him to do something different, and we thought the interest in KVN was temporary, that he would change, that he would choose a profession. After all, he's a lawyer. He finished our institute." Indeed, Zelensky had completed his studies and earned a law degree while performing in KVN. But he had no intention of practicing law. He found it boring. When he got back home to Kryvyi Rih, Zelensky and his friends staged a series of weddings, three Saturdays in a row. Olena Kiyashko married Volodymyr Zelensky in their hometown on September 6, 2003, and Pikalov and Pereverzev married their respective girlfriends. By the end of the year, when Olena was pregnant with their daughter, Zelensky moved to Kyiv to build up his new production company, Studio Kvartal 95.

Even at this early stage in his career, Zelensky's confidence went beyond the typical swagger of a young man smitten with early success. He betrayed no doubts in his team's ability to make it big, and if he felt any fear he hid it from everyone, including his wife. For an expectant father in his midtwenties, the job offered to him in Moscow must have been more tempting than he let on. Apart from the money, it would have placed him among the glitterati, the producers and showrunners in the biggest market in the Russian-speaking world. Instead he took a risk and struck out in a much smaller pond, relying on the team of friends who looked to him for leadership and made him feel at home wherever he went.

Upon arriving in Kyiv, Zelensky scored a meeting with one of the country's biggest media executives, Alexander Rodnyansky, the head of the network that produced and broadcast the KVN league in Ukraine. The executive knew Zelensky from that circuit as a "bright young Jewish kid," he told me. But he didn't expect the kid to stride into his office with a risky business proposition. Accompanied by the Shefir brothers, who were a decade older and more experienced in the industry, Zelensky did the talking. He wanted to appear with his troupe on the biggest stage in Kyiv for a nationally televised performance, and he needed Rodnyansky to give him the airtime and bankroll part of the production, marketing, and other costs. "The chutzpah on this guy, that's what I remember," the executive told me. "He had this bulletproof belief in himself, with these burning eyes." Many years later, Rodnyansky would come to see the danger hidden in that quality. It would lead Zelensky to the false belief that, in the role of president, he could outmaneuver Putin and negotiate his way out of a full-scale war. "I think that confidence of his betrayed him in the end," he said. But at the time, Zelensky's charm won out in the negotiations with Rodnyansky, who agreed to take a risk on the performance.

It proved to be such a success that, shortly after, the team at Kvartal 95 reached a deal to make a series of variety shows that would air in Russia and Ukraine. Their tone departed from the more wholesome, aw-shucks style of KVN. The jokes took on a harder edge, and they became much more overtly political. Pereverzev, who was a writer on the shows, told me their aim was to make a version of *Saturday Night Live* with elements of Monty Python. It was an untested concept on Ukrainian TV. There was no way to tell whether the audience was ready. "That was Green's style," he said, using Zelensky's nickname. (The word for "green" in Ukrainian and Russian is the same: *zeleny*.) "That was his main quality as a leader. He'd just say, 'Let's do it.' Then we'd all get scared, and he would just tell us to trust him. All our lives it was like that. And at some point we just started to trust him, because when he said it would work out, it did." From the writers' room in Kyiv, they soon saw history turn in their favor, as they could hardly have picked a better moment to launch a new breed of political comedy.

At the end of 2004, a popular uprising known as the Orange Revolution broke out in Ukraine, and the personalities involved were tailor-made for satire. For months the revolution topped the news across Europe, in part because the characters were catnip to the media. There was the dunderheaded villain, Viktor Yanukovych, a patsy to the Kremlin whose disputed victory in the presidential race set the rebellion in motion. There was the heroine, Yulia Tymoshenko, who commanded the protests on Independence Square with a golden braid wrapped around her head like a crown. And there was the telegenic leader of the revolution, Viktor Yushchenko, who fell victim to a poisoning plot involving former agents of the KGB that left his face grotesquely disfigured. The events were so operatic that it was hard to keep sight of what they represented for Ukraine: a popular rejection of Russian influence and a fundamental turn toward the West.

That is what the protestors demanded in the Orange Revolution and what the Kremlin tried to stop. For Vladimir Putin, who was then nearing the end of his first presidential term, the uprising presented a serious challenge. One of his advisers referred to it as "our 9/11." If the Kremlin allowed Ukraine to make a lasting break from Russia and integrate with NATO and the European Union, it would have no hope of restoring the power and influence Russia lost with the dissolution of the Soviet Union. Early in his tenure, Putin described the Soviet collapse as "the greatest geopolitical catastrophe of the twentieth century," and his plan for rectifying it depended on preserving the bonds between Kyiv and Moscow. The Orange Revolution threatened to tear them apart, and Putin was determined to stop it.

Ten years later, in 2014, this same dynamic would result in a second, far bloodier uprising on Kyiv's Independence Square. Eight years after that, it would culminate in the Russian invasion. But in its first manifestation, this standoff over language and history, corruption and accountability, made it easy enough to believe that Russia might let Ukraine go its own way, peacefully and without the need for blood. There was no blood on Independence Square during the Orange Revolution. There was just a sea of people, over a hundred thousand of them, standing on the square for weeks in the middle of winter, singing patriotic songs, giving speeches and listening to them, waving orange banners, the symbols of Yushchenko's presidential campaign, alongside the flags of Ukraine and the European Union.

There was also the rarest thing of all in Ukraine's political life: a happy ending, at least for the nation's westernizers. In January 2005, after two months of demonstrations in Kyiv, the Supreme Court overturned the disputed election results and ordered a new vote. No amount of support from the Kremlin could save Yanukovych from defeat in the rerun. Despite the effects of the poison on his face, Viktor Yushchenko pulled ahead, and he took power that spring with a promise to integrate his country with the West and make a final break from Russia.

But it was not a landslide victory. Even after the international media glorified his cause for months, Yushchenko got only 52 percent of the vote, with the strongest showing in Ukraine's western and central regions. Yanukovych, with all the charisma of a sack of potatoes, still got the support of 44 percent of the electorate. Solid majorities in southern and eastern Ukraine backed Russia's favored candidate, as did the people of Crimea. For the Kremlin, the divided vote served as a sign that Ukraine was not yet lost. Large parts of the country, especially the industrial region of the Donbas in the east, had little interest in Yushchenko's plans to join NATO and the European Union. Millions of people in these regions spoke the Russian language, watched Russian television, consumed Russian sources of news, and relied on trade with Russia for their livelihoods. If Putin could motivate them to resist their country's westward drift, he could achieve the influence he wanted in Ukraine through politics—and without the need for violence.

❖

In Zelensky's circle of friends and family, opinions were far from united in support of the Orange Revolution and its leaders. His parents voted for

Yanukovych, while his comedy troupe saw the deepening rift between the eastern and western regions as a serious professional dilemma. They were due to premiere their new variety series, *Evening Kvartal*, in the months after the Orange Revolution, and political comedy would be at its core. They could not afford to alienate or insult either side of the national divide. The project had financial backing from partners in Russia and Ukraine, and they wanted the audience to span both countries. When the show premiered in 2005, its first episode showed Zelensky's politics were not that different from his parents'. He had also grown up speaking Russian in a working-class town. Even if his years as a performer in Moscow had run up against a glass ceiling of prejudice against Ukrainians, he still believed the two countries were linked, for better or worse, by a shared culture and history.

In his response as a comedian to the Orange Revolution, he took jabs at both sides, though not with equal force. The premiere of his new show featured Pikalov's pitch-perfect impression of Yanukovych, the lilting, bumpkinish manner of speech, the frozen look to indicate the gears were turning in his head. But the treatment was mild, almost generous, when compared to the takedown of Yulia Tymoshenko, the icon of the Orange Revolution, who had just been appointed prime minister of Ukraine. Zelensky himself impersonated her. Right after his opening stand-up routine, he and three other members of the troupe changed into their Tymoshenko costumes: ratty braids perched on their heads, orange stripes running up their arms with the English word *revolution*. "I can't live without you, Putin," they crooned. "But without your love I'm going to NATO."

The humor was crude but also clever in the way it walked a political wire. The comics did not take a position, one way or the other, on the goals of the Orange Revolution. Instead they took aim at its heroine, depicting her as a two-timing opportunist, willing to shift her allegiances from east to west and back again. Fifteen years later, Tymoshenko would still remember the offense when, to her profound surprise, she faced Zelensky in a presidential election and lost. But the performance, when it aired, was not a statement of political purpose. It only made clear that Zelensky, in his comedy, would not go easy on any politicians, even if they were in power and in vogue. "We always reacted to political events, but it was based on the people's point of view," Olena told me. "We were not political experts. We joked about the things that people talked about in their kitchens. Our perspective was always from the outside in, and it was pretty superficial."

Not all of the material in *Evening Kvartal*, which ran in prime time every Saturday across the country, had to do with politics. There was also slapstick, dick jokes, celebrity impersonations. But the standout sketches were usually the ones that mocked the powerful. No one was spared. One sketch imagined all the main figures from the Orange Revolution with a case of amnesia, unable to remember which of them is president. It relied on a formula as old as satire: politicians have no principles, only a hunger for power. Watching such jokes on television from their old apartment in Kryvyi Rih, Zelensky's parents worried that his insolence would get him in trouble with the authorities. "It was scary, really scary," his mother, Rymma, later recalled. "My husband was opposed to it, very much so. He said, 'Vova, cut it out, stop joking about the president!'"

Younger viewers, having shed the Soviet instinct of deference before the state, found the satire exhilarating. The show became such a hit that, within a few years, Zelensky's production company became the envy of Ukraine's TV industry. It cranked out sitcoms and rom-coms, reality shows and cooking shows, stand-up specials and song contests. Zelensky worked on the Ukrainian version of *Dancing with the Stars*, first as a contestant (he won) and later a producer. Apart from their work on-screen, the troupe took their variety shows on tour across Ukraine and Russia, performing for sold-out crowds in theaters and banquet halls. "Two or three times on the road we almost died," Pikalov told me. Their tour bus once broke down in the middle of nowhere as the temperature dropped to forty degrees below zero Celsius. Another time, in the Russian city of Nizhny Novgorod, a knife fight broke out among members of the crowd, and the troupe got pulled into the melee. "Somehow we always got away clean," Pikalov said. But he remembers telling Zelensky: "'You live under a lucky star. Just watch out that it doesn't turn away from you one day.' The only thing we could do is pray to God—let it not be today, maybe tomorrow."

❖

The studio's success made Zelensky a wealthy man by the time he turned thirty in 2008. He and his business partners, the Shefir brothers, began to stash their wealth offshore around that time, primarily in Cyprus, a favorite tax haven for the Russian and Ukrainian elites. Millions of dollars flowed into their offshore companies, beyond the reach of Ukraine's tax inspectors, and much of it came from the oligarchs who owned the television networks that aired and financed Zelensky's productions.

The more capital he accumulated, the more bashful he became about the topic. "I don't talk about my income," he once said. "It makes me really ashamed." It troubled him that, as a rich celebrity, he risked losing touch with his audience. Most of the people who watched his shows and bought tickets to his movies were poor, at least by Western standards. Ukraine has one of the highest poverty rates in Europe. Zelensky's mother earned a typical pension of sixteen hundred hryvnias a month, worth roughly $200 at the time she retired. "People are down and out," Zelensky said when an interviewer asked about his wealth. "I don't want to rub it in their faces. They have it hard enough."

When the details of his offshore wealth were exposed in 2021 as part of a massive data leak known as the Pandora Papers, Zelensky, then in the second year of his presidency, was forced to make some awkward excuses. He denied laundering money or evading taxes on the millions of dollars he'd earned in the entertainment business. But he admitted to using offshore tax havens to "protect" his assets from the state. "All the networks had companies offshore," he said, "because it gave them a chance to avoid political influence."

As his viewership grew into the millions, Zelensky did face pressure from the politicians he satirized, and it grew worse after the 2010 presidential elections, which played out like a rematch of the Orange Revolution. The favorite to win was Yulia Tymoshenko, who promised to continue Ukraine's integration with the West. But Yanukovych also ran, and this time the Kremlin stepped up its support, relying on a group of friendly billionaires to grease his path to power. One of them hired a team of pollsters and image-makers to hone Yanukovych's message, while others used their TV networks in Ukraine to deliver that message to the electorate. In his speeches and TV appearances, Yanukovych argued that Ukraine had lost its way since the Orange Revolution, that it needed to get back on track, restore ties with Russia, and respect the rights of Russian-speakers in eastern and southern Ukraine. The message was blatantly divisive, making little effort to appeal to the western regions of the country, where most people speak Ukrainian and want little to do with Russia. Through extensive polling, the Yanukovych operation calculated that their promise of economic growth and appeals to Russian tribalism would get enough votes in the east and south to tip the scales in their favor. The strategy worked.

When the results came in, the electoral map was split down the middle. Western regions of the country voted overwhelmingly for Yulia Tymoshenko. But the more populous districts in the east and south handed Yanukovych a narrow victory in the race, which international observers deemed free and fair. For Putin, it was a triumph. All he needed to reverse the humiliation of the Orange Revolution was a few years of patience and some clever investments from the oligarchs in his court. The Kremlin's favored candidate now ruled over all of Ukraine, installed without bloodshed, both loyal and legitimate. As Putin phrased it during one of his meetings with Yanukovych that summer, relations between Russia and Ukraine had "acquired the character of a strategic partnership," while their militaries had come to enjoy an "atmosphere of cooperation." To maintain his popularity at home, Yanukovych had the support of Ukraine's biggest media tycoons, whose TV channels continued to shill for him and, on many issues, for Russia.

One of those channels, Inter TV, happened to be Zelensky's employer at the time, sending paychecks to his production company and its offshore accounts. After the elections, Yanukovych rewarded the channel's owner with one of the choicest jobs in his administration: director of the Security Service of Ukraine, the country's main spy agency. The following year, Zelensky became the general producer of Inter TV, in charge of all the programming except for the news. "I always had conflicts with the news side," he said. They would urge him to tone down the satire on *Evening Kvartal* and stay away from politics. One of Yanukovych's allies even offered to buy his loyalty. The price, Zelensky later claimed, was $100 million. "I didn't go for it. I'm not sick in the head," he said. "My life, my reputation, and my family are worth more than that sum."

In the second year of Yanukovych's presidency, Zelensky decided to move his productions to another channel. The politics at Inter TV, he said, made it "physically impossible" for him to work there. But his troupe continued to perform for the political elites, including Yanukovych and members of his entourage, who would pay upward of

$20,000 for a private show at one of their parties. Zelensky never liked these performances. He craved the laughter of a crowd when he took the stage, not the clinking of forks and knives against fine china.

Even by the gaudy standards of Eastern European plutocrats, the wealth amassed by Yanukovych stood out. Prosecutors would later allege that, during his four years in power, he and his allies siphoned as much as $100 billion into offshore bank accounts—a sum equal to about half of Ukraine's total economic output in the year before Yanukovych was ousted. His base of support in the east of the country saw a rush of government investment. Donetsk, the biggest city in the Donbas, got a new international airport just in time to host the 2012 European soccer championships, which gave Yanukovych a taste of international prestige and recognition. His allies took top posts across the country, filling the upper ranks of the police, the security services, and the courts, which promptly sent his nemesis, Yulia Tymoshenko, to prison for abuse of office. So many of these officials came from his base in the Donbas that a joke started going around about a homeless man sleeping on the streets of eastern Ukraine. Police run up and bundle him into a van. "Where are you taking me," he shouts. "To western Ukraine," the cops tell him. "A mayor's seat has become available." By the summer of 2012, Yanukovych felt so secure in his post that he agreed to give an interview to the Western press. One afternoon that June, his aides took me up to see him in the presidential chambers on Bankova Street, in the same set of rooms where I would later meet President Zelensky. "I remember your face," Yanukovych told me. We had seen each other on the campaign trail a couple of years earlier. "Especially that smile. The American smile."

There was no photographer with me that day. But the president had put on a layer of pancake makeup just in case, along with a boxy suit that shimmered a little in the glow of the chandeliers. The rooms around us, with their gold and ivory accents, a heraldic tapestry depicting a warrior and a lion—they suited Yanukovych well. Along with his shiny tie and lacquered bouffant, these were the accessories of power that he wanted to see in the mirror. What interested me most at the time was his decision to imprison Tymoshenko. Apart from the obvious violation of her rights, the case made no political sense. She posed no real threat to his rule. The charges against her were a petty vendetta. Didn't he see the precedent it set? Eventually his time would come to leave office, and his enemies would also want revenge. "Of course this is possible," he answered with a sigh. "We are now trying to stop this cycle."

But it didn't seem to worry him too much. He was only a couple of years into his first term as president. He had the backing of the Kremlin, and his hold on power seemed absolute. "When these trials end," he said, referring to the prosecutions against his opponents, several of which were still ongoing at the time, "then we should stop this practice. It should never happen again." Soon his assistant asked me to wrap things up, and I asked Yanukovych about the news. The previous day, his party had pushed through a law to make Russian an official language in eastern Ukraine. Ukrainian nationalists and supporters of the Orange Revolution had protested the law inside and outside the parliament. To them it looked like a bow of allegiance to Moscow. During one debate the previous week, they had blocked the podium in the plenary hall, and a brawl broke out. Dozens of parliamentarians punched and kicked each other in the very spot where Yanukovych had taken the oath of office two years earlier. When it was over, an opposition lawmaker had to be taken to the hospital, blood streaming down his face.

Over what? Ukrainians had always been free to speak Russian if they wanted. Their country's most successful production studio, Kvartal 95, made movies and TV shows in Russian that were broadcast nationwide. Why did Yanukovych need to ram this bill into law? The president answered with a question. "Do I like it when this goes on in parliament? Of course I don't like it," he said, referring to the violence. "It's a low level of culture. It's the language of ultimatums and force. But it goes on from both sides. First one side beats the other, then the other beats the first. At some point this too will end. We have to keep believing that it will."

CHAPTER 5

ANNEXATION

THE NEXT REVOLUTION BEGAN AS A VIGIL. FEW EXPECTED IT TO GROW INTO MUCH more. Street politics in Ukraine, particularly in the capital, had become a pastime in the years after the Orange Revolution, with protests and rallies serving as an antidote to cynicism and a showcase for the many frustrations of the young, the poor, the ambitious, or the voiceless. They happened almost every week, and the one that would evolve into an insurrection looked modest by the standards of protests in Kyiv, especially when compared to the upheavals it would bring.

On that first night, in late November 2013, about a thousand protestors gathered on Independence Square, the urban crossroads known around the city as the Maidan. Most of them were students from the city's universities, and they all felt duped and betrayed that night. For several months, President Yanukovych had been promising to sign an economic pact with the European Union. It did not offer much hope for Ukraine to join the E.U. anytime soon, but at least the deal held some promise of a lasting turn westward, toward the kinds of reforms that Poland, the Baltic states, and other former satellites of Moscow had already undergone since the fall of the Soviet Union, leaving Ukraine far behind in terms of living standards and the rule of law.

Yanukovych had promised to sign the deal that fall, during an E.U. summit in Lithuania. But, after a meeting with Putin in early November, he changed his mind. The Kremlin threatened an economic blockade if Ukraine went ahead with its European integration. It also promised a loan worth $15 billion to lure Yanukovych away from the West. For the students on the square, the reversal was painful in part because of how suddenly it came. They felt they had the most to lose from Yanukovych's decision to integrate with Russia. For them it meant their most productive years would be spent in the same Ukraine their parents had known. They called it *sovok*, their slang for all the shabby vestiges of Soviet existence—the lumbering economy, the corrupt bureaucracy, the doltish complacency and stagnation that Yanukovych embodied in their eyes. So they got together on the Maidan and built a protest camp of tents and banners, sang songs, and chanted, resigned not to leave until the president left office or signed the European deal.

The size of the demonstration quickly grew into the tens of thousands and spread to other cities nationwide. At first the mood was more festive than angry or fraught, and it stayed that way for about a week before the riot troops arrived. On the night of November 30, they stormed the encampment, swinging their batons, and began to stomp the tents and banners. It was the first of several turning points that winter. The crowds on the square began to multiply after that, more outraged over the treatment of the first group of demonstrators than any abstract political issue of Europe versus Russia. The camp was rebuilt and fortified with barricades made from whatever could be scavenged and thrown into a pile—old tires, trash bins, logs, and bricks. People descended on the square from different cities and all walks of life, chanting and singing and sleeping in their tents beneath the flags of Ukraine and the European Union. The national anthem was sung every hour. The revolution was underway.

It was the second one Ukraine had seen in a decade, and, once again, the Zelensky family watched it from the sidelines. Many of Ukraine's most famous entertainers performed for the protestors on Independence Square that winter, or at least came out to support them. But Zelensky stayed away. Throughout the uprising, he spent most of his time in Moscow. His production company had an office there, and he was working on a couple of big projects, a rom-com and a sitcom, both of which had Russian stars and sponsors. The sitcom, called *Matchmakers*, was due to air on the Kremlin-owned channel Rossiya-1, whose news division was busy describing the revolution in Ukraine as an anti-Russian coup orchestrated by the CIA.

The relationship embarrassed Zelensky at home, but he stuck with it. Once, during a press conference to promote his rom-com, a reporter asked what he thought about the uprising in Kyiv, which was then in its second month. The question seemed to annoy Zelensky. "We're with the people," he said without much conviction, reminding the reporter that the press conference was meant to talk about a movie, not politics. "Come on," he said. "We came here for a comedy."

Such deflections could only buy Zelensky so much time. By the end of 2013, the revolutionary movement was all around him. It was the main topic on all the biggest talk shows in both Russia and Ukraine. It led every news cycle and came up at every dinner table. Zelensky and his friends were having the same debates in private. But, from watching their comedy, their fans could only guess what side they were on. "It wasn't that we didn't sympathize with the supporters of the revolution," Olena told me. But the uprising felt too familiar, like a reboot of the Orange Revolution. In their comedy, Zelensky and his team sought the same middle ground they had occupied back then. They made fun of the politicians, all of them, while trying not to offend the people on either side of the political divide. They didn't always succeed. On the last day of 2013, Zelensky hosted the annual New Year's special on Ukrainian TV, and it included a joke that would come back to haunt him. During the opening sketch, one of the characters suggested the motion of police batons hitting protestors could be used as a source of alternative energy, like wind turbines. Some of the leaders of the revolution would later condemn the joke as an insult to the victims of police brutality. Beyond that slip, Zelensky and his team avoided cracking wise about the demonstrators.

A few members of his troupe spent time on Independence Square during the revolution. Pikalov, who was best known for satirizing Yanukovych, had many fans among the protestors, and several of his friends were living on the square. He and others from Kvartal 95 supported the protest camp. But they kept their involvement discreet. "We didn't do it for the photos, for the good P.R.," said Yevhen Koshovy, the comedian who made the joke about the swinging police batons. "Good deeds like it quiet."

They also had a financial motive for avoiding Independence Square during the revolution. Some 85 percent of their studio's income came from the Russian market. Its success depended on Zelensky's partners and audiences in Russia, and siding with the revolution would risk alienating both. Apart from the business case for neutrality, the leaders of the uprising turned Zelensky off. The energy on Independence Square derived from grassroots activism—what Ukrainians like to call "self-organization." But plenty of established politicians tried to harness it, just as they had during the Orange Revolution. Among the most prominent leaders of the uprising in 2014 was Petro Poroshenko, a former central banker and minister of trade who had earned a vast fortune in the candy business. He owned one of Ukraine's leading television networks, Channel 5, which had supported the Orange Revolution in 2004–2005 and, a decade later, became a mouthpiece for what became known as the Revolution of Dignity. Its other leaders included Vitali Klitschko, the former world boxing champion, and a melange of politicians and soapbox demagogues from the radical right.

From his career in political satire, Zelensky had an instinctive mistrust for populists who claimed to speak on behalf of the people, and many of the revolutionary leaders fit that description in 2014. Zelensky kept his distance from them. But as the standoff in Kyiv got more violent, it became harder for him to maintain an air of artistic detachment. Two months into the revolution, Independence Square began to resemble a medieval battleground. Vicious brawls broke out between protestors and police. The anti-riot troops, known as the Berkut, fired water cannons in the middle of winter, covering the square in sheets of ice. The protestors shot back with fireworks and petrol bombs. Some built wooden catapults to fling projectiles at police. When the troops approached, the protestors would often ignite their barricades, piled high with tires and soaked in gasoline, sending towers of fire and thick black smoke into the sky. Similar scenes played out in cities across the country that winter. Protestors armed themselves with clubs, shields, and helmets and took government buildings by storm. Police tried to beat them back with truncheons, tear gas, stun grenades, and rubber bullets. In most cases, they failed.

For Yanukovych, the clashes soon became untenable. The government quarter in Kyiv was paralyzed. Bankova Street was under siege. From the West, the president came under intense pressure to avoid violence, to negotiate with the protestors, and to grant concessions. From the east, the Kremlin urged him to put down the rebellion. To preserve his hold on power, his government rushed through a set of laws in January that restricted the freedoms of speech and assembly. But the crackdown backfired. The encampment only grew, and the clashes with police devolved into a grudge match, no longer driven by the political goals of the belligerents but by their raw desire for revenge. Firebombs were often hurled directly at the huddled troops, covering them in burning fuel.

Many protestors were snatched up off the street, beaten and tortured in custody. Some disappeared.

On Bankova Street, the sense of panic around Yanukovych grew as the violence escalated and his allies began to defect. The prime minister quit at the end of January, followed quickly by his entire cabinet. The president clung to his post for a few more weeks while attempting to reach a compromise with the revolutionary leaders. He was ready to call early elections and amnesty all the protestors. But it was too late. Too much blood had been spilled for all his opponents to accept a truce. Protestors overran several cities in western Ukraine, seizing armories inside police stations and threatening to march on the capital. Even if the political opposition in Kyiv was ready to make a deal, their more radical allies in the revolutionary movement demanded Yanukovych give up power. The deadlock lasted through the coldest days of winter, and it was only broken by a final spasm of violence.

On February 18, 2014, a mob of protestors set fire to the offices of Yanukovych's party and tried again to take the government district by storm. The riot troops and security forces responded with an all-out assault on the Maidan, burning down the House of Trade Unions, which had served as the revolution's headquarters. At least seven police officers and nearly a dozen protestors were killed in the mayhem. Two days later, the violence reached a horrifying climax when police snipers opened fire on demonstrators near the square, killing dozens of them. It was a massacre unlike any Ukraine had seen since World War II. Rows of bodies lay on the Maidan, their faces covered in bedding and blankets just outside the hotel where I was staying. On the opposite side of the square, the lobby of another hotel became a makeshift field hospital, its floor slick with blood. Up the street, the monastery of St. Michael offered shelter to protestors fleeing the bullets. The monks inside, some dressed in helmets and bulletproof vests, presided over vigils and funerals. In total, thirteen police officers were killed in those furious days of fighting. Among the protestors, the death toll topped a hundred.

For weeks the revolution had been building toward such a catastrophe. But the most common reaction was shock when it finally came. No one could believe that police fired live rounds at people armed with sticks and shields. It was the final turning point in the rebellion, and even Yanukovych seemed to realize he could not survive it. The night after the massacre, he boarded his helicopter and fled the capital, first to eastern Ukraine and then across the border into Russia, the only country that would offer him protection. The revolution had achieved its purpose. Soon Russia would exact a price.

❖

Few people paid much attention to the region of Crimea in the days that followed the revolution. There was too much turmoil everywhere else. Protestors stormed the lavish home of Yanukovych outside Kyiv, and their photos of his weird possessions went viral around the world: a pen full of ostriches, a golden loaf of bread, a private restaurant designed like a pirate ship, floors in the sauna complex inlaid with semiprecious stones. (To the disappointment of the protestors, the golden toilet long rumored to be in the house turned out to be a myth.)

From his exile in Russia, Yanukovych tried to maneuver his way back to power. Six days after he was overthrown, he gave a delusional press conference in the Russian city of Rostov. "Nobody overthrew me," he began. "I was forced to leave Ukraine due to an immediate threat to my life and the lives of those close to me." The people who had taken power in his place, he said, are "nationalist and pro-fascist hoodlums who represent an absolute minority of the residents of Ukraine." He called for a new presidential vote to be held that year. He called for urgent reforms of the Constitution. He called for an investigation of the massacre of protestors on Independence Square.

It wasn't clear whom he thought he was fooling. There was no way back for him now. In the eyes of most Ukrainians, the blood of those protestors was on his hands, regardless of whether he had given explicit orders to open fire. Most regions of the country had already sided with the revolution. Its supporters had taken control over state institutions, regional legislatures, and police precincts.

The main exceptions were in eastern and southern Ukraine, the Yanukovych strongholds. In those regions, and especially in Crimea, a counterrevolution had begun. A few days after the regime in Kyiv fell, a group of heavily armed men showed up at the regional parliament building in Crimea and rushed inside with guns drawn. They looked and moved like professionals, with masks and gear identical to those of Russian special forces. Only the patches were missing; all identifying insignia had been removed from their uniforms. The troops disarmed the parliament's security guards and took up positions in and around the plenary hall.

That morning, while the gunmen stood in the wings with assault rifles and rocket propelled grenades, the chamber's lawmakers held two critical votes, both recorded as unanimous. The first vote ordered a referendum to decide whether Crimea should break away from Ukraine. The second one appointed a new prime minister of Crimea, Sergei Aksyonov, a hard-line separatist whose political party, Russian Unity, held only four out of the chamber's one hundred seats. That was enough for Aksyonov to assume control. The following day, he issued a public appeal to the Kremlin: "I call on Russian president Vladimir Putin for assistance in guaranteeing peace and calm on the territory of the autonomous Republic of Crimea."

The appeal was just a pretext. Russian troops were already there. They had seized the main airport in Crimea and fanned out across the peninsula. Putin lied to the world about the gunmen, calling them "local self-defense forces," militiamen who stood up to defend their land from the "neo-Nazis" in Kyiv. In fact they were Russian commandos, and they hadn't traveled far. Many of them were based in Crimea as part of Russia's Black Sea Fleet, and they surrounded all the military bases Ukraine had in Crimea. The invaders came with sound intelligence about the troops inside those bases. They knew the names of the Ukrainian officers, the names of their family members, and where they lived.

"None of us imagined that our neighbors, our brothers, could come to our door with guns drawn," said Oleksandr Polishchuk, who served on Ukraine's national security council at the time, and later took a senior post in Zelensky's government. "But they came to us and said, 'You're not leaving. We know where your wife is. We know where your children are. You can decide to be a brave soldier, but then we'll go and kill them all.' That is what happened in Crimea." A handful of senior Ukrainian officers agreed to switch sides and join the Russians. Many others were prepared to fight back, but the orders from Kyiv never came. "The key reason was psychological," said Polishchuk. "Ukrainian soldiers were not mentally ready to shoot at Russians at the time."

❖

Within a few days, the Russian takeover of Crimea was complete. Putin's troops took over the government headquarters and handed the keys to Aksyonov. About a week into his tenure as the new leader of Crimea, I went to see him at one of the government buildings he had occupied. Sandbags covered the windows when I arrived, and two guards in full combat gear sat on either side of the doorway, staring at me through the holes in their ski masks. Aksyonov was up on the second floor, accompanied by a team of political advisers from Moscow who wanted to make him look less like a thug and more like a politician. But Aksyonov, a block of muscle in a baggy suit, was poorly cast for the role. Before going into politics, he ran with a crew of smugglers and racketeers who knew him by his gangland nickname, the Goblin. Now, with Moscow's blessing, he had taken the title of prime minister and was preparing to meet with Putin in the Kremlin. "I was chosen as a crisis manager," he said as we sat down. "I understand my historical role."

When I pressed him about the way he had taken power at the barrel of a gun, Aksyonov always reverted to the same deflection: If the revolutionaries in Kyiv could do it, why can't he? If they could use force to seize government buildings, what was wrong with his men doing the same thing in Crimea? If the uprising had the support of Western governments, why shouldn't he ask Russia to come to his defense? He didn't care about the sanctions that the U.S. and Europe had imposed against him and a long list of others involved in the Crimean power grab. "On what grounds should America tell us what to do?" he demanded. "Independence is what we want. It's what Crimeans want!"

The following week, he and his Russian backers organized a hasty referendum to test that hypothesis. The ballot did not offer voters the choice to remain in Ukraine. They could either agree to full independence for Crimea or unification with Russia. Around the region, campaign posters promised massive hikes in wages and pensions if Crimea chose to become a Russian province. The Kremlin's propaganda channels warned that, without the protection of Russian troops, gangs of fascists would come from Ukraine to subdue Crimea by force. In that climate, the results of the referendum were no surprise. The official tally was almost unanimous—97 percent of the vote—in favor of the Russian annexation of Crimea.

The next day, Aksyonov and a few of his fellow separatists traveled to the Kremlin for the annexation ceremony. Several hundred members of the Russian elite gathered under the soaring arches of St. George's Hall to hear one of the defining speeches of Putin's reign. It remains a singular moment of triumph for the Russian president, and a high point for the admiration he enjoyed among his people. The move to seize Crimea was illegal and condemned throughout the world. The U.S. and Europe imposed sanctions on the Russian economy and blacklisted dozens of Russian officials and oligarchs. But the vast majority of Russia's citizens celebrated the land grab. It had been swift and nearly bloodless. It added around two million people to Russia's long-declining population, and it expanded Russian territory by an area about the size of Belgium.

Not since the Second World War had a European power expanded its borders by force. In the pantheon of Kremlin leaders, the stick-up made Putin feel closer to the legacies of Peter the Great and other "gatherers of land," and the effect on his ambitions was clear in the speech he delivered that day. For a start, he said the Americans were long overdue for a challenge to their hegemony. "They came to believe in their own exceptionalism, in being the chosen ones," he said. "They feel they are allowed to rule the fate of the world." As for the wider battleground of Ukraine, Putin promised never to accept the outcome of the revolution. "The main perpetrators of the coup were nationalists, neo-Nazis, Russophobes, and anti-Semites." Before too long, Putin warned, they would all get their comeuppance.

❖

As the occupation of Crimea unfolded, Zelensky appeared on television in a way his fans had never seen. Political events in Ukraine had become too dramatic and dangerous for satire. The country stood at the edge of a war with Russia, and Zelensky felt his voice carried enough weight to make a difference, to change people's minds, including in Crimea and the eastern regions of the country. More than any of the politicians who had taken power in Kyiv that winter, Zelensky held sway over the people in those regions. They had followed his career, watched his movies, and appreciated his insistence on speaking Russian when he took the stage. Having worn a wry mask of neutrality throughout that winter's revolution, he decided it was time to make a political stand.

It took the form of a three-minute speech he delivered on one of Ukraine's leading news programs, sitting at the desk next to the anchorwoman, who seemed a bit confused about the presence of a comedian on her newscast. "Now a man who needs no introduction," she said, turning to Zelensky. Beneath his smile, the comedian looked anxious. "No jokes this time," he said into the camera. The first part of his appeal struck out at Yanukovych. "You're no longer the president of Ukraine," Zelensky said in Russian. "That's what the people of our country have decided. Believe me, in the west, in the east, in my beloved Kryvyi Rih, everyone believes that there is no more President Yanukovych in our history. Step aside. Above all, do not allow any chance of separatism. Stop appearing at press conferences. It's not interesting anymore. It's boring. I'm sorry. Just go."

One might have concluded from this introduction that Zelensky had taken the side of the revolutionary leaders. But his next appeal was aimed at them. Among their first decisions had to do with the language he was speaking. After taking power the previous week, they decided to repeal the law Yanukovych had enacted to make Russian an official language in eastern Ukraine. That decision, Zelensky said, would only stoke divisions in the country at a time when it needed to stay united. "In the east, in Crimea, if people want to speak in Russian, lay off of them," he told the leaders of the uprising. "Leave them alone. Give them the legal right to speak in Russian. Language will never divide our homeland. I have Jewish blood, I speak in Russian, and I'm a citizen of Ukraine. I love this country, and I don't want to be part of another country."

With the annexation of Crimea, Putin had used questions of language and ethnicity as pretexts for the use of military force. Zelensky saw the hollowness of that excuse for violence, because he knew there were no threats to his rights as a Russian-speaker in Ukraine, certainly none that might require any intervention from the Kremlin. In the third part of his speech, Zelensky pleaded with Putin to stop. "Dear Vladimir Vladimirovich, do not allow yourself even to hint at a military conflict. Russia and Ukraine, we really are brotherly nations," he said. "We are one color. We have the same blood. We all understand each other, regardless of language." Then he stuttered and hesitated for a moment before setting aside his pride. "If you need it, I can beg you on my knees," he said to Putin. "But please, don't put our people on their knees."

The statement put Zelensky in a role he had never occupied before. It marked the point when his political satire switched into political activism. Instead of holding a fun-house mirror to the faces of the powerful, he now used the power of his own celebrity to influence their actions and, he hoped, to shape events. Eight years later, with Kyiv under siege, Zelensky would make a similar statement from the barricaded rooms of the presidential compound. He would refer to his comedy as a means of making peace with Russia and Belarus, whose people, he said, had always been fans of his movies. "I have a perfect sense of the mentality of those nations," he said in the first week of the full-scale invasion. "I knew what we have in common, what differences there were, and where to find the points of contact that could prevent us from fighting wars and let us live in peace."

His career in show business had given him a way to reach across borders, to appeal to Russians in their own language, to convince them, if not also their leaders, that Ukraine posed no threat to their security. When he used that power for the first time in 2014, it had no effect on the course of history. Russia followed its invasion of Crimea with far deadlier attacks on eastern Ukraine and, eight years later, an all-out war that sought nothing short of Ukraine's annihilation. But Zelensky never abandoned the belief that his fame as an actor could help him as a peacemaker. Having learned to make Russians laugh, he thought he could also make them listen.

Part II

CHAPTER 6

BATTLE OF KYIV

THE NIGHTS WERE ALWAYS HARDEST FOR ZELENSKY IN THE BUNKER. PUSHED UP AGAINST a wall in his lower-level chamber, his cot was barely wide enough for him to toss and turn. The room was quiet, so deep underground that the howl of Kyiv's air-raid sirens could not reach the ears of the president. Even a direct hit from an aerial bomb on Bankova Street would not jostle him much at that depth. But Zelensky's phone was always beside him, and its buzzing rarely stopped for very long. When he reached for it, the screen made his face look like a ghost in the dark, his eyes scanning headlines and casualty counts, short videos and photos of the devastation, an unending newsreel of his country's nightmare. All of it was his to solve.

Later in the war, when we talked about those nights, he recalled the same thought turning over in his head: "I've let myself sleep, but now what? Something is happening right now." Somewhere in Ukraine the bombs were exploding, entire regions were falling under Russian occupation, thousands of his troops were pinned down in their trenches, bleeding and dying, with waves of shrapnel flying over their heads. In many places, especially in western Ukraine, missiles were the predominant form of Russian terror. One of them slammed into the side of an apartment block in Kyiv on the third morning of the invasion, ripping a hole into its upper stories. Footage of the strike led the news around the world, and people came from all over Kyiv to see the damage, staring at the pieces of furniture that dangled from the windows, private rooms torn open to the eyes of strangers, their occupants missing or dead. Another rocket landed in the central square of Kharkiv in the east, and soon the bombardment of that city turned much of its historical center into rubble. The strikes became so common they were condensed into statistics: more than 160 missiles in the first day, more than 400 in the first week.

Zelensky could do nothing to stop these attacks, but his desire to know about them was compulsive. "In those first days, I would wake everybody up," he said. "I didn't have the right to sleep until I knew what strikes had landed where." The bunker had no natural light, which meant no sunrise to mark the start of any day. But the ceiling lamps continued humming through the night in the upper-level conference room, as staffers stayed up to monitor the advance of the invaders. As early as 4:50 in the morning, Zelensky would also be up and on the phone, requesting an update from his military commander. "My day always starts with a call to Valery Zaluzhny, with his report," he told me. "Always."

General Zaluzhny, the commander in chief of Ukraine's armed forces, took these calls inside his own set of bunkers, located more than seventy meters below the headquarters of the General Staff, about three miles west of Bankova Street. The facility was not connected to the one beneath the presidential compound. But they resembled each other, with the same brown tiles on the floors, the same harsh light and glossy paint. The military bunker was quite a bit larger and, from the outset, a lot more crowded. Hundreds of people, including the families and children of high-ranking officers, lived down there during the early weeks of the invasion. Most of the top brass worked in the command center, where Zaluzhny spent much of his time. Bright and tidy, with the faint smell of vape smoke hanging in the air, the room contained a long table covered in battle maps, a bank of yellow secure-line phones, a ventilation shaft that ran along the ceiling, and not much else. For his early morning calls with the president, Zaluzhny would go to a smaller room, where he could keep their conversation private. "I don't like to share that moment with anyone," Zelensky said. "We start with his report tête-à-tête."

❖

The two men first met at the start of Zelensky's tenure, in the spring of 2019, when it fell to Zaluzhny to brief the incoming administration on military matters. About a head taller than the president and five years older, the general made a strong impression on Zelensky, both in his confidence as a commander and the easy rapport he enjoyed with his troops. The general's dream as a younger man had been to perform on the KVN circuit like Zelensky, but his military service did not leave him time, he later said, to pursue his gifts for comedy. As he rose through the ranks, he brought his sense of humor with him to the garrisons. "I'm always pranking, always with the gags," Zaluzhny told me. "It's more fun for me that way."

Zelensky took an early liking to him. But the months leading up to the invasion strained their relationship. Zaluzhny advocated for a full-scale mobilization of reserves and the fortification of Ukraine's borders with Russia to prepare for the coming attack. The president held him back, afraid that such measures would spread panic among the population and give the Russians an excuse to strike. The disagreement hung in the air at the start of the invasion, but they moved past it.

On the first day, Zaluzhny reported that thousands of enemy troops had broken through the northern border. By the second day, they had seized control of the Chernobyl nuclear power plant, where an accidental meltdown in 1986 had caused the worst nuclear disaster in history. The small detachment of National Guardsmen stationed at the facility surrendered to the invaders without a fight. The Russians then proceeded to set up camps, dig trenches, and mass heavy weaponry around Chernobyl, kicking up radioactive dust and taking the staff of the power plant hostage. From there, they intended to press on toward the capital, and Zaluzhny had a plan to stop them.

In his calls with the president, he explained that it would be costly. "We were pursuing two strategic goals," the general said. "We could not allow the capture of Kyiv. And on all the other vectors, we had to spill their blood, even if it meant losing territory." The military did not have enough equipment or manpower to confront the Russian forces head-on. Their best defense would be to set a series of traps for the enemy. "It's textbook stuff," Zaluzhny said. If the Russian columns keep moving toward Kyiv, their lines of supply would soon become strained. Their tanks would run out of fuel, blocking the advance of the vehicles behind them. "In some places we lose territory," Zaluzhny admitted. "We let their columns advance." But once their engines started to stall, he said, the Ukrainians would have a chance to surround the columns and tear them apart.

Though he kept the president informed about his strategy, Zaluzhny avoided sharing too many details. The risk of leaks and spies in the political leadership worried the general, and the decisions made in the lead-up to the invasion had not been forgotten. It was now obvious to the top officials involved in the national defense that the military leadership had been right to call for more preparations that winter. But Zaluzhny did not lord it over the president. Their tone was respectful and somewhat formal on the phone. They referred to each other by their first names and patronymics, and they did not dwell on past mistakes in those early conversations. Though Zaluzhny kept the president informed, both of them understood who was in charge of military matters.

"My aim was not to drag him into it," the general later told me. "What I hate more than anything else in the army is when a lower rank shifts part of the responsibility onto their superiors. That can get you killed straightaway in my command. And I didn't want to do that in this case with the president, because I am the commander in chief of the Armed Forces of Ukraine. I am commanding the operation." He asked Zelensky to have patience. It would take time to assess whether the defensive strategy could stop the Russian column from reaching Kyiv. "Those first days were really a bit difficult," the general said. "We had to understand how the operation was proceeding, whether it had a chance of surviving or not."

To the generals' relief, Zelensky seemed happy during this early phase of the invasion to let Zaluzhny take the lead on battlefield decisions. The president did not pretend to be a tactical savant. He focused instead on the aspects of the war where he could be most effective—inspiring Ukrainians to resist, and pressuring the West to help. His most frequent questions to the military command in those first days were pragmatic: What do you need? How can we support you? The armed forces asked for weapons, more of them every day, and their wish list quickly grew to include systems the West refused to provide: fighter jets, tanks, multiple-rocket launchers, heavy artillery.

Zelensky made it his mission to push these demands as forcefully as possible, and his days became a relentless succession of phone calls with foreign leaders. Most were frustrating. "They didn't believe in us," Oleksiy Danilov, the national security adviser, recalls of that period. "They were afraid that the weapons would fall into Russian hands." President Joe Biden dismissed Zelensky's pleas to impose a no-fly zone over Ukraine, as it could require U.S. or NATO forces to shoot down Russian aircraft. But Zelensky kept demanding more weapons for his military and more sanctions against Russia. Soon his message began to connect.

On February 27, the fourth day of the invasion, the European Union closed its air space to Russian planes, including the private jets of Russian oligarchs. The next day, the U.S. and its allies agreed to freeze some $300 billion in Russian gold and foreign currency reserves, blocking the Kremlin's access to a massive part of its war chest. Some of Russia's biggest lenders were cut off that week from the global banking system, while the E.U. set aside its rules against shipping weapons into conflict zones and agreed to arm Ukraine.

Zelensky was not the only impetus for these decisions. Many other factors were at play. The French, for instance, were livid with Putin for making a fool of their president, Emmanuel Macron, who had believed and even echoed the Kremlin's promises not to invade. Any gesture of appeasement toward the Russians would also come with serious political risks for European leaders. Their citizens pressured them to help Ukraine at least as much as Zelensky did. Nine out of ten Europeans surveyed in the first month of the war sympathized with the Ukrainians and welcomed their war refugees, and two-thirds supported giving Ukraine military equipment to defend itself. The U.S. saw an even stronger wave of outrage against Russia. Americans wanted the Biden administration to do more for Ukraine, even at the risk of sparking a wider war. Three-quarters of Americans said in a survey in early March that the U.S. and NATO should impose a no-fly zone to stop the Russian bombing raids, and four out of five people wanted to punish Russia with stronger sanctions.

Many Western leaders may have preferred to remain on the sidelines. Europe relies on Russia for much of the oil, gas, metals, and minerals that power its economy. But Zelensky's actions, and the power of his appeals, put to shame the politicians who refused to help him. His willingness to die for his country's independence challenged the rest of the democratic world to show how much they would sacrifice for the values they profess. Their failure to support Ukraine in that moment would make them look like hypocrites and cowards. Their inaction would look like complicity, and, if Zelensky died, he wanted his foreign allies to understand that his blood would be on their hands. "Do prove that you are with us," he said in a speech to the European Parliament at the end of the invasion's first week. "Do prove that you will not let us go. Do prove that you indeed are Europeans, and then life will win over death, and light will win over darkness." As they listened through their earphones, the European lawmakers could hear the interpreter choke back tears while translating Zelensky's words.

Even Switzerland came around, putting aside its tradition of neutrality to support the E.U. sanctions on Russia. The chancellor of Germany, Olaf Scholz, decided in the first days of the invasion to set aside the ethos of pacifism that had shaped Berlin's role in the world for three decades. In a speech to the German parliament on February 27, he promised to arm Ukraine, isolate Russia, and spend a hundred billion euros to revive the neglected German military. "We have entered a new era," the chancellor said. In the cities of Ukraine, "people are not just defending their homeland. They are fighting for freedom and their democracy, for values that we share with them." Enormous crowds had gathered in Berlin that day to denounce Putin and demand more support for Ukraine. Scholz could not ignore them; they were right outside the windows of the parliament building as he spoke. Nor could he ignore Zelensky, whose gaze stared back at him from the front pages of German newspapers and magazines. "The president understood that correctly in his gut," one of Zelensky's advisers told me. "He needed to show the world that the government stands, that we will fight. That broke through the initial shock in the U.S. and Europe."

❖

Amid all his pleas for assistance from the West, it was easy in those days to miss the softer signals Zelensky sent eastward to the Russians. He wanted to negotiate and was willing to make concessions. Whatever fury the president felt in those days, it was not enough to make him abandon the hope of reasoning with Putin and ending the war through diplomacy. "We are not afraid to talk to Russia," he said on the second day of the invasion. "We need to talk about the end of this invasion. We need to talk about a cease-fire."

The first response to these overtures arrived two days later, when Aleksandr Lukashenko, the dictator of Belarus, called Zelensky with an invitation. A former collective farm boss with a droopy mustache, Lukashenko was Putin's closest ally in Europe and a willing accomplice to the invasion. He had allowed Russian forces to gather and prepare on the territory of Belarus, which served as launching ground for the Russian thrust toward Kyiv. Now he was on the phone, offering to play the role of a mediator. He told Zelensky that a round of peace talks could be arranged as soon as the following day. A few hours later, Zelensky appeared in the briefing room to announce that he had accepted the offer. "I don't really believe this meeting will bring results, but let them try," he said. "So that no citizen of Ukraine can have any suspicion that I, as president, didn't try to stop the war when I had the chance, even a small one."

The man Zelensky chose to lead the delegation was his old friend Davyd Arakhamia, who had been living in the presidential bunker from the first day of the invasion. To many observers, the choice looked peculiar. Arakhamia was a member of parliament, the majority leader for Zelensky's party, but he had no experience in international affairs. His professional background was in the tech sector, where he had launched a successful start-up called TemplateMonster that built tools for making websites. In Zelensky's entourage, he was known as a slick talker and a problem solver, and he had no doubt in his own abilities to negotiate a truce as well as any professional diplomat. "All my life people said I could make a deal with anybody, even a corpse," Arakhamia told me. "So I was an organic fit."

His first challenge was reaching the venue. All civilian planes had been grounded, and the roads leading north from Kyiv toward Belarus ran through some of the most intense areas of fighting. In the end, Arakhamia and his team felt it safer to take a detour to the border with Poland, where a pair of Polish Blackhawk helicopters picked them up and got them to Belarus. Zelensky had given them simple instructions: "It doesn't matter what you say," Arakhamia recalled. "The main thing is for them to hear us, to get the signal that we can negotiate."

Late in the afternoon of February 28, the fifth day of the invasion, the delegates gathered at a venue in southeastern Belarus that did little to put the Ukrainians at ease. The negotiating room was inside the former palace of a Russian imperial field marshal, Count Pyotr Rumyantsev, who had conquered and ruled the lands of Ukraine in the late eighteenth century. The contrast between the two sides of the table could hardly have been starker. The Russians showed up in business suits and ties. Arakhamia wore a black baseball cap, cocked slightly to the side. "Our thing was anti-diplomacy, starting with the dress code," he later told me.

"They would start with the legalese, and I'd be like: 'I don't need this bullshit, break it down in normal terms.'"

The session ended with a mutual promise to continue talking—and not much else. Arakhamia returned home in the same roundabout way he had come, and he gave Zelensky a detailed summary of what had happened. The main goal of "establishing contact" with the Russians, he said, had been achieved. They now set out to build a more professional team of diplomats, lawyers, and military officers who could begin to draft the terms of a deal. Over the next few weeks, they came up with a list of proposals that centered around the idea of "permanent neutrality." Ukraine would agree to abandon its plans to join NATO or any other military alliances in exchange for "security guarantees" from Russia and a list of "guarantor states," potentially including the U.S., the U.K., China, France, Germany, Israel, and others. According to a copy of the proposals that was later leaked to an independent Russian journalist, the Ukrainian side called on Putin to meet with Zelensky and negotiate a treaty to end the war.

❖

In the first week of the invasion, reports and images of devastation continued to reach Zelensky at all hours: Dozens of fatalities, including children, as the Russians dropped cluster bombs on residential neighborhoods in Kharkiv, Ukraine's second-biggest city. Five others killed when a pair of missiles struck Kyiv's television tower. A kindergarten shelled in the northern region of Sumy, killing five adults and two children and wounding dozens of others. At least four killed by an aerial bomb in the suburbs of Mariupol in the south. A mortar strike on a maternity hospital near the capital.

But for every report of a Russian atrocity came news of Ukrainians standing their ground. In the city of Chernihiv, northeast of Kyiv, the armed forces repelled the Russian ground assault, capturing enemy vehicles and taking some of the first Russian prisoners of war. Two days later, civilians proved critical to the defense of southern Ukraine by acting as spotters for the military and guiding artillery fire to its targets. A few days after that, as the Russians approached Ukraine's biggest nuclear power plant in the town of Enerhodar, crowds of people stood in the roadways to stop them, facing down tanks with Ukrainian flags and improvised barricades. Similar scenes played out in the southern city of Melitopol, which the Russians occupied in the first days of the war. Local residents rallied in the streets of that city, chanting for the occupiers to turn around and "fuck off." Morale among Ukrainians surged as news of these confrontations spread on social media, each one chipping away at the myth of Russia's indomitability. But none of the early battles mattered more to Ukraine's survival than the one at the airport in Hostomel, near the western edge of Kyiv. On the first day of the invasion, the Ukrainian retreat from that airport looked like a crucial victory for the Russian airborne forces. They only needed to hang on long enough for reinforcements to arrive in military cargo planes, which soon took off from bases in Russia, packed with enough troops and weapons to march on Kyiv the next day. But the planes never came.

As soon as the Ukrainian forces withdrew from the airport, their commanders called in reserves of artillery to bombard it from multiple directions, making it impossible for Russian aircraft to land. The counterstrike lasted several days and involved a motley array of Ukrainian forces with no clear command or cohesion. Apart from professional military units—like the 72nd Motorized Brigade, which brought its heavy cannons to the fight—National Guardsmen descended on the airport, as did special forces troops, policemen, officers of the military intelligence service, and a large number of civilian volunteers. "Military theory does not account for regular dudes with track pants and hunting rifles," said General Zaluzhny, who monitored the battle from his command post. One of his aides in the bunker found the number of a man who lived in Hostomel, a friend of a friend, who agreed to get close enough to the airport to see where the Ukrainian shells were landing and correct their aim over the phone. Scores of enemy paratroopers wound up dead in the battle for the airport, their bodies scattered among the charred remains of their helicopters.

For the leadership in Kyiv, the courage of civilians in this battle, and many others across Ukraine, revealed one of the fundamental flaws in the Russian war plan. Putin counted on at least part of Ukrainian society to welcome his troops as liberators or stand aside and allow the occupation to proceed. "There was the expectation that we would be greeted with flowers," a Russian general later admitted. Instead vast numbers of regular Ukrainians joined the resistance in whatever ways they could, often at great personal risk and with little if any training. In Kyiv and many other cities, long lines formed outside of draft offices as people took up Zelensky's call to enlist. "We had grandmas making Molotov cocktails," said Oleksiy Reznikov, the defense minister. "And their grandsons were ready to throw them." One branch of the military, known as the Territorial Defense Forces, reported accepting one hundred thousand new recruits in the first ten days of the invasion.

At many points along the front, the Russians found themselves outnumbered. Their failure to seize control of any airports near Kyiv forced the invaders to pursue a cruder strategy—a ground assault that would seek to overwhelm Kyiv's defenses. On February 28, the fifth day of the invasion, commercial satellites spotted a vast column of Russian military hardware moving southward toward Kyiv from Belarus. It was over forty miles long and included thousands of military vehicles—towed artillery and anti-aircraft systems, tanks and armored personnel carriers, fuel trucks and mobile hospitals, all the steel machinery of war advancing in a chain that stretched to the horizon. News of the column led many to believe that Kyiv would soon be surrounded. General Zaluzhny saw it differently. The column was headed straight into his trap.

To slow its advance, the Ukrainians blew up the main bridge across the Irpin River, which flows along the western edge of Kyiv, and set off a series of explosions on the dam that holds the city's reservoir, releasing enough water to flood the banks of the Irpin and create impassable swamps in the column's path. The Russian formations continued their advance from the north, but soon their tanks and armored vehicles began running out of fuel, forming a giant row of sitting ducks on the highways north of Kyiv. For Zaluzhny, it was a turning point. "Whatever happens next," he said, "our plan had worked."

Mobile teams of Ukrainian special forces crept up to the column on foot, launched shoulder-fired rockets, and disappeared into the tree line. The weather was on their side. The ground was not frozen solid at the end of February, and the Russian tanks could not easily turn off the roads and advance through the fields and forests. The ones that tried would often get stuck in the mud, forcing other vehicles to tow them out or abandon them. Ukraine's fleet of combat drones, the Bayraktar TB2s, which had been purchased from Turkey in the lead-up to the invasion, began raining rockets down on the Russian vehicles, further stalling their advance. Aerial footage of the drone strikes went viral on social media and served as a major boost to morale.

As he monitored the operation from his bunker, General Zaluzhny could not believe the extent of the failures on the Russian side. He had studied the writings of his counterpart, General Valery Gerasimov, the commander of the Russian Armed Forces, who is seventeen years his senior. He even kept a copy of Gerasimov's collected works in his office. "He is the smartest of men, and my expectations of him were enormous," Zaluzhny told me. "I was raised on Russian military doctrine, and I still think that the science of war is all located in Russia." But the Russians did not perform as he expected. Their biggest flaw was a lack of imagination, an inability to adapt to changes on the battlefield. Their command structure still followed the Soviet model, which had no culture of initiative among the junior officers. They only did as they were told and faced censure for reacting to events without permission. Faced with heavy resistance or an inability to resupply, they did not retreat or shift to a different approach as the conditions of the war demanded. "They just herded their soldiers into the slaughter," Zaluzhny said. "They chose the scenario that suited me best of all."

❖

The idea that Ukraine could withstand the invasion soon ceased to seem delusional to Zelensky's most important allies. By the beginning of March, the U.S. and NATO leadership realized that the Russian military was not the juggernaut they had envisioned. The prized commandos of Putin's airborne forces had been mowed down all over the suburbs of Kyiv. Their losses mounted so fast it became difficult to keep any reliable count. Official figures from the Russian Ministry of Defense said almost five hundred of its soldiers had been killed and more than fifteen hundred wounded in the first ten days of the invasion, an alarming number by the standards of modern warfare. Independent estimates placed Russian losses at least an order of magnitude higher, including thousands of troops, hundreds of armored vehicles, and dozens of aircraft lost in the opening week of the war.

The military brass in Western capitals watched the battles intently, making adjustments to their understanding of the Russian threat. From his chambers in the military bunker, Zaluzhny stayed in close touch with his American counterpart, General Mark Milley, the chairman of the Joint Chiefs of Staff. By coincidence, a new interpreter had been assigned to Milley around that time, and the translations of their phone calls grew stilted and confusing, creating space for misunderstandings between the two commanders. As they tried to strategize and share intelligence, some of Milley's remarks struck Zaluzhny as offensive. "Milley asked these leading questions, about whether I'm planning to evacuate somewhere," he recalled. "I told him: I don't understand you." Zaluzhny had been commanding troops against the Russians since 2014, when Putin first sent his forces to occupy Crimea and seize parts of eastern Ukraine. From Zaluzhny's perspective, the war had been going on for eight years. "Only now it's gotten broader," he told Milley. "I didn't run away then, and I'm not going to run now. We are going to fight till the end." (A U.S. official who participated in these calls told me Zaluzhny delivered this point in even blunter terms: "He said something to the effect of: 'I'm going to die here. I'm ready to die.'")

When they discussed the battle for Hostomel, and the broader Russian failure to take Kyiv in less than a week, Milley did not ascribe the success to clever Ukrainian planning. It looked more like a military miracle. "He told me: 'Son, you just got lucky,'" Zaluzhny said. The comment stung. A range of unpredictable factors, starting with the weather, had favored Ukraine in the Battle of Kyiv. But its defense did not come down to luck alone. Zaluzhny had overseen the preparations, developed a strategy, and put it into action. One critical aspect of his plan involved moving and hiding Ukraine's air-defense systems and military aircraft in the days before the invasion. When these systems survived the initial barrage of missiles and aerial bombs, the Russian Air Force lost its chance to dominate the skies. Now the invasion entered a new phase, with Russian ground forces approaching the edge of Kyiv, and Zaluzhny needed help to stay alive. During a phone call with Milley on March 1, he explained that the Ukrainian forces could only hold on for a few more weeks without a massive influx of U.S. support. "In a month," he said, "I'm going to fall."

In particular, Ukraine needed aircraft. Its pilots had never operated NATO planes, but they had years of experience flying the MiG-29, a Soviet design that several European countries still had in their fleets. Poland had agreed to give these jets to the Ukrainians as long as the U.S. would compensate the Polish Air Force with a supply of American F-16s. The Biden administration refused to go along with that arrangement. They feared a cycle of escalation that could draw NATO into war with Russia or provoke Putin to use nuclear weapons in Ukraine. Milley also worried that Russia's modern fighter jets would outmaneuver the older Polish MiGs, which had not been designed to do what Ukraine needed most: provide air cover for troops on the ground and run bombing raids against the Russian forces.

As Zaluzhny tried to press the issue in their phone call, Milley insisted Ukraine still had enough planes in its fleet. Zaluzhny knew that wasn't true. "I said to him: 'No, General, if I tell you that I only have two bombers left, then that's the case.' And he said, 'No, according to our intelligence, you have seventy of them.'" Zaluzhny was speechless. He had a war to fight, and these calls took up precious hours of his day. "I wanted to spit on the ground and say, 'That's it, no more of these conversations.'" The Americans refused to budge on requests for other kinds of heavy weapons, such as long-range artillery to match what the Russians were using to bombard Ukrainian cities from afar. "In one month," Zaluzhny said, "we will urgently need to refill our stocks of ammunition and money. I asked Mark Milley about this two or three times, but I understood that his intelligence was misleading him."

As he hung up the phone, Zaluzhny sensed he was running out of options. In the first week of fighting, the Russians had seized about a fifth of Ukraine's territory. They had encircled the cities of Mariupol and Kherson in the south, while the cities Russia had tried and failed to capture, like Kharkiv in the east and Chernihiv in the north, faced relentless shelling and aerial bombardment. The front line now stretched for over twenty-five hundred kilometers, and the armed forces had no chance of holding it unless the West provided the necessary weapons. But Zaluzhny, in a moment of frustration, had just cut off contact with his most influential ally and refused to take any more of his calls. At that moment, he said, "I didn't know who else to turn to other than Zelensky."

The following day, the general left his command post and drove through Kyiv to see the president. The city felt deserted. More than a million of its residents had fled. Roadblocks made of concrete slabs and sandbags stood at many of the larger intersections. Not all of them were sturdy enough to complicate the advance of an enemy tank, but it seemed to be a point of pride for the volunteer fighters in every neighborhood to build these barricades and tend to them, burning barrel fires to keep warm and flying the national flag.

When Zaluzhny arrived on Bankova Street, the presidential staff gave him a hero's welcome. All of their hopes for defeating the Russians rested with the Armed Forces of Ukraine, and here was their commander, dressed in fatigues, ducking his head to fit through the bunker's door. Normally the guards did not allow photos down there. But a few of Zelensky's aides asked the general to pose for a picture with them in the conference room. As they sat down, facing one another around a lacquered wooden table, Zaluzhny told the president about his talks with the Americans and his decision to break off contact with Milley. "The president took that really badly," Zaluzhny later told me. So did some members of Zelensky's team, especially the ones in charge of diplomacy, who worried that the general could jeopardize Ukraine's relationship with its most important ally. But Zaluzhny would not be dissuaded. He was tired of asking the Americans for help only to be lectured about the needs of his own forces. The president would have to find another way to secure enough weapons to fight this war. "In a month," he told Zelensky, "we will be properly screwed. That means we have to do something now."

❖

Zelensky could not do much from the confines of his bunker. He had already appealed to the leaders of the world, at least the ones he could reach on a secure-line phone. His team needed to adjust their tactics, to make their demands more insistent and direct, even if it meant taking additional risks and breaking the rules of diplomatic courtesy. For a start, the president's bodyguards had to ease the terms of his confinement enough for him to start receiving guests and meeting journalists in person. He needed to stay in the headlines and shape the public's understanding of the war. Apart from Zelensky's talks with foreign leaders, he had to find ways to address the people who elected them, to win them over and keep them engaged.

"For us it's reality, but for millions of people around the world, it's still a reality show," Ukraine's foreign minister, Dmytro Kuleba, later told me. "Not in terms of fun, but it's something that you see through the screen." In an age of viral videos and perpetual newsfeeds, viewers could feel immersed in the tragedies unfolding in Ukraine from thousands of miles away. The president's goal, said Kuleba, was to keep the immersion going for as long as possible, for as many people around the world as possible, while doing everything he could to keep those viewers on his side.

"You have to follow certain rules if you want someone on the other side of the screen to keep watching you, and to remain sympathetic to you," he said. "These are the same rules that work everywhere, in marketing strategies and in military strategies. You have to be winning, because people love winners. From time to time, you have to impress them with something big and unexpected, because no one can follow routine," he continued. "Third, you need a clear character associated with the story to be visible to them all the time, and that's President Zelensky in our case. And last you need a good story to tell. It's the story of a smaller nation kicking the ass of a larger nation that invaded it. It's bad guys attacking good guys, and good guys winning. That's what people love."

On March 3, the day after Zelensky's meeting with General Zaluzhny in the bunker, his security guards relented, and the president's aides were allowed to organize his first press conference since the start of the invasion. Reporters from the U.S., Germany, Israel, Turkey, and other countries were brought in vans through the maze of military checkpoints and barricades to the rear entrance of the presidential compound, where they were thoroughly searched. The corridors inside were dark, the windows covered with sandbags, and the soldiers used flashlights to show the way to the briefing room on the first floor. Zelensky soon arrived with a few of his aides, dressed in their wartime attire of army-green T-shirts and fleeces. Instead of standing at the podium, the president grabbed a chair and placed it within arm's reach of the reporters in the front row, drawing anxious looks from the bodyguards who stood around the room with assault rifles.

Zelensky apologized for being out of sorts. "We've been sleeping three or four hours a night." But his spirits seemed high despite his pallor, and he commanded the room with an energy and openness that took some of the attendees by surprise. Many of the questions elicited flashes of anger, most of it reserved for the Western leaders who had refused to give Ukraine the weapons it needed. "How many people have to be blown to pieces, how many arms, legs, heads need to be torn off to get through to you?" Each day since the start of the invasion, he held twenty or thirty phone calls with foreign leaders, mostly his allies, and they still rejected his pleas to impose a no-fly zone over Ukraine. "If you don't have the strength, the courage, to close the sky, give me planes!" He mentioned the tentative deal for Poland to supply MiG-29s. "Give those to us!"

At times the performance seemed petulant, even spiteful. But the time for politesse had passed. To survive the war, Zelensky and his team needed to grab and steer the world's attention, to make as many nations as possible experience the invasion the way Ukraine did—as a threat to their lives, their values, their existence as democracies. Thoughts and prayers for Kyiv's fortitude would not suffice. Foreign governments and, crucially, their citizens would need to act, to make sacrifices, if not in terms of blood then at least one or two of their comforts. The methods Zelensky used to deliver this message would prove far more sophisticated than the bullhorn Russia carried into battle. On the propaganda front, Ukraine had an early advantage. It was the underdog and Russia the aggressor. But that did not guarantee the level of support Ukraine needed to stay in the fight. Past wars had shown how little the world's sympathies mean on the battlefield. Putin had, through the years, carpet-bombed Chechnya and Syria, invaded Georgia, and annexed Crimea, each time eliciting a wave of international revulsion and media coverage that would inevitably fade. The Russians had little reason to expect a different outcome in Ukraine. They tended to see their adversaries in this war as a bunch of pretenders and clowns. But they miscalculated. Zelensky and his team, as producers and performers, understood the power of perceptions as well as any Kremlin propagandist, and probably better. From their years in show business, they knew how to stir emotion, to inspire and captivate an audience, and they saw this as one of their most important tasks, perhaps their best way to support the valiant efforts of the military. While General Zaluzhny focused on the fighting, the president made it his mission to pressure the West for help, and that synergy in their relations would last for several months before the rift began to show between them.

For the moment, Zelensky had not attained enough confidence or experience as a wartime leader to override the decisions of the military brass. His role had less to do with the war itself than with the way it was perceived, and he had the skills to play it well. At the same time, he seemed to treasure the opportunity not only to witness history but to shape it. Many of his aides felt the same way; one told me that he derived a kind of "masochistic pleasure" from his life in the bunker and the vantage it afforded onto world-shaping events. Zelensky rarely talked about these feelings. But he also found it gratifying to be in this singular position of power and influence. Despite the danger and the stress, the separation from his family, the weight of the responsibility he bore, and the horrors he witnessed each day, the president felt privileged, even happy, to do the job that fate had put in front of him. Even on the hardest days it gave him a profound sense of purpose, and it made him feel alive.

"My life today is beautiful," he said at the end of the press conference, when a reporter asked how he was holding up. "I feel that I'm needed." The previous week, as horrifying and tragic as it had been for him and his country, was also among the most exciting and fulfilling of his life. He would not trade it for any of the comfort and security he knew in his old life as a movie star. "I think the main purpose in life is to be needed, not just to be a blank space that breathes, walks, and eats. But to live, to know that certain things depend on your being alive, and to feel that your life matters to others."

CHAPTER 7

THE BUNKER

ONE NIGHT IN EARLY MARCH, A COUPLE OF THE PRESIDENT'S AIDES STAYED UP LATE IN the bunker's conference room, drinking whiskey with cola and monitoring the news when a report from the southern front caught their attention. The Russians had started shelling the largest nuclear power plant in Ukraine—in fact, the largest in all of Europe. Located in Enerhodar, about a hundred kilometers from Zelensky's hometown, the facility had six nuclear reactors that produced power for much of southeastern Ukraine. A few days earlier, people from the nearby towns had confronted the advancing Russian troops with flags and barricades, and for a while the invaders stayed back. Now they had returned with orders to seize the facility.

"They were just blasting it with their tanks," said Kyrylo Tymoshenko, the first of Zelensky's aides to see the news that night. The plant's security cameras fed live footage of the attack into a government computer network, and Tymoshenko pulled it up on the big screen in the conference room. Machine-gun rounds showed up as white streaks through the darkness, slamming into the plant's administrative building. Incendiary bombs started a fire at the station. A small detachment of troops from the National Guard had been deployed to protect the facility, and they put up a ferocious fight. Tymoshenko got their commander on the phone and went to find his bosses in the bunker. "I was going around the corridors, looking for people, and I came across the president. He looked like he had just finished working out, and I told him, 'There's tanks shooting at the nuclear power plant. There's a battle going on.'"

The plant's administrators used loudspeakers to broadcast a message to the attackers: "Stop shooting immediately! You are threatening the security of the whole world!" It had no effect. No military units were available to reinforce the plant's defenders. All of them were tied down in other sectors of the front, which left Zelensky only one means of affecting the situation. He prepared a statement, sat down in front of a laptop in the bunker, and read it out loud. "Europeans, please wake up! For the first time in our history, in the history of humanity, a terrorist state has resorted to nuclear terrorism. There are six nuclear reactors there. Six!"

That night my phone lit up with messages from one of Zelensky's aides, pleading with me to report the story. "A possible start of the nuclear winter," she wrote. "Putin has completely lost his mind." News of the assault spread around the world as the sun rose over Kyiv. Large protests against the invasion gathered the next day in several European cities, and the head of the U.N. nuclear watchdog warned that Russia's attack on the power plant created "unprecedented danger" of a nuclear accident.

None of it had any discernible effect on the Russian forces. They seized control of the facility and took its staff hostage, forcing them to work at gunpoint. The occupiers later used the plant to store their ammunition, fuel, and fighting vehicles, secure in the knowledge that Ukraine would not lob shells toward a nuclear power station. Nearby towns came under intensive shelling from the Russian artillery based at the plant, and Zelensky could do nothing to stop them. The plant's managers told him that, in case of a meltdown, the devastation could be several times worse than the Chernobyl disaster of 1986. "The most horrible thing," Andriy Yermak, Zelensky's chief of staff, later said of that night, "is that you're trying to do everything you can, but physically you cannot do anything to influence what's happening."

❖

Despite the feeling of helplessness, no one in the bunker gave in to despair during that early phase of the invasion. They had too much to do, too many fires to fight and crises to manage. Zelensky and several of his aides would later describe the first week of the invasion as one endless day. But eventually all of them crashed. The adrenaline wore off, and the strain began to show. There was not much to eat at the time in the bunker. Some packaged sweets got passed around at meetings, and tinned meat with stale bread could be found in the communal kitchen. One minister told me he survived for days on chocolate bars and, in the process, gained several pounds. For the most part, though, anxiety suppressed the hunger of the presidential staff, and it started to wear them down. Zelensky's face became sallow, and he complained about the lack of sunlight and his inability to breathe fresh air.

When he did ride the elevator up to the main floors of the compound, he would usually stay just long enough to give a statement from the briefing room or record a video message, showing the world that he had not abandoned his post. He looked well enough in these clips, smiling and raising a fist in the air. But he was getting so little rest that some of his staff became concerned about his health. Early one morning, when he wandered into the bunker's conference room, one of his legal aides thought he resembled a walking corpse. "A living person cannot look like that," said the aide, Liliia Pashynna. The president mumbled good morning to no one in particular. "I couldn't even answer him," Pashynna later told me. "I have never seen a human being in that condition."

The rest of the team was no better off. Oleksiy Reznikov, the minister of defense, felt the last of his strength drain away in the second week of the invasion. He was healthy and athletic for a fifty-five-year-old. An avid scuba diver and parachute jumper, he had made a series of short films about his other hobby—riding all-terrain vehicles. But in March he realized the exhaustion might kill him sooner than the Russians. "I gave myself a psychotherapy session, an internal dialogue in which I asked myself: What's tormenting you the most?" It was the cycle of waking up at around five each morning, after one or two hours of sleep, and forcing himself to check the news and start returning messages. "My psyche was telling me that I can't take it." He needed to conserve his energy, to prepare, as he put it, "not for a sprint but a marathon."

Zelensky came to the same realization, and his life in the bunker soon settled into a more manageable routine. The first video conference on his daily schedule shifted to around seven a.m., enough time for him to have breakfast—invariably, fried eggs—before going down the hall and up the stairs from his chambers to the conference room. With some coaching from his staff, his days became a more structured series of statements, meetings, and interviews, usually conducted through the screen of a laptop or a phone. In line with their new communication strategy, Zelensky widened his target audience far beyond the circle of his peers in Western capitals. On March 4, the day of the Russian attack on the nuclear power plant, he appeared live via video link in front of large crowds gathered to support Ukraine in seven European cities, among them Frankfurt, Prague, Vilnius, and Vienna, where the U.N. nuclear watchdog is based. The next day, he gave a video address to over two hundred members of the U.S. Congress. A week later, he gave another lengthy press conference, his second in ten days, to a hall packed with reporters from around the world.

At night he still had trouble sleeping, in part due to a habit he developed of staring at his daily agenda even when the day was over. "It's pointless," he told me. "It's the same agenda. I see it's over for today. But I look at it several times and sense that something is wrong." He would text or call his aides to follow up about plans or promises, often rousing them out of bed in the process. It wasn't anxiety that kept him awake in those moments. "It's my conscience bothering me," he said. There were too many demands on his time, too many briefings and phone calls, too many requests from the armed forces and members of his government, too many tragic events that seemed to require his attention, his response. His chief of staff struggled to pick priorities without neglecting some crucial task or emergency. "After human lives the most precious thing we have is time," Yermak wrote me from the bunker in early March. "It's what we always have to economize. Every decision needs to be made as fast as possible. Some things for today should have been done yesterday. At this pace, under these kinds of pressures, only a reliable team could manage. There are no accidental people here."

Apart from the security guards and soldiers, around two dozen aides and advisers to the president lived in the bunker at the time. Pashynna, the legal aide, was among the only women. As a young lawyer in the office of the chief of staff, her peacetime duties had included reviewing legislation and other documents before they were sent for the president's signature. Now she was fielding calls about weapon shipments and coordinating the distribution of humanitarian aid. The role had not been thrust upon her; it was entirely her choice. On the morning of the invasion, when she arrived at work to find the offices swarming with soldiers, she decided to ask one of them for a weapon to defend herself in case the Russians broke through the gates. He agreed to show her how to operate his assault rifle. Pashynna then sent a text message to Yermak, her boss, telling him she knew how to shoot and had no intention of leaving the compound. He responded that afternoon, telling her to ask one of the security men how to reach the bunker. What she found had little in common with the atmosphere of the administration she had known. "No one was joking around," she said. "There was no laughter."

As a condition of living in the bunker, the staff had to sign nondisclosure agreements, forbidding them from leaking any details about the facility's design, location, or amenities. Though these restrictions were later relaxed, the bunker's inhabitants observed the pledge of secrecy as long as the risk of a Russian siege remained acute. Some decided to arm themselves. The president also had a handgun, though he never carried it around. Later in the war, when a reporter asked him about the pistol, Zelensky brought up the risk that he would be taken prisoner by the Russians. "That's a disgrace," he said. "I think it's a disgrace." Was that the purpose of the gun, asked the reporter? To make sure the Russians could not take him alive? Zelensky laughed. "No, come on. We wouldn't do that to ourselves. But shooting back?" he said. "Yes."

❖

As the weeks wore on, living conditions inside the bunker began to improve. Hot meals prepared in the kitchen of the presidential compound were brought down to the bunker's communal dining room two or three times a day. It was mostly standard cafeteria fare, a lot of boiled wieners and potato dumplings, goulash, buckwheat, and salads dressed with mayonnaise. Some of the staff grumbled that the portions were small, and they wondered how the burly presidential guards could survive on so few calories.

On the wall in the cafeteria, a flat-screen TV played the national news broadcast day and night. It was the same on all the major channels and, from the confines of the bunker, the president and his team had the power to influence the programming. All they had to do was call or text the studio directors, who had little choice but to comply with the orders from Bankova Street. Under the terms of martial law, the airwaves are treated as critical infrastructure, and the state can do whatever it wants with them in the name of national defense. For some of Zelensky's aides, this was a dream come true. They had long tried to develop a state-run news channel, a mouthpiece for the authorities that people would actually watch. "We never had that," said Kyrylo Tymoshenko, the presidential aide who was in charge of these efforts. The closest they came was Telekanal Rada, the parliament's official broadcaster, whose stock in trade was dreary footage of legislative sessions. Its ratings were abysmal. In the months before the invasion, the authorities invested heavily into that channel, building out elaborate sets and a stable of anchors for political talk shows and breaking news. But it never came close to challenging the established news networks in Ukraine. All of them were controlled by Ukrainian tycoons and politicians critical of Zelensky, and their programs attacked his government at every turn.

Now, with the nation at war, the office of the president asked all of these channels to set politics aside and fall in line behind the president. Some of the media executives resisted at first. "They said they wanted to broadcast separately, so that everyone would have their own news marathon," said Tymoshenko, who handled these negotiations. "From our side, we proposed a unified broadcast with a unified editorial council. When they heard our arguments, they agreed."

The only major holdout was Channel 5, which belonged to Zelensky's archrival, former president Petro Poroshenko. He did not agree to join the consortium. But all of its main competitors went along with the president's initiative. The result became known as the "United News" Telemarathon, a round-the-clock broadcast of news and commentary that aired on all the leading networks. It provided the latest updates on the fighting and essential advice on where to shelter, when to evacuate, and how to survive. It also carried Zelensky's message of defiance and resilience into every household in the land. Nothing of the sort had existed in Ukraine since the Soviet era, and critics complained that it smacked of wartime propaganda. The producers of the Telemarathon did not have editorial independence. Tymoshenko took part in their planning and strategy sessions and kept an obsessive eye on what they put on air. He was not shy about calling the studio to complain if the programming made Zelensky look bad or veered too far from the official line. As a result, the television news served up a sanitized picture of the president.

Ukrainians were not aware, for instance, that Zelensky and his team kept a supply of alcohol in the bunker even after the government restricted its sale across the country. Around the small table in his private chambers, the president would on occasion pour wine in the evenings for the aides who joined him there for a meeting or a meal. He understood that his staff needed ways to unwind and clear their heads, and he tried to preserve his sense of humor. "Without it, everyone's mood would be down in the dumps, and that's not where you want it to be if you want to win," Zelensky later told me. "Our goal, at least, was not to lose. So we couldn't succumb to the kind of weakness and panic that turns you into a blob."

With the president's blessing, his aides soon installed a small gym in the bunker, near the entryway, where the corridor was wide enough to accommodate the gear. It included free weights, dumbbells, and a bench press that Zelensky made a habit of using, often in the middle of the night. Later they put in a Ping-Pong table and started to have small tournaments. The only one who could reliably beat the president at table tennis was his old friend Davyd Arakhamia, the lawmaker and peace negotiator. When it came to lifting weights, Yermak, his chief of staff, served as a frequent companion, as did Zelensky's chief of security, Maksym Donets.

On a few occasions, the president would invite his staff to watch a movie in the conference room, which had the bunker's largest television screen. Lively debates took place about what to watch, though Zelensky got the last word. Among his heroes growing up were Soviet filmmakers like Leonid Gaidai, whose works were heavily censored at the time of their release but still charming and often hilarious. One of them depicted Ivan the Terrible swapping lives with a superintendent at a Soviet apartment building. These were the classics of Zelensky's generation, and watching them had been a ritual throughout his life. But in the bunker the president realized he could no longer stomach the Soviet comedies that had shaped his identity since childhood. "They revolt me," he said. The war had poisoned them. In place of the joy and nostalgia they had once evoked, Zelensky now felt a tepid, nauseating void.

Instead his staff tended to watch new releases from Hollywood. One of the first was an action-thriller called *13 Hours*, which depicted the tragic siege of the American diplomatic compound in Benghazi, Libya, in 2012. The plot hit uncomfortably close to home for some members of the administration. It depicted a group of government officials holed up in a fortified compound until they are dragged out and killed. The scenes of violence so closely resembled the worst fears of Zelensky's advisers that one of them left the room and went to bed.

When they needed to be alone, the staff had limited options. Only a few senior officials had rooms to themselves. Most bunked in pairs, even though the rooms were tiny. The standard ones contained a desk, a lamp, some shelving, and just enough room for two or three people to stretch out and sleep. In the early days, whenever the staffers felt exhausted, they would have to stumble through the corridor until they found an empty room to crash for a few hours. Later each of them took a more permanent spot, and the lumpy mattresses were replaced by sturdier cots, still narrow but a bit more comfortable. The ventilation ducts had metal grilles with a fish-scale pattern, but otherwise the only decorative elements were the Ukrainian flags they hung on the walls.

For the few women who lived in the bunker, there were additional inconveniences related to privacy and hygiene. Pashynna, the legal aid, did not even bring a change of clothes when she arrived at work on the first day of the invasion, and she did not return to her apartment for weeks. In the meantime, a member of the bunker's cleaning staff brought extra clothes and other essentials for her to use. The service personnel in the facility, nearly all women, had a separate bathroom with a shower that they welcomed Pashynna to use. The days passed in a constant rush of urgent tasks and emergencies. Hospital directors would call to demand an evacuation of their patients. Groups of paramilitary volunteers would call to ask for weapons and supplies. Pashynna arranged so many shipments of body armor to these groups that her colleagues began to call her Bulletproof Liliia. The nickname stuck.

To help the team cope with the endless demands on their attention, Zelensky invited more staffers to live in the bunker. Plenty of them volunteered. Among the late arrivals was Serhiy Leshchenko, a prominent journalist, commentator, and former lawmaker who had advised Zelensky's presidential campaign in 2019. Gangly and talkative, with a full set of orthodontic braces that made him look younger than his forty-one years, Leshchenko was serving on the board of the state railway company when the invasion broke out, and he spent the first few days riding around the country on makeshift reconnaissance trains, which turned out to be a valuable source of intelligence on the position and movement of enemy troops.

At the time, Ukraine's fleet of surveillance drones was not nearly large enough to monitor the entire front, and the military had limited access to satellite imagery. But there were thousands of railroad stations all across Ukraine, and the employees at many of them began to serve as lookouts, spotting the approach of Russian tanks and aircraft and reporting what they saw up the chain of command. Leshchenko's phone became a clearinghouse for these dispatches, which he forwarded to contacts in the presidential staff. By the second week of the invasion, Yermak invited him to come live in the bunker. His experience as a journalist and blogger, they decided, would be useful in combatting Russian narratives about the war. On his first descent, Leshchenko had no idea what to expect. He was surprised to find an atmosphere that looked and felt like a submarine in enemy waters. Everyone seemed stern and vigilant, exhilarated by the sense of danger. Though he had always been a demanding boss, Zelensky had even less tolerance for slacking in the bunker. He wanted to know what the members of his team were up to, what was next on their agenda, what they could or should be doing.

The usual backbiting and office politics had, to all appearances, been set aside. Old feuds were temporarily forgotten. Even the most mundane tasks—the drafting of a press release, say, or talking points for a presidential phone call—felt to the staff like matters of grave significance. Managing all of them created a level of stress that Leshchenko had rarely felt in his life, and it distended the passage of time in ways that could seem hallucinogenic. Days would feel like hours, and hours like days. The fear, he told me, only became acute in the moments before sleep. "That's when reality catches up with you," he said. "That's when you lay there and think about the bombs."

Though they knew the Russian forces had approached the capital, the fighting in the suburbs could feel remote at times. The president and his staff mostly experienced the front line through their screens, as footage of battles and rocket attacks often appeared on social media before the military could brief Zelensky on the details. It was typical for him to gather with his aides around a phone or laptop, cursing images of devastation or cheering a drone strike on a Russian tank. "This was a favorite," Leshchenko said, pulling up a clip of a Russian helicopter getting blown out of the sky. Some of the videos showed Russian soldiers writhing in apparent agony after a grenade or a shell exploded near them, but the president's aides felt no remorse for the Russian soldiers killed in these gruesome videos, no pity for the suffering of the invaders. Their deaths were among the only sources of optimism in the bunker, as were the war ballads that Ukrainians wrote, recorded, and posted online. Several of them went viral and played on repeat across the country. One of them went like this:

> Look how our people, how all Ukraine
> United the world against the Russians
> Soon all the Russians, they'll be gone
> And we'll have peace in all the world.

For members of the administration who remained aboveground, the action felt closer and the risks more severe. Many of them began to live like nomads, moving from place to place to minimize the chances of abduction.

Several of them told me the greatest danger at the time came from the Russian strike teams that had infiltrated Kyiv and were hunting Zelensky and his senior aides. But the state's decision to hand out weapons to its citizens also made it dangerous to move around the city. In Kyiv alone, the authorities gave out twenty-five thousand firearms to regular citizens, who helped man checkpoints or patrol the streets. Many of them had no training, and they were scared out of their wits. At night, they often opened fire at people who approached their positions by car or on foot, resulting in numerous casualties. Denys Monastyrsky, the minister of internal affairs, recalled one incident in which a Ukrainian general was pulled from his car at one of these improvised checkpoints, thrown facedown on the ground, and searched. Soon after that, his ministry ordered at least one police officer to take charge of every checkpoint.

Members of parliament were also entitled to firearms, with handguns at one distribution point in Kyiv set aside for female lawmakers while the men received assault rifles. Ruslan Stefanchuk, the chamber's speaker, stayed in close touch with the heads of parliamentary factions and committees, who mostly convened via video conference. "We all have to recognize one thing," he told them. "Not every generation of Ukrainians gets the honor of dying for the independence of their state." The remark inspired some of the politicians but horrified others. The parliament did not have the resources to provide them with security. They needed to fend for themselves.

Even Stefanchuk had to go into hiding with one of his assistants and a couple of guards. As the next official in the line of succession, the speaker could not remain in the government district with the president. Instead he moved around, staying with friends or in government buildings in the city and its suburbs. On the way to one of these safe houses, his security detail received word of Russian bombers overhead, and they turned off the highway onto a country road that led to a farmhouse. As they pulled up, the farmer came out to welcome them, a bit startled by the sight of men with guns. Then he went inside to prepare a hot meal for his guests. Stefanchuk, dressed in plus-sized military gear, decided to look around the homestead, and the stench of manure greeted him at the entrance to the barn. Inside, a small herd of goats and cows stood looking at him in the half-light, their eyes just about as bewildered as his.

❖

Zelensky's family remained in hiding for about two months, but their security guards gradually relaxed the rules enough to let them access the Internet and use their devices. By early April, they were no longer forced to move around as often as they had at the start of the invasion. Their social media accounts allowed them to experience the war through their screens, in much the same way as most Ukrainians. "We were all living in this condition," Olena recalled of that period. "From news item to news item."

Even as Ukraine began advancing on the battlefield and winning more support from the West, the daily tragedies of the war kept coming—the air strikes, the reports of rape and torture, the mass detention of civilians in Russian "filtration" camps. To fight off bouts of despair while following these events, Olena stuck to a strict routine: homework or reading with Kyrylo, cooking with Oleksandra, emails with her friends and staffers, scheduled calls with the president when he was able to set aside some time. "The nights were the most difficult," Olena said, "because everyone falls asleep"—the kids, the bodyguards—"and all you have are these stupid, unhappy thoughts, plus that disgusting habit of reading the news at night."

At one point she came across a post that was going viral around Ukraine. Several pages from the diary of an eight-year-old boy named Yegor had been published online, describing what he and his family had endured during the Russian siege of Mariupol in the south. On the first page, the boy wrote in capital letters, *WAR*, and then began his story: *I slept well, woke up and smiled.* But, in the very next lines, he reports that his grandfather had died and others in his family had been injured. *I have a wound in my back,* Yegor writes in the looping script of a second grader. *The skin was ripped off. My sister has a cut on her head. A piece of meat was ripped out of mama's arm and she has a hole in her leg.* The diary mentions the boy's new friend, a cheerful neighbor named Vika "with good parents," and the trips his grandmother took to fetch water for them. But the line that struck the First Lady came toward the end of the published pages: *My grandmother died. So did my two dogs and my beloved city of Mariupol.* The author of these words was only a year younger than Olena's son, and he had covered his diary in the same types of pictures that Kyrylo had taken to drawing: images of burning buildings, figures with guns and tanks, people bleeding on the ground.

"I couldn't imagine," Olena later told me, "what this child felt after living in modern society, going to school, playing sports, having hobbies, going online. He probably had a favorite Marvel hero, and then he's sitting in a basement, watching his loved ones die, watching people drink water from puddles." Yegor had been evacuated to safety by the time his diary appeared online. But Olena knew the experience would scar him for life. "There are thousands of these children and adults who saw how their relatives died, how their homes were bombed," she said. "They were saved, but they carry the guilt of being unable to return."

Her own guilt had to do with her isolation. It made her feel useless and helpless. She missed her husband, and she could not stand the rules that kept her from staying beside him and playing a greater role in her country's defense. At the same time, she wanted to do whatever was necessary to guard her children from the war, especially when she saw Kyrylo's brooding fascination with it. He had turned nine about a month before the invasion, and his old distractions, like dancing and playing the piano, no longer interested him much. The change made Olena feel another kind of guilt, that of a mother struggling to protect her child. No matter how hard she tried to distract him with music and drawing, the boy wanted to practice marksmanship and martial arts. He had fixed his mind on becoming a soldier.

When he spoke to his father, Kyrylo began to offer military advice, suggesting weapons systems that Ukraine should acquire. The president got a kick out of these conversations. He did not share his wife's concern about the boy's obsession with the military. "He studies it all. He looks it up online. He talks to the bodyguards," Zelensky told me with evident pride. "He's a fan of our armed forces, our army, and he knows deeply what our mission is, what we're liberating, what weapons we have, and what we're missing." If Kyrylo wanted to pursue a career in the military, that would be fine with his father. But not his mother. She wanted the boy to have his childhood back, and it pained her to watch the war draining it away, bleeding his innocence, no matter where they tried to hide or how hard they tried to protect him.

CHAPTER 8

BLANK SLATE

IN THE FIRST WEEK OF MARCH, AS BATTLES CONTINUED TO RAGE IN THE OUTSKIRTS OF Kyiv, the president insisted on leaving the compound to see the devastation for himself, driving out toward the Russian positions with a couple of his closest confidants. "We made the decision to go on the fly," said Andriy Yermak, who went along. They did not bring any cameras with them. The head of the presidential guards would only consent to the trip if it was done in total secrecy. Some members of the presidential staff only learned about it a month and a half later, when it came up during one of our interviews.

Heading out from Bankova Street, Zelensky drove north along the right bank of the Dnipro River, toward the road that runs along the top of a hydroelectric dam. To their left, the gray waters of the Kyiv Reservoir stretched into the distance. Barely two weeks had passed since the fleet of Russian attack helicopters flew over the reservoir on their way to Hostomel. Now it was still, the dull thuds of artillery audible in the distance as the president continued driving eastward, beyond the last of the Ukrainian positions, and came to a stop near a narrow bridge that marked the front line. The bridge had been destroyed to prevent the advance of the Russians toward Kyiv. Unable to cross, they lobbed shells across the expanse of water, aiming for the Ukrainian dugouts on the other side. One explosion had left a crater in the road, and Zelensky stopped to marvel at its size. It looked as though a giant claw had come and gouged the earth wide open in that spot. As he stood there, taking in the scene, he could sense his bodyguards getting nervous. "They were losing their minds," he later said. The Russian positions were close enough for a decent marksman to get a clean shot at the president, who had no pressing reason to be that close to the front. He was not there to command his forces into battle. He just wanted to get a sense of what his troops were experiencing. "I needed their emotions," he told me. "What are they feeling, what is their situation."

On the way back, they stopped at a checkpoint manned by a mix of soldiers and volunteers. It was close to lunchtime, and a local man had just brought a fresh pot of borscht for all of them. The cook lived nearby. Too old to serve in the military, building fortifications and running around with a rifle, he decided instead that feeding the soldiers would be his contribution to the national defense. His soup, a rich concoction of pork, beats, cabbage, and potatoes, had taken him most of the morning to make, and he insisted there was plenty to go around for the guests from Bankova Street. The president hesitated. "I can't take their food," he said. But his hosts insisted. No one seemed nervous around the president. They hung around for a while, within range of Russian artillery, and had a bowl of soup with bread, talking about the Soviet Union and what the Russians had become since its collapse.

The cook still had family in Russia. He had been a professional athlete decades ago, competing under the Soviet flag, and he went to the trunk of his car to retrieve some medals he had won in track and field. It was still hard for him to accept the fact that his former countrymen had come to kill and plunder here, and he told Zelensky how much he hated the Russians. As he got ready to leave, the president remembers asking the soldiers whether they needed anything, any additional support that he might be able to send their way. The men were armed with rifles and rocket-propelled grenades. Across the water stood an army with tanks and artillery. But they said they were fine. "They didn't want anything from me," Zelensky said. "They didn't complain. All they wanted was victory."

The conversation left a deep impression on the president. He had long felt a kinship with soldiers at the front, not only for their courage but their honesty. Eight years had passed since he first visited them in the war zone. Back then, in the summer of 2014, Zelensky was still a comedian with no political ambitions, and he traveled to the frontline regions to perform for the troops. At one point, when his tour bus pulled over somewhere in the east, Zelensky got out to talk to a soldier who had been manning the same checkpoint for months on end, living in the nearby trenches. His last real conversation with a civilian had been so long ago that he had trouble stringing sentences together. When Zelensky asked how he could help, the soldier told him: Talk to me. "Some things in life you remember," Zelensky later said of that trip to the front in 2014. "Maybe from childhood, or the brightest moments of raising your own children, when they say their first word, or go to school. This was a moment in my life like that."

At the time, the armed conflict in the east was just a few months old, but it had already seeded the violence and division that would erupt eight years later in a full-scale war. With the annexation of Crimea, Putin got his first taste of foreign conquest, and it was intoxicating. He began referring to other parts of Ukraine as *Novorossiya*, or New Russia. In a televised appearance that spring, he said Russia had "lost these territories for various reasons. But the people remained." And he intended to get them back. His agents and supporters across eastern and southern Ukraine soon began to replicate the tactics Russia used to take Crimea. They would seize government buildings, install separatist leaders, declare independence from Kyiv, and invite the Russian military to come to their defense.

In some places, the formula worked. Russian proxies and paramilitary forces took control of several cities and vast stretches of territory across the eastern Donbas region by the summer of 2014. But their victories were not as swift and frictionless as they had been in Crimea. The military fought back this time. Armed militias formed and deployed from across the country to defend the Donbas. Unlike the people of Crimea, the locals in the east and south were far from united in their desire to break away from Ukraine and support Putin's imperialist vision of a "Russian world" that stretched into every country where the Russian language was spoken. In Ukraine, Putin encouraged Russian-speakers to resist their own government, and he promised them protection if they did. "We are essentially one people. Kyiv is the mother of Russian cities," he said in a speech at the Kremlin. "Millions of Russians and Russian-speaking people live in Ukraine and will continue to do so. Russia will always defend their interests." The vast majority of people in these regions did not want Putin's protection. Many of them staged rallies and marches for Ukrainian unity that spring. In the southern port of Odesa, street battles raged for days between supporters and opponents of the revolutionary government in Kyiv. Dozens of pro-Russian activists wound up dead during one particularly gruesome day of clashes in

May 2014, most of them burned alive in a building where they had taken shelter.

As these events played out, the war became harder for Zelensky to sidestep. It was common in Kyiv to see armed men in camouflage uniforms, adorned with the patches of Ukraine's newfangled volunteer battalions. Lines of people formed outside draft offices, waiting to enlist. None of the famous comedians from Zelensky's troupe went to serve at the time, and some of them were more concerned about their future in the movie business.

When the Russians annexed Crimea, Zelensky's company, Studio Kvartal 95, still had a few projects in production with Russian partners, including a long-running sitcom and the sequel to a romantic comedy. He was bound by contracts to finish them but, in the meantime, felt free to make his feelings toward Russia clear. During his final months in Moscow, where he had lived for six years, Zelensky filmed a few segments of a weekly news parody at the edge of Red Square. He tried to keep the tone light, but the sense of betrayal he felt was palpable: "I'm reporting here from the heart of Russia," he said, "if it has any heart left at all."

After the annexation of Crimea, his production company shuttered its office in Moscow and began to wind down collaborations with Russian partners. Zelensky had worked with many of the biggest movie producers in Russia. He knew the heads of the major television networks. Some of them were his old friends. After Crimea, they stopped talking to him. "The feelings were mutual," he later said. "Everyone vanished, just like that."

By the end of 2014, he stopped working in Russia as a matter of principle. The effect on his business was devastating. He later estimated the studio's income shrank nearly sevenfold after the loss of the Russian market. For every hour of TV programming they produced, their revenue dropped, on average, from $200,000 to $30,000. It may have been possible for Zelensky to temper these losses. The censors in Moscow had not imposed any blanket bans on Ukrainian performers. The shows and films Zelensky's studio produced were still among the most popular and profitable in Russia at the time. In order to remain a player on that market, Zelensky would only have needed to keep quiet about politics and focus on entertainment. Many in Ukraine would have condemned him for that. Some would consider him a traitor. Then again, as a comedian, he was under no professional obligation to speak up about Crimea. He had already shown, during the revolution in Kyiv, that he was capable of batting away political questions and keeping his views to himself.

But Crimea was different. He took it personally. It felt as much a part of Ukraine to him as Kyiv did. His troupe had performed there throughout his career, and his family had gone there on holidays. The year before the annexation, Zelensky and his wife had bought a summer home in Crimea, and the pain of watching that region get ripped away was compounded by the applause and adulation Putin received from most of Russian society, including some of the artists and performers Zelensky had known and worked with since the start of his career. The vast majority of Russians saw the annexation as a brilliant and bloodless act of revenge against the insolent Ukrainians and their patrons in the West. Zelensky, like millions of his countrymen, experienced the theft of their land as a devastating act of betrayal. He could not imagine taking the stage in Moscow with a smile on his face after that. Even if it meant bankrupting the business he had spent over a decade developing in Russia, he made his position clear. "A lot of artists still go there to perform," he said. "I'm not judging them. It's their wish. It's all a matter of morals and what you feel inside. For me it hurts. It really hurts." When an offer arrived for him to perform a single show in Russia for $250,000, Zelensky refused it.

His personal relationships also suffered. During a night out at a restaurant in Moscow in 2014, he got into an argument with one of his close friends, a famous Russian actor. They had just made a movie together, then playing in theaters. "He was an awesome friend," Zelensky later recalled. "Then he started telling me how Crimea is theirs." The dispute got so heated that Zelensky grabbed the microphone from a karaoke machine and gave a speech to all the Russians in the restaurant. "Look here," he remembers telling them. "Your people are taking away *our* Crimea." Somebody called the police.

Even family occasions could not lure him back to Russia after that. One of Olena's relatives in Moscow invited them to a wedding soon after the annexation of Crimea. "We had no desire to go," Olena told me. Her father went in their place to represent the Ukrainian side of the family, and, as Zelensky later recalled, the guests wound up arguing about the annexation.

❖

That summer, not long after he returned home from Moscow, Zelensky went on the road to see the war up close for the first time in his life. It would change him. His comedy troupe, featuring several of Zelensky's old friends from childhood, organized a tour of the war zone, and they didn't travel light. A group of backup dancers came along for the musical numbers. Roadies brought a collapsible stage and a few trucks full of lights, speakers, props, and costumes. It resembled a USO tour, like the ones Bob Hope and his band of entertainers gave around the Pacific in the summer of 1944, flying from island to island to perform for American troops. The crucial difference was that, for Zelensky, this war was much closer to home. Departing from Kyiv, their bus could reach the front lines in less than a day on the highway. At some points they would be within a couple hours' drive of their childhood home in Kryvyi Rih.

In preparation for the tour, Zelensky wrote some new material to perform for the soldiers. Its centerpiece was a ballad that distilled his feelings about the revolution and the war. It included a few easy applause lines: "We've told Russia to get fucked." But the lyrics were neither optimistic nor very patriotic. They expressed a love for Ukraine that persists despite the country's endless foibles and disappointments. The song depicts the 2014 revolution, then only a few months old, as another act of mass deception, good for nothing but a lot of heartaches and another "government of nobodies." The song was a slap in the face of Ukraine's new president, Petro Poroshenko, who had just been inaugurated. But the soldiers in the war zone loved it.

During one performance at an air base near Mariupol, Zelensky watched a big crowd of them, more than a thousand in all, jump to their feet, some waving their assault rifles in the air, whistling, shouting, and dancing atop their armored vehicles. Afterward they rushed the stage for pictures and autographs, offering tokens of gratitude to the comedians. Yevhen Koshovy, who is completely bald, received a bottle of shampoo. Oleksandr Pikalov remembers a soldier stuffing something heavy in his pocket. He reached down to find that it was a hand grenade. "It's a gift," the soldier explained with a grin; he didn't have anything else to offer. Among the other gifts were a badge and balaclava that had been taken off the body of a Russian separatist. It felt macabre, but the comedians accepted.

From then on, touring the front would become a tradition for Zelensky and his troupe. The audiences they knew from years of performing in Kyiv were made up mostly of the pampered elites who could afford their ticket prices. Often the halls were full of the same bloated politicians Zelensky satirized onstage. No performance, no matter how funny or moving, could make those jaded bodies jump out of their seats. But here, out in the war zone, everything felt more sincere. The nearness of death made tears come easily. It made life in Kyiv feel shallow by comparison, devoid of purpose. Zelensky, after visiting the front, would never again be content to devote himself solely to show business and entertainment. At times he felt regret and a bit of shame for never taking up arms himself. Even when there had been no war to fight, his parents had protected him from the military. They were afraid that he would be hazed or picked on by other soldiers. "But I want to send my child to the military," Zelensky said after the first tour in 2014, when his son was just learning to walk.

That summer, he began raising money for the armed forces. The sums he collected were not huge. His first major donation in the summer of 2014 was a million hryvnia, roughly the value of one of the luxury cars Zelensky drove around Kyiv. But in the months that followed, he began to put pressure on his peers in show business to support the military, give money to the war effort, and visit soldiers at the front. "Go, just go and touch them, shake their hands," he recalled telling other actors and pop stars. Among the troops, he said he had observed a deep sense of estrangement from the rest of Ukrainian society. For the elites in Kyiv, the war in the east still felt far away. "They are protecting our future," Zelensky said of the armed forces. "And they don't have the feeling that everyone is proud of them."

❖

Zelensky's idea for a presidential run began to germinate during his trips to the Donbas in 2014. One of his companions was Yuriy Tyra, an old friend who served as a roadie, manager, and all-around fixer while the troupe was on tour in the war zone. Though never a performer, Tyra could entertain the crew for hours with his stories of the crooked cops and smugglers he met while running his many enterprises, from logistics and tourism to the import of luxury cars. Thickset, sharp-eyed, foul-mouthed, and chain-smoking, he was especially adept, through his connections in the customs service, at getting goods across the border, and he had an extensive network of friends inside the military, who often relied on Tyra to bring them high-end gear, such as night-vision equipment, that the armed forces could not afford to provide. When he first went with Zelensky to the war zone, Tyra helped arrange their shows at military bases, and he could see the way the troops affected Zelensky. "They would come up and say to him, straight up: 'Volodya, run for president.' They weren't kidding. It came from the heart."

While talking to the troops after his shows, Zelensky also absorbed their anger toward the leadership in Kyiv, especially President Poroshenko, whom he began to see as not only corrupt but criminally inept and avaricious. A few of the soldiers they met had been stationed in Crimea during the Russian occupation, and they told Zelensky that Ukraine would have been perfectly capable of mounting a defense against the Russians on that peninsula. "They just didn't get the orders," Tyra said. "They were just told to pack up and leave."

In August 2014, toward the end of Zelensky's first tour of the front, Ukrainian forces suffered another devastating rout that would later be blamed on the fecklessness of the military command under President Poroshenko. In the city of Ilovaisk, over a thousand Ukrainian troops found themselves encircled by Russian forces. When they agreed to withdraw, the Russians opened fire on their retreating columns, killing hundreds of them. It was one of the worst massacres of the war, and its participants would later tell Zelensky and his friends how it could have been avoided through better leadership. Once, after a concert near the front, Tyra saw the widow of a paratrooper come up to Zelensky and tell him to run for office. For good luck, she gave him the beret from her dead husband's uniform.

It would take a lot more pressure to convince Zelensky to change careers. But within a few months of his first trip to the front he began working on the script for a new sitcom called *Servant of the People*, which would become his gateway into politics. The show forced Zelensky to imagine himself in the role of the president. In the first episode, a high school history teacher uncorks his epic rant against corruption—*Fuck the motorcades! Fuck the perks! Fuck the fucking chalets!*—and one of his students films it and posts it on YouTube. The clip goes viral on the eve of a presidential election, prompting voters to install the teacher as a write-in candidate. The first season, with Zelensky in the starring role, showcased a common political fantasy: a regular schmo gets a chance to run the country, and he turns out to be better and more honest than all the lazy, self-serving elites. It made for good TV in part because it was cathartic. In one episode, Zelensky's character has a daydream of mowing down the entire parliament with a pair of submachine guns, Rambo-style. Premiering at the end of 2015, the show struck a nerve in the body politic. Fantasies of revenge against the ruling class were then fueling the rise of populism across Europe, and they would help Donald Trump take over the Republican Party the following year. In countries like Ukraine, where corruption often felt like the government's only demonstrable skill, the character Zelensky plays in *Servant of the People* was practically guaranteed to make him an icon.

Olena Zelenska, who worked as a writer on the show, insists the protagonist was not based on her husband. He conceived of the character himself, she said, and was deeply involved in the script-writing process. "It was an absolutely invented, fantastical persona," she told me. Even so, it did not take long for other writers and actors on the show to begin conflating that persona with the real Zelensky. At their office in Kyiv, the marketing team once reenacted a scene from the show, pretending it was Zelensky who had just been inaugurated president. "At first it seemed like half a joke to me," Olena said. "It was an idea I didn't even want to discuss, because it seemed too far-fetched." When any suggestion of a presidential run came up in conversation, the team around Zelensky tended to split into two camps. Olena led the opposition. Her husband had always been a workaholic. But, in that period, when the second season of *Servant of the People* was in production, he was juggling more projects than he could reasonably handle, and he had barely any time for her or their children.

"The process of raising them is just passing me by," Zelensky admitted while promoting one of his films. The only time he spent with Kyrylo, he said, was late at night, when Zelensky came home to find that the boy couldn't sleep. Olena was tired of caring for them on her own, and she knew that a second career in politics would eat up even more of his time and attention than show business. She made these frustrations clear to her husband in private for years. When the problem persisted, she made it public in spectacular fashion, during the taping of one of his game shows.

The show, *Make a Comic Laugh*, invited amateur comedians to do stand-up in front of Zelensky. Every time they made him laugh, the contestants would win cash prizes. Olena decided, in the spring of 2016, to have their daughter appear as a contestant on the show. She kept Zelensky in the dark about this plan, and he nearly walked off the set when he saw his daughter emerge from backstage, dressed in a glittery sweater and pigtails. "Your mother put you up to this," he said with annoyance, looking over at his wife, who gave him a devious smile from the studio audience. She'd written the jokes, and clearly intended them to send a message to an audience of one.

"Everybody thinks it's cool to be the daughter of Volodymyr Zelensky. There's nothing cool about it," Sasha said. "Papa is always at work." The only way to spend an evening with him, she said, was to turn on the TV. "Then it's almost like he's by my side." When the show was over, Olena and Sasha went home with a bunch of prize money, more than enough to buy a new TV.

❖

Among Zelensky's friends and business partners, the idea of a presidential run seemed more appealing than it was to his family. Gradually, they wore him down, Tyra told me, "like drops of water on his brain." One of their strongest arguments with Zelensky was the success of *Servant of the People* and the mass appeal of its protagonist, the accidental president he played on TV. But the point that carried the day made use of Zelensky's own self-confidence. It was not hard to convince him that he could do a better job than any of the politicians vying for the job. The next elections were scheduled for the spring of 2019, and polls showed that it would be a contest between two stalwarts of the political class: the incumbent, Petro Poroshenko, and the irrepressible Yulia Tymoshenko, who was the favorite to win the race. For nearly fifteen years, Tymoshenko had been the target of Zelensky's satire. He'd depicted her as a two-faced megalomaniac. Now Ukraine was facing the prospect of a Tymoshenko administration. "Let it be anybody," Tyra told me of their thinking at the time. "Just don't let that vamp become the president."

All told, it took about two years for Tyra's side of the debate to win Zelensky over. The first public inkling of their political plans came at the end of 2017, when one of Zelensky's oldest friends, Ivan Bakanov, registered a new political party. It was named after the sitcom: Servant of the People. Within a few months, Tyra sensed that Zelensky was starting to come around. One hint was a book Zelensky read around that time, about the life and career of Lee Kuan Yew, the authoritarian leader of Singapore. During his three decades in power, Lee won independence for his city-state and turned it into an economic powerhouse. But, in the process, he ruled through fear, jailing and silencing critics. "You ready to do that?" Tyra remembers asking Zelensky when he saw him with the book during a European tour.

He did not get a straight answer at the time. But, soon after, during a tour stop in Germany, Zelensky got into the passenger seat of Tyra's van and asked for a cigarette. It was one of the few places where he could still smoke without getting an earful about it from his friends. After a few long drags, he broke the news to Tyra: "I'm running." It was April 2018, more than half a year before Zelensky's wife and many of his closest friends would learn about the decision. Yet it was clear to Tyra that this was not a passing whim. Zelensky had carefully considered his chances.

"We knew what we were up against," Tyra told me. Both of the other candidates had been wealthy oligarchs before taking office. Poroshenko still owned one of Ukraine's leading television channels. Tymoshenko had earned a fortune in the European gas trade in the 1990s and knew Putin personally. From her days as a dissident and a prime minister, she also had clout in Western capitals. "They had power. They had resources," Tyra said. "And here was a dude from Kryvyi Rih, totally wet behind the ears."

There was, however, at least one influential backer Zelensky could turn to for support. The TV channel that aired Zelensky's programming, including Servant of the People, was owned by a billionaire named Ihor Kolomoysky, an oil and banking magnate with the looks of an oligarch from central casting. Crass and ill-tempered, he had once lashed out at a journalist for Radio Liberty, calling him a "prostitute" and a "fucking skirt" during a press briefing. Kolomoysky also had the rare distinction of being a fugitive from both the Russian and Ukrainian law. Authorities in Moscow wanted him for alleged war crimes in eastern Ukraine, related to the actions of a paramilitary unit Kolomoysky had bankrolled. Authorities in Kyiv wanted him for financial crimes, related to the alleged asset-stripping of his bank, which had required a government bailout worth $5.6 billion. Kolomoysky always denied these charges. To escape arrest, he moved to Switzerland in 2016 and later relocated to Israel, he said, "for family reasons." He and Zelensky were not especially close. But they had known each other socially and professionally for years before the start of the election season in 2018. Zelensky had once staged a private concert for the tycoon's birthday, and his movies and TV shows had earned a lot of money for Kolomoysky's media company.

When they discussed the idea of a political campaign, Kolomoysky was glad to support it, though not out of the goodness of his heart. He wanted to return to Ukraine and regain control of his bank, which the state had nationalized after the bailout in 2016. The idea of backing a dark-horse candidate for president had obvious appeal to Kolomoysky. It promised to make him a power player in the elections and, depending on the outcome, to give him substantial sway over the state's affairs. By late summer of 2018, he was actively helping Zelensky lay the groundwork for his campaign.

The person put in charge of the effort was a former lawyer for Kolomoysky named Andriy Bohdan, a cherub-faced operator with a cutthroat reputation. As a reward for victory, Bohdan would go on to serve as Zelensky's presidential chief of staff, a role endowed with enormous power. But early on, when their political plans were still a secret even to Zelensky's family, Bohdan kept his head down, his eyes on the data.

"To get elected in our country, you need two things," Bohdan told me. "A television network and recognizability." Kolomoysky had the first; Zelensky had the second. "The rest is up to the public relations guys, the political consultants, and so on." In other words, it was up to guys like Bohdan. To gauge Zelensky's electability, his team ran a series of nationwide polls, and the results were astounding. By the middle of September 2018, when Zelensky was still being coy about his political plans and, for the most part, laughing them off, the polls put him in second place in a field of potential candidates for president. He was already ahead of the incumbent, though still far behind his main challenger, Yulia Tymoshenko.

Bohdan then got to work on a strategy that could put Zelensky in the lead. According to surveys and voting patterns, the war against Russia and its proxies had polarized the electorate in Ukraine. The average voters in the eastern and southern half of the country were still under the sway of Russian propaganda. They had either given up on the political process in Ukraine, or they had taken the side of one of the pro-Russian parties, which had emerged from the ruins of the Yanukovych regime. The opposing side of the electorate had moved in a nationalist direction. They wanted Ukraine to be more assertive in defending itself against the Russians, and they would accept no concessions to Putin in the war. "The war had a centrifugal effect on the political spectrum," Bohdan told me. "Both sides went to their corners and got more extreme, and that created a vacuum in the center. Our candidate was designed to fill that vacuum."

In order to win, Zelensky's political advisers decided that he should not publish a detailed electoral platform or take any clear positions. "If you start taking positions," Bohdan said, "you lose one side or the other." It would be much more effective to keep Zelensky away from the issues. The plan, in other words, was to make him a blank slate, a canvas onto which voters could project their ideas of the perfect president.

❖

In December 2018, Zelensky was ready to make it official. During a tour of his variety show, he set aside some time backstage to record the video announcement for his presidential campaign. It was set to air on Kolomoysky's television channel on New Year's Eve. When the clip was ready, Zelensky wrapped up the tour and flew to France for a ski vacation with his family. Olena was still in the dark about his decision to run, and Zelensky neglected to warn her. Instead he and the kids went skiing that day, while Olena stayed in the lodge, none the wiser.

"Maybe it's better that he didn't tell me," she said later, when we discussed that moment in their marriage. "There was less worry for me. Instead of a few months of torment, there were just a couple of days being mad at him afterward." He had already made up his mind, she said, and there was nothing she could have done to change it. Zelensky understood as well as his wife that the campaign, to say nothing of the presidency, would be painful for their family. "I knew it would hit them hard," he later said. "But we did not talk about it." Though he listened to his wife's objections, Zelensky made up his mind in spite of them and saw no point in going in circles. It would later become a pattern in his administration. Those who questioned or opposed Zelensky's plans often found themselves pushed to the periphery.

On the night of the announcement, he did not stay up to watch it with his wife. It aired during a break between sketches in his annual New Year's comedy special. Olena woke up the next morning in their hotel room and saw a stream of messages from friends and colleagues. Some included links to her husband's political coming out, which looked like a practical joke. In the video, Zelensky stands next to a Christmas tree, as though lampooning the annual year-end address that Putin and his Soviet predecessors have made since the invention of color TV. "People have long been asking me, 'Are you running or not?'" he said, switching from Russian to Ukrainian for the official announcement: "I am running for president of Ukraine." Olena watched the one-minute speech, then turned to her husband and asked the obvious question: Why did she have to be the last to know? With a smile, he answered, "Oh, I forgot to tell you."

CHAPTER 9

THE FAVORITE

THE POLITICAL ESTABLISHMENT IN KYIV WAS NOT INCLINED TO TAKE ZELENSKY SERIously, at least not at first. The incumbent, Petro Poroshenko, dismissed his new challenger as a clown and a neophyte. He refused to believe Ukraine would choose a comedian as its commander in chief in the middle of a war with Russia. In the east, the front lines were mostly static as the elections approached in early 2019. But sporadic shelling and sniper attacks continued, and the death toll climbed every week. More than ten thousand people were killed in the first four years of fighting, and well over a million had been forced to flee their homes. During Poroshenko's tenure, the economy shrank nearly in half, largely due to the toll of the war. The national currency had collapsed in value by about 70 percent in 2014, and it had not recovered. Poroshenko could hardly be blamed for the economic pain of the war, but it left him with no easy path to reelection.

The slogan he chose—"Army, Language, Faith"—was emblematic of his hard shift to the right as the elections approached. He cast himself as a wartime president, the only one with the backbone to drive the Russians out. He pushed for new restrictions on the Russian language and urged the military to advance against Russian-held positions, even when it made little strategic sense. He also began an effort to strip the Russian Orthodox Church of its land and its standing in Ukraine, a process that Zelensky would carry forward after Russia's full-scale invasion.

Among the worst problems Ukraine faced at the end of Poroshenko's term was diplomacy. The U.S. and Europe provided a modest supply of weapons, military training programs, and billions of dollars in loans and financial assistance to help Ukraine defend itself. But in private, Western diplomats had long begun to talk about their "Ukraine fatigue," the deepening sense that the country was a lost cause, too corrupt and dysfunctional to save from Russia's clutches. Corruption had not abated since the downfall of the old regime. In some ways it seemed to grow worse. One of the country's top prosecutors under Poroshenko was recorded telling the targets of corruption investigations how best to avoid them. Another official close to Poroshenko was implicated in a scheme to smuggle military hardware from Russia and sell it at a markup to the Armed Forces of Ukraine.

No evidence emerged to implicate Poroshenko directly in these scandals, and his allies denied the allegations of corruption. But the frustration among Ukraine's allies was obvious whenever Poroshenko went abroad. In early 2018, about a year before the elections, he traveled to the annual security conference in Munich, and it was painful to watch the reception from his peers. Ukraine, even then, was the only European country with a war on its territory. Yet its president could not command an audience in Europe, not even in a room full of military types, not even at a summit devoted to matters of war. "I am the one who warned you that there are no limits to Russia's evil agenda," he said in a speech to the conference. "Ukraine is the shield and sword of Europe." To illustrate the point, Poroshenko brought out a tattered flag of the European Union and held it up for the delegates to see. It had been taken, he said, from the front lines in eastern Ukraine.

The theatrics had little effect. Apart from a few rows of journalists and diplomatic staffers, no one even bothered to attend the speech. Later that day, I found Poroshenko sulking in his hotel suite with a couple of his advisers, the curtains drawn against the snowstorm raging outside. "I hate the idea that this is a frozen conflict," he said, gesturing for me to write it down: "No! This is a hot war!" Of course he was right. His soldiers continued to fight and die. But the war had faded from the international agenda, and the West felt little urgency in trying to resolve it. Another round of peace talks between Ukraine and Russia was due to take place in Munich the next day. But the German foreign minister abruptly canceled them due to more pressing business he had in Berlin: a German journalist had just been released from prison in Turkey, and the minister wanted to be there for his homecoming. It would take another four months before the peace talks were rescheduled, and they would end in another stalemate for Poroshenko.

In his suite in Munich, we mostly talked about that impasse, and he thanked me for covering the war, as though my articles could make much difference. What he needed was a way to make the Europeans experience this war as their own, as a threat to their own security, not just some territorial dispute in the distant ruins of the Soviet Union. "Please, be my guest in Ukraine," Poroshenko said. "Maybe go to the front line and see with your own eyes what's going on there. I can organize it for you, because I'm very much interested in that." He'd been extending the same invitation to many of the leaders he met in Munich. There were not a lot of takers, and Poroshenko could not understand why his message failed to register. "I am a president of peace," he told me as we said goodbye. "I am not a president of war." But at the end of his first term in office, most Ukrainians saw him differently. They saw him as the man who had promised to secure a lasting peace and failed. They were ready to try someone new.

❖

By early 2019, when I arrived in Kyiv to cover the presidential race, Zelensky was already the favorite to win. In most polls, he had roughly twice as much support as Poroshenko, even though he refused to meet the incumbent in the typical arena of politics. Zelensky conducted the campaign on his own terms, and it left him nearly impervious to political attacks. He did not publish a detailed electoral platform. He did not even take a pause in his comedy career to focus on the race. The third season of *Servant of the People* was in production during the campaign, and Zelensky continued to tour his variety show throughout the winter and early spring.

One afternoon that March, a few weeks before the first round of the elections, Zelensky's aides invited me to visit the offices of Studio Kvartal 95, which they were using as one of their campaign headquarters. The offices occupied the top three floors of a high-rise just outside the city center, with views onto the sprawl of apartment blocks below and, in the distance, the TV tower that broadcast their productions. It could have passed for a large accounting firm—gray carpets, drop ceilings, generic kitchenettes—except the walls were covered with movie posters, many of them featuring Zelensky's blond, voluptuous costars from the studio's romantic comedies.

In a conference room on the twenty-first floor, Zelensky's childhood friend, Vadym Pereverzev, waited for me, his face difficult to recognize from the old videos of them performing together in the late 1990s. The eager teenager now looked jaded, his arms sinewy and covered in tattoos, an odd fit for his new role as a political campaign strategist. "Our work hasn't changed much since we went into politics," he told me. "We went from writing jokes to writing slogans. The difference is not that big." Some of their campaign promises, he said, started out as jokes in the writers' room. One of them offered cash rewards to people for turning corrupt officials over to the police. If the investigation recovered any bribe money, the tipster would get a slice of it. Billboards with this pledge went up around the country during the campaign: "Turn in a Corrupt Official, Get 10%!" (President Zelensky, true to his word, later signed an anti-bribery law that allowed for such payments.) But, beyond the gimmickry, it was hard to discern any coherent program. That was the point. A Gallup survey published during the campaign found that only nine percent of Ukrainians expressed trust in their government, fewer than in any other nation in the world. In that environment, Zelensky's strategy seemed obvious: avoid acting like a politician at any cost. He did not need a political vision. His comedy was his campaign.

On Kolomoysky's television channel, his stand-up and news parodies aired throughout the race. They allowed him to respond to criticism or to deflect it, often satirizing the people who attacked him. His rivals in the race complained that such programming gave him an unfair advantage, and they were right. Under Ukrainian law, television channels are obliged to give presidential candidates roughly equal amounts of airtime. But the law did not apply to the lineup of movies, reruns, and television specials that beamed Zelensky's image into every household in the land. "This makes our opponents go apoplectic," his campaign manager, Dmytro Razumkov, told me at the time. "But legally it does not count as campaigning."

Nor did the latest episodes of *Servant of the People*, which was among the campaign's most powerful means of persuasion. The hottest show on Ukrainian TV at the time, it invited the public to confuse Zelensky with the character he played, an eminently humble, likable, and good-hearted leader who, in the imaginary world of the sitcom, receives pep talks from his visions of Abraham Lincoln and Julius Caesar before forcing Ukraine's crooked politicians to straighten up and ride bicycles to work.

Outside Ukraine, Zelensky's advantage in the polls made a lot of people anxious, including the Western bureaucrats and bankers who had given the country emergency loans. They had also been watching *Servant of the People*, and they noticed that, in one episode, Zelensky's character tells a group of officials from the International Monetary Fund to go fuck themselves. In real life, the candidate was more gracious toward Ukraine's foreign allies, but not exactly reassuring. He agreed to meet with a group of Western diplomats not long before the vote, and many of them came away puzzled and concerned. "He wasn't in a position to specify what he intends to do when he wins," an official from the German foreign ministry told me afterward. "It seems clear that people want the president from the TV show," he said. "We don't know if Zelensky will be that president."

At the outset, the race looked like an easy win for Ukraine's most powerful woman. No other candidate, least of all Zelensky, could claim the credentials of Yulia Tymoshenko: two terms as prime minister, two years behind bars as a prisoner of conscience, and two popular uprisings that saw protestors carry her portrait through the streets like a talisman against corruption. When she invited me to visit her during the race, her office looked like a walk-in résumé. The walls were plastered with photos of her leading the Orange Revolution to victory in 2004 and 2005. There was a vitrine full of gifts from the envoys of China and a framed photo of her with the original Iron Lady, Margaret Thatcher.

On Tymoshenko's desk, next to a portrait of her daughter, there was a picture of her with Donald Trump, the blond crown of her braid somehow outshining his golden comb-over. Tymoshenko had no particular sympathy for Trump. But for a politician in Ukraine, no endorsement is more valuable than that of the U.S. president. During one of Trump's speeches at the National Prayer Breakfast in Washington, she got a seat in the front of the room, within the frame of the television cameras. Then she waited for him outside the bathroom for a quick chat and a photo, which she framed and placed on her desk.

A year later, as she watched Zelensky sprint past her in the polls, she thought about Trump, about the way he had pulled ahead of Hillary Clinton in 2016. The story felt familiar: a TV celebrity trouncing the nation's most experienced female politician just as she came within reach of the presidency. And it clearly pained her. This was her third presidential run, and it was likely to be her last. But she did not fault Ukrainians for supporting Zelensky. "We can't blame people for this," she told me in her office. "Their outrage is a sign of powerlessness. They are so disappointed, so unhappy with the system, that they start looking for new ways out. And when they don't find that, the rise of people like Zelensky is a protest, a response to the feeling of hopelessness."

Tymoshenko saw it as part of the wave of populist victories that had brought Trump and his many impersonators to power around that time. "It's not just Ukraine," she said. "This is a trend all over the world. It's the total degeneration of representative democracy." With the right gimmicks and enough followers on social media, she told me, "You could make a senator out of a horse." Or a president out of a comic.

❖

The final season of *Servant of the People* was made available for free on YouTube at the end of March, a few days before the first round of voting. It marked the climax of Zelensky's campaign, its final appeal to the electorate. The plot invited the people of Ukraine to imagine a dystopian future in which their country no longer exists. A series of coups splits the nation into micro-states, all governed by weird sultans, fascists, or kleptocrats. Zelensky's character, the imaginary president, ends up in prison, the victim of a plot. Then, in the series finale, he is released and sets out to stitch Ukraine back together again. With a bit of hard work and some rousing speeches—"Everybody needs to do their part!"—he inspires all the Ukrainian splinter states to reunite under his leadership. The final sequence presents a vision of their distant future. Their great-grandchildren live in prosperity, speaking a multitude of languages, amazed and a bit confused when they are taught in their clean and spacious classrooms about Ukraine's tumultuous past.

By no means was this Zelensky's best work, either as an actor or a screenwriter. It wasn't funny, and the fairy-tale ending reeked of agitprop, which seemed to be the point. His goal for the final season was to win over voters, not TV critics. The timing of the release gave Ukrainians a Friday and a Saturday to binge-watch the new episodes before heading to the polls, and the results on that Sunday were unequivocal. In the first round of voting, the ballot had a total of thirty-nine candidates, and Zelensky trounced them all, knocking Yulia Tymoshenko out of the race and winning nearly twice as many votes as his closest rival. Three weeks later, in the runoff vote, Zelensky went head-to-head against Poroshenko and won with a staggering 73 percent of the vote. Out of the twenty-four regions of Ukraine that took part in the elections, all but one went to Zelensky. The electoral maps shown on TV looked like a sea of green, the color of his campaign.

Historically the result was not the best of any candidate for Ukraine's highest office. After leading the uprising of 2014, Poroshenko fared better, winning a snap ballot that spring with a clear majority in the first round. Ukraine's first presidential election in 1991 also ended in a more resounding victory for Leonid Kravchuk. But the outcome of the race in 2019 still felt like a singular moment of consensus for Ukraine. Throughout its history as an independent state, political power had swung from one side of the national divide to the other, from east to west, through war and revolution, and now the voters in almost every region had rallied around a single candidate. In the process they exposed the hollowness of Putin's lies about Ukraine, his claims that the country had been a historical mistake, stitched together from incongruous parts, incapable of unity and led by neo-fascists, with millions of citizens and vast territories that belonged by right with Russia. It took the victory of a Russian-speaking Jew from Kryvyi Rih to show that Putin's theories about Ukraine were not only false but ridiculous. In the eastern regions that Putin liked to describe as parts of the "Russian world," Zelensky got nearly 90% of the vote.

But the winner did not dwell on such lessons on election night. As the confetti fell from the ceiling at his victory party, he did not use the moment to expound on his plans for the country or his vision of its history. "We did it together," he declared from the stage, where his wife stood clapping, her misgivings hidden behind a fixed smile. "Thanks to everyone! Now there will be no pompous speeches." He knew he didn't need to make any. His momentum felt unstoppable. Three months later, Zelensky's political party, Servant of the People, became the only party ever to win an absolute majority in the Ukrainian parliament. The party now had enough seats to pass legislation and, if it wanted, to rewrite the Constitution. "It was scary," said Bohdan, who became the presidential chief of staff. "I was sleeping three hours a night, and I was really afraid." The race itself had felt like a dream, a hilarious experiment in the wizardry of mass communication, and now they woke up to the consequences. Voters had entrusted Zelensky with enough power to rule as a despot if he chose. "Our mistakes," Bohdan told me, "would now be their mistakes."

CHAPTER 10

TRUST NO ONE

THE INAUGURATION FELL ON A MONDAY IN MAY, WHEN THE WEATHER WAS ALREADY warm enough for crowds to gather outside the parliament in their T-shirts and sunglasses, waving Ukrainian flags and watching the ceremony on a giant screen. Hundreds of lawmakers, diplomats, and delegates from around the world gathered inside, beneath the glass dome of the plenary hall. Zelensky's parents beamed with pride from the gallery, Rymma dressed in a smart pink suit, seated in the same row as her son's predecessors, the dour men who had gone through this ritual before. There was the founding father, Leonid Kravchuk, a former propaganda man for the Soviet Communist Party who won freedom for Ukraine in 1991 and believed so firmly in a peaceful future that he agreed to give up Ukraine's nuclear arsenal, then the third biggest in the world. Next to him sat the elfin figure of Leonid Kuchma, boss of Ukraine through the years of gangster capitalism, who clung to power even after his own bodyguard revealed a plot to kill a journalist. Next came Viktor Yushchenko, stately and distant, his face still scarred from the poison that nearly killed him during the revolution he rode to the presidency.

What could Zelensky learn from these men if not a lesson in the toxicity of power, the way it grinds you down, blackens your name, offers trades and gambles that get you in the end. On the campaign trail, he showed open disdain for such politicians, and he had no intention of emulating their leadership or even seeking much of their advice. "They go backstage and they're all buddies with each other," Zelensky told me. "Then they enter the arena and they're gladiators." He didn't want to be that kind of leader. "I'm not interested in being their buddy," he said. "I already have a world of friends." Many of them showed up in the parliament that day to see him take the ceremonial mace in his hand, the symbol of the Ukrainian presidency. Some were set to take up jobs in his administration, comedians and writers, actors and spin doctors, morphing into technocrats and politicians. Zelensky promised their work would be different. His team would be younger. Their priorities were new.

"Our first task," he said in his inaugural speech that day, "is a cease-fire in the Donbas." This should have been a bigger applause line than it was. Five years into the war against Russia and its proxies, Kyiv's political class was not ready for a cease-fire. They feared it would cost Ukraine too dearly. Zelensky didn't seem to care. "I have often been asked," he said, "'What price are you ready to pay for the cease-fire?' It's a strange question. What price are you ready to pay for the lives of those you love? I can assure you that I'm ready to pay any price to stop the deaths of our heroes."

As a first step, he wanted to win the release of Ukrainian prisoners of war. He also wanted to push aside the politicians who had allowed the war to drag on for half a decade. During his address, he ordered the parliament to fire the defense minister and the head of Ukraine's main intelligence service. Once that was done, he ordered the entire parliament to dissolve itself. New legislative elections would be held in two months' time.

With that, Zelensky had set the agenda for the first part of his presidency: peace at any cost, and a total renewal of power. His approval ratings were astronomical in the months after he took office, approaching 80 percent in some polls. The vast majority of Ukrainians wanted their leaders to pursue peace with Russia. So it was not just pacifism that drove Zelensky's agenda. It was also a form of populism, and he needed to show results.

One of the key figures he put in charge of enacting this agenda was Andriy Yermak, the movie producer and former lawyer for his production company. Yermak would oversee international affairs within the new administration, including relations with the Americans and the Europeans and any peace talks with the Russians. Before the snap parliamentary elections, it would also be his job to organize an exchange of prisoners of war.

First, their team needed to settle into their new offices, and that's where the problems began. The look of the place did not appeal to Zelensky and his entourage. The compound on Bankova Street felt shabby

and gaudy at the same time, the drapes heavy with the air of past ad-
ministrations, whose habits Zelensky had promised to clear away. He
was surprised to learn that his new chambers had been designed to
include a secret elevator. Its sole purpose, Zelensky told me, was for
people to deliver bribes without being seen. Like what? I asked him.
Suitcases of cash? "Let's call it a rumor," he said with a smile, "so I don't
offend anyone."

From the start, his team began looking for alternative places to house
the administration. One was just a few blocks away, a vast exhibition
space called the Ukrainian House on European Square, which they considered renovating into a futuristic dreamscape. Andriy Yermak told me
that he wanted to model it on the Apple headquarters in Silicon Valley.
But security protocols got in the way. It would be expensive and difficult
to wire the new office with secure lines of communication. Then there
was the issue of the bunker. The presidential guards insisted this facility
would prove essential in case of a war or some other catastrophe. Zelensky and his team thought it was pointless. When they first took a tour
of the tunnels that spring, it felt like returning to the past, to the nuclear
stalemates and paranoias of another era. "It was all that Soviet history,"
Yermak told me of that visit to the bunker. "I felt like none of this would
ever be needed. They had built it. Okay. But for what?"

In the end, the bookkeepers and security guards won the argument.
The costs were too high, and the risks too severe, for Zelensky to move
to another building. "It's impossible to be here," he told a group of journalists while giving them a tour of his office. "It drives me insane." The
old yellow telephones that looked like museum pieces, the freestanding
crystal lamps that nearly reached up to the ceilings, the tapestries of
hunters and their prey, the hardwood tables with feet like tiger claws, all
of it clashed with the image Zelensky wanted to project. Still, the reporters seemed glad to see him occupy these rooms. Even if the space looked
old, at least the occupants were new.

For a while, the press gorged on the Cinderella story of the comedian sweeping to power. But Zelensky's honeymoon with the media was
brief. On the day of his inauguration, May 20, 2019, the law obliged him
to declare his assets, which became the subject of lively debate. Everybody knew that Zelensky had earned a fortune in show business, but
the details made for delicious headlines. Apart from his family's sum-

mer home in Crimea, the president had a rental apartment in London, a house in Italy, a handful of luxury watches, and several offshore companies. The leading news outlets in Ukraine gave ample coverage to such revelations, in particular the fact that the president's property in Crimea, a three-bedroom penthouse apartment, had been sold to them for well below the market rate. Zelensky defended the terms of the sale, but his critics used it to suggest that he was just as corrupt and out of touch as his predecessors. Some of the worst attacks came from the TV channel that belonged to Poroshenko, himself a billionaire. His electoral defeat had placed a massive chip on his shoulder. Now among the leaders of the opposition in parliament, the ex-president made it his mission to undermine his successor at every turn.

None of this should have surprised the incoming administration. But, from his first days in office, Zelensky showed a painful sensitivity to criticism. His old friends knew that he suffered from the actor's malady—an abiding need to be liked and applauded. But they hoped he would grow thicker skin after transitioning to politics, where his rivals could not be expected to spare his feelings. Zelensky's chief of staff, Andriy Bohdan, soon understood the importance of keeping the president away from his accounts on social media. Even the comments Zelensky got from strangers could upset him. "Some no-name, totally fake account, and he's losing sleep over it. He's shaking. He's on the phone with his mom," Bohdan told me. "In politics people get used to this stuff and don't make it into a tragedy. It's part of the political process. But for him it was a tragedy, a personal affront."

His wife also suffered from the wave of attacks their family faced in the press and on television. She was not accustomed to all the scrutiny. The summer home in Crimea was registered in Olena's name, which dragged her into the center of the scandal. Whenever she appeared in public, tabloids dissected what the First Lady wore and how she carried herself. "The tension was constant," she told me. It often depressed her to read what the blogs wrote about her and her husband, but she had trouble avoiding them. "I stressed out when they would bite him, criticize him," she said. "You want to answer, but you know that it's pointless to try." Given how touchy her husband could be, she usually avoided giving him advice or even discussing his work when he came home. "Better for me not to criticize him," she said in one of her first TV interviews as First Lady. "It puts him in a bad mood."

Having tried to talk him out of running for office, Olena now found herself trapped with him and their children inside the presidential bubble. She tried to escape it, clinging to her old life as a comedy writer, and in the first months of Zelensky's tenure she spent more time at the offices of their production company, Studio Kvartal 95, than she did at the presidential administration. One of Zelensky's aides recalled asking the First Lady to come to Bankova Street and meet a foreign guest as a courtesy. The president had been called away on official business and was unable to do it himself. Olena refused. "She was busy writing a script," the aide told me.

For the past fifteen years, the studio's stock-in-trade had been political satire, and now Olena felt uncomfortable writing in that genre. It would require making fun of herself, her husband, and many of their friends, who had either joined the administration or taken seats in parliament. Their sketch comedy show, *Evening Kvartal*, had mocked every president in the history of Ukraine, but Olena could sense the writers pulling punches when it came to lampooning Zelensky. It frustrated her. "It's hard to have no mercy when joking about your friend," she told me. "We didn't want to lose our trademark as people who always told the truth about politics, but it's difficult to maintain the necessary distance." One of the actors on *Evening Kvartal* managed to do an impersonation of Zelensky that Olena found passably funny but not nearly harsh enough. To avoid clashing with her colleagues over these issues of pride and politics, honesty and friendship, she decided to stop writing for *Evening Kvartal* and to work instead on other productions that came out of Zelensky's old studio. She did not put her name on the programs and movies that featured her work, because she did not want viewers and critics to see it through a political lens, searching for hidden meaning in scenes and sketches written by the wife of the president.

Zelensky knew better than to pull Olena into the spotlight. "At first my husband never made me feel obligated to do anything as First Lady. I was told right away: You can do your own thing, live your own life, nobody needs to see you." Over time she agreed to ease into the role, as long as she could do it her own way, not under the dictates of convention and protocol. "I understood right away that I will not be an accessory for his appearances and handshakes, standing next to him and smiling," she told me. "That's not what I wanted to do." But that was often what the role required. In June she accompanied Zelensky to Paris, one of the first foreign trips of his tenure, and posed for pictures with her husband, standing next to him and smiling, during their formal reception at the Élysée Palace. Even if the stiffness of it all annoyed her, some of the pageantry felt strange and charming, the military band playing to welcome them, the ceremonial guards marching around with red-feathered plumes sticking out of their hats. Who else gets to experience Paris this way?

During the visit, Brigitte Macron, the First Lady of France, invited Olena to a private meeting and gave her a sense of what they could achieve. The spouses of European leaders rarely have any formal title or responsibilities, and their duties tend to be poorly defined. That changed in France after Emmanuel Macron took office in 2017. His wife took on official status in the administration, with her own staff, budget, and office space. Olena took careful note of that approach and, with Zelensky's support, pushed through the same changes on Bankova Street, establishing the Office of the First Lady as an institution with its own resources. The new status helped free Olena from what she called her "decorative" function—"looking pretty in the background." It still felt odd and somewhat demeaning for her to occupy a role derived not from her own achievements but those of her husband. But, granted the chance, she wanted to make the most of it.

❖

For President Zelensky, the trip to Paris had been a fallback option. The top priority on his travel schedule for the first year of his tenure was to arrange a trip to the United States, Ukraine's most important ally. His team wanted to make a full tour of it, not just the usual stops in New York and Washington but swings through Texas and California to talk about cooperation in the energy and tech sectors. Above all, Zelensky needed to demonstrate that Ukraine's alliance with the U.S. would only grow stronger under his leadership. The Armed Forces of Ukraine relied on American assistance, and the president understood that any sign of weakness in U.S. support would tempt Russia to get more aggressive in the Donbas. The trip would not just be a vanity tour for Zelensky. The lives of Ukrainian troops depended on it. So did the success of the president's peace plan.

His aides believed the trip would not be hard to organize. President Donald Trump, then in the third year of his tenure, had called to congratulate Zelensky on election night and invited him to Washington. Trump's envoys to the inauguration then delivered a written invitation for Zelensky to visit the White House. The Ukrainians took it seriously. But every time they tried to agree on a date, the Americans gave them the runaround. "It's ridiculous," said Igor Novikov, a presidential adviser involved in trying to arrange the trip. "Something is incredibly wrong."

No one on their team, least of all Zelensky, picked up on the signs that a serious scandal was brewing, one that would lead only seven months later to the impeachment of a U.S. president. Few of them paid much attention to foreign affairs during their first weeks in office. They were too busy assembling a government and figuring out how to run the country. "It was incredibly chaotic," said Novikov, a young tech entrepreneur and motivational speaker who stumbled into the administration around that time. The process of interviewing and hiring staff, he said, resembled a "very unique political crowdsourcing experiment . . . creative and very Californian, I would say, in its approach."

In practice, this often meant friends and colleagues of the president got pulled into roles for which they had little if any preparation. Novikov was a case in point. Young and suave, with flawless English from his studies at a British boarding school, he was known around the tech scene in Kyiv for holding seminars on "futurism," focusing on the way new technologies would change humankind. Zelensky attended one of these sessions in 2018, while he was preparing to announce his run for the presidency. "And we clicked," Novikov told me. Soon he found himself advising Zelensky's campaign on issues of energy and innovation. After they won the election, the entourage around Zelensky ballooned, attracting a varied cast of power brokers and opportunists. "It's that usual post-election window of opportunity to skip a couple of steps on the career ladder," Novikov said. "The old people, the new people, the neophytes, the corrupt elites, everyone was running around trying to get their piece of the cake."

Novikov tried to blend in among them, taking every chance to hang around the offices on Bankova Street. One night, soon after the inauguration, they were sitting around in Zelensky's office and discussing how to deal with the Trump administration and arrange a visit to the White House. Novikov expressed surprise that no one in the presidential staff had yet been assigned to manage the task. Zelensky turned to him and said, "Do you want to do it?" The response came just as quickly: Why not? If a comedian could figure out how to be president, a tech guru could figure things out with the Americans. Later that night, when he got in his car to drive home, Novikov opened a search page on his phone and typed: *U.S. political system.* "I started teaching myself," he later told me, "the intricate workings of how the U.S. actually works."

Zelensky's expertise on the subject was not much more sophisticated. Once, on the campaign trail in Kyiv, he asked me to enlighten him about the character of Donald Trump, as though every American reporter had some special insight on the matter. "What's he like?" Zelensky said. "A normal guy?" The question made me stammer. Even a basic awareness of Trump's pronouncements would be enough to know his feelings toward Ukraine. Since the start of his tenure in 2017, Trump had expressed admiration for Vladimir Putin and undermined NATO. He had repeated Putin's claims that Ukrainian politicians, not Russian spies, meddled in the 2016 presidential election. He also echoed Russian talking points about Crimea, once claiming the peninsula belongs to Russia because most of its residents speak the Russian language. Zelensky had seen these reports in the news, but he did not seem worried about them. He believed his similarities with Trump—their shared background as TV celebrities, their status as outsiders to politics—would allow him to change Trump's mind about the Ukrainians with little more than a joke and a smile. He had no idea what he was walking into.

❖

Inside the White House, a group of advisers to Trump, led by his personal attorney, Rudy Giuliani, had already developed an obsession with Ukraine. Giuliani was convinced that Ukraine held the keys to Trump's reelection in 2020 and, from a certain vantage, he was right. Their main opponent in the 2020 race would be Joe Biden, and any close observer of Biden's career understood Ukraine to be among his vulnerabilities.

During his tenure as vice president, Biden made it his mission to help Ukraine defend itself from the Russian incursions in Crimea and the Donbas. On behalf of the Obama administration, he oversaw billions of dollars in U.S. financial and military aid to Ukraine. He also pushed the government of Petro Poroshenko to fight corruption, strengthen institutions, and appoint officials the U.S. believed to be clean and competent. At the same time, Biden's son Hunter went to work in Ukraine's energy sector, a notorious swamp of corruption and self-dealing. In the spring of 2014, Hunter Biden accepted a lavishly paid seat on the board of Burisma, a Ukrainian natural gas company. The arrangement looked awful for the Bidens, like a classic case of influence peddling. Even if Joe Biden did nothing to help Burisma, his son's seat on the board exposed both of them to accusations of corruption, and it was only a matter of time before Trump and Giuliani exploited that weakness. In 2018, as they prepared to face Joe Biden in a presidential race, Trump and his team began looking for dirt on the Bidens in Ukraine.

Their main goal at the time was to pressure the authorities in Kyiv to investigate Hunter Biden for corruption, and Giuliani made that request explicit in a phone call with Andriy Yermak. "Let these investigations go forward," Giuliani said during the call on July 22, 2019. "Get someone to investigate this, who is honest, who will not be intimidated, and then we can get all the facts." Yermak agreed to cooperate. In return, he only asked that Giuliani help set a date for Zelensky's visit to the White House. But the tone of the conversation worried the Ukrainians. Novikov, who listened to the call and recorded it, said Giuliani sounded like a mobster on the phone, especially when he passed along a warning for Zelensky to "be careful."

Three days later, President Trump took much the same tone during his call with Zelensky. After a few pleasantries, Trump suggested that any further U.S. assistance to Ukraine would be contingent on Zelensky's willingness to do the Americans a favor. He mentioned Hunter Biden and Burisma and urged Zelensky to investigate them. "There's a lot of talk about Biden's son," Trump said on the call. "It sounds horrible to me." Zelensky agreed. He seemed willing to play along, at least when it came to assigning a prosecutor to study the issues Trump had raised: "We will take care of that," Zelensky said, "and will work on the investigation of the case."

A White House transcript of that conversation would become Exhibit A in the case for Trump's removal from office later that year. But, at the time, Zelensky saw the phone call as a breakthrough. "There was a certain amount of jubilation when it was over," Novikov told me. Trump had promised at the end of the call to set a date for the White House visit, which remained a key priority for the Ukrainians. To celebrate, Zelensky and his aides moved to another room in the presidential chambers, where a waiter brought out bowls of ice cream, offering a choice of chocolate or vanilla. They began to imagine their big trip to America, which finally seemed within reach.

The need to satisfy Trump's demand for investigations seemed like a manageable problem at the time. Zelensky was not opposed in principle to investigating Burisma. As one of the biggest natural gas producers in Ukraine, the firm had often been involved in corruption scandals. Its founder and controlling stakeholder was a former minister in the Yanukovych regime, and he was widely suspected of using his influence to secure drilling rights and concessions from the government. It may have been possible for Ukraine to investigate the company without implicating Hunter Biden. But that approach would still risk entangling Ukraine in U.S. presidential politics. William Taylor, who was then the top U.S. diplomat in Kyiv, warned Zelensky to avoid that. "I said over and over and over that they should just stay out of our politics," Taylor told me. "It makes no sense for them."

Zelensky agreed, so his team stalled for time. When pressed to make a statement about the investigations, they tried to keep the language vague, pledging to fight corruption in broad terms without singling anyone out for suspicion. One night in August, Novikov went up to Zelensky's office on the fourth floor to discuss a statement he had helped to draft about the investigations, and he found the president in miserable form. Less than three months into his tenure, he looked exhausted, as though the demands and dangers of the job had already drained the life from his eyes. When he looked at the statement, Zelensky winced and asked a question: "Do we really need to do this?" The draft made no mention of Hunter Biden or Burisma, and Novikov assured his boss that, with these omissions, they could not be accused of meddling in American politics. "God forbid there is anything about Burisma," Novikov recalls Zelensky saying in response. "That is the ace up our sleeve, and we will play it only when we have no other cards left to play."

They soon ran out of other options. On August 28, 2019, Politico broke the news that Trump had blocked $250 million in military aid to Ukraine. The stakes for Zelensky were now much higher than any visit to the White House. Trump had decided to leave Ukraine at Russia's mercy, cut off from the assistance it needed to defend itself. Zelensky's team could no longer stall and deflect, and they began preparing for him to announce the investigations Trump wanted during an interview with CNN. What stopped them was the rush of news out of Washington that week. Congressional leaders were outraged over Trump's decisions to block the aid. A whistleblower complaint inside the White House accused Trump of coercing Zelensky for political favors. Even Trump loyalists on Capitol Hill urged Trump to release the aid package. So did many of the top officials in the Trump administration. On September 11, Trump relented. His administration released the aid to Ukraine, and Zelensky's team promptly canceled their CNN interview. But the crisis was far from over.

On September 24, the Democratic leadership in the House of Representatives launched a formal impeachment inquiry against Trump for his treatment of Ukraine. That same day, Zelensky and his entourage arrived for their first official visit to the U.S., though not on the terms they had envisioned. The purpose of the trip was to attend the U.N. General Assembly, where Zelensky would meet with many of his peers, including Trump, for the first time. He was also due to deliver the first major speech of his presidency on the biggest stage in international affairs. But all these points on his agenda were overshadowed by the impeachment scandal.

When they landed in New York City, the story of Trump and Ukraine led the news broadcasts on every channel. At the airport and the hotel lobby, Zelensky saw his own face reflected back at him from every television screen, depicted as the victim of Trump and Giuliani's scheme. The White House had just released its transcript of Trump's phone call with Zelensky, and the media were poring over every detail.

"It was everywhere," said Bohdan, the chief of staff, who'd helped organize the trip. "We knew that one wrong word, even a misplaced accent on a word, could lead to an all-out crisis for our country."

Under those circumstances, it may have been wiser for Zelensky to keep away from the cameras. But he chose not to hide. On the sidelines of the General Assembly, he agreed to appear at a press briefing with Trump. He even insisted on speaking in English, which all but guaranteed he would misplace a word or two. Seated beside the man who had just tried to blackmail him, Zelensky thanked Trump for extending an invitation for him to visit the White House. Then he flashed a grin and cracked a joke: "I think you forgot to tell me the date."

❖

In the end, Zelensky never got his visit with Trump in the Oval Office. As the impeachment saga unfolded that fall and early winter, he did his best to stay out of it. But the story was difficult to shake. A parade of witnesses, many of them highly regarded diplomats and military veterans, testified in Congress about the plot that Trump and Giuliani pursued in Ukraine. Every aspect of Trump's call with Zelensky came under scrutiny. For the team on Bankova Street, the political theater was painful to watch, and often humiliating. It served as a crash course in the meanness of U.S. politics and the gauntlet of international affairs. Bohdan described the experience to me as a "cold shower." The White House did not even consult with the Ukrainians before declassifying the transcript of Zelensky's phone call with Trump and sending it out to the press.

In the weeks that followed, the confidential messages Zelensky's aides had sent to U.S. officials were projected onto the screen inside the hearing room on Capitol Hill and dissected live on television. Their private conversations with U.S. diplomats became the subject of fiercely partisan debates. Yermak found it infuriating. He had spent most of his time on Bankova Street trying to figure out a way to make peace in the Donbas, and the foreign media only wanted to know about his conversations with Giuliani and his views on Burisma and Hunter Biden. "The entire time you've been talking about this, we've had people dying in the war out east," Yermak told me in his office as the impeachment hearings carried on in Washington. The breakdown in relations with the U.S., he said, played right into Russia's hands. Putin could see that Kyiv was getting kicked around by its most powerful ally. "Every day," Yermak said, "that costs us human lives."

Zelensky had a different reaction. His temper didn't flare when we talked about the scandal. For several weeks, the president declined my interview requests. It was too dangerous for him to speak during the impeachment inquiry, when his every word could be used as ammunition in the partisan warfare on Capitol Hill. But in late November, as the inquiry prepared to release its final report, Zelensky invited me and a few other reporters to his office. We had not seen each other since the campaign trail, and he had aged and changed far more than I expected in the span of eight months. He was not only more tired and more of a realist, he seemed to have caught a strain of the political disease he once detested and wanted to cure: cynicism. "I live here," he said as we sat down in his office, "like in a fortress that I just want to escape."

The frustrations had started with the little things. He was not allowed to use the apps on his phone to communicate with anyone he wanted. Instead there was the bank of yellow telephones, the secure lines leading to the protocol department, the executive assistants, the presidential guard, and others across the bureaucracy. "When we found out how much the country spends on servicing all these secure lines, I was very surprised," he said. "It requires a huge amount of manpower." It bothered him to have employees of the state open the door for his wife when they arrived at an official function, to remove her overcoat and put it on for her. "Thank you," he would snap. "Don't bother." He could do it himself. There was constant friction between the ways he had been raised to behave and the rules that now governed his movements, his contact with other human beings. They made no sense to him. "All these protocols," he said, "they destroy me as a person."

It was the same with all his plans, all the reforms he had in mind when taking office. His party had won an overwhelming majority in parliament, but the process of passing laws was still taking forever. There were weeks of debates, thousands of amendments, endless squabbles over technicalities. "Everyone needs to discuss everything for a very long time," Zelensky said. He was trying to speed things along, telling the lawmakers: "Go to work! When you enter the chamber to vote, then vote, whether you like the law or not." But it did little good. The rules were stubborn.

In foreign affairs, the system felt even more convoluted, and the impeachment saga shattered Zelensky's faith in his supposed allies. "I don't trust anyone at all," he said. "I'll tell you honestly. Politics is not an exact science. That's why in school I loved mathematics. Everything in mathematics was clear to me. You can solve an equation with a variable, with one variable. But here it's only variables, including the politicians in our country. I don't know these people. I can't understand what dough they're made of. That's why I think nobody can have any trust. Everybody just has their interests."

Trump had known all along that Ukraine was at war with Russia, that its soldiers were sitting in trenches in the Donbas, taking sniper fire and sleeping in the mud. He knew that people were dying out there, and he still decided to block the military aid Ukraine needed to defend itself. "I don't want us to look like beggars," Zelensky said when I asked him about this. "But you have to understand. We're at war. If you're our strategic partner, then you can't go blocking anything for us . . . I think that's just about fairness."

The brief suspension of military aid did not, in itself, cause much harm to Ukraine. But Trump had done enormous damage to Ukraine's reputation. His incessant talk of corruption had signaled to the world's financial institutions that the new government in Kyiv was not a reliable partner. "That is the hardest of signals," Zelensky said. "It might seem like an easy thing to say, that combination of words: 'Ukraine is a corrupt country.' Just to say it and that's it. But it doesn't end there. Everyone hears that signal. Investors, banks, stakeholders, companies, American, European, companies that have international capital in Ukraine. It's a signal to them that says, 'Be careful, don't invest.' Or, 'Get out of there.'"

The message to the world's political leaders was just as hurtful. Trump had treated Ukraine as a pawn, and it was only through a mix of luck and fortitude that Zelensky avoided the role of his accomplice. When he reflected on that experience, the world looked different to Zelensky. He had felt what it is like to lead a country trapped between the world's great powers—"in essence," he said, "these empires, the United States, Russia, China." He had hoped to win their respect as an equal, and the best he could manage so far was to maneuver between them, trying not to get crushed. This was never the role Zelensky envisioned for himself or his country. "I would never want Ukraine to be a piece on the map, on the chessboard of big global players, so that someone could toss us around, use us as cover, as part of some bargain," he said. "I want Ukraine to have agency." But if the first six months of his tenure had taught Zelensky anything about the world, it was a lesson in the ease with which alliances could shift. "That's why," he said, "on the question of who I trust, I told you honestly: No one."

Zelensky with his mother, Rymma, an engineer by training, who doted on her only child much more often than she disciplined him. *(Office of the president)*

Zelensky with his fifth-grade class at School No. 95 in Kryvyi Rih, the city he would later call "my big heart, my big soul." He and several of his classmates, including Denys Manzhosov, seated to Zelensky's right, would later name their comedy troupe after the neighborhood where the school stood, Kvartal 95, or District 95, a reminder to all of them never to forget their roots. *(Courtesy of Denys Manzhosov)*

Zelensky and his crew stood out on the streets of Kryvyi Rih when they were kids in the 1990s, often wearing ties and blazers in a throwback to the Beatles and other idols of early rock and roll. *(Courtesy of Denys Manzhosov)*

A flier for a performance of Zelensky's comedy troupe soon after it was formed in the late 1990s. A gifted physical comedian and dancer, Zelensky often wore tight leather pants during his stage acts at the time. *(Courtesy of Denys Manzhosov)*

Zelensky watches the premiere of his variety show from backstage in Kyiv in March 2019, during his presidential campaign, alongside his longtime friends and partners in show business, Serhiy Shefir (left) and Oleksandr Pikalov. *(Anastasia Taylor-Lind)*

Combining slapstick, sketches, musical numbers, and stand-up, Zelensky's stage acts defy easy comparison to contemporary styles of comedy in the West. They are in many ways closer to the flashy and raucous vaudeville shows popularized in the U.S. in the early twentieth century. *(Anastasia Taylor-Lind)*

Zelensky during his first interview with the author, backstage after his comedy performance in March 2019, in the middle of his run for president. "I don't want to change my life," he said that night of his transition into politics. "If you lose yourself, you'll sink into the swamp." *(Anastasia Taylor-Lind)*

Even though she had opposed his plans to enter the race, Zelensky's wife, Olena, stayed by his side on election night as the results came in. *(Vadim Ghirda, AP Photo)*

After Zelensky took office, his parents, Oleksandr and Rymma, continued living in their old apartment in Kryvyi Rih, declining invitations to move to the capital. Later, at the start of the full-scale invasion, they would need to be evacuated as Russian forces advanced toward the president's hometown from the east and south. *(Office of the president)*

A portrait of the first family released on the president's social media accounts soon after he took office in 2019. The face paint was intended to protect the privacy of Zelensky's son, Kyrylo, who was six at the time. With his fifteen-year-old daughter, Oleksandra, known in the family as Sasha, the same security measure was not taken, as she had already appeared on some of her father's TV shows and was known to the public. *(Office of the president)*

At their first meeting, held in Paris in December 2019, Vladimir Putin seemed cold and irritable as he confronted Zelensky with a litany of historical grudges. The European mediators, Chancellor Angela Merkel of Germany and President Emmanuel Macron of France, could do nothing to break the deadlock. *(Charles Platiau, AFP pool photo via Getty Images)*

In September 2019, Zelensky met with Donald Trump in New York, on the sidelines of the U.N. General Assembly, days after the world learned of Trump's attempts to pressure Zelensky for political favors. His encounters with Trump weakened Zelensky's faith in Ukraine's alliances. "I don't trust anyone at all," he said amid the impeachment scandal. *(Saul Loeb, AFP via Getty Images)*

First Lady Olena Zelenska poses inside the presidential compound on Bankova Street with one of her bodyguards. "You absorb it," she said of the war. "Each of us, including myself, have felt that our psychological state is not what it should be." A few months into the invasion, she said, "None of us are OK." *(Maxim Dondyuk)*

In trying to dominate Ukraine, Putin aimed to install his closest friend and ally in Kyiv, the wealthy politician Viktor Medvedchuk, in place of Zelensky. Instead, during the Russian invasion, Medvedchuk was arrested by the Ukrainian security services, forced to pose in shackles for this mug shot, and later sent to Russia in a prisoner exchange. *(Left: Vyacheslav Prokofyev, Tass pool photo via AP; right: Security Service of Ukraine, handout via Getty Images)*

During his first trip with the author to the war zone, in April 2021, Zelensky visited the scene of a battle near the frontline village of Shumy, in eastern Ukraine. Tens of thousands of Russian troops had already deployed by that point to the border with Ukraine and stood poised to invade. But Zelensky continued to downplay the threat of an invasion until the day before it began. *(Office of the president)*

In July 2021, Zelensky appointed a new commander of the Ukrainian armed forces, General Valery Zaluzhny, who would go on to lead the country's defense during the full-scale invasion the following winter. Disputes over strategy and rumors of the general's political ambitions would later deepen a rift between him and the president. *(Valentyna Polishchuk, Global Images Ukraine via Getty Images)*

The invasion began on the morning of February 24, 2022, with a barrage of Russian missiles launched at cities and towns across Ukraine, often striking residential areas and forcing civilians to flee or take shelter in basements, bunkers, and subway tunnels. Many were killed as they tried to escape. *(Maxim Dondyuk)*

As the Russians approached Kyiv, Zelensky called for mass resistance while the authorities handed out weapons to regular citizens. Many thousands of them volunteered to guard checkpoints and face the Russians in combat, often outgunned and with little training. *(Maxim Dondyuk)*

In the first days of the invasion, commercial satellites spotted a vast column of Russian military vehicles, at one point stretching for some forty miles, as it moved south from Belarus toward Kyiv with the aim of encircling the capital. *(Maxar Technologies via Getty Images)*

Through a series of battles and ambushes, Ukrainian forces picked off parts of the advancing column with attack drones, artillery fire, and shoulder-fired missiles. *(Maxim Dondyuk)*

The roads leading toward Kyiv were soon littered with the charred remains of Russian troops and military hardware that the Ukrainians had to clear away. *(Maxim Dondyuk)*

As the Russians retreated from the suburbs of Kyiv in late March 2022, they left behind evidence of mass executions, torture, and other atrocities in towns like Bucha, which the president visited on April 4, 2022. He would long remember it as the most painful day of that tragic year. *(Ronaldo Schemidt, AFP via Getty Images)*

Though many European leaders may have preferred to stay out of the war in Ukraine and salvage relations with Russia, Zelensky managed to rally them to his side. Several of them took the train to visit him in Kyiv in June 2022, including, from left to right behind Zelensky, Romanian President Klaus Iohannis, French President Emmanuel Macron, German Chancellor Olaf Scholz, and Italian Prime Minister Mario Draghi. *(Maxim Dondyuk)*

On his frequent trips into the war zone, Zelensky would meet with senior officials and military brass in underground command posts like this one. Accessible through a solid-metal door, the bunker was hidden beneath a factory near the southern front. *(Maxim Dondyuk)*

During their second trip to the war zone together, President Zelensky and the author traveled by train to the frontline city of Kherson two days after it was liberated from the Russians in November 2022. *(Maxim Dondyuk)*

Zelensky in the spring of 2019, two months before taking office . . .

. . . and in the spring of 2022, two months after the full-scale Russian invasion. *(Top: Anastasia Taylor-Lind; bottom: Alexander Chekmenev)*

"I've gotten older," he said on the day the second portrait was taken. "I've aged from all this wisdom that I never wanted. It's the wisdom tied to the number of people who have died, and the torture the Russian soldiers perpetrated. . . . To be honest, I never had the goal of attaining knowledge like that."

Part III

CHAPTER 11

THE CHURCHYARD

BEFORE THE RUSSIAN TROOPS ARRIVED, THE TOWN OF BUCHA AT THE WESTERN EDGE of Kyiv was a well-to-do place, tidy and green, its real estate in high demand among young couples who had made it in the capital and wanted more space and cleaner living for their kids. The commute to the city took less than an hour even in heavy traffic. The schools in Bucha were good, some of the best in the region, especially the one on Vokzalna, or Station Street, and there were plenty of ways to relax on weekends or holidays, to go hiking or ride bikes in the overgrown parks, to drop the kids off at summer camp or take them to a local ropes course called the Crazy Squirrel. For generations of people in Kyiv, the word Bucha evoked memories of summer in the countryside. Mikhail Bulgakov had a dacha there at the turn of the twentieth century, and an old photo survives of the great writer's siblings, sun-kissed and smiling in their garden full of flowers. My grandmother spent summers in Bucha as a girl, and she always remembered the cottage our family rented there, with its broad veranda, the goat they kept in the yard, and the berries they picked to cook jam in the summer kitchen. This was in the late 1930s, a few years before the Nazis tore through and occupied Bucha along with the rest of Ukraine. But in those summers before the war, no place felt safer to her than that yard.

When the next great war arrived in winter of 2022, Bucha again felt so sheltered and remote that a lot of people moved from Kyiv to stay there for a while, just to play it safe. The warnings that reached the public through the news did not mention the detailed predictions Zelensky heard from the Americans—about Kyiv being encircled, columns of tanks coming down from Belarus. The idea of Bucha becoming a battleground seemed preposterous to people in Kyiv, about as likely as a missile barrage over the Poconos. Even on the morning when the bombing started, the local priest in Bucha, Andriy Halavin, did not cancel services at the Church of St. Andrew the Apostle, whose golden domes reach upward from a hill near city hall.

Young and gaunt, with a handsome face and tired eyes, the priest could hear the explosions coming from the airport in Hostomel, which borders Bucha to the north, and he could see the Russian helicopters passing overhead in swarms. The defenders shot them down in such numbers, he said, that the sky flashed red with flames that night. With a bit of foresight and a look at a map, it should have been possible to guess that Bucha was in trouble. "We were the gateway into Kyiv," said Father Andriy.

The first group of Russian military vehicles drove into the center of town on the morning of February 27 and took up positions on Station Street. From there, they fanned out and fired at random. One volley hit the Church of St. Andrew, leaving gashes in its outer walls. An explosion damaged the pumping station that brought water into town. But that first wave of the invasion was quickly forced back. Within a few hours, Ukrainian fighters swept in and destroyed the Russian column with attack drones and shoulder-fired rockets, leaving the husks of their vehicles smoldering near the school. The victory gave residents a few extra days to evacuate Bucha, and many of them made their way over a makeshift bridge by foot toward Kyiv.

In the first days of March, the Russians arrived in far greater numbers, and the monthlong occupation of Bucha began. A few thousand people remained in the town, many of them elderly, sheltering in their homes or hiding in basements. The water and power supplies were cut, and it was well below freezing most nights in early March. Once in a while, the priest walked to the church to get some candles or to pray, occasionally spending the night in his quarters there. On his way back home one day, he stumbled upon a group of Russian soldiers doing searches house to house, kicking in the doors and pulling families into the street. They had set up a checkpoint at the intersection, with armored vehicles parked at each corner. Father Andriy decided not to turn back. He approached them on foot and showed his hands. "They asked me what I was doing," he later recalled, "and I said I was getting some food, some candles. 'Do you boys need candles? Here you go.'" They took a handful and let the priest go.

It was still early in the occupation then, and the first wave of Russian troops seemed to be more disciplined, better trained, and far less cruel than the detachments that followed. Some of the residents even recalled the early arrivals bringing food to elderly shut-ins in Bucha. "The first ones that came in, they weren't so rude, so shameless," Father Andriy said. "They did search people, forced them to undress." Men were stripped naked and searched for tattoos that the Russians seemed to associate with military service or neo-Nazi sympathies. Even a trident, the state symbol of Ukraine, could be treated as a mark of extremism by the interrogators. "They went into houses, took the people out, seized their phones and looked at the numbers they had called, what photos they had taken, and so on. They were afraid that our people were passing information to the military."

A few of them were. Even in early March, Ukrainian fighters hid in the basements of Bucha and coordinated ambushes. As the fighting intensified, the Russians took heavy losses, and they began to brutalize the town, torturing civilians and killing them at random. People would be shot while going out to look for food or firewood, their bodies left in the street. Many others were taken to interrogation rooms, tortured, and executed. From their checkpoints around town, the Russian troops would open fire at anyone who approached. "Men, women, children. They didn't care," said Father Andriy. One woman got shot when approaching a Russian checkpoint in her car. Some locals pulled her out and buried her right there, in a patch of grass by the sidewalk, marking the grave with her license plate so she could later be identified. It was far too dangerous to take the bodies to the cemetery. By the second week of the invasion, the sight and the smell of death became unbearable, and a member of the town council asked Father Andriy whether they could stage a mass burial in the churchyard. The priest agreed. The morgue was only a few hundred yards away from St. Andrew's.

On the morning of March 10, under a clear blue sky, a yellow excavator arrived at the church and dug a long, deep trench. Then a truck came from the morgue with thirty-three corpses zipped into black bags. A handful of men, among them a local real estate agent, dragged the bodies into the trench and laid them down side by side. There were no prayers at the grave, and only a simple marker was placed atop the soil when they were finished. "You have to understand," Father Andriy told me. "We could not think of funeral rites in that moment. We could only think of staying alive."

At the end of March, the priest came out of his home to find the Russians abandoning Bucha. Starved of supplies and exhausted, they loaded their vehicles with loot from local homes—televisions, computers, even a few washing machines—and drove north toward Belarus, the same way they had come. The scenes they left behind would soon turn Bucha into a byword for war crimes, with dozens of corpses scattered around town, one next to his bicycle, another killed in her vegetable patch, some covered with just enough dirt to keep the hungry dogs away, others left in the open to decompose for weeks before the Kremlin gave up on its plan to take Kyiv. In an attempt to save face, the Ministry of Defense in Moscow declared on March 29 that Russian troops had achieved their "main tasks" in the region of Kyiv and would move their forces to other sections of the front. They lacked the courage to admit their defeat. But the world could see it. The Armed Forces of Ukraine, with support from many thousands of civilian spotters and volunteers, policemen and guardsman, pensioners with hunting rifles and teenagers with drones, had forced one of the world's most powerful armies into retreat.

The toll on both sides was enormous. A pro-Kremlin newspaper in Moscow, citing classified figures from the Russian military, reported at the end of March that 9,861 Russian soldiers had been killed in action in Ukraine and 16,153 had been wounded. The paper quickly removed these figures from its website, but they seemed to confirm the conclusions of Western analysts that Russia had lost more troops in Ukraine in one month than the Soviet Union lost in ten years of war in Afghanistan. In those first weeks of the invasion, several towns in the Kyiv suburbs saw intense fighting, street to street, but nowhere else in the region did the Russians massacre as many civilians as they did in Bucha. Local authorities would later find 458 bodies there, including 12 children, the vast majority bearing wounds from gunshots or shrapnel, many showing signs of torture.

In the yard of St. Andrew's, a few dozen parishioners walked past the mass grave on the morning of April 10 and gathered for their first Sunday service since the Russian retreat. Some of the bodies had already been exhumed and sent to the morgue for identification and a proper burial. A long plastic sheet covered those who remained in the pit, keeping away a group of crows. Inside the basement chapel, I found Father Andriy performing the rites in his gold-and-purple robes, chanting as he took sips of wine from a goblet and made the sign of the cross. We talked for a while after the service, and he suggested I drive around to see what happened in Bucha for myself. The many scars of the occupation, he said, would not be difficult to find.

On Station Street, the Russians had set up a garrison inside a summer camp for children. It was called Promenystiy, which means "radiant," and the groundskeeper was standing at the gate with his bicycle as I pulled up. His name was Volodymyr Roslik, a cheerful man of sixty-five, and he agreed to show me around. The camp served children from the ages of seven to sixteen, with enough beds for about two hundred of them to stay at the camp at a time. College students from Kyiv often worked as counselors here, teaching the kids to dance, paint, and play soccer. At the end of every session they would celebrate with a big bonfire and a singalong. Roslik had worked there for about half his life, tending to the dorms, making repairs, and he had just come back to assess the damage from the occupation and figure out whether the camp could ever be used again. He wasn't sure. The physical damage could be fixed, but he didn't know whether anyone would ever send their children here after the occupation. One of the neighbors from across the street believed it would be better to raze the place, because, as he put it, "It's a place of killing now."

To the left of the entrance, Roslik let me into the administrative building, which the Russian officers had used as their headquarters. Dirty mattresses and cigarette butts lay on the floor, and, in the main room upstairs, there was an odd trove of loot apparently taken from local homes: an old boom box, some costume jewelry, a leather briefcase—none of it valuable enough for the soldiers to carry as they fled. In one room, the Russians had left a pile of hair shorn off with clippers. On the floor of another sat two dried lumps of human shit. "This was no army," Roslik told me. "This was a horde."

From the wreckage they left behind, it was easy to imagine the habits of these creatures. Some scenes suggested the handiwork of teenage boys left to explore the limits of their cruelty. Toward the back of the summer camp, in front of a mural of children dancing in the sun, we came upon a cherry-red sedan that a group of Russian soldiers had apparently stolen. The car had been crashed at speed into a stump, mangling it beyond repair. Its open trunk was full of wine bottles, most of them broken, one still intact. The tableau was so fresh that we could almost hear the music blasting on the radio and the sound of drunken laughter as the soldiers ended their joyride this way. It did not look like the work of a few young conscripts who had snuck away for a night on the town. This was at the center of their makeshift garrison, in a spot where the commanders would have seen it happening. The commanders' quarters were also covered in filth, loot, and liquor. There had been nothing and no one to hold these men back, no sense of law or military discipline. The leadership had simply let them loose on this town and its people, with absolute license to kill and destroy. Roslik stood there and shook his head without a word, then gestured for me to follow him to the basement, where the bodies had been found. It was underneath one of the dormitories in the back of Camp Radiant, and the steps leading down were lousy with trash from Russian army rations: dried macaroni, empty juice boxes, tins of meat. Standing at the bottom of the stairwell, Roslik looked up at me and raised an eyebrow, as if to offer one more chance to reconsider going in.

The airless tunnel behind the door resembled a series of torture chambers. They were divided by concrete walls, with a room for executions at the front, its walls pocked with bullet holes. The next room was dark. The light from the doorway no longer reached it, and we used our phones to illuminate the scene. On the far wall, a single word had been written in big black letters: *SENYA*. It was my name—rather, the pet name my mother has called me since I was a baby. The coincidence stunned me. Had one of the Russian occupiers, or maybe one of their victims, marked this wall with the name that we share? The room contained two chairs, an empty jug, and a wooden plank, the implements needed to waterboard someone. In the next chamber the Russians had brought in two metal bedsprings and leaned them against the concrete wall. They may have tied people to those frames, Roslik suggested, and used a car battery to apply electric shocks. In the front room, the bodies had been found in civilian clothes. They had burns, bruises, and lacerations. When we went there, shining our lights on the floor where they had lain, we could see pools of dried blood running down the wall into the dirt. Next to one of them was a fleece hat with a jagged bullet hole. It was also caked in blood.

❖

President Zelensky visited Bucha a few days after the Russian retreat, and he would long remember it as the most terrifying moment of that tragic year of war, another turning point for him and his country. It showed him, as he later put it, that the devil is not far away, not a feature of our myths and nightmares. "He's here on this earth," Zelensky said. Among the items on his agenda in Bucha was a walk along the blown-up bridge that led into town, a visit to an overcrowded food pantry, and a few conversations with locals in their yards; Zelensky wanted to hear what they had witnessed. His bodyguards got dressed for the trip in full battle gear before piling into their fleet of armored cars. The president agreed to put a bulletproof vest over his hoodie, its camouflage pattern matching the color of his low-top sneakers. But he declined to put a helmet on his head.

He knew on that day the world would be watching. Before his entourage left the bunker in the morning, Zelensky's aides informed reporters of where he was headed, and a bank of news cameras waited for him in Bucha, on the street where some of the worst atrocities occurred. "It's very important for us that the press is here," Zelensky said in front of the cameras. "That's the most important thing. We really want you to show the world what happened here, what the Russian forces did." With that, a strange new period began for Bucha, a period of healing under a magnifying glass.

From the center of Kyiv, buses full of journalists would depart every morning for weeks, ferrying hundreds of reporters to Bucha and other liberated towns outside the capital. It was sometimes difficult during these press tours for the photographers to get a shot without their colleagues crowding into the frame. Oleksiy Reznikov, Ukraine's defense minister, understood after his visit to Bucha that it was not unique among the towns that had been liberated. The Russians withdrew by early April from an area of northern Ukraine that was roughly the size of Denmark. "The crimes of the Russian orcs took place all over Ukraine, the looting, the murders, the rapes. But the world heard the word 'Bucha,'" Reznikov told me. "Bucha became the black swan that shook the world, and everyone saw the images from Bucha."

On the day after Zelensky's visit, he made Bucha the centerpiece of a landmark speech to the U.N. Security Council. Appearing on a massive screen above the hall, the president dedicated the speech to the civilians "who were shot in the back of the head or in the eye after being tortured, who were shot just on the streets, who were thrown into a well so that they die there in suffering, who were killed in apartments, houses, blown up by grenades, who were crushed by tanks in civilian cars in the middle of the road, just for fun, whose limbs were cut off, whose throats were cut, who were raped and killed in front of their children." He warned the delegates in his speech that Russia would try to shift blame for all these crimes, inventing alternative theories for what had happened in Bucha, and he was right. Putin would later refer to Bucha as a "fake," while his propaganda channels asserted, among other ridiculous theories, that some of the bodies found in the streets were crisis actors pretending to be dead. "We are dealing with a state that turns the right of veto in the U.N. Security Council into a right to kill," Zelensky said. If that does not change, he added, "the U.N. can simply be dissolved."

The president then asked the members of the council to watch a short video, which was so graphic that some of them had to avert their eyes. On the screen at the U.N. headquarters in New York City, there appeared the burnt remains of Ukrainian children, limbs and heads sticking out of mass graves, a man's body at the bottom of a well. Most of the images were taken in Bucha, some inside the basement at the children's summer camp, where those men were lined up against the wall, their hands bound behind their backs, and shot. The effect of the images was so powerful that, in the weeks that followed, Zelensky's team sought new ways to show them to their allies, hoping to stop them from looking away. "I confess," said Andriy Yermak, the president's chief of staff, "I would get these horrific photographs from our intelligence services, showing dead children, and in the night, when nobody living down here with us was sleeping much, I would send them to a long list of recipients in the White House." The mailing list stored on his phone would eventually grow to more than fifty names, he said, including senior officials in Europe. "I would send it to them, and most of them, about ninety percent, would respond, call me back, write a message, and so on," he told me. "That served as a really serious motivation."

In the days after Bucha was liberated, the yard behind the Church of St. Andrew became a kind of pilgrimage site. Diplomats and statesmen came from across Europe to see it and to pay respects. Only in the summer would their embassies begin to reopen in Kyiv. But when the Russian forces withdrew in April from the city's suburbs, the foreign envoys felt safe enough to visit Zelensky in his capital. A steady stream of them began to arrive, often bringing along a group of reporters to document their journeys. For many of them, the political benefit was obvious. These trips played well for their constituents back home. Across Europe, Zelensky had become a symbol of courage, and it turned into a political rite of passage for his European allies to stand beside him for a photo on Bankova Street. If they did not make the trip to meet him in person, they risked looking weak, their support halfhearted.

Zelensky and his aides were quick to recognize the trend. "We don't accept guests empty-handed," Kyrylo Tymoshenko, the president's close adviser, told me. "They can't just come here and take selfies." When the foreigners arrived, Zelensky's team would always invite them to take a trip to Bucha and other liberated suburbs of the capital, letting them see for themselves the evidence of Russian atrocities committed there. It would encourage them to help Ukraine, to commit more aid, and to keep the war on the global agenda long after they went back home. Among the most frequent guides on these tours was Ruslan Stefanchuk, the speaker of the parliament, who told me that he personally brought more than thirty foreign delegations on these trips in the spring and summer of 2022. "It caused a unique transformation in these people's brains," he said. "I saw it with my own eyes."

During one of the earlier trips, forensic experts and war crimes investigators were still working behind a line of police tape in the churchyard, and the smell of the mass grave became overpowering as the foreign guests approached it. Stefanchuk got permission to bring them closer, right up to the edge of the pit, where the Europeans could see the bodies and inhale the stench of death. "It changed them," he told me. When they were driving back to Kyiv, one of the visitors, a lawmaker from Poland, seemed particularly shaken. He had seen the images of bodies on the news; they all had. But the visit to the grave site "turned his consciousness inside out," Stefanchuk said. The Polish lawmaker later referred to Bucha and other liberated towns in the vicinity of Kyiv as the "Golgotha of the twenty-first century."

❖

The atrocities in Bucha came to light at a turning point in the peace process. Only a few days earlier, on March 29, the warring sides had held a round of negotiations in Istanbul, their first in about three weeks, and they finally seemed to be making progress. The Ukrainian delegation, led by Zelensky's close friend, Davyd Arakhamia, had presented the Russians with the outlines of a peace deal. It said that, in exchange for reliable "guarantees of security" from Russia and other countries, Ukraine was willing to accept the status of a neutral state on Russia's western border. It would abandon plans to join NATO and would not allow any foreign bases to be built on its territory. Even military exercises with foreign troops would not take place on Ukrainian soil if Russia saw them as a threat.

The offer, known as the Istanbul Communique, gave Putin a chance to claim at least a partial victory. One of his main excuses for launching the invasion had been to stop Ukraine from seeking to join the NATO alliance, and Zelensky now offered to grant him that wish, though he knew it would not be easy. Ukraine's commitment to joining NATO had been written into its Constitution. In February 2019, a few weeks before the presidential elections, Petro Poroshenko had signed this amendment, which was widely seen as an act of populism and desperation on the part of the incumbent president. He knew he was likely to lose the race. He also knew NATO had no intention to accept Ukraine in the foreseeable future. The amendment, which was approved by parliament, served little practical purpose other than to put Poroshenko's successor in a difficult spot. It enshrined in the fundamental law of Ukraine a promise that no one could keep.

By the time Zelensky took office that May, Article 102 of the Constitution had been changed to include the following line: "The president of Ukraine is the guarantor of the implementation of the state's strategic course toward full membership of Ukraine in the European Union and the North Atlantic Treaty Organization." Sidestepping this commitment would be politically costly for Zelensky. But, in the first two months of the war, he was ready to pay that price for peace. He was, in effect, willing to change his country's Constitution at the barrel of a Russian gun. This was no minor concession, but the president made his position clear.

"Security guarantees and neutrality, the non-nuclear status of our state. We are ready to go for it. This is the most important point," Zelensky told a group of Russian journalists two days before the talks in Istanbul. "That was the first principal point for the Russian Federation, as far as I remember. And if I remember right, they started the war because of this."

Other points of contention, however, were left open to debate in the Istanbul Communique. On the delicate question of Crimea, the Ukrainians suggested taking a pause of fifteen years. The two sides would use that time to find a peaceful solution to their dispute over the peninsula, committing to avoid the use of force. The most difficult issue of all— the status of the occupied territories in eastern and southern Ukraine— would be left for the leaders of the warring sides to figure out. "We are leaving all the territorial questions to the heads of state," Arakhamia told me at the time. "These are the most difficult questions. They're really tough, and our positions do not align at all."

The Russian negotiators seemed to agree that the only way to break the impasse would be to get the two leaders in a room together. With a gesture upward at the heavens, they would often say that only "the boss" had the power to address Crimea, the Donbas, and other territorial disputes. Zelensky still believed the best way to end the war was to look his enemy in the eyes and level with him. "There is only one person who launched this war, and only one person who can stop it," Zelensky's closest adviser on foreign policy, Andriy Sybiha, told me. "That is why Zelensky gave clear signals that he is ready to talk to Putin."

From his partners in the West, Zelensky was also facing a great deal of pressure to negotiate, even if it meant granting more concessions. Sybiha recalls some unpleasant phone calls from Western leaders around that time. "Their recommendation was to accept Russia's terms," he said. It was already obvious that Russia would use oil and gas supplies to put pressure on the Europeans, especially during the winter heating season, and politicians across the Continent understood that public sympathy for Ukraine had its limits. Would millions of voters in Western Europe be willing to lower the thermostats in their homes for the sake of Ukraine? Would they sacrifice jobs at their local factories to keep up the sanctions pressure on Russia? Would they accept an economic recession at home as a consequence of someone else's war? And if so, for how long? No European leader could answer these questions with any certainty.

But they all understood the need to keep the peace talks going, and to keep Zelensky in a frame of mind to negotiate.

At the end of March, five weeks into the full-scale war, the Ukrainian negotiators believed they were within reach of organizing a meeting with Putin. The Russians seemed to take the offer seriously. Emerging from the talks in Istanbul on March 29, Alexander Fomin, Russia's deputy minister of defense and the most recalcitrant member of the negotiating team from Moscow, made an astonishing announcement to the reporters gathered outside. The Russian military, he said, would pull its forces away from Kyiv "in order to increase mutual trust and create the conditions required for further negotiations." The Russian withdrawal, which began the next day in the suburbs of Kyiv, was not just a goodwill gesture from Moscow. Ukraine's resistance had forced the Russians to abandon their plans for seizing Kyiv. They were withdrawing because they had been defeated. Still, given the timing of the announcement, it looked like a breakthrough had come out of Istanbul: Ukraine had offered a road map to peace, and Russia was pulling troops away from the capital. The Turkish foreign minister, who acted as mediator, called it "the most meaningful progress since the start of the negotiations."

The sense of relief did not last long. As the Russians withdrew, images began to emerge from the liberated towns near Kyiv, and the optimism among Ukraine's negotiators gave way to horror, then to anger. "After what happened in Bucha, when it became known to the world, our natural desire was to leave the negotiating table," Arakhamia told me. "That was our consensus." On April 5, the day after Zelensky visited Bucha, he convened a meeting with about a dozen officials and aides over dinner in the Situation Room. Arakhamia and most of the other members of his team urged the president to suspend the peace process and abandon his plans for meeting Putin. The discussion grew tense. The images of dead civilians were so fresh in the minds of everyone present that it was hard for them to hold back their emotions. Still, Zelensky was adamant that the talks must move forward, even as the scale of Russian war crimes continued to emerge. "You guys understand that this is war," Arakhamia recalls the president telling them as he tried to win over the room. "There could be many more victims, and even more terrible stories could later emerge. But if there is even one chance for us to find some kind of mechanism for ending the war, then we need to use that chance. We can't miss it."

As a compromise, the president agreed to curtail some parts of the negotiations. They had been progressing along three parallel tracks—legal, diplomatic, and military—with three groups of negotiators. Zelensky decided to cut off the military track and to take a brief pause in the other two. But, within a couple of days, Arakhamia resumed his daily video conferences with Putin's envoys. At first, their behavior seemed off, as though they were disoriented or ashamed. "You could see it in their faces," Arakhamia told me after one of these sessions. "They were fumbling, like they couldn't put into words" what had happened in Bucha. It gave him the sense that some officials in Moscow were also shocked by the scale of the atrocities. "For one day, they were in a daze," he said. "Then their propaganda machine started working, and they began to say we had staged it all with help from the Americans."

Such claims were deeply insulting. But the Ukrainians pushed ahead through their rage, and Arakhamia was proud of the progress they made. After Bucha, the negotiations were still proceeding based on what was written in the Istanbul Communique. The document did not include the preposterous notions Putin had used to justify his invasion—de-Nazification and demilitarization—and the Russian negotiators did not insist on using these terms in their revisions of the document. For Arakhamia, this felt like an encouraging sign. In the middle of April, he told me they were still planning to finish a draft agenda for the leaders' summit within two weeks.

Zelensky kept urging them to press ahead, still clinging to his belief that, with enough concessions, he could salvage Ukraine, its land, and its sovereignty. "Every such tragedy, every such Bucha will just make it harder as regards any negotiations, and here we still need to find ways to move forward," the president told reporters. "We believe that this is genocide. We believe that they must all be punished. But we have to find opportunities to meet. And, during these meetings, to find a way out of this situation, while not giving up any of our territory."

❖

On the morning of April 8, a private train arrived in Kyiv bearing one of Zelensky's most influential allies, Ursula von der Leyen, the president of the European Commission. Before she was taken to meet the president, a convoy of armored cars drove her to Bucha for a tour of the crime scenes. It was raining hard that day, and a plastic canopy had been erected in the churchyard of St. Andrew's, at the edge of the mass grave. When the Europeans reached it, trailed by a crowd of reporters and surrounded by guards, von der Leyen did not expect the corpses to be there. She gasped when she saw them: more than a dozen black body bags had been arranged in a row on the muddy ground. The blood drained from her face, and she placed a thin hand on the front of her bulletproof vest. Father Andriy then took her inside to light a candle in memory of the dead.

Soon the delegation made its way back toward the presidential compound, where Zelensky's aides had asked reporters to gather for a briefing. I arrived in the afternoon and found a few dozen of them huddled in the usual gathering place, under the awning of a firehouse, waiting for the vans that would take us inside the security cordon. The largest group was from Germany, the homeland of von der Leyen, where she had served as the minister of defense before being appointed the E.U.'s most senior official. At the checkpoint, the soldiers stood under the rain and watched us, their rifles slung over their shoulders, retreating every now and then to a little hut they had built out of tarps and cinder blocks. Six weeks into the war, their fortifications still had an improvised look, as though they had been slapped together from the stuff left behind at a construction site.

The vans soon picked us up and took us through a narrow tunnel and into a courtyard with a few more soldiers. One of them stood guard with a grenade launcher, his firing position camouflaged amid the lower branches of a tree. There were no military vehicles standing in the yard, just a few cars parked near the back entrance, where a German shepherd sniffed our bags for explosives. At the metal detectors, we were all asked to surrender our smartphones, laptops, and other devices. A large cluster of phone signals, all transmitting at the same time, would allow an enemy surveillance drone to pinpoint the location of the gathering. "And then, kaboom," one guard explained, tracing the arc of a rocket with his hand.

Before surrendering the phones, we all checked the news one last time. There had been another missile attack that morning in eastern Ukraine, and the details were still coming in. Two rockets, each more than twenty feet long and weighing over two metric tons, had struck a train station in the city of Kramatorsk, one of the most important garrison towns in the Donbas. Zelensky had been urging civilians to leave that area, and more than a thousand of them had gathered at the station to catch evacuation trains, mostly women, children, and elderly people. The Russian missiles landed right outside the crowded station late that morning. Sixty people were killed and over a hundred wounded. Several children lost limbs. The news reached Zelensky just before eleven a.m., when he was preparing for his meeting with von der Leyen. He knew it would be a pivotal moment for his country and his presidency. At the start of the invasion, Zelensky had seized his chance to apply for membership in the European Union, and its leaders had now come all the way from Brussels to move the process along. Von der Leyen, as head of the E.U.'s executive branch, had also come with a fresh package of aid: one billion euros' worth of military assistance and another billion to prop up the economy.

But, once the first images from Kramatorsk flashed up on the screen of Zelensky's phone, it became difficult for him to focus. The aftermath of the explosions horrified him. The puddles of blood on the pavement. The severed limbs among toys and suitcases. In one of the photos forwarded to him that morning, Zelensky saw a woman who had been beheaded by the blast. "She was wearing these bright, memorable clothes," he later told me, gazing inward at the image in his mind. His aides had planned to release the photographs on social media that day, but the president forbid it. "We can't do that," he said. "What if children see this?" That afternoon, he was still struggling to shake the images when the presidential staff ushered in the Europeans. They were to spend the afternoon together, discussing the package of aid, the process of joining the European Union, the liberation of Kyiv's suburbs, and the atrocities that Russian forces had committed there. It was getting dark by the time they came out to speak to the reporters.

"Dear Volodymyr," von der Leyen told him in front of the cameras. "My message today is very clear: Ukraine belongs to the European family. We have heard your request loud and clear, and today we are here to give you a first positive answer. In this envelope, there is an important step toward E.U. membership." The envelope contained a questionnaire that Zelensky's office would need to fill out, justifying its application for

E.U. membership. "It is where your path towards Europe and the E.U. begins," von der Leyen said. In fact Ukraine had begun its path toward Europe decades earlier. It had lived through two revolutions and eight years of war. Tens of thousands of lives and millions of acres of occupied territory were among the prices Ukraine had already paid in its struggle to integrate with Europe. And now, when the moment finally came to fill out the introductory questionnaire, the president's face was a shade of green, and he could not stop thinking about that headless woman on the ground. At the podium, Zelensky's usual gift for oratory failed him. He could not even muster the presence of mind to mention the missile attack on Kramatorsk. "It was one of those times when your arms and legs are doing one thing, but your head does not listen," Zelensky later told me. "Because your head is there at that station, and you need to be present here."

At the end of the briefing, when von der Leyen and her staff left the presidential compound, Zelensky sat down in the briefing room with a reporter from her native Germany. The first question was about the images from Kramatorsk, which were leading the news around the world that night: "Did you cry," the reporter asked Zelensky in English, "when you saw these pictures?"

The president gave a tired smile and stared off into space for a moment. "I don't cry anymore," he said. "I have not cried in a long time." The first days of the invasion had often left him close to tears, and he tried to stop himself from growing accustomed to the sight of death. But over time, he admitted, his skin was getting thicker. "You get used to it," he said.

"Do you feel hate?" the reporter continued.

"Yes, I feel hate. I feel hatred for the military. Against the Russian troops, I do. There's no secret here. You feel it when you see these images, or you go to the places, you drive out to the site of an explosion, and see what is left. You see the people. You see the dead children. You are shown photographs of children without limbs, and you are horrified. As a father, I think about my own children, and what that must be like."

Yet even then, even after his visit to Bucha four days earlier, and the images he had seen that morning from Kramatorsk, Zelensky did not allow himself to express personal hatred toward Putin. He even argued, in response to the reporter's next question—What does Putin want?—

that the Russian leader may not be fully aware of all the suffering his invasion had caused. "I'm not sure he knows what is happening," Zelensky said. "I'm sure he lives in a different world of information. He doesn't have all the information. He gives the order to advance, yes, to occupy this or that town. But in what way? How many people died in the process?"

The statement astonished me. It was as though Zelensky was still clinging to the illusion he brought with him to the presidency. He seemed to believe that if he could only take Putin on a tour of Bucha, if he could bring him to the edge of that pit in the churchyard and let him peer down at the bodies, the war might stop. "I don't think we have any other choice," he said. "Even though we're fighting very hard, I don't see any option, other than to sit with him at the negotiating table and to talk."

CHAPTER 12

TROJAN HORSE

VOLODYMYR ZELENSKY'S ATTEMPTS TO REASON WITH VLADIMIR PUTIN BEGAN IN THE first days of his tenure. On the campaign trail and in his inaugural speech, he promised in the spring of 2019 that restoring peace in eastern Ukraine would be the central mission of his presidency, and he understood that achieving it would require compromising with the Kremlin. Putin, for his part, kept an open mind about the prospect of negotiations. Though he never called to congratulate Zelensky on his election victory, he wanted to see what the TV-show president might do in real life. "It's one thing to play somebody," Putin sneered in June 2019, roughly two weeks after Zelensky took office. "It's another thing to be somebody."

For Zelensky and his team, the success of their whole presidential agenda hinged on the need to make peace. Ukraine's gross domestic product collapsed after the Russian annexation of Crimea and the start of the war in the Donbas, shrinking from a high of over $180 billion in 2013 to $90 billion two years later, and it was far from recovering to prewar levels when Zelensky took office. "To return to a state of economic development, we had to somehow end this conflict," said Andriy Bohdan, who served as Zelensky's chief of staff at the time.

Zelensky would tell his advisors, "We need a move"—a catchphrase that many of them recognized from their days in the writers' room at Studio Kvartal 95. Back then, Zelensky would use it to demand a plot twist or a joke that would grab the audience. Now he needed a move to convince the Kremlin he was serious about ending the war. They came up with several options. During the first full month of his tenure, Zelensky ordered the withdrawal of troops from three points along the front line in eastern Ukraine. They were told to pull back by one kilometer, clearing away mines and dismantling their fortifications. Zelensky's Western allies, especially the Americans, were concerned that he would give too much ground. They warned him not to speak with Putin directly, because they were afraid Zelensky could be outfoxed. One senior American diplomat recalled warning the new president: "Don't get sucked in." Zelensky's own advisers offered similar advice. The chairman of the foreign affairs committee in parliament, Bohdan Yaremenko, told Zelensky that Putin would never give up his obsession with controlling Ukraine, that he would never grant a peace deal acceptable to most Ukrainians. Zelensky took offense. "He felt I was contesting his abilities as a diplomat, as a leader," Yaremenko told me.

Despite his total lack of experience in international diplomacy at the time, Zelensky had no lack of confidence in his ability to break an impasse that some of the world's best diplomatic minds had tried and failed to overcome. In the middle of July 2019, two months into his presidential tenure, he ordered his staff to arrange a phone call with Putin. "Everybody tried to scare me about having this call," Zelensky said. "But I told our people, why should we be worried? Why be afraid if the truth is on your side?"

Putin and Zelensky agreed during that call to organize a prisoner exchange to demonstrate they were serious about the peace process. By the end of that month, a cease-fire took effect throughout the war zone, the first in three years, laying out strict rules for the use of weapons in the war zone. It barely held for a week before a fresh spasm of fighting in early August led to the deaths of four Ukrainian marines. But Zelensky did not retaliate. He arranged another phone call with Putin and lodged a complaint. "This does not bring us closer to peace," he recalled telling Putin. The restraint paid off. The number of cease-fire violations plummeted in the weeks that followed. Soon the warring sides carried out the prisoner exchange that Putin and Zelensky had negotiated. In early September, each side released thirty-five captives. Among the Ukrainians was the filmmaker Oleh Sentsov, a native of Crimea, who had been sentenced to twenty years in a Russian prison on bogus charges of terrorism. Zelensky waited at the airport to meet the plane when they came home. "As you can see," he told the news cameras, "we don't just talk, we have results."

That November, the Russians granted Zelensky another one of his wishes. They agreed to return three Ukrainian naval vessels that they seized in 2018 in the waters near Crimea. "They were showing the world that they're sweethearts," said Oleksiy Reznikov, who was then one of Ukraine's lead negotiators in the talks. "And that built expectations for the world that, well, things are alright with the Kremlin." The gesture made Zelensky more eager than ever to hold an in-person meeting with Putin before the end of the year. Their aim, Reznikov told me, was to talk to the Russian despot with no preconditions, to leave behind the animosity that had built up during Petro Poroshenko's tenure. "The president really believed deep down that he could end the war. Maybe in the past people just weren't listening," Reznikov said of Zelensky's thinking at the time. "Maybe there were hard feelings that needed to be discussed. That's why we had this goal. Set a meeting. Face-to-face."

Soon they settled on a format for the summit. It would be held in Paris that December. As the date approached, Zelensky held out hope that the Americans would have his back. Despite the damage the impeachment saga had done to his relationship with Trump, Zelensky knew that no one had a better chance of encouraging Putin to negotiate in good faith. But the U.S. had no formal role to play in the peace process. There would be no Americans at the negotiating table. The mediators in the talks were Germany and France, and Zelensky was not sure he could trust them to stay in his corner.

Angela Merkel, the German chancellor, had encouraged Putin to participate in the talks. But her support for Ukraine grew weak when it came to her country's economic interests. Throughout that year, Germany rushed to finish an energy project with Russia that could cripple Ukraine's economy. The new gas pipeline, known as Nord Stream 2, would bypass Ukraine by carrying Russian fuel under the Baltic Sea to Germany. The estimated loss for Zelensky's government would be about $3 billion per year, which Ukraine would otherwise expect to earn from shipping Russian gas to Europe through its pipelines. Germany and Russian were, in effect, cutting Ukraine out of the European gas trade. The French did not seem much more reliable. The host of the peace talks would be French president Emmanuel Macron, whose recent appeals to Putin had worried the Ukrainians. He had suggested that Russia should be seen as a partner of the NATO alliance, not a threat. In an interview with the *Economist*, Macron also said NATO was "experiencing brain death" and may no longer be willing to defend its member states from a Russian attack.

During their infamous phone call in July, Zelensky had complained to President Donald Trump about the Europeans. He had questioned their resolve in isolating the Russian economy. "They are not enforcing the sanctions," Zelensky told Trump. "They are not working as much as they should work for Ukraine." But these were the only allies Zelensky would have by his side in Paris, and he was still convinced the talks could lead to a breakthrough. Throughout the fall, his aides would bring him the minutes of previous rounds of negotiations, going all the way back to the start of the war in 2014. "Here's what I know from studying them," Zelensky said when we met to discuss the preparations that November. "People have come to these meetings intending for nothing to happen." I asked what he meant by that. The negotiators were pretending? "That is how I felt," he said. "Often these meetings go in circles, with people repeating the same things to each other."

❖

Ukraine and Russia set down their terms for peace in the Donbas long before Zelensky took power. Their first peace deal, known as Minsk-1, dated back to the first months of the war, when the wreaths were still fresh on the graves of protestors killed during the 2014 revolution. Poroshenko was elected president that May, and his aim in the first weeks of his tenure was the same as Zelensky's would be five years later. "I am absolutely certain of one thing," Poroshenko told me in an interview two days after his inauguration. "My first actions as president will be effective in bringing peace to the eastern regions."

Many towns and cities in those regions had already descended into lawlessness by then. Russian paramilitaries, local gangs, and well-armed militias had seized control of government buildings and turned parts of the Donbas into separatist strongholds intent on breaking away from Kyiv's control. Every arm of the central government, from the traffic police to the tax inspectors, had abandoned these areas to Russia's proxies. When Ukraine tried to hold a presidential election that spring, militants armed and supported by Moscow blocked the ballot from taking place in the parts of eastern Ukraine they controlled. Two election officials in the region of Luhansk were kidnapped and held hostage during the campaign. One of Poroshenko's surrogates got shot in the Donetsk region. During a whistle-stop tour of the separatist enclaves, a group of militants chased Poroshenko's convoy out of town, forcing his driver to cut through a field to reach the airport, where a plane was waiting to evacuate him. Poroshenko's tone was flat, nearly emotionless, when he told me about the incident: "The separatists," he said, "made an attempt to take me and my staff hostage."

Within days, the Ukrainian military went on the offensive. Helicopter gunships swept down over separatist positions near the city of Donetsk on May 26, the day after Poroshenko won the presidential ballot. By nightfall the local morgues filled up with the bodies of pro-Russian fighters. It was the deadliest day of combat since the war had started, and Poroshenko seemed to think the show of force would strengthen his hand. "Russia has understood the danger of its policy toward Ukraine," he told me. "Dozens of coffins are going back to the Russian Federation. What are they dying for?"

Putin did not seem to know the answer. The Kremlin continued to deny the presence of Russian soldiers in the Donbas, and the Russian military treated their deployment, and their deaths, as closely guarded secrets. Putin also showed no interest in annexing the eastern regions of Ukraine the way he had done with Crimea a few months earlier. He did not even recognize the legitimacy of the separatist leaders in the Donbas. Instead he supplied them with weapons and fighters, content to let the conflict fester as the peace talks got underway. The first round was held in early June 2014, during the ceremony to mark the seventieth anniversary of the D-Day invasion in Normandy. President Barack Obama attended that event and helped to broker the talks between Putin and Poroshenko. But the most active mediators were Germany and France, whose leaders pushed both sides to agree on a truce.

At the time, Poroshenko was eager to convince the people of the Donbas that their rights would be protected under his leadership. Most of them still got their information from the Kremlin's propaganda channels, which claimed that Kyiv was intent on eradicating the Russian language and persecuting ethnic Russians. Poroshenko did his best to counter that narrative. "There must be a guarantee of people's right to speak whatever language they want," he said a few days after the talks in Normandy. "Crucially, we need to elect representatives of the Donbas with whom we can have a dialogue." These issues—language rights, local elections, the legal status of the Donbas—were at the center of the peace talks that began that summer and continued into early 2015. Russia and Ukraine both sent envoys to those talks, which were held in Minsk, the capital of Belarus. The separatist leaders from eastern Ukraine also sat at the negotiating table, even though they were, in essence, under Moscow's control.

All sides agreed to stop fighting for the duration of the peace process. But none of them honored that commitment. On the contrary, the bloodshed intensified. Russia did not seem satisfied with the amount of territory its proxies controlled at the outset of the negotiations. So its forces pushed forward, seizing more cities and towns and, in the process, killing hundreds of Ukrainian soldiers that summer and early fall. On multiple occasions, the Kremlin deployed regular Russian troops equipped with tanks and heavy artillery to carry the fight when its paramilitary forces proved insufficient.

Moscow also provided the separatists with anti-aircraft missiles, which they used in July 2014 to shoot down a civilian jet, Malaysia Airlines Flight 17, apparently by mistake. All 298 passengers and crew members were killed, their bodies scattered across fields of wheat and sunflowers in the Donbas. A few weeks later, the Russian military surrounded and massacred hundreds of Ukrainian troops around the town of Ilovaisk, mowing them down as they tried to retreat in surrender. The brutality of these attacks put enormous pressure on Kyiv to strike a deal. Western leaders understood that Ukraine had no chance of defeating the Russians on the battlefield. Poroshenko understood that, too. "Don't forget: we had no army only two months ago," he told me that summer. "The Ukrainian soldier was in effect naked, barefoot, hungry, and unarmed."

Germany and France, as mediators in the war, urged the Ukrainians to grant concessions, and Poroshenko agreed to many of Russia's demands. He would allow the separatists to govern many of their own affairs inside the territories they had seized. These terms were included in the peace deal he signed in early September 2014. But the armistice did not last. The Russians kept up the pressure through the autumn and winter, culminating in a battle that would cost well over a thousand lives. In early February 2015, a combined force of Russian troops and paramilitary units encircled thousands of Ukrainians in the city of Debaltseve, including many civilians, and bombarded them with artillery and multiple-rocket launchers. The slaughter continued even after Ukraine agreed, in the middle of that battle, to sign another version of the peace accords.

The new deal, known as Minsk-2, was more detailed than the first and, in the eyes of many Ukrainians, more onerous. One of its provisions obliged Ukraine to enact a new Constitution by the end of 2015, enshrining the principle of "decentralization" in its fundamental law. In practice, this would shift power from the capital to the regions, eroding Kyiv's authority over the Donbas. The breakaway regions in the east would remain a part of Ukraine, but the central government would allow them to build stronger ties with Russia, to run their own courts, their own education systems, and their own "people's militias" to keep the peace.

Poroshenko would later come to see the terms of the deal as a kind of creeping annexation of Ukraine's eastern territories. He believed the idea of decentralization would allow the Donbas to drift ever further into Moscow's grasp. When Zelensky studied these agreements four years after his predecessor signed them, he came to much the same conclusion. The Minsk accords, Zelensky told me, "were a means to hold Ukraine in a constant state of instability."

The Russians admitted as much. At the outset of the war, Putin had no plans to swallow up eastern Ukraine the way he had done with Crimea. He wanted the Donbas to be a part of Ukraine that Russia could control. "It's a typical Trojan horse," one of Putin's close associates told me. "Let them give these regions a special status, some autonomy, and have the Western partners convince the Ukrainians to go along. That would be what we call a suitcase without a handle." Ukraine would be burdened with a region devastated by war and influenced by Russian propaganda. Its residents—some 3.5 million of them—would support a strong pro-Russian bloc inside the Ukrainian parliament, and they would hinder any of Kyiv's attempts to integrate with the West. Over time, they might even field a candidate strong enough to take power across the country, just as they had done with Viktor Yanukovych during the elections in 2010.

Embedded in the fine print of the Minsk agreements, this was Moscow's plan, and the Russians talked about it openly. A few weeks after the Minsk-2 accords were signed in 2015, I arranged to meet in Moscow with one of its architects, Konstantin Zatulin, a proud imperialist with a brush mustache. The mood in Russia was tense at the time. A year had passed since the annexation of Crimea, and the sense of euphoria in Moscow had faded. Western sanctions had started to bite, sapping the value of the ruble and scaring a lot of investors away. Many Russians started to realize that the war in Ukraine would come at a price. The regime had tasted conquest in the Donbas, and it would not behave the same way toward its citizens at home.

A few days before my arrival in Moscow, one of Putin's most influential critics, Boris Nemtsov, was shot dead near the walls of the Kremlin. His friends and followers were in a state of shock. They had been planning another massive march near the Kremlin to protest the war in Ukraine that week. Now it would become a march of mourning. But Zatulin, the consummate hard-liner, was having the time of his life. He received me in his cluttered office a short walk from the spot where Nemtsov had been killed. It was full of antique weapons, ceremonial sabers, and other military bric-a-brac, the shelves packed with books about Russia's imperial history. This was Zatulin's specialty. As one of the founders of Putin's political party, he had long been a fixture at the Kremlin. His work in the Russian parliament, where he had served since 1993, focused on the affairs of the "near abroad," the countries of the former Soviet Union.

Like Putin, Zatulin dreamed of restoring Russia's hold over these nations. But his efforts on this front did not amount to much during the first two decades of his career in politics. He would pontificate on state TV about the fraying bonds of language and faith that had once kept Ukraine within the "Russian world." Few people took him seriously. In 2006, the Ukrainian authorities deemed him *persona non grata* and charged him with inciting ethnic violence. Only in 2014 did Zatulin really get his chance to shine. At the start of the war, he became a liaison between the Kremlin and its paramilitary proxies in Ukraine, funneling money to their leaders and instructing them to rise up and seize control of local governments. Their success was mixed. Zatulin and his cohorts hoped to take over all of southern and eastern Ukraine, at least a third of the country. They were forced to settle for Crimea and parts of the Donbas. But Zatulin seemed content with these limited victories. They would be enough, he told me, as long as Ukraine agreed to implement the Minsk agreements.

The crux of that deal, he said, was the concept of decentralization, which would allow Russia to control the regions of Ukraine that "share the Russian point of view on all the big issues." The local authorities in these regions would remain loyal to Moscow. The Kremlin could assist them in running political campaigns and launching TV stations. In a pinch, their loyalty could be bought or extracted through blackmail. "Russia would have its own soloists in the great Ukrainian choir, and they would sing for us," Zatulin said. "This would be our compromise." If the government in Kyiv accepted this arrangement, he told me, "We would have no need to tear Ukraine apart."

To Ukraine's most powerful allies in the West, that compromise looked reasonable enough. Angela Merkel, the chancellor of Germany, pressured Poroshenko to accept the deal, and the Americans urged him to implement it. Joe Biden, who was then the U.S. vice president, paid a visit to Kyiv at the end of 2015, hoping to advance the peace process. One of his first stops was Independence Square, where he stood and stared at the memorial to protestors massacred during the revolution. The next day, Biden delivered a speech to the parliament in which he gave a firm endorsement of the Minsk agreements. They would be difficult, Biden said, for both sides of the war to accept. The Russians would need to withdraw their troops and disarm their proxies. They would need to give Ukraine back control of its border with Russia. But the authorities in Kyiv would also need to show determination. Ukraine would need to change its Constitution, Biden said, and accept the idea of decentralization. He even compared it, however inaccurately, to the American political experiment. "This issue of federalism is the thing that almost prevented our nation from coming into being," Biden said. "Autonomous, independent states. Their determination to have their own police forces. Their determination to have their own education system, to have their own government under a united Constitution."

Above all, he urged Ukraine to hold elections in the Donbas and allow its people to choose their own leaders. Those elections were part of the peace process spelled out in the Minsk agreements, and Biden believed they would only strengthen Ukraine in the long run. "Free and fair elections are exactly what the Kremlin fears the most," he said. "It's not just your territory they covet, it's your success they fear. For if free elections occur, and the people determine, as I'm confident they will, that they are an integral part—that they are Ukrainians first—that's what Russia fears. That's what Putin fears."

❖

When he took office four years later, Zelensky agreed with the premise of that speech. He also wanted to hold elections in the parts of the Donbas that Russia controlled. Zelensky recognized that, since the war began in 2014, these separatist regions had become deeply isolated, wildly dysfunctional, and firmly reliant on Moscow. They were ruled by a rotating cast of warlords and spin doctors who routinely killed one another, only to be replaced with new appointees of the Kremlin. One commander, known as Batman, was ambushed and sprayed with bullets on a roadside in Luhansk. Another was blown to pieces inside his favorite cafe. A third, nicknamed Motorola, was killed by a bomb in an apartment building. A fourth was incinerated with a flamethrower. A fifth was shot dead at a restaurant near Moscow. The list was long.

Neither of the two separatist regions, which called themselves the People's Republics of Donetsk and Luhansk, had anything like a functioning economy. They were cut off from legal commerce with the world. They dealt in contraband, particularly the smuggling of weapons and coal, with some meager subsidies from Russia. No country in the world, not even Russia, recognized the independence of the People's Republics. Yet they were home to well over three million Ukrainian citizens, and they had not been allowed to participate in a Ukrainian election since the Russians took over in 2014. Zelensky figured he could win them back, at least enough of them to make a difference in the war. What if the people in these regions began to reject Russian control over their towns and cities? What if they rose up against the separatists? What if they were given a chance to vote in a free election and decided to reunite with Ukraine?

Reliable surveys of public opinion were hard to come by in these regions. The best polling available suggested that, in the fall of 2019, just over half of the people in the separatist enclaves were not, in fact, separatists at all—they wanted to reintegrate with Ukraine. Around 45 percent wanted to become a part of Russia. Any plebiscite on this issue would be a major risk for Zelensky's government. The task of ensuring a fair vote would be daunting, and the result could end up legitimizing the Kremlin's control over these territories. But Zelensky wanted to try. He felt a kinship with the people in these regions. Like them, he hailed from the industrial east of the country, and some of his strongest results in the presidential race had come from the parts of the Donbas that were still under Ukrainian control.

In his first months as president, Zelensky began reaching out to the people living under the separatists. He promised to pay their pensions and restore their infrastructure. New roads across the front line were opened, making it easier for them to visit friends and family in other parts of Ukraine. "People should cross over and see that it's better here, and slowly their opinions will change," Zelensky said. "We need to bring them back and fight for them." He also wanted the separatist regions to hold elections and choose legitimate leaders, who might then represent their interests in talks with the government in Kyiv. A few months into his tenure, Zelensky publicly committed to a plan that would allow for such elections to be held under Ukrainian law. As a precondition for such a ballot, he said that Russia would need to withdraw all its forces from the region and disarm all the local militants. "There will be no elections under the barrel of a machine gun," he said in announcing this decision on October 1, 2019. "There won't be any elections there if troops are still there."

Officials in Moscow welcomed the announcement. They saw it as a major step toward implementing the Minsk agreements, which explicitly called for Ukraine to hold elections in the separatist territories. But many people in Ukraine were outraged by Zelensky's decision. Among the political opposition, it was seen as an act of appeasement toward Russia and its proxies. Tens of thousands of people protested in Kyiv and other cities in the fall of 2019, accusing Zelensky of preparing Ukraine's capitulation in the war. One rally was held on Bankova Street, right outside the windows of his office. Among the leaders of the demonstrations were Zelensky's former rivals for the presidency, Poroshenko and Tymoshenko, who both controlled sizable factions in parliament. The rallies also attracted the far-right wing of Ukrainian politics, including many veterans of the war. Together they posed the first popular challenge to

Zelensky's rule, and it began to erode his popularity. When we met in his office that November, the protests were still breaking out across the country, under banners that read, "No to capitulation!"

Zelensky, still sensitive to criticism, found these attacks deeply unfair, and he condemned the rally organizers as political opportunists. His staff in this period tried hard to keep him away from social media, where countless memes and comments cast him as a chump, even a traitor. But he stuck to his guns on the issue of letting the Donbas vote: "We need to hold elections there," he said. "They must take place." They would give Ukraine a chance to win the Donbas back by democratic means, and Zelensky had no patience for the politicians who would prefer to accomplish that goal by force. "I will not agree to go to war in the Donbas," he said. "I know there are a lot of hotheads, especially those who organize rallies and say, 'Let's go and fight to win it all back!' But what's the price? What is the cost? It's another story of lives and land, and I won't do it. If that doesn't satisfy society, then a new leader will come who will satisfy those demands. But I will never go for that, because my position in life is to be a human being above all. And I cannot send them there. How? How many of them will die? Hundreds of thousands, and then an all-out war will start, an all-out war in Ukraine, and then across Europe."

❖

The small, round table at the Élysée Palace was set for four people when Putin and Zelensky arrived on the appointed afternoon, December 9, 2019. They would be seated across from each other, close enough to reach for a handshake if they chose, while the two mediators, Merkel and Macron, would sit on either side of them. In front of each participant, the organizers had placed headphones and microphones to ensure simultaneous translation in all four languages: Russian, Ukrainian, German, and French. But Zelensky, to the surprise of some of his aides, decided to break the language barrier.

Early in the conversation, once the journalists and news cameras were asked to leave the room, Zelensky made his opening remarks in Ukrainian and then, with a smile, switched to his native language to recite a Russian proverb. In rough translation, it meant: "The path on paper looked so smooth, we all forgot about the pitfalls."* It seemed like an apt description of the Minsk agreements, which may have looked straightforward on paper—the entire document fits on a few printed pages—but turned out to be full of trapdoors.

"From there, he began to speak in Russian for the duration of the talks," said the Ukrainian negotiator, Oleksiy Reznikov, who was seated behind Zelensky. This was a breach of the usual protocol for such talks. As a matter of principle, each nation's representatives typically used their national language. But Zelensky wanted to be understood, and to show that he would not be bound by the way things were done in the past. The proverb also seemed like an attempt to break the ice with Putin. But that would not be easy.

Putin seemed irritable and impatient with Zelensky, having arrived in Paris with all the baggage of his past negotiations with Ukraine. His talks with Poroshenko had broken down in 2016. After that, the two presidents never spoke to each other. They only traded insults and threats through the media as the war in the Donbas dragged on. Zelensky now hoped to convince the Russians that his election would mark a clean slate. Putin was unwilling to accept that. "The Kremlin's representative voiced accusations that Ukraine had not kept some of its promises," Reznikov told me. In particular, Putin insisted that Kyiv had not met its obligations under the Minsk agreements. This was true of all parties to the deal. Ukraine had not amended its Constitution, and it had not held elections in the separatist regions of the Donbas or granted them more autonomy. Russia had not withdrawn its military forces from these regions. Nor had it observed any of the cease-fires.

Merkel, a fluent Russian speaker, did not need an interpreter to understand what Putin and Zelensky were saying, and Reznikov had the impression that she agreed with the Russian president's complaints. "I saw in Merkel's reaction that, in essence, she concurred with his displea-

---

* The saying in question—Было гладко на бумаге, да забыли про овраги—originates from a satirical poem that Lev Tolstoy wrote during his service as a soldier in the Crimean War. That war ended in 1856 with the Treaty of Paris, a humiliating capitulation for the Russian Empire. In Tolstoy's poem, the line about paper and pitfalls refers to the battle plans that Russia's incompetent officers would draw up in their headquarters, only to have their soldiers realize, when it was far too late, that their maps had little in common with the real shape of the battlefield.

sure, that she also had the same impression." Merkel had been a mediator in the peace talks since their inception in 2014, and she had urged Poroshenko to sign the Minsk agreements. That was not true of Macron. The French leader, who took office in 2017, was the only one at the table in Paris who did not speak Russian, and he seemed to have a harder time following along.

Zelensky also seemed confused by Putin's litany of grudges and complaints. "My president did not understand what was at issue," Reznikov told me. He could not overcome Putin's fixation on the promises Ukraine had made under its previous leadership, and there was no way for Zelensky to get through to Putin, at least not during their first conversation. At their press conference afterward, the two leaders pledged to continue talking, and they focused on their main point of agreement at the talks: another prisoner exchange, even bigger than the last one. The outcome was hailed as a partial victory for Zelensky. The *New York Times* reported that the former comedian had played "to a draw" against Putin, the "seasoned master of no-holds-barred global intrigue."

Zelensky might have felt relieved. But the talks in Paris troubled him deeply. It was one of the rare moments in his life when he found the limits of his gifts as a communicator. He had expected to discover a creature of flesh and blood in Putin, a man with a sense of humor and pragmatism that Zelensky could turn in his favor. "With his charisma, his talent as a negotiator, he thought he could break through that armor," said one of Zelensky's closest aides, Iryna Pobedonostseva, who saw the president upon his return to Kyiv. For years, she had worked alongside Zelensky at his movie studio before taking over the presidential press service, and she had rarely seen her boss as dejected as he was after coming face-to-face with Putin for the first time. "He probably thought there would be more humanity in him," Pobedonostseva told me. "We're all inclined to project our own qualities onto other people. But some people are different. There are those with whom it's just not possible to make a connection."

Putin's demeanor, however cold it may have seemed to Zelensky, was not enough to hold up the peace process. Three days after their talks, Zelensky's majority in the Ukrainian parliament made another important concession to the Russians. They passed a law that would pave the way for the separatist regions of the Donbas to hold local elections. It came with a deadline of one year; the law would expire at the end of December 2020. With that, the clock was set for Zelensky to deliver the peace he promised.

The Russians continued to encourage him. They soon agreed to pay Ukraine back nearly $3 billion in debts, settling an old financial dispute. They also signed a five-year contract for Russia to ship gas through Ukrainian pipelines to Europe. Under that arrangement, Ukraine stood to earn billions of dollars per year in fees for the use of its pipelines. In the months that followed, Zelensky threw himself into the peace process. He promoted his lead negotiator, Andriy Yermak, to the role of chief of staff in the presidential administration, replacing Andriy Bohdan, and they pushed ahead on multiple tracks at once, assigning different teams to work with the Russians on issues of security, economic relations, prisoner swaps, and elections in the Donbas. The strategy created the illusion of progress. Even when most of the negotiating tracks stalled, Yermak could point to some success on one of the easier issues, supporting the narrative that things were moving forward on the whole. In reality, they were stuck from the start. One member of Yermak's team said the process felt like sinking into a vat of jelly that made it impossible to move or maneuver. On the issue of holding elections in the Donbas, she told me, "there was no way to agree, and we had to just sit there and play along, listening to their nonsense." Once again, as Zelensky had observed in old transcripts from such talks, Ukraine and Russia were pretending to negotiate, circling around the issues that mattered most.

The fundamental problem with the Kremlin's position was that it was based on a lie. Putin had always denied the deployment of Russian forces in the Donbas. Their presence in the war zone was well-documented. The world had seen them in news footage, in satellite images, even in the social media posts of the Russian soldiers themselves. But Putin continued to claim, as he had done in Crimea, that these were all local rebels and "self-defense forces," which Moscow could not disarm.

Until Ukraine granted the Donbas permanent autonomy, the Russians refused to pull out of the region. They would not take Zelensky at his word. They wanted him to issue a formal decree to allow elections in all of the Donbas. More than that, they wanted the parliament in Kyiv to ratify the Minsk agreements and commit to carrying them out in full. The Ukrainians refused. Their aim was to amend the agreements, at least the parts that were outdated, unworkable, or made no sense. "We said we were ready to modernize Minsk," Reznikov told me. In the original deal signed in February 2015, Ukraine was supposed to change its Constitution by the end of that year, granting additional rights of autonomy to the separatist regions in the Donbas. The deadline had come and gone five years ago. Under Zelensky, the Ukrainians offered to set a new time frame for these constitutional reforms. "And while we're at it, let's fix a few other points," Reznikov said to the Russians. But they would not change anything about the deal, "not even a comma," he told me. "That's when the legal battles started. That was the moment of degradation."

Even if they wanted to give more ground, the Ukrainians were hamstrung by political forces at home. The backlash to the talks was ferocious from the start. Opposition leaders in parliament accused Zelensky of treason, and his approval ratings took a hit. Many members of his own party were not willing to go along with his approach to the peace talks. His plan for winning over the people of the Donbas by paying pensions in separatist-controlled areas got bogged down in the legislature, which did not like the price tag of $4.2 billion and rejected the plan in February 2020.

Yermak, as the lead negotiator, found himself depicted in the media as a Russian spy, as though he were scheming with the Kremlin to divvy up the lands of eastern Ukraine. "His hands were really tied," said his close adviser, Dasha Zarivna. "They were labeling him a traitor." The opposition wanted Yermak to publicly reject the Minsk agreements and refuse Russia's demands. But he kept quiet about the talks, only insisting that progress was slow but steady on the path to peace. "He had to keep playing the game," Zarivna said.

No matter what they said in public, both sides understood by summer that the game was all but over. The Ukrainian parliament made it official in the middle of July, when it voted to block the elections that Ukraine and Russia were negotiating over. Toward the end of a long and boring plenary session on July 15, 2020, Zelensky's party proposed a plan to hold local and municipal elections across the country in the fall. The plan explicitly excluded the Donbas. To justify the measure, the lawmakers argued that it would be impossible to hold a proper vote in areas that were either under Russian occupation or in close proximity to the conflict zone. Before any elections could proceed in these places, Russia would need to withdraw all its troops and weapons, disarm all the separatist fighters, and give Ukraine back control of its eastern borders.

By then Zelensky had also concluded that he had no chance of winning support in these regions. "The people of the Donbas have been brainwashed," he told me. "They live in the Russian information space." The Kremlin and its proxies had long shut off their access to Ukrainian television channels. The propaganda they received from Moscow had convinced them that Russia had come to protect the Donbas from the "fascist regime" in Kyiv, and Zelensky felt he had no way to change their minds. "I can't reach them," he said. "There is no hope of making those people understand that Russia is really an occupying power."

When it came time for the parliament to vote on the plan for local elections, 225 members of Zelensky's party were in the hall, a clear majority, and every one of them voted to block the elections from taking place in the Donbas. Reznikov knew right away what this would mean for the peace talks with Russia. "It blew apart the Kremlin's expectations," he told me. After five months of talks, the Russian negotiators would need to explain to their boss in the Kremlin why things had fallen apart. The Ukrainians did not expect the Russians to blame their own inflexibility for the failure. They would blame Zelensky, and Putin would be furious. "It would be the same disappointments, the same hurt feelings toward Ukraine and the Ukrainian authorities," said Reznikov. In the minds of the Russians, he imagined, "that brings out aggression and a desire for revenge. Quite simply, it's the formula for every conflict."

CHAPTER 13

THE DARK PRINCE

THE COLLAPSE OF THE PEACE TALKS MARKED A MAJOR SETBACK FOR RUSSIAN INTERESTS in Ukraine. About eighteen months later, Vladimir Putin would cite Kyiv's refusal to hold elections in the Donbas as one of his excuses for launching the invasion. But for the moment, the Kremlin still had a range of options short of war to achieve the influence he wanted. The most promising ones involved Putin's old friend Viktor Medvedchuk, who had emerged as Zelensky's main political rival. A wealthy power broker with an array of media properties in Ukraine, he had the plastic look of a Ken doll's father—stiff, tanned, and manicured, with an angular jaw. His role in Ukraine's political life had earned him a nickname in the press, "The Dark Prince," to match his reputation on Bankova Street.

By the time Zelensky took office, Medvedchuk had been in politics for well over two decades, most of that time as Putin's not-so-hidden hand. Only two years apart in age, Putin and Medvedchuk belonged to the last generation of leaders forged by the Soviet empire and nostalgic for its achievements. Both had ties to the Soviet security services. Putin had been a KGB spy in Germany; Medvedchuk had allegedly helped Soviet authorities silence dissidents in Ukraine. But the story of their friendship began in the early 2000s, during the first years of Putin's presidency. At the time, Medvedchuk served as the chief of staff to Putin's counterpart in Kyiv, President Leonid Kuchma, and they would often see each other at official functions. They got along well, as did their governments. Kuchma, the former head of the Soviet Union's biggest missile factory, prized his country's independence, publishing a book toward the end of his tenure called *Ukraine Is Not Russia*. But their economies were tightly intertwined. Ukraine relied on supplies of Russian oil and gas, and the elites in both countries were bound by business interests, family, and corruption.

Putin's relationship with Medvedchuk exemplified these ties. In 2003, when Medvedchuk married a famous TV personality in Ukraine, Putin was the guest of honor at their wedding in Crimea. The following year, Medvedchuk's bride asked Putin to become the godfather of their newborn daughter, Daria. The girl's christening at a cathedral in St. Petersburg, Putin's hometown, was attended by many of the oligarchs, courtiers, ministers, and spies who ruled Russia and Ukraine at the time. Daria became a living symbol of the union between these elites. In one interview on Russian state TV, Medvedchuk recalled how Putin doted on the girl, bringing her a bouquet of flowers and a teddy bear when he visited her family's villa in Crimea for a holiday. "Our relationship has developed over twenty years," Medvedchuk later told me. "I don't want to say I exploit that relationship, but you could say it has been part of my political arsenal."

Putin could say the same about him. Through the years, as relations between Ukraine and Russia cycled through periods of crisis and comity, Medvedchuk remained Putin's faithful surrogate in Kyiv, the only politician in Ukraine known to have a direct line to the Russian president. It served him well. Through his connections in Moscow, his family received stakes in Russian gas fields and a Russian oil pipeline, which gave Medvedchuk the money to fund his political parties and charity projects. In 2014 and 2015, during the bloodiest days of fighting in the Donbas, he served as a mediator in the peace talks, helping to convince Ukraine to accept the terms of the Minsk agreements. He then began assembling a coalition of forces in Kyiv willing to implement those agreements. It was not an easy feat. Most Ukrainians saw the terms of the deal for what they were—an act of acquiescence to the Russians and a poison pill for Ukraine's goal of joining the European Union. The only politicians eager to implement the Minsk accords came from Ukraine's pro-Russian parties, an assortment of grifters and oligarchs who were usually at one another's throats, brawling over finances, voters, and the blessings of the Kremlin.

In 2018, Medvedchuk finally managed to unite them under a political alliance called Opposition Platform—For Life, which took up the Kremlin's narratives of unity between the people of Russia and Ukraine. It wanted to cut ties with NATO and turn Russian into an official language in Ukraine, and its financial resources were formidable. Apart from Medvedchuk's fortune from the oil trade, his party had support from several billionaires with ties to Moscow. Most important, they controlled three major television channels in Ukraine that allowed them to win a solid base of support, especially in the Russian-speaking regions in the east and the south. In December 2018, just before Zelensky announced his plan to run for president, Medvedchuk's party launched its own campaign.

The candidate they fielded for the presidency, Yuriy Boyko, had a decent showing in the race against Zelensky, taking fourth place with 12 percent of the vote. A few months later, Medvedchuk's party fared even better in the parliamentary race, coming in second place and winning forty-three seats in the legislature. For Russia's proxies, the comeback looked encouraging. Only five years after Putin ordered the annexation of Crimea and started the war in eastern Ukraine, his friend became the leader of the opposition in the Ukrainian parliament. In order to take power, Medvedchuk would need to overtake Zelensky in the polls. His chance arrived in a form no one expected—a novel respiratory virus called COVID-19.

❖

By the fall of 2020, when Zelensky's peace talks with Putin collapsed, the spread of the new coronavirus had eclipsed all other issues of concern. Most of the world was in lockdown. In Ukraine, as in most of Europe, the government ordered all restaurants and most shops to close while banning public events to avoid what officials described as the imminent collapse of the health-care system. Even if Zelensky had wanted to hold another round of talks with Putin at the time, it would have been nearly impossible. The Russian despot had quarantined himself.

Though he had long been obsessive about his health, the risk of infection with this disease seemed to trigger an advanced spell of hypochondria in Putin. He retreated to his vast estate on Lake Valdai, about four hours' drive northwest of Moscow, near a medieval monastery. The property had been designed to accommodate Putin's wellness routine, which became increasingly elaborate in the second decade of his reign. According to the leaked floor plans of his spa complex at Valdai, it included a room for cryogenic therapy, mud baths and salt baths, a cosmetology clinic, and a twenty-five-meter pool where Putin could take his morning swim. Very few people were allowed to visit this property. In years past, Putin held regular sessions with a circle of advisers, oligarchs, and other members of his retinue. The pandemic put a stop to those. "It's an extremely limited circle of people he talks to," said a Russian billionaire who used to attend the meetings. "People are waiting a few weeks in quarantine just to see him," he told me. "He's very cut off from the world."

Putin did, however, make some exceptions to the rules of his seclusion. In October 2020, he invited Medvedchuk to visit him. Russian state TV showed the two men dressed in business suits and slumped into armchairs, side by side, unmasked and with no social distance. The main topic of their meeting, at least in the televised version, was the coronavirus. A couple of months earlier, Russia had unveiled a new vaccine against it, and Medvedchuk was among the first to get the shot. "I took it on the second day after it was approved," he told me. "My wife didn't even ask about any side effects." The Russian vaccine, branded as Sputnik V, would later turn out to be safe and effective. But injecting it seemed like a risky decision at the time. It had not gone through clinical trials before the Kremlin rushed it onto the market. The World Health Organization had not approved its use, nor had any government other than Russia. Even Putin refused to take a dose. But Medvedchuk saw it as more than a health precaution. It was also a means of winning voters. At his meeting with Putin, he struck a deal for Russia to supply Ukraine with millions of doses of Sputnik V.

The offer was timed for maximum political effect. The local and municipal elections were due to take place across Ukraine in about three weeks. Zelensky was at a summit in Brussels at the time, pushing to accelerate Ukraine's membership in the European Union and lobbying for vaccine supplies from the West. "The European Union confirmed that it will help Ukraine get a real vaccine when it appears and does not cause doubts among scientists," Zelensky said in response to the offer from Putin and Medvedchuk. "So I would not recommend putting too much faith in the pre-election 'initiatives' of certain cynics, who have already vaccinated themselves by untested means."

As the elections approached, Zelensky realized the wave of support that brought him to power had crashed. In a nationwide survey released on the week of the ballot, only 17 percent of respondents said they would vote for Zelensky's party, a devastating climbdown for a leader who had upward of 70 percent support when he took office the previous year. On the day of the municipal elections, October 25, 2020, poll workers wearing masks and gloves tested voters for fevers before letting them cast their ballots. The turnout was dismal. The mayor of Kyiv was unable to vote for his own reelection because he had tested positive for the coronavirus. The nation's biggest worry was no longer the peace process with Russia. In the first ten months of the pandemic, the virus would claim more Ukrainian lives than the war in the Donbas had taken in five years.

When the results of the vote came in, the candidates from Zelensky's party ended up losing all nine of the mayoral races held in major cities across Ukraine. The most painful of these defeats for Zelensky was in his hometown of Kryvyi Rih. In most of the races for municipal councils, his party did not even make it to second place. Whatever his achievements in the first year of his tenure, the need for vaccines now eclipsed other demands from voters. But Zelensky had no way to provide them. In November, after a German company announced that its vaccine was safe and effective, he appealed directly to chancellor Angela Merkel. It was no use. Every country in the world was scrambling to line up supplies for its citizens, and manufacturers would not be able to meet global demand anytime soon. The biggest vaccine makers in the U.S. and the E.U. would supply their own people first. Poorer countries like Ukraine would have to wait their turn. Zelensky found it deeply unfair. "With COVID it was like this: You're a good country, here's your vaccine," he later told a German journalist. "You're not such a good country, head toward the back of the line."

Voters in Ukraine were just as frustrated, and many of them blamed Zelensky. On their television channels, Medvedchuk and his allies berated the president over the failure and argued that his alliances with the West meant nothing. In Ukraine's time of need, they said, it was Russia that stepped up to offer vaccines. "And the authorities in Kyiv ignored them," Medvedchuk told me. In early November, he went to meet with Putin for a second time, and he returned with yet another offer. The Russians would allow Ukraine to produce the vaccine on its own soil, at a laboratory in Kharkiv, near the Russian border. "Putin said: Help yourself! We are ready to give you the raw material. We are ready to set up the production facilities," Medvedchuk said. "It would be made in Ukraine!

It's a Ukrainian product!" There was no good reason, he argued, for Zelensky to reject the offer. "It was purely political."

Zelensky tried to push back against these accusations, insisting that Russia's vaccine was unsafe, and that the Kremlin intended to use it as a weapon in the information war to support Medvedchuk and his political party. But the president's office had trouble getting its message across. All of their key rivals, including Medvedchuk, controlled their own media empires. Zelensky did not. "We don't have a single channel of our own," Yermak told me. "Because we're not oligarchs." By the end of 2020, they had fallen out with their former patron Ihor Kolomoysky. The tycoon had been disappointed with his reward for supporting Zelensky's presidential campaign, as he appeared to have little influence over the administration. His bailed-out bank remained under state control, and his former lawyer, Andriy Bohdan, had been fired from his position as chief of staff to Zelensky. As their relations grew tense, then hostile, so did the coverage on Kolomoysky's television channel. It fell in line with the rest of Ukraine's major news networks, which were relentless in their criticism of the president.

Zelensky's family was not spared. About a year into Olena's tenure as First Lady, her staff on Bankova Street organized a series of focus groups to gauge her popularity. Hidden behind a one-way mirror, she stood and watched as regular Ukrainians gave their unvarnished opinions about her. "Some things upset me," she later recalled. If she was so rich, they wanted her to give money to the poor, and they knew almost nothing about the work she had done over the previous year. Her biggest project as First Lady, modeled in part on the work of Michelle Obama, tried to improve the quality of school lunches. But it received paltry coverage in Ukrainian media. "Every step I took, it was up to the goodwill of the media to show it or not. And the media was not always on our side." The head of Zelensky's press service, Iryna Pobedonostseva, put the problem in starker terms: "It was an information war," she told me. And Zelensky was losing.

Throughout the fall of 2020, his ratings continued to deteriorate, and mass protests broke out against him. Some of the biggest ones involved nationalist groups and veterans of the Azov movement, a paramilitary force with ties to the radical right. But the leaders of the opposition in parliament, including Petro Poroshenko, were only too happy to help organize the protests and participate in them. Among the most memorable ones took place right after Zelensky and Yermak came down with the coronavirus. The infection was serious. Both of them had to be hospitalized. On November 21, Yermak's birthday, a crowd of protestors gathered outside the hospital in Kyiv where they were being treated. From their rooms in the COVID ward, the president and his chief of staff could hear the demonstrators blasting music and chanting slogans. Some of the protestors called for Zelensky to be overthrown and arrested for his pursuit of peace with Russia. Anti-riot police guarded the hospital. What seemed to shock Yermak the most was the cynicism of the organizers. Long afterward, he would recall how one of them sent him a message while the protest was happening: *Happy birthday*, it said. *Get well soon.* No matter how two-faced the Russians may have been at the negotiating table, Yermak could see, looking out of his hospital window, that many of Zelensky's domestic enemies were no better. "For them," he told me, "nothing is sacred."

❖

By the end of 2020, Zelensky's approval ratings reached an all-time low. Polls released at the end of December showed that his party was no longer the most popular in the country. Medvedchuk's party had taken a narrow lead. Some surveys suggested it could win against Zelensky's party in a head-to-head race. There was now a real risk that the pro-Russian forces could come to power in Ukraine by democratic means. "And what's bad about that?" Medvedchuk asked me. "We stand up for restoring relations with Russia. That's what our voters want. And that platform brought our party into parliament."

For Putin, the shifting political winds in Kyiv represented a momentous opportunity. Having spent several years and considerable resources supporting Medvedchuk's political project, the payoff for Russia now came into view. With enough seats in the Ukrainian parliament, his allies could block any attempt by Zelensky to integrate with NATO and other Western institutions. They could also push ahead with the process of "decentralization," weakening the central government in Kyiv and allowing Russia to tighten its hold on the eastern and southern regions of Ukraine without the use of military force. Putin, always a spy and never a soldier, preferred as a rule to achieve his ends through subterfuge before turning to violence. If Medvedchuk continued gaining popular support, he would not only deliver the influence Putin wanted in Ukraine. He would also solidify the reputation Putin had long cultivated, that of a cunning operator who could outwit and outlast his rivals in the West.

On Bankova Street, Zelensky and his close advisers held a series of crisis meetings that winter to discuss the threat from Medvedchuk, and they settled on a response that was born as much of the president's emotions, his wounded pride, as any measured assessment of the risks involved. On February 2, 2021, Zelensky banned the three television channels that Medvedchuk and his party controlled. There was no legal precedent for such a move in Ukraine. Instead of going through the justice system, the president tapped one of his most senior allies, Oleksiy Danilov, to help shut the channels down. Danilov, as secretary of the National Security and Defense Council, signed off on a series of sanctions against the channels' ownership, a novel form of political attack. Sanctions are normally meant to punish foreigners outside of a country's legal jurisdiction. Here they were used against a Ukrainian member of parliament, an opposition leader, and his private media conglomerate. Some of Zelensky's closest allies tried to dissuade him from taking this course. "This is an illegal mechanism that contradicts the Constitution," said Dmytro Razumkov, the speaker of the parliament, who had served as a manager of Zelensky's presidential campaign. "The law cannot be replaced by political expediency," he told me.

When I asked Zelensky about the decision, he grew defensive, his eyes shifting between anger and embarrassment. He acknowledged how strange it looked for a former comedian and political satirist, a star of the screen and the stage whose own productions had faced censorship over the years, to begin shutting down television networks by decree. "We are very liberal people in our views, in our philosophy," he told me with faint conviction in his voice. But Russia's information war against Ukraine, its use of political proxies and propaganda, had pushed Zelensky to set these liberal values to the side. The danger from Medvedchuk and his television channels felt existential to Zelensky. "I consider them devils," he told me. "Their narratives seek to disarm Ukraine of its statehood."

The argument stank of paternalism. Could people not be trusted to watch TV and form their own opinions? For almost thirty years, ever since Ukraine became a free and independent country, its media landscape had been messy, rife with spin and outright disinformation as various moguls and politicians vied for control of the popular narrative. But it was also a free and competitive arena for public debate that had largely maintained its independence from government censorship. Now Zelensky decided to shut down the media conglomerate of his main political opponent, the one whose channels he saw as a threat not only to his popularity but, he said, to the existence of Ukraine. "What are pro-Russian politicians? They are elected. People voted for them. We have to take that into account. When people vote for them, it's their right. But here's the issue," Zelensky told me. "Once they are elected, they do not do what they promised. They promise one thing, they do another. They pull a bait and switch. To put it very crudely, you can't go on Ukrainian TV and say that everything in Ukraine is bad, and everything in Russia is good."

In a democratic society, Zelensky conceded that such statements—Ukraine bad, Russia good—would not justify an outright ban on the media that broadcast them. But their sources of financing, he said, obligated the state to get involved. "When it became clear that these channels are being financed through business deals with the occupying Russian forces, we said, that's enough. They take this Russian money and they pump it into these channels." Medvedchuk stood accused of doing business with the Russian-backed separatists in eastern Ukraine, whom the government in Kyiv regarded as terrorists. "That's out of bounds," Zelensky said. "That's financing terrorism. Al Capone killed a lot of people, but he got locked up over his taxes. I think these channels also killed a lot of people. Not directly," he said, "but through information."

The rhetoric seemed out of character. The soothing tones of the unifier who took office in 2019 seemed to dissipate when it came to these TV networks. Zelensky had decided to go to war with them, though he still seemed uncomfortable with the way it made him look. His tactics resembled the ones Putin used in the early 2000s. At the time, Russia's media industry was mostly free, though it also functioned as a battleground between rival political clans and oligarchs. Soon after taking power, Putin went after the media tycoons that criticized his rule. He accused some of them of defending terrorists in Chechnya and seized their TV channels. Human rights groups and free-speech activists had condemned Putin for those actions, and they condemned Zelensky for his move against Medvedchuk. The European Union warned him that the fight against Russian propaganda should not "come at the expense of freedom of media." But the Biden administration, which had taken office only two weeks earlier, applauded Zelensky. "We support Ukraine's efforts to protect its sovereignty and territorial integrity through sanctions," the U.S. embassy in Kyiv said in a statement. Officials at the Department of State told me they were impressed with how decisively Zelensky had acted against Russia's "malign influence" in Ukraine. "He turned out to be a doer," one of the officials said. "He got it done." The American response seemed to anger Putin at least as much as the ban on his friend's TV channels. It played right into some of the Kremlin's favorite narratives about Western double-dealing and hypocrisy. "In Ukraine," Putin said, "they just went and shut down three leading channels. With one stroke of the pen. And everyone is silent! Some are even giving them supportive pats on the back."

Zelensky soon went a step further. On February 19, 2021, his government announced the confiscation of the Medvedchuk family's assets. Among the most important, it said, was a pipeline that brings Russian oil to Europe through Ukraine. This was the main source of Medvedchuk's fortune. Not only had the pipeline enriched him and his family—including Putin's goddaughter, Daria—it also helped bankroll the political party that represented Russian interests in Ukraine. Putin gave no public statement about the seizure of these assets.

But a sign of Russia's response came two days later, at seven a.m. on February 21. In a little-noticed statement on its website, the Russian Ministry of Defense announced that it was sending three thousand paratroopers to the border with Ukraine for "large-scale exercises." Their arrival would mark the start of a major military buildup along the borders of Ukraine. Within two months it would grow to more than one hundred thousand Russian troops and thousands of military vehicles. The purpose of their exercise, according to the Ministry of Defense's statement, would be to train Russia's elite commandos to "seize enemy structures and hold them until the arrival of the main force." Almost exactly one year later, Russian paratroopers would put these drills into practice during their assault on Kyiv.

CHAPTER 14

WELCOME TO RAGNAROK

B Y THE END OF MARCH 2021, RUSSIA HAD POSITIONED MORE TROOPS ALONG ITS BORders with Ukraine than at any point since the annexation of Crimea. Along the edges of the territory Russia occupied in the Donbas, the fighting intensified that spring, and one firefight would later stand out in the minds of President Zelensky and his team as a milestone on the road to all-out war. It began with the booms and whistles of Russian mines landing near the village of Shumy. Launched from miles away, the weapons had a diabolical design. When they hit the ground, instead of exploding, they popped open to release a web of nearly invisible wires. Anyone who came along and touched one of the strands—a soldier, an animal, a child—would cause the mine to detonate, spraying a hail of shrapnel in every direction.*

On March 26, 2021, the task of clearing these mines around Shumy fell to a group of sappers from a nearby base, Demining Center 2641, whose motto read, "Mistake is not an option." Among their more experienced officers was Serhiy Barnych, a senior sergeant with a long nose and a distinctive dimple in his chin. The armor he wore that day covered his head and most of his body. In case he tripped one of the wires by accident, he could trust the gear to withstand small shards of shrapnel and, more than likely, keep him alive. That week, the cold of early spring had lifted, and the sun had melted most of the snow in the field that Barnych was assigned to clear. As he scanned the ground for wires, the sound of a bullet cut the air. It struck Barnych from behind in his upper thigh, ripping a hole in his femoral artery. He fell to the ground, cried

---

* Under international law, these weapons have been banned for decades. Russian forces have deployed them in eastern Ukraine throughout the war.

out, and tried to stop the flow of blood. It was already pooling in the dirt around him.

With that first shot, the Russian snipers had set a trap, and they waited for other soldiers to come running through the field. The first one to reach Barnych was his commanding officer, Lieutenant Colonel Serhiy Koval, who tried to staunch the bleeding and drag Barnych back to the trenches. They couldn't see where the shots were coming from. They could only hear the whistle and thwack of the bullets as they landed. Within minutes, both men were dead. Two other soldiers who came to help them were soon killed the same way, one shot through the neck and the other the heart. No one ever saw the snipers.

Pinned down in a set of nearby trenches, the Ukrainian troops radioed to the high command for permission to shoot back. Under the rules of the cease-fire that Zelensky had agreed to the previous summer, the officers first had to send a message to the Russian side, asking them to call off the attack. This game of telephone took time, and it drove the soldiers mad. Minutes passed. The snipers continued firing, and the Ukrainians continued bleeding in the field. Their comrades could only watch and wait for the signal to respond. When it finally came, the Ukrainian side launched mortars toward the approximate position of the snipers. Only then the shooting stopped, and they were able to retrieve the bodies of their comrades from that field.

At around eight p.m. that evening, President Zelensky issued a statement from his office in Kyiv. There was restraint in the word he chose—*escalation*—to describe the killing of those four men, and he made clear that his preference was not to retaliate. "For war you need courage," he said. "For peace you need wisdom. Ukraine still has plenty of both." The leaders of Germany and France, Zelensky added, must organize an emergency round of talks with Putin to discuss the fighting near Shumy. "All that we have toiled to build, piece by piece, for over a year," he said, referring to his fragile cease-fire with Russia, "it can be destroyed in seconds."

A few days after the sniper attack in Shumy, the Ukrainian parliament called an extraordinary session to discuss what had happened. General Ruslan Khomchak, then the commander of Ukraine's armed forces, showed up in full regalia, with a series of maps to illustrate the dire situation at the front. The Russians near Shumy showed "particular cynicism," he said, in their use of a water pumping station as a sniper's nest. Damaging that station would have cut off the water supply to several towns in the area, which is why the Ukrainians took so long to fire back. In the middle of his speech, Khomchak proposed a minute of silence to honor Barnych and the other victims. Then he moved on to explain much graver threats. As of March 30, 2021, he said, Russia had gathered 32,700 troops along the border. Some of them had come from their bases in Siberia, thousands of miles away. The annual Russian war games in Belarus had also been used as cover to station more troops and military hardware to the north of Ukraine, within a few hours' drive from Kyiv. The nation was thus surrounded on three sides. "Our common purpose is to defeat the aggressor at war," Khomchak concluded. But that would require "colossal efforts from the entire Ukrainian nation."

The speech, which lasted a little over ten minutes, did not cause alarm among the lawmakers. If anything, it seemed to elicit a collective yawn. Yulia Tymoshenko, one of the leaders of the opposition, continued to talk on her phone during the general's presentation. The speaker was forced to turn on his microphone and instruct the chamber to stop gabbing and pay attention. In any other capital, the scene would have looked preposterous. Here was the top military officer in the country, declaring that a foreign power was ready to invade from three directions, and the legislature could barely summon the patience to listen to him. They had long grown numb to such assessments. Flare-ups along the front lines felt too common to inspire outrage. The encounter at Shumy had been particularly bloody, but it was not enough to create a sense of unity or urgency among the parties represented in parliament. Their political squabbles resumed as soon as the general took his seat.

Among the first to give a rebuttal was Petro Poroshenko, who spoke with some authority about the situation in Shumy. He had been president when Ukrainian forces took that village back from the Russians in 2018. At the cost of at least one soldier's life, they had managed to shove the front line forward by a few kilometers, even as many officers questioned the wisdom of doing so. The purpose of the operation seemed to have more to do with politics than military strategy. Poroshenko was getting ready to launch his campaign for reelection at the time, and he was keen to prove himself as a wartime commander. It didn't help him much in the end. Zelensky still trounced him at the polls. But two years later, when Shumy came under attack, Poroshenko put the blame on his successor.

"I want to begin," he said from the podium, "by thanking the Ukrainian warriors for their courage in resisting the aggressor, and for the resilience they show whenever it gets hard to understand the maneuvers of Zelensky, who has spent the last two years gazing into Putin's eyes." The cease-fire Ukraine had reached with Russia during the first year of Zelensky's tenure was based on the "false hypothesis," said Poroshenko, "that a truce can lead to peace." After Shumy, Ukraine needed to counterattack, he said, to send its own snipers into the field and launch drones to hunt Russian artillery systems. "Putin is a killer!" Poroshenko shouted. "I hope you, Volodymyr," he said, teasing the president, "even you will manage to squeeze that statement out of yourself." The speaker soon cut off Poroshenko's microphone, and the chamber erupted into a shouting match, by then a regular occurrence.

Footage of the session topped the news in Ukraine that day, and Zelensky and his team were livid when they saw it. Poroshenko was in his element, wagging his finger at the chamber as he spoke. He understood that his best chance to win back power was to paint the comedian as a pushover. With polls showing that most Ukrainians did not trust their president, Zelensky faced intense pressure to make a show of strength in response to the Russian attacks. At the same time, he could not abandon the promise he had made to engineer a lasting peace. The day after Khomchak appeared in parliament, Zelensky summoned him to a closed-door meeting with other generals and all of Ukraine's top spies. They talked until late in the evening about the bloodshed along the front lines, but the office of the president kept the meeting quiet. They did not want to create the impression of a crisis.

Through spy satellites, U.S. intelligence agencies had been watching the Russian troops gather at the border, and Joe Biden called Zelensky that week to pledge the "unwavering support" of the U.S. in any confrontation with the Kremlin. The NATO alliance offered similar assurances when Zelensky spoke to its secretary general, Jens Stoltenberg, a few days later. "NATO is the only way to end the war," Zelensky said on the call. He urged the alliance to hurry up and offer Ukraine a formal path to membership, which would mark a "real signal to Russia." For the Krem-lin, that appeal was enough of a signal. It elicited a warning from Putin's spokesman, Dmitry Peskov, that any talk of NATO membership would "only make the situation worse."

❖

The following week, Zelensky and his team decided to visit the front. They needed to show support for the troops and to recognize the horror of what happened in Shumy without letting it trigger a wider war. On the eve of the trip, Zelensky gave a posthumous medal of valor to Sergeant Barnych. Then he set out to visit the site of his death, and he invited me to come along.

The president's plane, an An-148, landed the next morning at the air base in Chuhuiv, about fifty kilometers from the Russian border, and we walked across the runway toward the military helicopters that would take us into the war zone. My ride was with the bodyguards, who spent most of the flight changing into their battle gear, loading their rifles, adjusting their helmets. The roar of the blades made it impossible for us to hear one another. Through the windows, we could see the presi-dent's helicopter, a Soviet-designed Mi-8, painted in camouflage, with a blue-and-yellow circle that looked like a bull's-eye painted on its rump. We were headed southeast toward enemy territory, our course roughly parallel to the border with Russia. To avoid ground fire, the pilots flew low enough to bend the treetops as we approached the town of Severo-donetsk.

About a year later, during the full-scale invasion, news anchors and diplomats around the world would struggle to pronounce the name of this backwater, population 120,000. For several weeks in the spring of 2022 it would be the epicenter of the war, its streets leveled with artillery and subsumed in urban combat. For the moment, it was still peaceful and obscure, not close enough to the fighting to prevent life from continuing as normal. At the local airport, General Khomchak waited on the tar-mac with a few air-conditioned vans for our ride to the town of Zolote, where part of the 92nd Separate Mechanized Brigade had set up a base in a commandeered building. One might have expected them to spruce the place up for the arrival of the president, but they had mostly preserved its natural state, with bowls of food for stray dogs in the courtyard and piles of sandbags where the soldiers sat and smoked. The younger ones had grown up watching Zelensky's comedies, and some could not suppress a chuckle at the sound of his husky voice. The lower ranks were glad to see him. Whatever the inconvenience of hosting such a delegation, it was still a welcome break in their routine of guarding trenches and going on patrols. The officers were the ones who had to game out the risk of a Russian attack, and they seemed uneasy that morning. "Let's hope the cannons stay quiet today," one of them remarked during a cigarette break.

The trip to Shumy was scheduled for the afternoon. It was not an easy place to reach. Armored trucks got us most of the way, passing old cabins that looked uninhabitable but had fresh piles of firewood stacked outside. Zelensky rode near the front of the convoy, wearing a bulletproof vest. Khomchak was in another vehicle, riding shotgun, with me squeezed in the back behind him. True to form, the general stared straight ahead at the road and kept his answers to my questions brief: "We've been at war with the Russians since 2014. We're used to it. We're ready." The recent battles were par for the course, Khomchak told me, and they had no logical explanation apart from the enemy's familiar treachery.

The drive took more than half an hour, and, for the final stretch, we crept along country roads, swerving to avoid the potholes. The cars in front of us came to a stop in the middle of nowhere. It wasn't possible to drive to the place we were headed. As we climbed out, Khomchak gestured toward a narrow footpath through the fields, and the rest of us followed him in single file. Behind Zelensky, and just ahead of me, one of the guards lugged a massive assault rifle, its ammunition boxes clattering on his belt with every step. The weapon looked impressive, but it would not be our salvation in case of an ambush. We were out in the open now, hiking through dry grass and leafless bushes. Less than a mile to the east was the edge of Horlivka, a Ukrainian city that the Russians had occupied and fiercely defended for years. The warlord Russia installed to rule that city at the start of the war was a sociopath who went by the nickname Demon, best known for staging summary executions and bragging about them to the media. One of the Russian scouts in Horlivka would only need a pair of binoculars to spot us in that field, a perfect little daisy chain of high-value targets: the president, his chief of staff, his top general, and, ambling along toward the rear, a man with a notebook and a foppish black overcoat under his bulletproof vest.

As we approached the village, Khomchak stopped in the middle of the path. The Russian positions were just to our right, he said, on the other end of some sagging power lines. The snipers who killed Sergeant Barnych and his comrades had taken aim from the pumping station just beyond. The general paused to let the president absorb the scene. Then he suggested we head back toward the armored cars. Zelensky looked confused. "Our guys are over there, right?" he said to Khomchak. "They'll hear I came all this way and didn't come to see them. They'll be upset." Maybe the general had not made clear that Russian snipers could still be working in the area. Maybe he did not describe in detail the nature of the mines they had dropped in these fields. But it seemed more likely that Zelensky understood the risks when he spun around and continued hiking through the brush. Khomchak, like the rest of us, had little choice but to go along.

The path led to a clearing where troops had set up a forward operating base, a target so close and tempting to Russian artillery that its survival seemed miraculous. The soldiers had built themselves a little sauna, which they would heat in the evenings with stones from a campfire. Though no women served in this place, the wooden outhouse was labeled with a big red *M*. At the eastern edge of the encampment, their system of trenches formed an arrow pointing straight toward the Russian positions. The troops had placed a wooden sign at the entrance that read "Vietnam," a nod to the mud and morass of a war they had seen in the movies. Zelensky ducked underneath it to enter the trench, which was deeper than he was tall, and just wide enough for us to pass through, our shoulders brushing the walls of dirt on either side. When it rains, the troops told us, the water pools at the bottom and turns the trenches into tubs of mud. At the far end of the dugouts, Zelensky asked to have a word in private with a few of the troops. They looked surprised and a little starstruck but kept their composure, answering his earnest questions about what they had seen. When he emerged, the president went with Khomchak to the place where Sergeant Barnych had been shot. Nothing was alive on the ground this close to winter. Only dry reeds and bushes sticking out of the dirt.

"So, this is Shumy," the general said. Its population twenty years ago had been around a hundred people. Nearly all of them fled or died as the front lines shifted back and forth during the war. All the brick homes had long been shelled into rubble, and graffiti from the soldiers marked the few walls that still stood. One inscription said in English, "Welcome to Ragnarok," an old Norse term for a mythical apocalypse. The lone resident preventing this village from becoming a ghost town was an old woman. Her son fought on the Russian side. "For the separatists?" Zelensky asked in disbelief. The general nodded.

Shumy, he pointed out, lies in a depression, "in the palm of the enemy's hand." There is no way to hold it without taking losses, and no way to advance "even one centimeter" from here in any direction. It had been a senseless move to take this territory, and now it forced the Ukrainians to confront a painful question. Khomchak spelled it out for Zelensky as they stood there, looking around: "Is this place worth the lives of so goddamn many men?" Just that morning, another Ukrainian had been killed at the front, bringing the death toll to twenty-six troops in the first three months of 2021. One of them had tripped the wire on a Russian mine, and it blew him apart.

But Zelensky did not promise to avenge their deaths. Instead, like Khomchak, he questioned the wisdom of sending men to die for these muddy dugouts. The decision to seize the terrain around Shumy had been the mistake of his predecessor. "They pushed forward just to show that they could do it," Zelensky told me. "For some that meant we were the tough guys. For others it meant their sons would not be coming home." He had no intention of making such trades again. The stakes were too high, and he had no desire to test his own abilities as a wartime commander. "Right now," he said, "I can't understand why we had to fight over this empty field."

In the distance a dog started barking. Khomchak said it was time to go, and we set off toward the military base in the town of Avdiivka, where we would spend the night a few miles from the Russian positions. On a bulletin board near the entrance to the base, the troops had posted portraits of Sergeant Barnych and the men who died with him. Zelensky bent down to look at his face and read the details of his life. The cause of death was rendered clinically: "perforating gunshot wound to the left leg that was incompatible with life." Zelensky grimaced. *Incompatible with life.* Barnych was only three years older than the president when he was shot. Their birthdays were a couple weeks apart.

❖

The next day, as we were flying back to Kyiv, I went up to the front of the plane to talk to Zelensky. He sat at a table with a starched white tablecloth, his back to the cockpit, drinking coffee and gazing out at the fields beneath us. He seemed in good spirits, not overly concerned about the escalation at the front. That morning, after we woke up near the garrison, the president showed up in the mess hall for breakfast in his running clothes, fresh from a jog through the war zone. His cheeks still had a healthy flush as I sat down across from him and asked the flight attendant for coffee. We had spent two days in the Donbas, and it wasn't clear what the president made of the recent sniper attacks, the mortar fire, the Russian troops arrayed along the border. Why did the Kremlin want to escalate? What was Putin's aim? Why now?

Zelensky disagreed with the premise of the question. "You say it's Putin, it's the Russians," he told me. "It's very hard to tell in the Donbas where the fighters are Russian, where they're separatists, and where they're something else." He recalled a story he had heard from some of the troops earlier that day. There had been a shoot-out before the latest cease-fire came into force. The enemy was hammering the men with artillery and heavy fire, trying to beat them back from their positions. "It was tough," Zelensky said, "just awful, the dirt, the shooting. Our guys were dying, and so were theirs." At one point, when the guns fell quiet for a little while, the Ukrainian troops found the bodies of some of the men they had killed. They searched their possessions and found fresh parole papers in the pocket of a Russian fighter. "He'd been let out of prison," Zelensky told me, widening his eyes. "So there were convicts fighting in this war. They have nothing to lose. Where else can they go? They are told to go and fight, so they do it. Who are they? The citizens of what country? It's not even clear."

Zelensky seemed to pity them, sounding more like their defense lawyer than the leader of the country they were fighting. As his plane reached cruising altitude and the war zone disappeared beneath the clouds, the president tried to convince me that the conflict in the east was a lot more nuanced than it seems. There was no way to tell for sure who was fighting on the Russian side, he suggested, and what their motives might be.

In a narrow sense, he had a point. Russia has long used criminals to prosecute its war in eastern Ukraine. The mercenary force known as the Wagner Group, led by one of Putin's lieutenants, would later begin a widely publicized recruitment drive inside Russian prisons, offering clemency to murderers and rapists in exchange for military service in Ukraine. Such fighters had been involved in the war since its earliest days. The very first Russian unit to seize control of towns in the Donbas in the spring of 2014 was staffed in part with ex-convicts and fugitives from Russian law. I once met the most famous fighter in that unit. He went by the nickname Babay, which means "bogeyman" in Russian, and he told me that he faced charges in southern Russia for threatening to stab someone to death. To avoid prison time, he had volunteered to join a unit of Russian irregulars that took part in the occupation of Crimea that spring. When we met a few months later, his crew of about a dozen fighters had just taken over the Ukrainian city of Kramatorsk. They met no armed resistance and, on the whole, seemed to be having an easy time of the war, riding around in an old van whose fender had been stenciled with the words "People's Militia of the Donbas." "Before the American menace comes to my homeland, I came here to stop it," Babay told me. Eventually, he said, they would take Kyiv, "and then we'll go back and celebrate." His buddies had a good laugh at the remark. But, scrappy as they looked, their unit was not roaming around Ukraine unsupervised. Babay was a Russian military veteran. His commander at the time, Igor Girkin, was a retired officer of the Russian intelligence services. They were part of an invading Russian force that was there with the Kremlin's blessing and support. Even if their rap sheets and army-surplus uniforms made them seem more like pirates than commandos, they were still fighting for the Russian side, killing Ukrainian citizens and seizing Ukrainian land. Babay showed me his Russian passport. He was Russian born, hailing from the city of Krasnodar. He had crossed the border to conquer Ukraine. What did it matter that he was a fugitive or a convict? Did that not make him a Russian invader? Was he not part of Putin's strategy?

"You keep asking about Putin or Russia," Zelensky told me on the plane. "I'm not sure we need to think in those terms." The Kremlin's role in the recent attacks around Shumy and other places in the Donbas appeared to be an open question for Zelensky. He was willing to give Putin the benefit of the doubt, and at least to consider the possibility that the shelling and sniper fire along the front lines had not been sanctioned in Moscow. And what about the Russian troops gathered at his eastern border? Was that just one big chain gang? Lost souls released from prison yards and handed the keys to some wheeled artillery?

"Okay, the troops on the border," Zelensky said. "They're doing exercises. That's their official position." Indeed, the Kremlin's official position was that its troops pose no threat to Ukraine, and they had gathered at the border as part of a regular military drill. "They happen every year," Zelensky reminded me. Maybe the Russians were going overboard this time. They had parked their fighter jets and military hardware on the territory of Belarus, just to the north of Kyiv. But the deployment still fit the established pattern of Russian posturing and bluster. "They want us to be afraid," Zelensky told me. "They want the West to be afraid of Russia's might, of her power. There's no big secret here." No one could tell what Putin was thinking, and Zelensky agreed that Russia might have more aggressive intentions this time. "There could be a broader military plan," he told me. "Sure, yeah, maybe." But he was not convinced that Russia's maneuvers amounted to anything more than a bluff. "I just don't think their decision is that primitive: 'Let's go and attack!' Of course not," he told me. "They are playing different games."

At least for the moment, Zelensky believed it was still possible to salvage the cease-fire and continue working toward peace with Russia. Maybe he was right. After visiting Shumy, he would have loved to tell those young men in the trenches to pack up their gear and go home to their families. But he understood that any withdrawal would tempt the Russians to try the same maneuver elsewhere, taking more lives and claiming more territory. It would give his political opponents a fresh excuse to claim that the president lacked the chops for war. Poroshenko would call him a coward, forced into retreat after just a few shots from a Russian sniper rifle. Such attacks in parliament and on the TV talk shows seemed to worry Zelensky at least as much as the risk of a Russian invasion. Ukraine's enemies, he said, "are working on different fronts, with information, disinformation, and the military."

The flight attendant came around to collect our coffee cups, and the pilot began to descend. If nothing else, our trip had made the risk of war seem less abstract to both of us. We had seen the troops in their trenches and shared a couple of meals with them. But the threat from Russian propaganda still felt more immediate to Zelensky, who kept returning to the ways that Russia's political proxies had been "destroying Ukraine's information space." The decision in February to close the television channels of Viktor Medvedchuk had stabilized the president's position in the polls. Some surveys showed him climbing by a few percentage points. When the plane touched down, Zelensky returned to the political battles of the capital, where he planned an escalation of his own.

❖

A few days after we got back from the Donbas, I went to see Viktor Medvedchuk at his office in Kyiv. It took me a while to find the place amid the alleys of the city center. The address led to an old apartment block near the end of a steep slope, with no outward sign of its political significance. Behind the unmarked door, a handful of armed guards looked at me in silence. One proceeded to search my bag, demanding to know whether it contained a knife or "any kind of shiv." Medvedchuk, dressed in a fitted blue suit, looked even more artificial in person than he did on television, his skin taut and face chiseled as though he had also availed himself of Putin's cryogenic chambers at the villa on Lake Valdai. Upon entering the conference room to meet me, he strutted over to a thermostat and asked, "Are you warm enough?"

It was the middle of April 2021. His television channels had been off the air for over a month, and there were by now tens of thousands of Russian troops standing near the border of Ukraine. A year later, when the invasion would be in its second month, the Kremlin would confirm that its decision to attack had been related to Medvedchuk and his political party. "If his ideas and the ideas of his party had been taken into account at the time, and formed the basis of the state policies of Ukraine, then there would be no military operation," Putin's spokesman, Dmitry Peskov, told reporters in April 2022.

But the connection was not yet clear when Medvedchuk agreed to meet with me. The chance of an invasion still felt remote. Even Medvedchuk tended to believe his friend in the Kremlin was merely using his troops as a means of extortion. "Maybe this demonstration of force has a different aim," he suggested. Its true intent may be to force Zelensky back to the negotiating table, and to remind him of the consequences if he refused. "The path of escalation is pure suicide for Zelensky. Pure suicide," Medvedchuk told me. No one could tell for sure whether Putin was bluffing, and if Zelensky saw the slightest chance of a Russian invasion, "even a one percent chance, then he needs to do everything in his power to keep his country and his citizens safe. But he's not doing that."

Leaning forward, Medvedchuk checked the table for flecks of dirt before planting his elbows on top of it. Then he began to describe his disappointment with Zelensky. At the outset, their views did not seem that far apart. Both wanted to hold elections in the Donbas under the laws of Ukraine. Both wanted the separatist regions to choose leaders that the world would recognize. Both believed they could win the support of the people in these regions. It was a valuable pool of potential voters for both of them. "As a politician," Medvedchuk said, "I want these people back. Our party wants them back as supporters." The political math looked compelling. In the summer of 2019, his party had won a total of around 1.9 million votes nationwide, enough to make it the second-largest faction in the Ukrainian parliament. If everyone in the Donbas, including the 3.5 million people living under Russian occupation, were allowed to participate in the next elections, Medvedchuk believed his party's electorate would at least double in size. It would take enough seats to shape the agenda in parliament and, over time, to win power through the ballot box.

When Zelensky took office, he promised to let these people vote, believing he could win their support. But he soon realized he could not reach them. They had been brainwashed, he said, by years of Russian propaganda. Instead of holding elections in the Donbas, Zelensky tried to go after the source of Russian propaganda in Ukraine—the television channels that Medvedchuk used to spread the Kremlin's message. Putin's response did not surprise Medvedchuk. "When they close TV channels that Russian-speaking people watched, when they persecute the party these people voted for, it touches all of the Russian-speaking population," he said. "And Putin gave a promise to protect them."

Is that why he had sent his armies to the border? To protect Medvedchuk and his television channels? "My personal assets, no, nobody cares," he said. "But the party, the TV channels, yes. Millions of citizens voted for us. We are the party that represents the Russian-speaking population of Ukraine." Without its TV channels, the party did not stand a chance in the political arena. Its approval ratings went into decline soon after they were taken off the air. "This is political repression," Medvedchuk told me. "All my bank accounts are frozen. I can't manage my assets. I can't even pay my utility bills."

His problems had just begun. A few weeks after our interview, Ukrainian authorities issued an arrest warrant for Medvedchuk. Prosecutors accused him of using profits from the oil trade to fund separatists in the Donbas, and they charged him with treason and financing terrorism. A court ordered him to remain under house arrest pending trial, cut off from the airwaves and forbidden from attending sessions of parliament. To enforce the order, Medvedchuk was fitted with a tracking device on his ankle, and police officers were stationed outside his home around the clock. His daughter Daria, Putin's goddaughter, remained with her parents in Kyiv, surrounded by private security guards.

Medvedchuk's allies in parliament were outraged, and they warned Zelensky of the consequences. "Russia either gets the influence it wants by peaceful means, or it gets it by force," said Oleh Voloshyn, a prominent lawmaker from Medvedchuk's party. "There is no third option." But the U.S. continued to support the crackdown against them. When Voloshyn visited the U.S. that summer, two agents of the FBI approached him at Dulles International Airport and asked to have a word in private, away from his wife and infant son, who were traveling with him. Voloshyn spent the next three hours answering the agents' questions and allowing them to search his phone. "You have to understand," he later told me. "There are hawks around Putin who want this crisis. They are ready to invade. They come to him and say, 'Look at your Medvedchuk. Where is he now? Where is your peaceful solution? Sitting under house arrest? Should we wait until all pro-Russian forces are arrested?'"

Three days after Medvedchuk was charged with treason, Putin gave his response during a virtual meeting with his national security council. He urged its members, including Russia's spy chiefs and the minister of defense, to prepare a response to the legal assault on Russia's allies in Ukraine. The government in Kyiv was attempting to "purge the political playing field," Putin said. Their ultimate goal was to transform Ukraine "into Russia's antithesis, a kind of anti-Russia," which would serve as a permanent threat to Russian national security. "We will need to react," he said, "with these threats in mind."

But, at that moment, Putin had not made up his mind to attack. His immediate goal, as Medvedchuk suggested, was to use the threat of force to extract concessions—not only from Ukraine but, more importantly, its allies. Throughout the spring of 2021, as Russian troops stood at the border with Ukraine, U.S. intelligence sources and satellites monitored their numbers and guessed at their intentions. The White House found them alarming enough for President Biden to get involved. In the middle of April, he called Putin to propose their first presidential summit, offering an agenda that would go far beyond the standoff in Ukraine. Biden wanted to talk about cyber warfare and nuclear arms control, as well as broader issues of European security. The list included many of the threats and grievances Putin had raised over the years, and he seemed eager for the chance to discuss them with his American counterpart.

To pave the way for their summit, the Russian military wound down its maneuvers near the Ukrainian border and sent its troops back to their bases at the start of May. Many of their tanks and other military hardware stayed in place, signaling that Russia could resume the standoff on short notice if it chose. Putin also made clear that he was done talking directly to the Ukrainians. He refused Zelensky's invitation to meet in the Donbas that spring. Zelensky's offers to hold a summit with Putin in Vienna, Jerusalem, or the Vatican were also rebuffed, and the Kremlin's negotiators declined to recommit in writing to a cease-fire in the Donbas. Those talks were dead.

Now Putin wanted to hear out the Americans, who signaled their willingness to offer major concessions to Moscow. In the middle of May, the Biden administration lifted sanctions against a Russian gas pipeline to Germany, Nord Stream 2, which Ukraine and the U.S. had long opposed. A month later, the presidents of the world's two biggest nuclear powers met at a villa on the shores of Lake Geneva. But after nearly two hours of talks, the gulf between them remained so vast that Putin declined to participate in a joint press conference with Biden. They had not even managed to agree on the terms of a prisoner exchange between the U.S. and Russia, let alone a European security architecture that might assuage Putin's fears of NATO enlargement. "He still is concerned that we, in fact, are looking to take him down," Biden said after the meeting.

Indeed, the depth of Putin's fear and resentment toward the West became clear a month later, when he published a lengthy essay on the subject of Russian relations with Ukraine or, as he put in the title of the piece, the "historical unity" of these two nations. Relying on a mix of dusty tropes from the Russian nationalist and imperialist writers whom Putin had apparently been reading and rereading in his isolation, he again described Kyiv as the mother of all Russian cities who had been corrupted and lured away by the conniving West. He expanded at length on his idea of Ukraine as an "anti-Russia," not really a country at all, he suggested, but an instrument, a platform from which the West hoped to weaken and destroy the Russian state. This plot would persist, he wrote, regardless of who came to power in Kyiv. "The Western authors of the anti-Russia project set up the Ukrainian political system in such a way that presidents, members of parliament, and ministers would change, but the attitude of separation from and enmity with Russia would remain."

The failed peace talks with Zelensky served as proof of this theory in Putin's mind. "Reaching peace was the main election slogan of the incumbent president," he wrote of Zelensky. "He came to power with this. The promises turned out to be lies. Nothing has changed." Putin had given up on Medvedchuk's plan for remaking Ukraine through television, corruption, and politics. If Russia intended to restore its "historical unity" with Ukraine, it would need to do so by other means.

CHAPTER 15

SHOOT TO KILL

I N THE FINAL SUMMER BEFORE THE INVASION, PRESIDENT ZELENSKY DECIDED THAT Ukraine's armed forces, rather than its negotiators, needed to play a greater role in staving off the Russian threat, and he appointed a new commander to advance that goal within the military. The decision came as a surprise to most of the top brass, and it shocked the man selected for the job. Major General Valery Zaluzhny was still in his forties when he got the call from Bankova Street on the morning of July 23, 2021. His rank and stature at the time were far below the position Zelensky offered him: commander in chief of the Armed Forces of Ukraine, the nation's top military title, outranked only by the president himself. The height of that perch, the general told me, induced a feeling in his gut like vertigo. "Time and again I've looked back and asked myself: How did I get myself into this?"

None of Zelensky's decisions, certainly none in the personnel department, would have a greater impact on Ukraine's defense than his decision to appoint Zaluzhny. At the time, the choice seemed rash. Zaluzhny was a bold and ambitious commander, but he was also a bit of a goofball, better known for clowning around with his troops than disciplining them. A staffer had once photographed the general in uniform, picking daisies in the courtyard of the Ministry of Defense, and, with a flourish and a kiss, delivering the bouquet to his wife, who had come to visit him.

Such antics made him stand out among the older and stiffer cadres of the General Staff, nearly all of whom were about a generation older and had come up through the ranks of the Soviet military before Ukraine became independent. The call from Bankova Street caught the general when he was getting ready for a long-anticipated break. His wife's birthday, July 24, was always a big event for the family, and Zaluzhny had reserved a venue for a two-day celebration that weekend at a restaurant in Brovary, a suburb of Kyiv. On the eve of the party, he got a call from the president's office, instructing him to drop whatever he was doing and come to Bankova Street straightaway. He did not have the permission of his commander to leave their base. But he soon found himself back in Zelensky's chambers, inside the same rooms where he had briefed the new president two years earlier.

This time, though, the president was joined by the minister of defense and the chief of staff, Andriy Yermak. The conversation went on for hours, far longer than Zaluzhny expected, and it made him nervous. The questions from Zelensky and his team had little to do with his work in the military or his dream of commanding the troops in eastern Ukraine. They were asking bigger, more ambitious questions, touching on the nature of leadership and trust. When they finally finished, the president and his aides shook the general's hand and told him to come back again the next day. Zaluzhny squirmed. The restaurant was booked. The guests were coming. "Screw the guests," he remembers thinking. "How am I going to tell her that it's off?" The wrath of his wife, he told me, seemed more dire than any punishment his political bosses were likely to inflict. "Just tell me what you want," he recalls pleading with the presidential aides, "and we'll figure it out right here."

They considered it for a moment and proposed a compromise. Their team would come to the birthday party and settle things there. Sure enough, on the second day of the celebrations, Zaluzhny was in his shorts with a beer in his hand when another call came in from the presidential administration. They were already nearby, eager to deliver some important news. With the Russians hauling tanks to the border and the Americans warning that Ukraine could soon face a full-scale attack, the president had decided to name Zaluzhny as the nation's top military commander.

The general remembers asking, "What do you mean?" His buzz from the festivities evaporated, and he returned to the party looking as though he had just been punched, he says, "not just below the belt but straight into a knockout." It wasn't the military side of the promotion that scared him. His concern had to do with the public backlash and the media attention. The president was about to dismiss General Khomchak, his top military commander, in the middle of a war scare. As his replacement,

Zaluzhny would be leapfrogging over the heads of several of his commanders, potentially earning enemies inside the General Staff. "A lot of people will be shocked by that," Zaluzhny said. "And that'll come down hard on me and my wife." But that was Zelensky's wish, and he wanted to move fast.

As ever, he trusted his gut when it came to hiring decisions more than he listened to the measured advice and analytics of his aides. The key difference in this case was the weight of responsibility Zaluzhny would need to carry. This was not like appointing a central banker. The new commander of the armed forces would need to take charge at a critical moment in the war. Even amid the summertime lull in hostilities, the officer corps in Ukraine understood that a Russian invasion could start at any time. "Me and my guys immediately began preparing for war," Zaluzhny told me. "We understood what we needed to do, and we were trying to comfort ourselves with the idea that our political leaders also knew what to do. But, in reality, we had our doubts."

As soon as Zaluzhny took charge, Ukraine's military posture became more assertive. Rather than avoiding escalation in the event of Russian shelling or sniper fire in the Donbas, his goal as commander was to dissuade the enemy from attacking in the first place. Ukrainian troops would not only seek to hold their ground against the Russians. Whenever possible, they would begin to advance, Zaluzhny said in his first speech after taking up his post. "The Armed Forces must develop, must improve their tactics." Most important, he said, they must "prepare for conducting offensive actions to liberate the occupied territories."

Zelensky soon made clear that he was fully aligned with the general's new approach. On the morning of August 24, 2021, the president treated Ukrainians to a display of military power like they had not seen in the streets of Kyiv since he took office. Ukraine's arsenal of ballistic missiles, anti-aircraft batteries, multiple-rocket launchers, and tanks rolled through Independence Square that morning to mark the thirtieth anniversary of Ukraine's independence. Troops from the U.S., Canada, and several of their NATO allies took part in the parade. Standing on a stage in the middle of the square, Zelensky craned his neck and clapped as attack helicopters and fighter jets appeared in the sky. Toward the rear of the column came the Bayraktar TB2, an attack drone that Ukraine had purchased from Turkey, its wings spanning four lanes of traffic as it moved along the boulevard on the back of a truck. The spectators cheered. The mood was festive, but the display seemed starkly out of character for Zelensky.

Two years earlier, during the first Independence Day of his tenure, Zelensky had made a point of banning heavy weapons from the streets of Kyiv. The tradition of military parades, he said, "is very pompous and definitely not cheap." Instead he ordered a round of bonuses to be paid to Ukrainian servicemen that year and, on the day of the celebrations, he presided over a "March of Dignity," featuring teachers and nurses walking in formation. The few soldiers invited to take part were asked to walk instead of marching. But by the summer of 2021, the times had changed, and so had the president. "What is a powerful country? A country that dreams ambitiously and acts decisively," he said from the stage. "New tanks and helicopters with Ukrainian blades are being built for the army this year. A powerful country is reviving its naval fleet and naval bases and building corvettes. A powerful country is a country that adopts a missile program for ten years."

Only four months had passed since our trip to the eastern front that spring, but the president had changed. He had given up hope of preserving his hard-won cease-fire with the Russians. Their military proxies in eastern Ukraine had violated the truce dozens of times in those four months, and the peace talks with Putin had fallen apart. By August, Zelensky and his team concluded that the Kremlin would only respond to the language of strength and military power. So Zelensky decided to put that power on display.

"The idea for the parade belongs to the president," Yermak told me. "He was its ideologue." Zelensky now understood that he could not protect Ukraine by agreeing to bend and grant concessions. His chief of staff put the realization this way: "You do not have to build relationships on your willingness to debase yourself." But they also knew the risks involved in taking this approach. "Many people, and especially the Russians, I think, could not get over that parade," Yermak said. "It was a demonstration of national greatness, and, in my view, it was one of the reasons why they could not forgive us in the end."

Ukraine's new military leadership soon gave the Russians another reason to worry. When the parade was over, all those weapons systems were not just sent back to their bases and stored away. General Zaluzhny had plans to use them. Soon after taking up his post, he gave officers on the ground the freedom to return fire "with any available weapons" if they came under attack. They no longer had to request permission from senior commanders or fill out any "unnecessary" paperwork to document what they had done. "Maybe I'll get criticized for that," Zaluzhny said later, when we discussed these decisions. "But yes, I really did give the orders, in the war zone: shoot to kill," he told me. "This was also part of the plan, because we needed to knock down their desire to attack. We needed to inflict losses, not only because we wanted to save the lives of our soldiers. We also needed to show our teeth, because the enemy did not abide by the terms of any cease-fire."

Under these new directives, Ukrainian forces would not need to hesitate the way they did during the battle at Shumy and other flare-ups along the front line. They could return fire at will. "It is possible and necessary to cause death to the enemies," Zaluzhny said at a closed-door briefing at the end of September 2021, when he announced this new order of battle. The next day, President Zelensky followed up with an announcement that infuriated the Russians. After months of negotiations, he had agreed to a deal not only to buy more drones from Turkey, but to build a factory in Ukraine that would manufacture them. Never before had a NATO member state approved such a deal with the Ukrainians. The drone's inventor—incidentally, the son-in-law of Turkish president Recep Tayyip Erdoğan—traveled to Kyiv to sign the deal on September 29. "We have been waiting for this moment for a long time," Zelensky said at the signing ceremony in his office. "It's a big, real step forward."

By then the drone had earned its reputation as a tank killer. During a brief war in 2020, the armed forces of Azerbaijan had used their fleet of Bayraktars to crush the army of Armenia, a Russian ally, in little over a month. Although Russia could outgun Ukraine in other forms of military tech, it had no analogue to the Bayraktar in its arsenal. (Much later, in the midst of the invasion, Putin would need to ask the Iranians to sell him attack drones.) Zaluzhny was an avid supporter of these weapons. Only a few weeks before he took charge of the armed forces, Ukraine had signaled that it would keep its Bayraktars in storage and use them only to defend against a "large-scale" Russian attack. The new commander was quick to change that approach. In the fall, under General Zaluzhny, the Bayraktar flew its first combat mission over the battlefields of eastern Ukraine.

On October 26, 2021, Russian-backed separatists shelled a Ukrainian position near the front, killing at least one soldier—the latest in an escalating pattern of Russian cease-fire violations. This time, Ukraine sent up one of its Bayraktar drones and dropped a twenty-two-kilogram bomb on the Russian artillery position, destroying it. An aerial video from the drone, released by the Armed Forces of Ukraine, showed several fighters running and stumbling away from wreckage of their howitzer. The Kremlin took notice. The arrival of the Bayraktars signaled to Putin that his military advantage over Ukraine would erode over time, giving him a finite window of opportunity to launch a swift and decisive attack. "Our fears are unfortunately being realized," Putin's spokesman said in response to the Bayraktar's appearance over eastern Ukraine. The Russian Air Force scrambled jets to defend Moscow's separatist proxies in that area, an unusual display of firepower. A few days later, when Zelensky was asked about the incident, he made clear it was not a case of some rogue commander overstepping the bounds of his authority. "It is in this format that Ukraine will continue to operate," the president said. "When the Ukrainian army feels the need to defend its land, it does so. And it will further act under this principle."

❖

At the start of November, within days of the Bayraktar's debut in combat over eastern Ukraine, the Americans informed Zelensky that Russia was again preparing to invade. The warnings this time were surprisingly detailed, and the messengers more adamant than they had been in the spring. The U.S. claimed the invasion would start in January 2022 with a certainty of between 75 and 80 percent. That gave the Ukrainians about two months to prepare.

Zelensky's top security advisers soon found their schedules filling up with visits from U.S. diplomats and intelligence officials. At the headquarters of the National Security and Defense Council, Oleksiy Danilov would offer them coffee in his sunny office and listen to them predict Ukraine's demise. "They were telling us that we would be conquered in four to five days, that there would be concentration camps," Danilov told me. "And the entire political leadership would be killed." Once, he went to meet Kristina Kvien, the most senior diplomat at the U.S. embassy in Kyiv, who looked at him like a man condemned to death. "She felt so sorry for me," Danilov recalled. He was touched but also offended, and he tried his best to convince the Americans that Ukraine would hold its ground. Kvien countered that Zelensky and his team were in mortal danger. "None of them believed it," she later told me. "Not even the ones who pretended to believe it to my face." The usual response from Zelensky's administration, she said, was that the Russians were using the threat of force to squeeze concessions out of the U.S. and its allies. "They said we were being fooled. The Russians were fooling us."

To back up their predictions, the Americans began to share a variety of intelligence with Zelensky, including intercepted phone calls and messages in which the Russians appeared to discuss their plans. Satellite images showed entire Russian armies gathered along the border. They had come from all over Russia, linking up with elite troops and tank formations dispatched from the Moscow region. They had set up field hospitals, warehoused provisions, even brought supplies of refrigerated blood. In classified briefings, the Americans also referred to a high-level source inside Russia. The source, they said, had provided the U.S. with details of Putin's plan to invade. The identity of this apparent mole was kept confidential, but the U.S. officials offered some hints. "Remember Tom Clancy's *Cardinal of the Kremlin*," one of Zelensky's top foreign policy advisers said in describing this source to me at the time.* "The ultimate spy. The ultimate insider. It's that guy."

Though they did not believe the American intelligence, Zelensky and his team were not inclined to dismiss it outright. "Every crisis is an opportunity," said the foreign policy adviser, who was closely involved in talks with the Americans. Ukraine, he noted, had been trying to get more of the West's support against Russia for years. If the Americans now wanted to start paying attention, the upside was obvious: "Ukraine could get more aid," he said. "Ukraine could get more assistance."

---

* In the novel, published in 1988 as a sequel to *The Hunt for Red October*, CIA analyst Jack Ryan tries to save the agency's most valuable source inside the Soviet Ministry of Defense, a war hero code-named Cardinal, who had been passing military and political intelligence to the Americans for decades.

To keep the talks going, Zelensky dispatched his chief of staff to Washington in early November to better understand what the Americans were putting on the table. At the White House, Yermak was due to meet with Jake Sullivan, the national security adviser to President Biden. His expectations were low. A few years younger than Yermak, Sullivan was polished, stiff, and not known for his deep interest in Ukraine or Russia. His top priority in foreign affairs was China, followed by Iran and Afghanistan. (In the words of one frustrated U.S. diplomat in Kyiv, the National Security Council under Sullivan "didn't give a fuck about Ukraine" when Biden took office.)

"I was prepared for a rather dry, tough conversation, and knew it was very important to make an impression," Yermak told me. He and Sullivan seemed to get along. It was clear the Americans wanted to help. "We spoke the same language," Yermak said. After that meeting on November 10, they started texting and calling each other, opening a direct line from the White House to Bankova Street that would prove invaluable to Zelensky in the months that followed. "We can tell each other anything," Yermak would later gush about Sullivan during one of our interviews. "We can call each other at any time of day or night."

About a week later, Zelensky sent another delegation to Washington to get into the details of weapons supplies. It was led by the newly appointed minister of defense, Oleksiy Reznikov, who had been on the job for less than two weeks at the time. A highly regarded lawyer, he had been Zelensky's top negotiator with the Russians for years, and he knew the conflict inside out. But, apart from his service in the Soviet Air Force back in the 1980s, he had little experience in the military. The trip to Washington was organized in such haste that Reznikov had no time to study the types of weapons Ukraine needed. "I didn't know the difference between a 155 caliber and a 152," he admitted, referring to different kinds of artillery shells.

At his meetings with U.S. Defense Secretary Lloyd Austin and other top officials, Reznikov urged the Americans not to exaggerate the threat. Putin, he said, was convinced that the people of eastern Ukraine sympathized with Russia and would greet Russian troops as liberators. The idea that Putin might bomb Kyiv made no sense to Reznikov and other senior officials on Zelensky's team. "I was convinced," the defense minister told me, that Putin "would not bomb Russian Orthodox Churches" in Ukraine. When the Americans showed Reznikov the range of Russian troops arrayed along the borders—well over one hundred thousand by that point, the middle of November 2021—the defense minister did not dispute that it looked serious. But Putin had sent the same force to Ukraine's borders in the spring, just in time for Easter. "And what did Putin get?" Reznikov asked. "He got two phone calls with Biden and a personal meeting in Geneva." The Kremlin's most likely motive this time was the same: to get more concessions from the Americans, more discussions about the future of Europe, more prestigious summits with the leaders of the free world. "As I said then, Putin wanted to dance, but not with us," Reznikov explained. "The ones on his dance card were the White House, Paris, Berlin, and London."

Still, if the U.S. was so convinced of an imminent Russian invasion, then the next move seemed obvious to Reznikov: start flooding weapons into Ukraine. For a start, the military needed shoulder-fired rockets that could kill tanks and shoot down planes and helicopters. Citing legal restrictions and other red tape, the Americans told him it wasn't possible. But Reznikov sensed there was a deeper reason. He called it "the Afghan syndrome." Only three months earlier, the U.S. had pulled all its forces out of Afghanistan after two decades of war. Trillions of dollars from U.S. taxpayers had been spent on arming and training the Afghan military to prevent the Taliban from returning to power. As soon as the Americans left, the military collapsed.

Images of Taliban fighters strolling through U.S. bases and arming themselves with U.S.-supplied weapons marked a low point for U.S. policy in the region. The U.S. Department of Defense later estimated that over $7 billion in U.S.-funded equipment wound up in the hands of the Taliban, including vast numbers of weapons, vehicles, and aircraft. The Biden administration did not want to risk a similar scenario with the Russians in Ukraine. And it wasn't just the Americans, Reznikov said. "The West was certain that Ukraine would lose the opening phase of the war in seventy-two hours."

❖

In early December, Joe Biden tried to defuse the crisis with another presidential phone call. It worked the last time, in the middle of spring, when the prospect of a summit with the Americans encouraged Putin to pull his troops away from the border for a while. Biden now made a fresh offer to hear out Russia's "strategic concerns" about security in Europe, opening the door for a round of talks that might delay the invasion if not prevent it. He even promised to discuss the future of the NATO alliance, a topic the U.S. had long preferred to address only among member states.

The response from Russian diplomats left no room for serious negotiations. Not only did they demand a written guarantee from the U.S. that Ukraine would never join NATO, they also told the U.S. to withdraw its military forces from Eastern Europe, retreating to positions they held before Putin took power. As the lead Russian envoy put it, "NATO needs to pack up its stuff and get back to where it was in 1997." The demands were so outrageous that the Americans could not even pretend to take them seriously. They rejected Putin's agenda out of hand. Instead of scheduling another presidential summit, the U.S. threatened a raft of sanctions that would cut much of the Russian economy off from the rest of the world. "The gradualism of the past is out," said one senior official from the Biden administration. "And this time we'll start at the top of the escalation ladder and stay there."

The threat of sanctions rippled through the global economy that winter, as stock markets adjusted to the risk of Russia, the world's largest exporter of oil and the second largest exporter of natural gas, launching a catastrophic war. The price of oil climbed to a seven-year high in the lead-up to the invasion, forcing Biden to reach for strategic fuel reserves to "provide relief at the gas pump" for Americans. The value of Ukraine's currency fell sharply as capital fled and investors pulled out. The president's approval ratings also continued to slide, prompting his aides to focus more of their attention on domestic problems. "Energy prices, the economy, inflation, all of that will be bad," one of them told me over dinner in Kyiv at the time. "Those are the immediate risks right now." The risk of an invasion went unmentioned in this list.

While downplaying the threat from Russia, Zelensky ramped up his attacks against political opponents at home. In December, authorities in Kyiv filed charges of treason against Petro Poroshenko, accusing the former president of doing business with Donbas separatists at the start of the war in 2014 and 2015. Poroshenko said the case was an act of political persecution, and nearly half of Ukrainians agreed with him, according to a survey taken around that time. Western officials also voiced concerns about the case, urging Zelensky not to deepen political divisions inside Ukraine when, just outside its borders, he faced a Russian force of over 150,000 troops. But he refused to listen. When a reporter asked Zelensky about the case against Poroshenko, the president accused him and other wealthy politicians of staging protests against the government by paying poor people to take to the streets. "We see all this," Zelensky insisted. "Our country is not blind, and we are starting to deal with this, step by step."

By the end of January, the U.S. took steps to guard the eastern flank of NATO in anticipation of the Russian attack, placing over 8,500 troops on high alert in Eastern Europe, prepared to deploy alongside naval ships and warplanes. The Department of State ordered nonessential staff and family members to leave the U.S. embassy in Kyiv. Most European diplomats quickly followed. Zelensky took it hard. "This ain't the *Titanic*," he told reporters. From satellite images, he said, it was not possible to tell what Russia might do with the troops surrounding Ukraine. Some of their tents, he said, appeared to be empty. "It's psychological," he said of the Russians. "They are trying to build up psychological pressure."

CHAPTER 16

THE BLIZZARD

AT NINE A.M. ON FEBRUARY 12, A COLD AND CLOUDY SATURDAY IN KYIV, VALERY ZALU-zhny called his subordinates to a meeting at the headquarters of the General Staff. They had spent the last few days overseeing an ambitious set of military exercises, known as Blizzard-2022, which were then playing out around the country. Many thousands of Ukrainian troops were involved in the drills, and their performance had been disappointing. Basic maneuvers meant to simulate a Russian attack had exposed deep flaws in Ukraine's defenses, and, in Zaluzhny's view, the commanders had failed to address them. His response was out of character: "I spent an hour yelling." The men seated around the table were mostly older and more experienced than Zaluzhny, and he did not have a reputation for losing his cool, much less in the company of senior officers. "But that time I lost it," he told me. "These were respected people, generals. And I explained to them that if they can't pull this off, the consequences will not only cost us our lives, but also our country."

For Zaluzhny, the exercises were a centerpiece of Ukraine's defensive strategy, its best chance of survival. Their stated purpose, as described in a bland statement on the Facebook page of the General Staff, was to "acquire and expand the operational capabilities" of various branches of Ukraine's armed forces. The statement suggested that these exercises had long been planned, just the latest of many drills and maneuvers the military had undertaken in the past year. In reality, Zaluzhny told me, the exercises were a cover story, intended to hide Ukraine's preparations for war.

As part of the drills, the military began moving troops and weapons out of their bases and sending them on tours around the country. They included aircraft, tanks, and armored vehicles, as well as the anti-aircraft batteries Ukraine would soon need to defend its skies. "We were constantly cycling them around," Zaluzhny said. At the start of February, there were roughly 110,000 military personnel deployed in Ukraine. One-third were stationed permanently at the front lines in the east, where the invasion seemed most likely to start. But the rest of them—around sixty-five thousand troops in total—had been ordered to pack up, leave their garrisons, and start running drills in preparation for a Russian attack. The commander expected it to start at any time. The Russians had already imposed a naval blockade on Ukrainian ports in the Black Sea, and at least thirty thousand of their troops were training in Belarus, around one hundred miles north of Kyiv. "There's no mistaking the smell of war," the general said, "and it was already in the air, believe me."

But, even then, President Zelensky fastidiously held his nose, more worried about the economic impact of the war scare than the risk of Russian bombardment. In their frequent phone calls and meetings around that time, the military leadership urged Zelensky and his aides to prepare more intently for a full-scale war. "The biggest problem was that we lacked strategic reserves of ammunition, reserves of fuel, uniforms, and body armor," Zaluzhny told me. The president agreed to help fill those gaps as long as they could do so quietly, without provoking the Russians or scaring the public. Through diplomatic channels, they convinced the U.S. and its allies to send Ukraine a large cache of weapons that had been stored in Bulgaria and intended for the army in Afghanistan. "This ammo was left without a home" after the Taliban took over Kabul in August 2021, "and we pounced on it," the general said. "All credit to the president, because he heard me out, and by some enormous miracle we managed to get the Afghan cache." Arriving in planeloads in the middle of February, the arms were a godsend, amounting to an estimated 1,300 tons of equipment from the U.S. alone. The U.K. also stepped up to provide 2,000 anti-tank missiles. Taken together, the West sent around $1.5 billion in military aid in the run-up to the invasion, helping to give Ukraine a fighting chance.

But even as they pleaded for these weapons and celebrated their arrival, Zelensky and his government continued to dismiss the Russian threat. "Don't worry, sleep well," Oleksiy Reznikov, the minister of defense, said in a speech to parliament at the end of January. "No need to have your bags packed." After a ski vacation that week to the Carpathian mountains, Zelensky put out a soothing video message for which he would later be ridiculed. "Take a breath, calm down," he said in the clip. "Don't wind yourselves up." Come spring, Zelensky promised, Ukrainians would all be grilling shashlik in their gardens like they do every year. A few days later, the state tourism board launched a new campaign slogan: "Keep Calm and Visit Ukraine."

At a meeting with top military and security officers around that time, one of Zelensky's aides yelled at them to stop freaking people out with their predictions of invasion. The outburst put Ukraine's armed forces in an awkward spot. The office of the president had placed what General Zaluzhny would later describe to me as "political barriers" around the military's efforts to prepare. The Armed Forces of Ukraine could not mobilize for a Russian invasion without alarming investors and piling more strain on the economy. They could not act on the dire warnings of U.S. intelligence while Zelensky, their supreme commander in chief, poured cold water on these same warnings. "We couldn't even allow ourselves to move a column of armored vehicles in broad daylight. We did it by cover of night," Zaluzhny told me. "In that political situation, my men and I were doing everything possible." Some of their preparations went outside the political parameters Zelensky had imposed. As the general put it, "We were finding loopholes."

The most important loophole was Blizzard-2022, which gave the military an excuse to move forces into position. As the troops left their bases on February 8, it became much easier for Zaluzhny and the other generals to assess their vulnerabilities. "We understood which indicators were really flashing red," he said. "If the Russians had attacked us at that time, the outcome would have been very different." After their meeting with Zaluzhny four days later, the generals rushed to relocate and camouflage a lot of the country's military hardware, making it more difficult for the Russians to strike from the air in the opening hours of the invasion. They also tried to ensure that any bombs dropped on Ukrainian garrisons would not find the troops asleep in their beds.

No less valuable to Ukraine's defense was the psychological effect the drills had on the soldiers involved. For weeks, virtually all of Ukraine's armed forces trained for a possible attack, including the worst-case scenario of a full-scale invasion. "They were psyching themselves up," said Denys Monastyrsky, the minister of internal affairs, who oversaw one of the most effective branches of Ukraine's armed forces: the National Guard. As the preparations played out, the General Staff kept the president informed about the exercises. Zelensky even flew to the city of Rivne, in western Ukraine, on February 16—nine days before the invasion—to observe how Blizzard-2022 was playing out. Zaluzhny gave the president a tour of the training base that morning and showed him some of the weapons that the West had been providing to Ukraine, including anti-tank and anti-aircraft systems.

But when it came to the details of his strategy, Zaluzhny did not share everything with the president and his aides. The risk of a leak worried him. "I was afraid that we would lose the element of surprise," Zaluzhny told me. "We needed the enemy to think we are all sitting in our usual bases, smoking grass, watching TV, and posting on Facebook." It was impossible to know how deeply Russian spies had infiltrated the military and the political leadership. If they learned where the Ukrainian troops and hardware had been placed outside their bases, there was no fallback option, no way to protect them from a hail of missile strikes. "I knew that I only had one shot," Zaluzhny said. "It was my only chance and, while we were getting ready, I kept it close to the chest."

As the Blizzard drills played out, he stayed in close touch with his American counterpart, General Mark Milley. The two men had gotten to know each other well that winter, and Zaluzhny admired the American for his toughness and experience. Like the rest of the Biden administration, Milley had been urging the Ukrainians to call up their military reserves and mobilize all available forces. He also recommended a strategy that harked back to European wars of a previous era: start digging trenches and laying down minefields, the more the better.

Zaluzhny tried to explain the political sensitivity of that approach. Trenches and fortifications are difficult to hide, and a mass mobilization of troops would be sure to drive an exodus of civilians, businesses, and anyone looking to dodge the draft. "He kept telling me that there is going to be a war, that there are going to be missile strikes, and he wanted me to take certain measures," Zaluzhny recalls. "But I couldn't, because I'm just the commander in chief of the armed forces. Above me is the supreme commander"—President Zelensky—"and many questions were tied up with him."

As the argument went back and forth, Milley asked to see the plan that Zaluzhny had concocted. "I tried to explain the strategy to him, but then I got scared: What if I'm telling him things that I'd better not say?" He was afraid the strategy might leak, either to the Russians or the Ukrainian public. He was also afraid it would get back around to Zelensky. Instead of sending the real details of his strategy to Milley, Zaluzhny decided to show him a fake one. "I couldn't come up with a better idea." He would later feel bad about deceiving his most important ally. When the war ends, he said, Milley would have every right to "bend me over his knee and give me a fatherly spanking."

❖

Early in the morning of February 19, Zelensky boarded the presidential jet for what would be his last foreign trip in many months. Leaving Ukraine was not an easy decision under the circumstances. Close to two hundred thousand Russian troops now stood at the border, and the flow of warnings about their plans had never been more dire. By going abroad, Zelensky risked giving the Russians an immediate advantage. Their propaganda would claim the president had fled in the event of an all-out war. Their jets could block him from returning, and their proxies in Kyiv, led by Viktor Medvedchuk, could quickly move to fill the power vacuum. Worse yet, officials throughout the government would feel far less pressure to remain at their posts at the start of an invasion if their president was not around.

But the occasion seemed worth the risk to Zelensky. In southern Germany, political and military leaders from around the world were gathering that weekend for the Munich Security Conference, the favored venue for members of NATO to discuss the threats they saw in the world, and to invite their adversaries for some spirited debate about the dangers they saw in each other. During the last three decades of the Cold War, it had been the premier venue for East and West to stare each other down and, on occasion, hear each other out. This was the summit where I had seen Zelensky's predecessor, Petro Poroshenko, plead for Western support in 2018, during a speech he delivered to a mostly empty hall.

It was also the venue Vladimir Putin had chosen in 2007 to declare the start of a new cold war. "NATO has put its frontline forces on our borders," the Russian leader told the Munich conference at the time, addressing a crowd where Senator John McCain, who was then about a year away from his run for the U.S. presidency, sat in the front row. From

Russia's perspective, Putin said, the expansion of NATO into Eastern Europe, through the admission of Poland, the Baltic States, and other onetime satellites of Moscow, "represents a serious provocation . . . And we have the right to ask: Against whom is this expansion intended?"

From his perspective, the collapse of the Soviet Union had allowed the rise of the global order dominated by the Americans, a system where there is only "one center of authority, one center of force, one center of decision-making. It is a world in which there is one master, one sovereign." That master and its allies felt empowered to use force against their adversaries and to get away with it, Putin said, referring not only to the wars in Iraq and Afghanistan but to the NATO bombing campaign to stop the Serbs in Yugoslavia, Russia's allies, from committing genocide in Kosovo in 1999. "Today we are witnessing an almost uncontained hyper-use of force—military force—in international relations, force that is plunging the world into an abyss of permanent conflicts," Putin said. "And of course this is extremely dangerous. It results in the fact that no one feels safe. I want to emphasize this—no one feels safe!"

It did not make Putin feel any safer when, the following spring, at a summit in Romania, the leaders of NATO promised someday to grant membership to Ukraine and Georgia. "These countries will become members of NATO," the alliance said in a formal declaration in April 2008. Four months later, Russia invaded Georgia, bringing its tanks right up to the capital, Tbilisi, and occupying about a fifth of Georgia's territory. It was the first foreign war of Putin's tenure, and it did not result in any serious consequences for his regime. He warned the West in Munich that he was tired of NATO expansion, and the war in Georgia showed that he was willing to challenge it with military force.

Fifteen years later, on the eve of another Russian invasion, it was Zelensky's turn to address the gathering in Munich, and he had trouble finding the words. Even on the plane, as he flew over Europe in his An-148, the president and his aides struggled to craft a speech that could inspire the West to stop Russia from sending its tanks across the border. "We were making corrections," recalled Reznikov, the defense minister. "Weighing every word."

Before delivering the speech that afternoon, Zelensky had to meet with the American delegation, which was headed that year by Vice President Kamala Harris. Her session with the Ukrainians seemed awkward from the start. The Bayerischer Hof hotel, which has hosted the conference since its inception in 1963, has no shortage of pleasant if outdated rooms where allies would normally sit and talk. Zelensky's meeting with Harris, however, took place around a formal negotiating table, with the two sides facing off. In contrast to Zelensky's other dates in Munich, the Americans also avoided shaking hands and insisted on wearing masks, a pandemic protocol that added to the sense of distance between them. According to the officials who sat on either side of President Zelensky, the Americans declared that the invasion was inevitable, as though U.S. intelligence agencies had gazed into the future and prophesied it thus. It was not the first time Zelensky had heard this warning; he had spoken by phone with President Biden only a few days before. Stories in the U.S. media were full of White House sources suggesting the Russian assault was set to begin with an "imminent" wave of cyber attacks, a barrage of missiles and aerial bombardment. President Biden, on a call with European allies, was even reported to have named a specific date for the invasion: February 16.* That date had come and gone. But the American warnings had not abated. Zelensky's answer to Vice President Harris was well rehearsed by the time they sat down in Munich on February 19. The threat of Russian aggression had been around since the annexation of Crimea in 2014, and he was glad the Americans had finally recognized it. "Thank God you've now seen the same thing we see," Zelensky told her. "So let's respond to it together."

The Ukrainians suggested, for a start, a set of sanctions strong enough to make Putin reconsider his decision to invade. The Americans could close their ports to Russian ships. They could impose an embargo on Russian oil and gas and urge the Europeans to do the same. They could short-circuit the Russian banking system. Apart from that, Zelensky asked for specific weapons, including Stinger and Javelin missiles, warplanes, and anti-aircraft batteries, at least enough of them to protect Ukraine's nuclear power plants from aerial bombardment. None of these proposals seemed acceptable to Harris. The U.S. could not impose sanc-

---

* After a call with Biden to discuss these forecasts, Zelensky decided to make light of them. He urged Ukrainians to mark the date by hanging flags out of their windows and singing the national anthem in unison at ten o'clock that morning. "They tell us February 16 will be the day of the attack," he said in a televised address to the nation. "We will make it the Day of Unity."

tions, she said, because the punishment could only come after the crime. She also appeared eager for Zelensky to acknowledge that the full-scale invasion was coming. Zelensky asked her: "What will that give you? If I acknowledge it here in this conversation, will you impose sanctions?" Reznikov recalls the president asking this several times throughout the meeting, but he never got a clear reply.

"It's interesting," the defense minister later told me. "Why did they need us to say this? If we had told them, 'Yes, he will attack,' then what? Should we surrender? Or were they preparing us to say: 'Okay, we understand that [Putin] will attack. We understand that we will not win.' That means there is a reason to capitulate, to sign another set of peace accords like we did in Minsk. Then we concede to some more of the Kremlin's demands. The world avoids a hot phase of the war." Bitterly, he added: "Then everybody gets a gold star. Everybody is a wonderful peacemaker."

Zelensky and his team were not ready to follow that script. They were not going to capitulate, certainly not without a fight. But as their day in Munich wore on, they became convinced that some of their Western allies wanted them to face the certainty of Ukraine's defeat. It was, in their view, a first step to accepting peace on Putin's terms. Olaf Scholz, the German chancellor, had visited Moscow two days before the start of the Munich summit for another round of talks with Putin. He would have been glad to mediate some kind of deal. The Ukrainians would need to make concessions. They would likely need to give up hopes of joining NATO, and Zelensky was prepared to discuss a compromise on that particular point. He understood that Ukraine had no real chance of joining NATO anytime soon. But he was not ready to give up Ukraine's claim to the land that Russia had already occupied.

On the sidelines of the Munich conference, several Western leaders urged Zelensky not to return home that day, and instead to begin the process of forming a government in exile. The president responded to one such offer with a smile: "I had breakfast in Kyiv," he said. "And I'll have dinner there." Andriy Sybiha, who witnessed the exchange, did not believe the pressure to leave Kyiv was malicious. It came from some of Ukraine's closest and strongest allies, and its intention was not to strengthen Russia's chances of taking Ukraine without a fight. "It was about the importance of the president in this struggle with the enemy," Sybiha told me. "The survival of the state as embodied in the president."

Still, the offer to flee added to Zelensky's impression in Munich that even his closest allies had written him off, and the frustration showed when he took the podium that afternoon. It reminded me of his condition in November 2019, on the eve of his first talks with Putin, when he told me he could not trust any of his allies in the West. Back then, the loneliness of his position pained him. Now it seemed to anger him. "It was here, fifteen years ago, that Russia announced its intention to challenge global security," he said. "What was the world's response? Appeasement." NATO had failed to keep its promise to put Ukraine on a path to membership. "We are told the door is open. But so far outsiders are not allowed inside. If not all members of the alliance want us, or if all members don't want us, then tell us honestly. Open doors are good, but we need open answers, not years of open questions."

He ended his speech by thanking the leaders who stepped up for Ukraine and showed genuine support. Among the allies he meant, according to his aides, was Boris Johnson, whom Zelensky also met during his trip to Munich. But he did not name Johnson in his speech. "I'm not calling you by name," he said. "I don't want some other countries to feel ashamed. But this is their business, their karma. And this will be on their conscience."

What did Zelensky imagine the attack would look like? Would it be led by paramilitaries, like in the Donbas in 2014? Would there be Russian special forces, like in Crimea, with no insignia on their uniforms? Or, like in Syria, would the Russian campaign be waged from the air, with indiscriminate bombing of civilians? Would Putin send tanks across the border, and if so, how far would they go? All the way to the edge of the capital, as they did in Georgia in 2008? Or would they stick to the borderlands in the east and the south?

Zelensky didn't know. He wasn't even sure what his allies would consider an invasion, as opposed to, say, another skirmish somewhere at the edge of Europe. In an offhand remark in the middle of January, President Biden suggested that Russia would only be held accountable if the scale of its attack were big enough. "It's one thing if it's a minor incursion," he said, "and then we end up having to fight about what to do and not to do." The remark appeared to leave Russia some room to scale back its ambitions, to avoid the full package of Western sanctions by showing some restraint. Zelensky did not appreciate that strategy. There is no such thing, he said, as a minor incursion. "Just as there are no minor casualties and little grief from the loss of loved ones."

In truth, Zelensky wanted to have it both ways. He was betting on a minor incursion and hoping it would provoke a major response from the West. The scenario at the front of his mind was a Russian push from the east, where he believed Putin might try to seize more territory. That is where the Kremlin still had a chance of finding allies and sympathizers. The city of Kharkiv in northeastern Ukraine was particularly vulnerable. Its suburbs touch the Russian border, and its historical center is wide open to Russian artillery fire, which could pummel the city without even crossing into Ukraine. In passing, during an interview with the *Washington Post* in January, Zelensky even acknowledged that Kharkiv, the second-biggest city in the country, "could be occupied." This was about as close as he came to leveling with the public.

When he returned from Munich on February 19, his statements betrayed nothing of the dangers he had discussed with Western leaders. He did not acknowledge any serious threat of aerial bombardment or the possible encirclement of Kyiv. He knew the West had sent him home with nothing—no package of sanctions, no security guarantees—that might stop or even delay an invasion on any scale. And so, Zelensky waited, carrying on with a more or less normal agenda in the days before the invasion began. He honored the victims of the 2014 massacre of protestors on Independence Square. He had a call with the leader of Slovenia. The president of Estonia came to visit, and Zelensky urged him to invest in Ukraine's IT sector.

Two days after Zelensky's trip to Munich, Putin delivered an hourlong speech that sounded like a declaration of war. He accused Ukraine of committing torture, genocide, and other crimes against the people of the Donbas. He claimed that Ukraine had nuclear ambitions that posed a direct threat to Russia. He denied the viability and even the existence of Ukraine as an independent state. And he returned to the theme of NATO expansion, rehashing the arguments he had first presented in Munich a decade and a half before. "They completely ignore our concerns, protests and warnings," he said of the alliance. "They spit on them and do whatever they want." But, at the end of the diatribe, Putin stopped short of declaring war. He announced that Russia would recognize the breakaway regions of eastern Ukraine, the so-called People's Republics of Donetsk and Luhansk, as independent states. It was a bureaucratic half measure, and it offered some room for Zelensky to hope that the gravest predictions had been wrong. Putin was laying a claim to regions of Ukraine that Russia had partly controlled for eight years. He was not explicitly setting his sights on Kyiv or anything outside the Donbas. But U.S. officials had no illusions about Putin's true intentions.

Ukraine's top diplomat, Dmytro Kuleba, happened to be in Washington that day, and President Biden invited him to the Oval Office after they had both seen the news of Putin's speech. "He was comforting me," Kuleba later told me. "It's like when you see someone who has cancer, the last stage of cancer, and you know the person is doomed, but you really sympathize with him, and try to help him, and you do your best while knowing that nothing is going to help. That was basically the atmosphere in the meeting." Kuleba was deeply moved, but also terrified. He understood the war was about to begin, and he asked for Biden's advice, not as a diplomat but as a father. Would it make sense for Kuleba to evacuate his children? Or was it his duty as a government official to lead by example and keep his family in Kyiv? Biden placed a hand on his shoulder and answered, "Be a good father." That night, as he rushed back home to Ukraine, Kuleba called his family and told them to leave the capital right away.

On Bankova Street, Zelensky and his aides were meanwhile huddled in his office, preparing their response to Putin's speech. It aired after midnight on February 22, once again seeking to lull the people of Ukraine back to a sense of security. "There is no reason for you to have a sleepless night," the president said in a televised address to the nation. "We will never hide the truth from you. As soon as we see a change in the situation, as soon as we see an increase in risks, you will know it." With the release of that statement, Ukraine and its leader had about twenty-four hours left to prepare. Months later, they would debate what could have been done in that time. How many orphanages or retirement homes could have been evacuated near the borders with Russia. How much food, fuel, and other supplies could have been stockpiled. How many lives could have been saved. But, in the moment, Zelensky and his team believed that panic posed the greater danger. "If we sow chaos among people before the invasion," he said, "the Russians will devour us." Millions of people would flee. The economy would collapse. The country would be hollowed out, with no one left to defend it from the enemy. Those were the fears that drove Zelensky in the days before the bombs began to fall. Until the very end he thought the attack would be limited in scale, certainly not as catastrophic as the Americans predicted. And he continued to imagine that the bigger threat to Ukraine's survival was an exodus of people and capital. Only on the eve of the invasion, at around noon on February 23, the president and his security council met to declare a state of emergency around the country. It would allow the authorities to conduct searches, limit transport, tighten security around critical infrastructure, and take other wartime precautions. But, even then, the message to citizens was not to worry. "These are preventative measures so that the country remains calm and the economy works," Oleksiy Danilov said in announcing the state of emergency.

That evening, the last major item on the president's agenda was a meeting with Ukraine's wealthiest businessmen, with whom Zelensky had been at war for over a year. He had recently signed a law to strip the oligarchs of their power, curtailing their ability to own media, hold public office, and influence politics. Now, seated around a vast table with some of the men he suspected of treachery and treason, the president tried to call a truce. "The main point was not to fuel the atmosphere of panic," said one of Zelensky's closest aides, Iryna Pobedonostseva, who attended the meeting. "You should all be here," she recalls the president telling them. "Anyone who is not just earning money in this country but wants to live here, to continue employing hundreds of thousands of people, you need to be here, because those people are watching you."

Danilov and other members of the security council then gave the oligarchs an update on the Russian threat. It was serious, they said, but manageable, because Russia would not resort to an all-out invasion. "We were told with great confidence that it won't happen, don't worry, don't fret," metals tycoon Serhiy Taruta told me afterward. But many of the businessmen still had plenty of connections in Russia. They were getting information from their Russian sources that, as Taruta put it, "did not match the official position here." It was already dark when the meeting adjourned, and the oligarchs filed out to their cars on Bankova Street, their chauffeurs running the engines in the cold. Zelensky, his official agenda finished for the day, went back upstairs to his office with Yermak, his chief of staff, and drafted a speech to the nation.

Throughout the evening, fresh intelligence arrived from the U.S. and other allies, warning that an invasion would start that night. Hackers had taken down government websites. From the east, Russian military hardware was moving into the occupied parts of the Donbas, where separatist leaders had appealed to Putin to defend them. For Zelensky and his staff, the Russian move into those territories marked the formal start of the invasion, though they still held out hope the Russians would not go farther than those borderlands, at least not yet. Sitting at his desk, the president ordered his protocol office to connect him to the Kremlin. He wanted to try one last time to speak to Putin. But the call was ignored, said Yermak, who was by his side. "There was no answer on the other end."

Only then, with all options for peace exhausted, Zelensky shifted away from his attempts to calm the public. He wanted to appeal directly to the Russian people, and his speech to them was not coated in the reassurances he had been feeding to his own citizens. It went live soon after midnight. "Between us," he said, speaking in Russian, "there are more than two thousand kilometers of common borders, where your troops are standing today, almost two hundred thousand of them, and thousands of military vehicles. Your leadership has ordered them to advance on the territory of another country. And that step could be the start of a Great War on the European continent."

"You are told that these flames will bring freedom to the people of Ukraine. But the people of Ukraine are already free," Zelensky said. "You are told that we are Nazis. But could there be support for Nazism among a people who gave more than eight million lives for the victory against Nazism? How could I be a Nazi? Put that question to my grandpa, who fought the whole war as an infantryman in the Soviet army, and died a colonel in an independent Ukraine.

"We know for sure: we don't want war. Not a cold war or a hot war or a hybrid war. But, if we are under attack, if someone tries to take our country, our freedom, our lives and the lives of our children, we will defend ourselves." If the Russians invade, Zelensky told them, "you will see our faces, not our backs."

Part IV

CHAPTER 17

BATTLE OF THE DONBAS

THE RUSSIAN SOLDIER LAY DEAD NEAR THE VILLAGE OF MOSHCHUN, HIS BODY MORE OR less intact, not burned alive or ripped apart by an exploding shell like so many of the other men who fell while trying to capture Kyiv. From the markings on his uniform, the Ukrainian troops who found his corpse on the second or third day of the invasion could tell he belonged to one of Russia's elite commando units. Among his possessions they found a set of maps, creased and dirty but still legible enough to reveal a lot about his mission in Ukraine. He came from unit 07264, part of the 76th Guards Air Assault Division, based in the city of Pskov, in western Russia. Hundreds of its men took part in the initial assault on the airport in Hostomel, at the western edge of Kyiv. The map was labeled "Secret," and it bore a handwritten date indicating when the commanding officers released it to their troops: February 22, 2022, two days before the start of the invasion.

"That's how much warning they had," said Oleksiy Danilov, the secretary of Ukraine's National Security and Defense Council. "Two days before they came here to die." In the first week of the invasion, a Ukrainian special forces officer brought the map to Danilov for safekeeping. What astonished him most was the date printed on the upper right-hand corner. It said the map had been published in 1989, two years before the collapse of the Soviet Union, and well before many of the Russian soldiers killed in the invasion had been born. The Russian military, in its attempt to satisfy the expansionist urges of Vladimir Putin, had apparently been so badly prepared that it failed to update its maps of the land it was invading. They simply reached into the archive, pulled out what they had, and drew a red line running along the old highways from Belarus in the north, through the radioactive zone around Chernobyl, all the way down to the center of Kyiv. As a result, Russian commandos arrived like travelers from the past, forced to learn however they could about the changes Ukraine underwent after the Soviet collapse, the new bridges and highways it had constructed around Kyiv, the forests cleared to make way for new homes, the schools and shopping malls built over the course of Ukraine's history as an independent state. None of these things were marked on the map. "Can you imagine it?" Danilov asked me one afternoon, a few months into the invasion, as we stood over his conference table and studied the document. Their maps, he explained, were from a different era, just like their strategy and their mentality.

The error likely cost a lot of Russian troops their lives. At one point in the Battle of Kyiv, an assault group parachuted onto a wide-open clearing, which their maps had marked as a forested area. As a result, the paratroopers had no cover when they landed. They had nowhere to hide, and the Ukrainians cut them down with machine-gun fire and artillery. Waves of Russian troops went the same way, advancing in columns of tanks and armored personnel carriers toward Bucha and Irpin on the outskirts of Kyiv. Ukraine's armed forces had so few fighting vehicles in the area that Danilov gifted them his armored Land Cruiser, the one he drove to Bankova Street on the morning of the invasion. A few days later, one of his friends in the special forces sent him a photo of the SUV, riddled with shrapnel and bullet holes. "It's alright," Danilov said as he showed it to me. "It probably saved someone's life."

The Battle of Kyiv, which raged through the end of March 2022, had a greater impact on the course of European history than any since the end of World War II. Had it ended differently, the Kremlin could have replaced Zelensky with a marionette and pushed the edge of Moscow's dominion right up to Poland's eastern border, effectively erasing Ukraine from the map. Instead the defense of Kyiv shattered Russia's image as a military powerhouse, an image that had shaped the balance of power in Europe for generations. The confidence of Ukraine's defenders soared after their victory, because the turning point in any fight comes when the victim hits back and draws the blood of the attacker. The Battle of Kyiv was that moment, exhilarating but also terrifying. It came with the split-second awareness that the counterpunch is coming, and there is no way back.

❖

Though they succeeded in defending the capital, the Armed Forces of Ukraine lost vast amounts of territory in the east and south of the country. Some of the most devastating setbacks took place around the port of Mariupol, a center of metallurgy and shipping on the Azov Sea. With a prewar population of around 450,000, the city's location at the southern edge of the Donbas, right between Crimea and the Russian border, made it a strategic target for the Russians. It nearly fell under Russian control in the spring and summer of 2014, when Putin set out to secure a land corridor through Mariupol to Crimea. The Ukrainian armed forces lacked the means to stop him at the time. So the city's defense fell to paramilitary units that formed after that winter's revolution. The strongest ones had backing from Ukrainian oligarchs and financiers, who sponsored these volunteer forces as a way to defend their own cities and enterprises from going the way of Crimea. In Mariupol, this role belonged to the billionaire Serhiy Taruta who paid for the creation of the Azov Battalion, a fighting force that drew many of its early members from Ukraine's far-right and neo-Nazi underground. The battalion took its name from the Azov Sea, and their successful defense of Mariupol in 2014 earned them the status of heroes across the country. The Ukrainian National Guard soon absorbed the Azov Battalion into its ranks, turning it into a fully fledged regiment within the armed forces, with thousands of troops and several military bases.

Eight years later, the main base of the Azov Regiment outside of Mariupol came under intensive bombardment in the opening hours of the invasion. Because of the regiment's ties to far-right extremists, Kremlin propaganda became fixated on Azov, depicting its fighters as "Satanists" and radicals that needed to be "de-Nazified." The invaders devoted a lot of their firepower and resources to surrounding and destroying the Azov Regiment, whose troops fought valiantly to defend the city that had become their home. But in early March, Mariupol was surrounded. The Russians began shelling it relentlessly, decimating neighborhoods and cutting off supplies of water, heat, and electricity. In the middle of March, a Russian jet dropped a heavy bomb on the Mariupol drama theater, where thousands of civilians had taken shelter. As many as six hundred of them were killed, their bodies buried beneath the rubble in what became the worst known atrocity of the war up to that point.

The city's defenders, including hundreds of fighters from the Azov Regiment, fell back to the territory of Mariupol's largest factory, a giant metallurgical plant called Azovstal (Azov Steel). Founded by the Soviets in 1930, the plant occupied four square miles along the city's waterfront. It was equipped to function as a fortress, with enough supplies to withstand a lengthy siege. Around twenty-five hundred Ukrainian soldiers and civilians took refuge in the bunkers beneath Azovstal, turning it into a symbol of Ukrainian defiance. Russian forces besieged and bombarded the plant with artillery, fighter jets and warships stationed in the Azov Sea. One of the commanders attempting to storm Azovstal called for the Kremlin to use chemical weapons, like sarin gas, to force its surrender and, as he put it, "to smoke the moles out of their holes." In the second week of April—more than a month into the siege—Ukrainian officers reported that a noxious gas had seeped into Azovstal, burning the eyes and airways of the troops trapped inside. Even then they tried to fight back, staging raids on Russian positions around the factory and refusing to surrender. Nearly two months into the siege, Putin gave orders to seal off the factory so tightly that "a fly cannot get through." At the time, there were hundreds of women and children sheltering inside its bunkers with thousands of Ukrainian troops.

Their supplies of drinking water soon ran dry, and their daily rations were so meager that some soldiers fainted from lack of food. But, in a remarkable feature of war in the twenty-first century, their communications gear continued working. They had diesel generators and enough fuel to run Starlink Internet terminals, which allowed them to get online, make calls, and broadcast their story to the world in real time. It also gave them a chance to speak directly to the Ukrainian high command, including President Zelensky, who began taking their calls in March. "We know each other well by now," he told me the following month. Most days he would exchange messages with them on his phone, sometimes in the middle of the night. Early in their correspondence, the president received a text from Major Serhiy Volynsky, commander of the 36th Separate Marine Brigade, one of several units that had retreated to Azovstal. The message included a selfie that the two men had taken before the invasion, during a visit the president made to Volynsky's base.

"We're even embracing there, like friends," Zelensky said of the photograph.

These exchanges had a profound effect on Zelensky. Like his earlier trip to the checkpoints north of Kyiv, they gave him a chance to connect with his troops and to understand their suffering with an immediacy that few political leaders experience in a time of war. On most days, the Starlink signal was strong enough for the president to see the faces of the men at Azovstal on the screen of his phone. They pleaded with him to break the blockade, to send more weapons or reinforcements. "It was a catastrophe," Zelensky told me of the battle for Mariupol. "No food, no water, no weapons. Nothing. It had all run out. They had it really hard, and we tried to support each other."

Over the phone, the officers explained to the president that they could not surrender or leave their positions. It would mean abandoning the wounded and bringing shame onto themselves. Zelensky tried to reassure them, to remind them of their importance to Ukraine. "It's not just about that piece of Azovstal, about the factory or even Mariupol. It's the symbolism of the situation," he said. The Russians were trying to make an example of the holdouts in that city, to demonstrate what happens to those who resist. "It's their desire to break one of the bones in our back," he said. "For the Russians, it's a symbol."

Ukraine now stood on the verge of losing it. The armed forces did not have the weapons to break the Russian encirclement of Mariupol. They could only send helicopters to evacuate some of the wounded and drop off supplies and ammunition. But Russian air defenses kept shooting these helicopters down, eroding the meager ranks of Ukrainian pilots and their fleet. After one of these pilots was killed over Mariupol, his mother wrote to General Zaluzhny, looking for her son. The commander tried to explain to her what happened, but he was unable to restrain his emotion. "I didn't have the strength to do it." It was the only point in the invasion when the general broke down and cried.

If there was any chance of rescuing the troops and civilians who remained at the factory, the president believed it would come through negotiations. Zelensky still hoped to meet with Putin and agree on a way to evacuate the wounded from Azovstal, the women and children. Ukraine's lead negotiator, Davyd Arakhamia, raised the issue many times with Russia's envoys, and Zelensky asked for help from the president of Turkey, Recep Tayyip Erdoğan, one of the few leaders in the world who still seemed to have sway over Putin. None of it worked. "The Russians just continue to play their bloody games," Zelensky told me during these negotiations. "They say they want to make a deal, but they don't follow through."

❖

On the morning of April 19—the fifty-fifth day of the invasion—Zelensky took his seat in the Situation Room on the second floor of the presidential compound, just down the hall from the office of the chief of staff. It had become his preferred place to work and confer with his team, a windowless boardroom with gray carpets and recessed lights. Instead of the oil paintings and chandeliers that surrounded him in his office upstairs, this room had only one embellishment: a trident on the wall behind Zelensky's chair. Large monitors ran along the other walls, and a camera faced the president from the opposite side of the conference table.

At around nine a.m., the faces of Ukraine's top generals and intelligence chiefs filled the screens around him. The previous night, Zelensky had announced the start of a new phase in the war. "Russian troops have begun the battle for Donbas," he had said in his nightly address to the nation. "A very large part of the entire Russian army is now focused on this offensive." He wanted the generals to report on their progress at the eastern front, where the fighting was most intense, where his troops had retreated, who had deserted, what help they needed, and where they had managed to advance.

Russian tactics in the east did not resemble their blitz offensive against Kyiv. This time their aim was to trap the bulk of the Ukrainian forces in what they called a *kotyol*—a cauldron—that would stretch for hundreds of miles across the Donbas. From Mariupol in the south, the Russian columns would advance northward once the last of the resistance in that city had been crushed. The other side of their pincer would advance southward from the Kharkiv region, attempting to cut off Ukrainian supply lines and bombard the defenders into submission. During Zelensky's call with the generals, the battles were most intense around the city of Izyum, in the Kharkiv region, where the Ukrainians had launched a counterattack and liberated several villages, hoping to block or at least delay the Russian encirclement of the Donbas.

"What do you need? What are you missing?" Zelensky asked the officers, inviting them to list the exact type of weapons, the caliber of ammunition. He did not offer advice on battlefield tactics, said Oleksiy Reznikov, the defense minister, who participated in the call. "He doesn't teach them how to fight, because he's a civilian," Reznikov told me. "He just gives them a feeling of freedom and support." Armed with his notes from the briefings, Zelensky devoted part of his day to securing what the commanders requested. "He starts calling presidents, prime ministers of different countries, and saying, 'Let me borrow what we need. Just let me borrow it. I'll give it back,'" Reznikov said. "There are no factors holding him back, no protocols, no rules of behavior, no politeness. He is fixated on getting results."

On that particular day, he had a call with Mark Rutte, the prime minister of the Netherlands, whom the Ukrainians considered a problematic partner at the time, requiring extra pressure to increase supplies of weapons. Zelensky also spoke with Ursula von der Leyen, the president of the European Commission, who was still fresh off her trip to Bucha and pushing the E.U. to support the Ukrainians in every way possible. Apart from these private conversations, the president spent time in the Situation Room drafting a speech. "Very often people ask who is Zelensky's speechwriter," said his adviser on communications, Dasha Zarivna. "The main one is him," she told me. "He works on every line." His performances won applause and pledges of support, but they also frustrated Zelensky. He fumed over the dithering among his allies. "It is unfair that Ukraine is still forced to ask for what its partners have been storing somewhere for years," he said in his daily video address, which channeled the frustration of his call with the generals that morning. A few hours later, when he was at least six meetings into his agenda for that day, Zelensky invited me up to his office to talk.

His aides warned that his schedule was erratic. Lately, they said, so was his mood. There was seldom an evening without some new emergency, and he could be pulled away at any time to deal with it. The compound felt deserted and a little spooky when I got through security. The only light in the main corridor came from a desk lamp that stood on the floor, casting a faint glow over the paintings on the walls. They all looked so cheerful, a row of vivid relics from an early phase of the administration, incongruous now in that barricaded gloom, hanging over piles of sandbags where the soldiers might duck and cover in case of a siege.

On the fourth floor, outside the executive offices, I had just placed my bag on the belt of an X-ray machine when a voice from one of the soldier's radios reported that the president was coming up. Everyone took a step back to make way, and soon Zelensky emerged from the elevator with his bodyguard, laughing at something on the screen of his phone. He looked up and wiped his eyes, a little startled by the crowd. A handful of us stood on the landing, a variety of staffers, soldiers, and senior aides, and it was curious to see the way they stood at attention, not afraid of him but tense, a little wary of his gaze.

His circle had not always acted that way. Early on, his associates and members of the administration often called him by his schoolyard name, Volodya, and kept their seats when he entered a room. By now they had switched to the formal manner of address, Volodymyr Oleksandrovych, or used his title in Ukrainian, Pane Prezidente. The change reminded me of something he had said on the campaign trail three years earlier. "The scariest thing is to lose the people you have around you," he said back then, a few months before he was elected, "the ones that keep you grounded, that tell you when you're wrong."

It wasn't clear whether anyone still played that role in Zelensky's entourage. His wife was still in hiding, as were his parents. None of his childhood friends were by his side. No one in the bunker was from his years in KVN. Even the Shefir brothers, Zelensky's mentors and confidants for his whole adult life and most of his presidential tenure, fell out of sight when the invasion started. Those who remained, like Yermak, Reznikov, and Sybiha, were not the type to question his instincts or contradict him. Zelensky was not their pal. He was their boss, and it showed in the way the air grew tight when he arrived.

The demands of the war, the need for the president to live in isolation from everyone but his most essential staff, had accelerated a process that began long before—the whittling away of advisers who tried to argue with his intuition, to offer data or arguments that might change his mind. His confidence grew as the circle around him tightened, and by the time we sat down to talk in the second month of the invasion, he no longer searched the room for his advisers when considering the answer to a question. He knew what he wanted to say, and there was no one around to contradict him.

❖

The room set aside for our conversation was the same one where I had interviewed Ukraine's previous leaders, Yanukovych a decade earlier, Poroshenko after the revolution in 2014. We even sat at the same table, only the gold leaf on its surface had flaked away over the years. In the fall of 2019, the first time I had met Zelensky in these rooms, he had described them as a fortress that he wanted to escape. Only a year removed from his life as an actor, he looked so vulnerable then, so wounded as he exposed his disgust with politics to say, "I don't trust anyone at all." Now, when he was truly vulnerable, one Russia missile strike away from death, the president carried an air of invincibility, as though the war had made him grow some stubborn armor that no weapon in the world could break. If this was an act, it looked convincing right down to the details, the way he settled into the seat across from me like a sovereign into a hereditary throne. The presence of all these aides, all these bodyguards, no longer made him feel self-conscious. He saw no need to maintain an ironic distance between himself and the symbols of power around him. The role was his now. He had accepted it. On his request, an assistant brought him a glass of sparkling water, and he teased her for not bringing the entire bottle. "You see," he told me, "this is how they're trying to conserve around here." His aides exhaled, as though the joke was a sign of the boss's good mood.

"So then," he said, his palms on the table, "are we speaking Russian or Ukrainian?" It was a touchy question. My Ukrainian is far from fluent. We had always spoken in Russian before, and the choice this time was a symptom of the war. The language of the invader was quickly becoming taboo. For most of his life, Zelensky had struggled with Ukrainian. It was not his mother tongue, and his attempts to learn it proved embarrassing for him on the campaign trail. Now he was so accustomed to the official language of the state that he had trouble remembering Russian words. Ukrainian had supplanted them. As we started talking, he seemed to forget the Russian word for *understand*, then he apologized, corrected himself—and slipped back into Ukrainian a few seconds later.

The first questions in our interview came from him. He wanted to understand the purpose of our conversation, what it was meant to achieve for Ukraine. "What do you want to get across to people?" Before I could open my mouth to speak, he offered an answer: "It is very important for the world to understand exactly what is happening. For me, personally, it is not about making people in the world feel more emotions." He was not out to exaggerate or manipulate. "We just want the truth," he said. "The more people see the reality, the more they will sense that this war is not somewhere far away. It's near them."

Next he wanted to know about my readers, as though I had any insight into the ways they had collectively experienced the war. "Do you think the American audience feels the same pain that you do here?" Zelensky asked. "The same that we do?" I told him I wasn't sure. In the last couple of weeks, the attention of the world did seem to be flagging. Other events were crowding Ukraine off the front pages, and the major networks were not as fixated on the war as they had been in March. "I feel that way, too," the president said, looking around at his aides as though they had just been discussing this problem. "It's only a matter of time. Sadly our war is perceived through the big social networks. People see this war on Instagram. When they get sick of it, they will scroll away. It's a lot of blood, a lot of emotion, and that tires people. For them it's a source of entertainment that has sadly claimed a lot of lives, and when people get sick of looking at the same image, the same blood, from the same nation, some of them will want to turn away."

A form of entertainment? It seemed like a harsh thing to assume about the way people absorbed this tragedy, even the people who only saw it through their screens. But this appeared to be the way Zelensky imagined his audience, and mine. His aim, as he saw it, was to keep them engaged, to pry open their eyes and point them toward the picture of the war he wanted them to see. My work was useful to him as a means to that end. He took a pause and cleared his throat, realizing he may have crossed a line in telling me how to do my job. Then he continued to do exactly that. "Forgive me for saying this, but I think the aim of journalism, of the media, is to keep people from getting sick of this," he said, referring to the story of the war. "When they do get sick of it, that brings about fatigue, and fatigue causes a loss of interest. For our country, that leads to the loss of support."

His bluntness was commendable. In all my years of reporting on Ukraine, no politician had ever been so direct about his motives for speaking with me. They had nothing to do with his vanity, much less to do with my charms. He did not care about clarifying the historical record or enlightening readers about his plans. Here the truth was simpler and uglier. The lives of his people depended on his ability to keep the spotlight on Ukraine. For his nation to survive, the Americans and Europeans could not be allowed to get bored and change the channel. The president saw this as part of his mission, maybe the most important part. It was hardly unique in the history of warfare. Many leaders spend their days pleading with foreigners to notice the suffering of their people and to help. Most of them are ignored. Sometimes the world takes an interest only when it's far too late, when the massacres have ended and it's time to talk about tribunals or commissions on truth and reconciliation. Zelensky was not even the first leader of Ukraine to face this problem. His predecessor also needed to take the war on tour across the world's political stages, like the time in 2018 when Poroshenko waved that tattered European flag in front of a half-empty hall at the Munich Security Conference.

Now it was Zelensky's turn, and he was not ashamed or coy about this aspect of his job. He knew he was good at it, and in the new phase of the war, the one he had announced in a speech the previous night, the president also understood that he needed the world to pay attention more than ever. In the Donbas, the Russians had a clear advantage. They could fire ten or twenty times more shells than the Ukrainians. The battle would be slow and bloody, intended not only to break Ukraine's resolve but to tire out its Western allies. "At certain points in the east, it's just insane," Zelensky told me. "Really horrible in terms of the frequency of the strikes, the heavy artillery fire, and the losses." The generals warned him that morning to prepare for a full-scale battle in the east, "bigger than any we have seen on the territory of Ukraine," Zelensky said. "If we hold out, it will be a decisive moment for us. The tipping point."

The next few weeks would prove him right. By the end of April, the Russians would outnumber Ukrainian forces by a ratio of at least three to one in the Donbas, having concentrated as many as sixty thousand troops in that region alone. The Ukrainian counterattack around Izyum managed to stop them from advancing southward and creating a cauldron across the Donbas. When the invaders tried the same maneuver on a smaller scale, the Ukrainians fought their way out again and again. During one battle, their artillery destroyed an entire Russian brigade as it tried to cross a river in the Donbas, killing nearly five hundred enemy troops, according to one estimate, and destroying scores of Russian military vehicles. The death toll soon reached a scale unlike anything Europe had seen since the Second World War. At the end of May, Zelensky said up to a hundred of his troops were dying every day in the Donbas, with another five hundred wounded. The losses on the Russian side were estimated to be even higher.

But the tipping point remained elusive. Even as the Russians failed to make any dramatic gains or to encircle large formations of Ukrainian troops, they maintained an overwhelming advantage in men and firepower that allowed them to push forward mile by mile, using artillery to bombard entire towns before rolling over them with tanks and mechanized infantry. Joseph Stalin had once referred to artillery as the god of modern warfare, and in the Donbas it became the engine of the Russian strategy. The only way to even the odds would be a massive influx of weapons from abroad. Without them, Ukraine stood no chance of holding its ground in the east.

CHAPTER 18

ABOVEGROUND

AT THE END OF APRIL, ABOUT A WEEK AFTER OUR INTERVIEW, ZELENSKY RECEIVED A visit from two American officials whose support would change the course of the war. Antony Blinken, the U.S. secretary of state, and Lloyd Austin, the U.S. secretary of defense, tried to keep their travel plans secret until their train pulled into Kyiv's central station. But Zelensky announced their arrival a day before, on the eve of Orthodox Easter Sunday. "We are expecting specific things," the president told reporters during a briefing held in the subway station closest to his compound. "Specific weapons."

His guests obliged. An additional $700 million in aid was announced during their visit, including some of the arms Ukraine needed to withstand the Russian assault in the east: howitzers, counterartillery radar systems, and a consignment of exploding drones known as the Phoenix Ghost. Standing among crates and boxes of these supplies in a warehouse in eastern Poland, Lloyd Austin clarified his vision for the war in terms that unnerved his more cautious colleagues in the White House. "We want to see Russia weakened," he said, "to the degree it cannot do the kinds of things that it has done in invading Ukraine." The U.S. objective, in other words, was not merely to help Ukraine survive this war but to destroy Russia's ability to fight another one.

The statement underlined the evolution of U.S. policy. Only two months earlier, Austin was among the American officials explaining to the Ukrainians that supplies of more powerful weapons, such as howitzers, were out of the question, and that the Ukrainians should instead dig trenches to slow the Russian advance. But the Russian withdrawal from the suburbs of Kyiv had changed the conversation in the White House. As Antony Blinken put it during the trip, "Russia is failing. Ukraine is succeeding." Even with the risks of an escalatory response from the Russian side—such as a strike against NATO supply lines into

Ukraine or even the use of a tactical nuclear weapon—the U.S. and its allies calculated the payoff would be worth it. They had a chance to wreck the Russian war machine, and Secretary Austin made clear that the U.S. and its allies would "keep moving heaven and earth" to help Ukraine achieve that goal.

Two days after his visit with Zelensky, Austin convened a summit of defense officials from forty nations at the Ramstein Air Base in Germany to coordinate assistance to Ukraine. The head of the delegation from Kyiv was Oleksiy Reznikov, the minister of defense, who had been working for weeks to put such a coalition together. On his return to Kyiv, he explained to Zelensky that the outcome of the summit was far better than any weapons shipments. It was, as he put it, a "tectonic philosophical shift" in the world's most powerful military alliance. Ukraine still had no clear path to joining NATO, but its leaders had finally agreed to train and equip Ukraine's armed forces as though they were on the same team, fighting the same enemy. "It's that beautiful English word," Reznikov said. "*Interoperability!*"

With a few exceptions, like the Bayraktar drones from Turkey and the Javelin missiles from the U.S., Ukraine's military relied on Soviet weapons systems, and it was expending them at a rapid rate. The same was true of the Russian military, which had also stuck to Soviet standards and designs. But Russia's arsenal was vastly larger, and its military industry could churn out replacements much faster than Ukraine. To make up the difference, Ukraine tried to tap foreign stockpiles from countries like Bulgaria and South Korea. "We were knocking on every door," Reznikov told me. But they were coming up short. The countries who possessed these weapons either didn't have enough of them, he said, "or they were friendly with the Russians."

The summit at Ramstein offered a long-term solution. Ukraine would need to break its dependence on Soviet hardware and adapt to the use of NATO weaponry. Rather than searching the world for outdated guns to plug the holes in the Ukrainian arsenal, the alliance could then ramp up supplies of new systems from its own factories and stockpiles. Over time, the strategy promised to even the score between the warring sides. It also came with major risks. One of Putin's stated goals for the invasion was to prevent Ukraine from ever joining NATO. Only a few weeks before the Ramstein conference, Zelensky was still offering to grant that concession to Putin in the peace talks. He was ready to give up Ukraine's bid for NATO membership even if it required an amendment to the Constitution. Now Ukraine was moving in the opposite direction, and the Russians were furious.

The Kremlin's propaganda channels began to insist that Russia was now at war with all of NATO or, as they often put it, "the collective West." Foreign Minister Sergei Lavrov, a relatively moderate voice in Putin's circle, warned that the flow of weapons into Ukraine would raise the risk of a nuclear war. "The danger is serious, real," he told Russian state TV on the eve of the Ramstein conference. "And we must not underestimate it." Such warnings did not dissuade Zelensky or his supporters in the West. They had begun a rapid process of integration. "De facto," Reznikov told me, "Ukraine is becoming a part of NATO. We are fighting with NATO weapons. Our soldiers are starting to train with NATO instructors."

The minister was getting ahead of himself. It would take months to enact the vision that Austin had spelled out in Ramstein. But the momentum was shifting in favor of Ukraine on multiple fronts. With his decision to invade, Vladimir Putin had unleashed the very forces he intended to stop. Finland and Sweden, two of the last militarily neutral powers in Northern Europe, applied to join NATO within three months of the invasion of Ukraine, and the alliance put them on a fast track to membership. With Finland's accession the following spring, the length of Russia's border with NATO would double. Zelensky asked to be next in line and, after nearly two decades of banging on NATO's door for protection against the Russians and receiving little more than hollow promises in response, Ukraine was now on its way to interoperability with the alliance. Even if full membership remained out of reach, Ukraine's military would be tightly intertwined with NATO, as would its spy agencies.

Within a week of the conference in Ramstein, the U.S. announced that it was sending vast amounts of intelligence to the Ukrainians. "We have opened up the pipes," said General Mark Milley. With the help of U.S. satellites and surveillance systems, Ukraine could see where the invading forces had set up command posts and what officers were stationed there. In early May, the *New York Times* reported that the flow of U.S. intelligence had helped Ukraine kill as many as twelve Russian generals in targeted strikes. Not since the Second World War had a major military force lost that many senior officers in such a short time.

As the sharing of intelligence improved, so did the relationship between Milley and Zaluzhny. The generals were in touch at least once a week, often planning operations in detail. "For me this person is almost godlike," Zaluzhny told me around that time. The need for interpreters continued to garble some of their conversations. But Zaluzhny, hunched over the speakerphone in his command center, could feel Milley's passion for fighting and winning this war. "His heart was really in it with us," he said. Their March dispute over faulty intelligence was soon forgotten, and Zaluzhny regretted his refusal back then to take the American general's calls. "Of course I'm young and was a bit stupid," he told me, "and I wanted to wind the tape back and talk to him in a new way."

❖

By the middle of spring, Zelensky and his team began spending most of their time aboveground. They continued to sleep some nights and hold a few key meetings in the bunker, but the Russian retreat from the suburbs of Kyiv made the risk of a siege feel remote. The president asked his staff to prepare a bed for him in a little room behind his office on the fourth floor. It was a single, about the same size as his bed in the bunker, with a wooden headboard and a TV suspended on the wall above his feet. In the closet, he kept several changes of clothes from local military outfitters, who gave him an ample supply of the T-shirts and fleeces that turned Zelensky into an unlikely fashion icon. "I had to tell them to stop," he said. "They all wanted me to wear their T-shirts." Hanging next to them in his closet he kept a single business suit, pressed and ready, he said, for the day when the war would end in victory for Ukraine.

In the streets outside, victory felt a long way off. The government district was a maze of checkpoints and barricades. Civilian cars could not get close, and soldiers standing at intersections would ask pedestrians for secret passwords that changed each day. They were usually nonsense phrases, like "філіжанка залицяльник" ("coffee cup suitor"), Ukrainian tongue twisters that would be difficult for a Russian to remember or pronounce. Many of the street signs and house numbers had been removed to confuse outsiders. But beyond the security perimeters in the center of the city, the broad boulevards were open to traffic, and the city slowly came alive. The dry cleaners reopened a few blocks from Bankova Street. The panhandlers and buskers came back to the sidewalks, as did the street chanters from the cult of Falun Gong, who invited passersby to meditate with them across from city hall.

Andriy Sybiha, the president's foreign policy adviser, recalls squinting up at the sun and smiling when he first emerged from the bunker that spring to take a walk around the neighborhood. He hadn't seen the sky in weeks and was astonished to find a crowd in the local pizza parlor. "There were a lot of foreigners around," he noted with amazement. "And the bazaar was selling imported stuff, berries, vegetables." Sybiha soon made it a habit to stroll through the city when he had the chance.

The presidential guards did not object to staffers leaving the compound or working in their usual offices upstairs. Some of their rooms had been occupied by soldiers, the floors covered with their blankets and sleeping mats. For the most part, though, they looked the same, full of the same long conference tables and leather sofas, the same printers and copy machines. One obvious difference was the darkness. Many of the windows were covered with sandbags, and lights were kept off throughout the compound to make it harder for an enemy sniper to get a clean shot from outside. Other precautions made no apparent sense. At the start of the invasion, guards ripped the lights out of an elevator leading up to the executive suites. A tangle of wires protruded from the holes where they had been, and Zelensky's aides rode up and down in the dark. Nobody remembered why.

On the fourth floor, Zelensky's office remained a cocoon of gold leaf and regal furniture, and his staff still found it oppressive. "At least if the place gets bombed," one of them joked, "we won't have to look at this stuff anymore." On quiet days, when there were no important visitors or meetings on the schedule, the mood was relaxed. Custodians dusted the cabinets and put fresh lining in the wastebaskets. Once it surprised me to find the metal detector and X-ray machine unplugged at the entrance while a janitor worked around them with a mop. Later it felt normal for a tired guard to glance in my bag and wave me through with a nod of recognition.

Upstairs, the war felt far away. When the wailing of the air-raid siren started, the staffers would often ignore it and continue with their work. Some of them believed that Kyiv's air defenses were strong enough, at least around the government quarter, to shoot down an incoming rocket. But this seemed more like a coping mechanism, the offspring of defiance and denial. At that point in the war, Ukraine had no way to stop the type of hypersonic missiles that Russia fired at targets in Kyiv and other cities. The Kh-22 "Kinzhal," or "Dagger," can travel at more than five times the speed of sound while zigzagging to avoid interceptors. It can also carry one of Russia's nuclear warheads.

Faced with that threat, the most frequent response among Zelensky's aides was a kind of fatalism, which soon began to function as an organizing principle. Some crude precautions—barricaded gates, bulletproof vests—had felt necessary during the war's opening stage. Now, when there was no longer a risk of Russian commandos bursting through the doors, Zelensky's team understood that such defenses were pointless. They were facing an invader with a nuclear arsenal. They had decided not to run. What was the point of hiding?

❖

One afternoon in early April, I paid a visit to one of Zelensky's closest aides, Mykhailo Podolyak. He had lived in the bunker from the start of the invasion, and now he was back in his office on the third floor, his nameplate affixed to the door and light pouring in through the windows. There were no sandbags to prevent a blast wave from shattering the glass. Podolyak hadn't even closed the drapes. When I pointed this out, he told me with a shrug that the missiles would come sooner or later: "They'll hit us here," he said, "and it'll all be ruins." But there was no fear in his voice as he said this. There wasn't even much concern. "What can we do? We've got to keep working."

Clean-cut and well-spoken, with a penchant for blasting heavy metal through his earphones while at work, Podolyak was a relative latecomer to the administration. He had spent most of his career as a muckraking journalist before transitioning into the field of political PR and crisis communications. In the spring of 2020, when the COVID-19 pandemic began to erode Zelensky's ratings, Podolyak joined the team as a spokesman. Even in that crowded field, he stood out for his openness and bluntness with the media. His views on Russia were hard-line from the start. But when the invasion broke out, he began to espouse a program of total and uncompromising victory that seemed, at least at first, out of sync with the intentions of the president. "It's very important for you to understand," he said as we sat down at his conference table, pushing aside a pile of documents and a recent map of the fighting near Kyiv. "There can be no talk of any normalization of relations with Russia. Their crimes have completely changed the emotional backdrop of how Russia is perceived. For Ukraine, Russia is a country that has ceased to exist. They are nonhumans, monsters."

He mentioned the "filtration camps" that Russia had been using to detain and interrogate civilians in eastern and southern Ukraine. Entire families were disappearing into these camps. Women and children were taken there before being deported to far-flung regions of Russia, often against their will. Reports of torture and degrading conditions in the camps were rampant, and Podolyak was right to point out their resemblance to Dachau and Buchenwald. "The difference is that these wounds won't heal the way they did after World War II," he told me. "Today the Russians see what they are doing in Bucha, and they are only inspired by it. They demand mass murder. It's a totally different level of understanding. For the Germans there was repentance. For the Russians there will not be." It struck me as strange that Podolyak would stake out this position. It seemed too early at the time to judge the level of Russian popular support for the invasion. Surveys had found that around 60 percent of Russians backed it, while roughly a quarter disapproved. But most Russians knew better than to criticize the state when a pollster called them on the telephone. In early March, the Kremlin had enacted a law banning open opposition to the war. The mere act of calling the war a war, rather than a "special military operation," could get you locked up in Russia for up to fifteen years.

Besides, there were still a few Russian dissidents speaking out online and trying to organize protests. One of them, Ilya Yashin, would later send me a letter from his prison in Siberia. "We are resisting," he wrote, listing a few isolated cases of dissent that had swiftly been repressed. In Yashin's case, a Moscow court gave him eight and a half years for posting a video about the atrocities in Bucha. "Those who have remained in Russia," he wrote, "live with all the rights of hostages . . . The silence of a hostage with a terrorist's gun to his head does not make him an accomplice to the terrorist."

Zelensky, at least in his public pronouncements, seemed to agree. He had not yet begun to accuse all Russians of complicity. There was still hope that the war in Ukraine might end with a popular revolt in

Moscow, and Zelensky wanted to believe it would. But the tone inside his administration changed by the middle of spring. Podolyak, the presidential spokesman and one of the lead negotiators in the peace talks with Russia, was doing all he could to convince me that Russia was a race of savages with whom there could never be a lasting peace.

"They are not like you and me," he said. "This is a completely barbaric country that stayed back in the sixteenth or seventeenth century, waging a war against humanity as such. It wants to kill off everything human in us, to turn us into animals." Then what about the peace process? Why was the president still pursuing talks if he also believed the Russians were barbarians? Podolyak paused and leaned back in his chair. "President Zelensky uses all possible instruments to defend his citizens." His voice had suddenly lost its vehemence and reverted to the placid tone of a press attaché. "It's an instrument. Nothing more." He glanced at his phone, which had been buzzing with a steady stream of messages. None of Zelensky's advisers could turn away from their devices for long. The relentless flow of news always pulled them back, demanded their attention. This time the messages did not seem to upset Podolyak. He told me to expect good news as we parted ways. That evening, after I got back to my apartment at the edge of the government district, it became clear what he meant. My phone also filled up with ecstatic messages. Viktor Medvedchuk had been caught.

There was his photo on Zelensky's social media page, a disheveled figure in handcuffs and a camouflage uniform. The turn of fortune seemed too dramatic to believe. When the invasion started, Medvedchuk came within reach of taking power at the head of a Russian military parade. A few months before that, he had commanded the second-largest force in the Ukrainian parliament, a party that Moscow had spent a fortune promoting and nurturing. There was seldom a night before the invasion when the leaders of that party were not on the prime-time talk shows in Ukraine, calling for unity with Russia and denouncing Zelensky as a clown, a weakling, or a despot. Where were they now?

A few of them, including the party's cochairman, Yuriy Boyko, had switched sides, condemned the invasion, and declared allegiance to Ukraine. Others continued to cheer on the Kremlin in their posts on social media, offering up the perverse argument that Zelensky's refusal to surrender to the Russians had resulted in the senseless killing of Ukrainians. When it came to their own whereabouts, these politicians were vague. The backdrops in their selfies tended to be neutral, difficult to place. Most of them had simply fled. Some landed in friendly jurisdic-tions like Serbia or Dubai. The lucky few with open visas to the European Union might be spotted in Prague or Berlin. The more prominent ones stopped picking up my calls as soon as the Russian tanks crossed the border. For months I had not been able to reach anyone close to Putin's old friend Medvedchuk. All that had been reported of his fate was that, in the opening hours of the invasion, he had disabled his ankle monitor and escaped from house arrest. His wife had been spotted crossing the border into Belarus a few days earlier. The location of their daughter Daria, Putin's goddaughter, was a mystery.

Their abandoned mansions did not offer any clues. In the middle of March, a group of activists got inside one of them, and they found it under renovation, with piles of paintings and antiques on the floor. At the edge of the property was a mock train station named Dalnyaya—The Faraway Place—that housed a replica of an old Pullman dining car, the ceiling made of stained glass, the bar stocked with dishes marked with the Russian imperial eagle. Medvedchuk and his family, in their leisure hours, apparently liked to pretend they were riding the rails after the fashion of nineteenth-century aristocrats. The photos of the dining car went viral, and Medvedchuk became a punch line. In my conversations with lawmakers or security officials, I made a habit of asking where he'd gone. The answer was usually a shrug, sometimes a look of suspicion. "Why do you even care?" one member of Zelensky's party asked me. "Such figures have no future in Ukraine. The Russian political project is dead."

He was right, and now the proof was hanging on Zelensky's Face-book page: a mug shot of Medvedchuk with tousled hair, a far cry from the polished image he had always cultivated. Ukraine's main intelligence agency, the SBU, soon came forward with some details. Putin's friend had been trying to flee Ukraine while disguised in the uniform of a Ukrainian soldier. SBU officers caught him in a suburb of Kyiv when he was on his way to meet the Russian agents tasked with evacuating him. The response on Bankova Street was ecstatic. Some of Zelensky's advis-ers wanted to bring Medvedchuk in shackles as a trophy to their first meeting with Putin, which the two sides were still hoping to arrange.

"We've got a lot of Russian prisoners, and our hope is to trade them, all for all," said Davyd Arakhamia, the lead negotiator. He wasn't sure how much Medvedchuk would be worth to the Kremlin. How many Ukrainian prisoners of war would Putin trade for him? "There are two theories," Arakhamia told me. "The first is that, as a close friend, as a member of the family, he's very valuable. The second theory is that he's worthless. Everything he stole, all the money sent to him, the billions of dollars meant to create all these networks of people, these loyalists who could take over in the event of an occupation—all of that money was spent on yachts and furs, cars and corruption. So maybe he doesn't have any value at all. We don't really know the Russian position."

The value of his capture to Ukrainian morale was, however, difficult to overstate, and it was only compounded a few days later, when Zelensky's generals brought him more good news. On April 14, the Ukrainian Navy launched two torpedoes at the *Moskva*, the flagship of the Black Sea Fleet. This was the pride of the Russian Navy, with a crew of over five hundred sailors, and now it was on fire and sinking fast. The attack gave new meaning to the Ukrainian battle cry—*Russian warship, go fuck yourself.* It was soon printed on T-shirts and postage stamps along with images of the *Moskva* engulfed in flames.

That same week, Ukraine's armed forces carried out a series of precision strikes on Russian targets, killing at least one general. Intelligence from American satellites proved instrumental in these attacks, which laid bare a structural flaw in the Russian military. It still relied on the rigid hierarchies of the Soviet Union, which gave junior officers little authority to make decisions on their own. When a problem arose on the battlefield, the top brass arrived to straighten things out, leaving them exposed to Ukrainian strikes.

Taken together, these victories had a dramatic impact on Zelensky and his team. Only a few weeks earlier, holed up in their bunker, their chances of survival did not look much better than even. Now they could see the losses mounting on the side of the invaders. Russian commanders were coming home in boxes, and more of their troops were dying in two weeks of fighting in the Donbas than the U.S. lost in twenty years of war in Afghanistan. Even if the credit for this shift in the war belonged most of all to the Armed Forces of Ukraine, Zelensky's skills as a communicator had played a crucial role. He and his team secured the supplies of weapons that the military needed to stay in the fight. Throughout the spring, Zelensky averaged one speech per day, addressing venues as diverse as the parliament of South Korea, the World Bank, and the Grammy Awards. Each one was crafted with his audience in mind. When he spoke to the U.S. Congress, he referenced Pearl Harbor and 9/11. The German parliament heard him invoke the history of the Holocaust and the Berlin Wall. As these efforts began to pay off with a steady supply of weapons from the West, it became far easier for Zelensky and his team to imagine a path to victory. "We are not just surviving anymore," his adviser Oleksiy Arestovych told me a few days after the sinking of the *Moskva*. "We are winning, and the president feels a powerful drive from this new role. He's swimming in it, giving orders like Napoleon before a battle. I think it's woken something up inside him," he said. "Some inner strength."

Months later, Zelensky would use the same phrase—"inner strength"—to describe what he felt at this point in the war. He compared it to an arm-wrestling match, when your wrist is just about to touch the table. "And then, to everyone's surprise, you pick your head up and hear the applause, and you start pushing back." The reversal gave Zelensky an abiding sense of confidence that the war would now proceed along the same trajectory, even though its culmination remained far out of sight. Privately, away from his advisers, Zelensky tried to discipline himself to be humbler about his chances of winning the war. "The higher a person climbs up that mountain," he told me, "the more painful it is to fall."

❖

In early May, as the eastern front became the epicenter of the fighting, Olena Zelenska managed to leave her isolation and resume at least some of her work as First Lady. She began on Mother's Day, when her American counterpart, Jill Biden, made a trip to eastern Poland to visit Ukrainian refugees. Olena, who had been in hiding for more than two months by that point, seized the chance to welcome her in the town of Vyshhorod, just inside the Ukrainian border. They had never met before but, as Biden recalled, "instinctively, we embraced." They spent a few hours together at a school that doubled as a shelter, making bears out of tissue paper with a group of children displaced by the war. Olena did her best to seem natural and relaxed among the cameras and unfamiliar faces. But Jill Biden could sense her anxiety. "In the strain of her smile," she later said, "I could see the weight she carried." Her time on the run had taken a toll, and Olena could not just leave that trauma behind when she left her final safe house.

Though her children remained out of sight, Olena soon returned to work in her office at the presidential compound, where her movements and her schedule were not quite as tightly restricted. The adjustment proved difficult. She had trouble defining her place in the wartime administration, and the security around her remained tighter than for anyone else at the compound, including the president and his military commanders. Guests to the First Lady's office were not allowed, for example, to pour a glass of water from the same carafe as her.

In her first days back, she struggled to find ways to be useful. The program she had launched in 2019 to improve the quality of school lunches seemed senseless now, as most of the schools in Ukraine were closed. Some of them had been destroyed by Russian air strikes and shelling. In Bucha, the Russians had parked their artillery pieces in the courtyard of a primary school and used them to launch rockets at neighboring towns. Reading about these horrors, watching footage of the victims on the news, Olena experienced the kind of paralysis that many Ukrainians felt at the time. "You hear the constant sirens. You hear what's happening in other regions," she told me. "It doesn't put you in the best of moods."

Some of the most valuable guidance she received in this period came not from her husband or the presidential staff but from the women she had once regarded as the "accessories" of powerful men. She met a handful of them during a summit in Kyiv the year before the invasion, and the First Ladies of Poland, Lithuania, and Israel stayed in close touch with Olena, as did the spouses of other foreign leaders who had rushed to Ukraine's defense. They spoke on the phone as often as possible. "This club is really helping me right now," she told me. "We understand each other." But arranging more than a few of these conversations a week proved difficult, Olena said with evident frustration, "because any contact on the level of First Ladies has to go through the protocol service."

Then again, so did her calls to President Zelensky during her time in hiding. By now she was used to all the protocols, which only seemed to grow more severe after her return to Bankova Street. She and her husband did not return to living together. Zelensky and his security detail insisted that it would be too dangerous for them all to sleep in the same place, and his schedule gave him little freedom to spend time with his family. "We don't watch movies together," Olena told me with a smile. "We watch them separately."

They saw each other two or three times a week, even less frequently with the children. Once in a while, Olena would run into her husband in the hallways of the presidential compound as he rushed to another one of his meetings, and they would exchange a few hurried words. Most of the time she was surrounded by aides and advisers who encouraged her to do more interviews, appear on magazine covers, and amplify the president's calls for international assistance. On a few occasions, Zelensky agreed to appear on television for an interview with his wife, and she sometimes used these conversations to interrogate him about his feelings, as though the journalists doubled as marriage counselors.

"Thank you for this TV date," she told one British broadcaster. "Every time we really enjoy these interviews, because we get to see each other." It sounded like a rebuke, and Zelensky stared at his hands with an air of embarrassment as she revealed some details of their family life. Their daughter, Sasha, was applying to college and would have her final exams in a couple of days. "She really needs her papa, to talk to him, so she can more easily get through this period in her life, when she is entering adulthood," Olena said, speaking as much to her husband as to the television cameras that surrounded them. "Unfortunately, we are not allowed to do that."

Zelensky tried stiffly to shift the topic back to the war, pointing out that many Ukrainian families have it far worse than theirs, such as those living under Russian occupation. His first priority, he said, was the liberation of occupied territory. "My second side is my family, my wife," Zelensky said. He missed them and could never get used to being apart. But they needed to be strong, he told her. Olena smiled and looked into the distance. All of their life together, Zelensky had put his work first, starting with those nights when their children were still small, and he would wrap up a movie shoot or finish a performance before coming home too exhausted to do anything but sit on the couch and watch TV. The demands of the presidency, and now the war, had taken this quality to an extreme that Olena found hard to accept. Then again, many of the officials who fled Kyiv in the first days of the invasion did so because they needed to get their families to safety. Zelensky stayed. "I couldn't have done otherwise," he said later in the interview. "The president is the leader of the nation. The nation chose me."

But now, in this new phase of the war, his family had returned to Kyiv to be near him, and he still chose to live apart from them, to devote himself more fully to the role. The interviewer noted that such situations could ruin a marriage. Would it make theirs stronger? The question made Olena smile and look over at her husband. "What do you think?" she asked him in English, and for a few long moments he fumbled for an answer, having suddenly misplaced his gift for finding the right words. "We're all living people," he said. "Probably there are such moments in every family over of the years. But I never felt that there is something wrong in our relationship." Then, turning the tables, he asked his wife: "Are you ever sad with me?"

"With you—never," she answered. "Without you, it's always very sad."

CHAPTER 19

RETURN OF POLITICS

Late one evening in the middle of June, the president and a group of his close advisers boarded a train near the center of Kyiv and settled in for an overnight ride. From the outside, their private carriage looked like a regular passenger car, an old Soviet design painted in blue with yellow details. But the interior was freshly renovated, with gleaming fixtures, beige carpets, and golden curtains on the windows. The state railway company had long kept a handful of these luxury cars in its fleet to shuttle its executives around the country. At the start of the invasion, when air traffic over Ukraine shut down, the company put them in the service of the presidential administration, which began using them to transport senior officials and foreign dignitaries.

That spring, they became Zelensky's primary means of long-distance travel, and he usually enjoyed them. The trips gave him time to read, and the smell of the smoke from the engine brought back memories of his childhood. When he was growing up, air travel had been too expensive for his family, and he would sometimes go to visit his father in Mongolia by train. The trips would take eight days on the railroad from Kryvyi Rih, passing all the way through Russia and Siberia, with stopovers in Moscow and Ulan Bator. On those long days, sitting beside his mother in the sleeping car, he would stare out the window at the vast expanses of the Soviet empire, drinking glasses of tea in metal cup holders embossed with the hammer and sickle. Many years later, when such memories surfaced during the war, Zelensky admitted to feelings of nostalgia. But it tasted bitter now, tainted by one of the defining ironies of his life. He had been raised by the same empire whose revival he was now fighting to stop.

On this trip, the longest the president had taken since the invasion started, he headed south toward the city of Mykolaiv, about as close as the train could safely bring him to the southern front. Most of the compartments were taken up by the security men, who rested their assault rifles on the luggage racks, kicked up their feet, and watched videos on their phones. Wartime protocols required the locomotive to chug along at a dreary pace. In case of a rocket strike on one of the wagons, the others would sustain less damage at that speed, and more passengers would be likely to survive. For long stretches, as they passed through the country's rural heartland, communications on the train were spotty. Some of their phones did not have enough signal to send a text message or read the news. "It gives us a chance to speak in peace," said Denys Monastyrsky, the minister of internal affairs, who accompanied the president.

In Zelensky's private car, they sat around a conference table or sank into a narrow sofa upholstered in green. The space was cramped, but the table was big enough for a handful of Zelensky's aides to join him over glasses of tea, still served in metal cup holders, but with the railway company's logo in place of the hammer and sickle. For Monastyrsky, the trip was a particular treat. Unlike most of the officials on the train, he had never lived in the presidential bunker, and his wartime interactions with Zelensky tended to be rushed and formal. At security briefings, they spoke in short bursts of information, delivering status reports on the crisis of the day. But on the long journey south, Monastyrsky told me, "We talked about our private worries, how our families are coping, our kids."

It was also their first real chance to discuss the future of the war and how it might end. In the event of a Ukrainian victory, they knew the nation's troubles would be far from over. The national economy was in tatters, much of its infrastructure damaged or destroyed. Nearer their destination, they passed empty stations and half-abandoned villages, naked trees ripped apart by mortar fire. Nearly a third of the population had been displaced. Many of them would return with expectations of government support. At least a million veterans of the war would also come back to their towns and cities in need of work, social services, and psychological support. They would be armed, and more than a few would have grievances against the government. "What are we going to do about mass demonstrations?" asked Monastyrsky. The restrictions imposed under martial law would sooner or later result in a backlash. "It will lead to mass protests," he said. "What do we need to put in place that will allow us to talk to the people? Who's going to talk to them? Clearly it needs to be someone who has experienced this war, who went through it and can talk to the veterans in their own language."

In his nightly speeches to the nation, the president tended to focus on the issues of the day. But in private he and his aides had begun to consider the political threats of the future. "We're not just talking about the war and the immediate challenges," Monastyrsky said. "We also need to calculate the risks coming around the corner. What will happen in half a year? What sorts of crimes? What actions do we need to take today to deal with issues six months from now?" They all believed in Ukraine's ultimate victory, but they understood the war would leave wounds and fissures in society that could take many years to heal. Political leaders would need to address public demands for recovery and reconstruction at a time when state resources will have been depleted. For a while they could count on the nation's sense of unity and common purpose to hold out in the postwar period of deprivation. But for how long? Millions of displaced Ukrainians would return to find their cities damaged or destroyed, cut off from basic services, and they would not have endless patience with official promises to rebuild.

In particular, Zelensky and his aides worried that the war could spark popular unrest, even another revolution in Ukraine. Kyrylo Tymoshenko, who was also on the train that night, understood that Ukrainians were losing patience with the war as spring turned to summer. The ratings of the Telemarathon had begun to crater as millions of viewers tuned out. "People were always going to get tired sooner or later with the flood of news," he said. In an effort to win them back, he urged the producers to air more entertainment, popular movies, and documentaries. "We tried that several times, but it did not work in the marathon. It was wrong to think it would give people a chance to exhale. The numbers showed that it hurt the ratings."

As the main source of news in the country, the marathon remained a powerful tool for the government to shape perceptions of the war. For nearly half the population it was the primary news source, often the only one available. Its coverage was broadcast around the clock on all the major networks, and it skewed hard toward the patriotic and the reassuring, another form of national sedation. Zelensky's speeches, posts, and public appearances ran throughout each day. Voices critical of his decisions rarely made it on the air. But the marathon did not amount to a monopoly on information.

Social media apps, like Instagram and Telegram, rivaled the popularity of TV news, and some of the most prominent voices on these platforms had begun to question the government's handling of the war. One particularly fierce debate emerged around the siege of Mariupol. Its last defenders, speaking to the media from the bunkers of Azovstal, blamed the authorities for allowing the Russians to encircle the city in just a few days. Military leaders and the rank and file also remembered how Zelensky had downplayed the threat of an invasion and did little to prepare for it. Denys Prokopenko, the commander of the Azov Regiment, pulled no punches in his condemnations of the state. "We've been left on our own," he told *Ukrainska Pravda*, the nation's leading online news outlet, in early May.

By then, the reporters at *Ukrainska Pravda* had gotten wind of a secret survey that the presidential administration commissioned in the spring. Its purpose was to assess the political playing field and how it was evolving at a time of war. The results offered some good news for Zelensky. His traditional rivals, like Petro Poroshenko, had withered to near-irrelevance in the polls. But other figures had gained in popularity. General Zaluzhny, the commander of the armed forces, had earned enough adoration among voters in the first two months of the invasion to challenge Zelensky in a presidential race. The next elections were not due to take place for another two years, in the spring of 2024, and the president's approval ratings left him no urgent reason to worry. They had reached above 90 percent in March. The only institution with more popular support was the military, which Zaluzhny had come to embody in the eyes of most Ukrainians.

Although he rarely appeared in public, the general had attained cult status in Ukraine. Memes and videos of him went viral. Images of Zaluzhny holding up the victory sign could be found stenciled with spray paint on walls across the country. In April, he created a foundation to help raise money for the armed forces, and some officials on Bankova Street saw it as a sign of Zaluzhny's political ambitions. They were not being paranoid. While the general denied having plans to run for office, some of his closest aides told me he was open to the idea. "I'd say it's possible," one of them said. "There are a lot of dead, a lot of wounded, and he feels a great deal of responsibility for them, for their families. He would not be able to sit on the sidelines if he sees that the country is going in the wrong direction."

For the moment, Zaluzhny focused all of his energy on winning the war, and he had made no firm decisions about his future in politics. But a group of his advisers within the General Staff set out to calculate what it would take for him to launch a political party or run a presidential campaign. His spokeswoman, Lyudmila Dolgonovska, was collecting material for a book about Zaluzhny, an authorized biography that he was helping her to write. "He understands that becoming president would be straightforward enough with the right team, the right program," she told me. "He's prepared. But I'm not sure he'll go for it. If everything goes all right, if he sees that the right steps are being taken, the right attitude toward veterans, toward the families of the dead, if the efforts to fight corruption are really tough and the army is getting stronger, he might decide against it."

That was cold comfort to Zelensky and his aides. As they surveyed the field of political competitors, past or future, real or imagined, the office of the president did not appear to be taking any chances. News networks that declined to show the Telemarathon were taken off the air by the end of spring. Poroshenko's channel, once among the top broadcasters in the country, could still be found on cable and YouTube. But its viewership shrank precipitously, as did popular support for the former president and his party. As one of Zelensky's advisers put it, Poroshenko and his allies had been relegated to the "digital fringes" of the Internet.

Even allies of the president found themselves under suspicion if they grew too popular. Vitaliy Kim, the charismatic governor of the Mykolaiv region, attained the status of a national hero in the first days of the war, when he taunted and trolled the Russians on social media even as they tried to storm his city. In one viral post, he offered to buy Russian soldiers some food and a ticket home if they surrendered all their weapons. As Kim's celebrity grew, the media began to mention him as a possible successor to Zelensky. The president's aides were not amused, and they urged Kim to lower his public profile. "It was getting annoying," one of them told me.

Those tensions passed by the time Zelensky's train pulled into Mykolaiv. Governor Kim, dressed in the camo-green T-shirt that was now de rigueur among politicians in Ukraine, came out to meet the presidential entourage and to take them on a tour of the city and its ruins. The first Russian assault on Mykolaiv took place on February 26, the third day of the invasion. Pushing northward from Crimea, the invaders took control of a nearby airport, intending to use it as a base for their onward drive across southern Ukraine. The airport had just been completed the previous year. At its unveiling, it served as a showcase for what Zelensky had called "the Big Build," his administration's plan to develop the nation's infrastructure. Kyrylo Tymoshenko, who oversaw the project, worried at the start of the invasion that the airport would become a battleground, and he wrote a text message to General Zaluzhny: *Please be very careful when working around it. The runway is new.* The general responded: *Of course, understood.* A few days later, Ukrainian attack drones and artillery laid waste to Russian forces at the airport, destroying scores of enemy vehicles and aircraft. Zaluzhny sent Tymoshenko a photo of the damage. The runway lay in ruins. The terminal building had collapsed. The general added: *Sorry.*

For weeks afterward, the Russians kept trying to seize and hold the airport, pushing wave after wave of their columns into the crosshairs of Ukrainian artillery. At least one Russian general and hundreds of troops wound up dead, and the name of the nearest village, Chornobaivka, became a byword for Ukrainian defiance and a symbol of the Russian failure to learn from their costliest mistakes. In a video posted on March 5, Vitaliy Kim announced that the invaders had been expelled from Mykolaiv. "They're just running away," the governor said. But they didn't go far. Digging in around the city of Kherson, about forty miles to the southeast, Russian rockets and artillery took revenge for the defeat by bombarding the city where their advance had been stopped. One missile struck the regional government headquarters in Mykolaiv on March 29, killing at least thirty-one people and destroying the governor's office. Kim happened to be away at the time and survived the attack. When he took Zelensky to see the building in June, the president winced at the scale of the destruction. The central section had collapsed, leaving a gaping hole in the middle of the building.

The barrage went on for months. In every city that managed to hold back the enemy, from Kharkiv in the east to Zaporizhzhia in the south, vicious bombing raids ensued, killing hundreds of civilians, as the

Russians terrorized the people they had failed to conquer. At least four rockets hit Mykolaiv during Zelensky's visit. The day before, a missile struck one of the city's biggest factories. Still, the president chose not to make these attacks the focus of his trip to the southern front. He gave out medals to those who led the defense of the region, including Governor Kim. Most of all, he looked ahead to the process of reconstruction and recovery. He and Kim talked about restoring the water supply, which the Russian bombs had cut off months before. They discussed the harvest in the region, how to provide farmers with enough fuel for their combines, enough storage for their grain, and the logistical routes to move it. Later that day in Odesa, the country's biggest seaport, Zelensky focused on his plan to resume the export of food, which would require convincing the Russians to ease their blockade of shipping routes through the Black Sea. On the ride back to Kyiv, he stepped out of his private car after midnight and recorded an address in the gangway, where the clatter of the train forced him to raise his voice. "The losses are significant," he said into the camera of his phone. Around Odesa and Mykolaiv, "a lot of homes destroyed, civil logistics interrupted, a lot of social questions." He had ordered regional officials to concern themselves not only with matters of defense but with recovery, with social services and support for victims. "We will definitely rebuild all that has been destroyed," he said. "Russia does not have as many rockets as our people have the will to live."

Four months into the war, around three million refugees had returned to Ukraine from the European Union, arriving at a rate of roughly thirty thousand per day. Zelensky wanted to make sure they would at least have light and heat, schools for their children, a chance to work and provide for their families. The demands of the war did not free him from the more mundane responsibilities of leadership, nor from his concern that his people would run out of patience eventually and turn against him. The state did not have nearly enough resources to offer social support to military personnel, whose numbers had roughly tripled since the start of the invasion, to more than seven hundred thousand people. The need to pay their salaries, to say nothing of their medical bills, had begun to strain the federal budget to the breaking point by the middle of summer, and Zelensky's aides understood the political risks of failing to care for them. Davyd Arakhamia, the president's close friend and the leader of his party's faction in parliament, estimated that

Ukraine would have two million active or retired military personnel by the end of the war, equal to about 15 percent of the economically active population. "We will not have enough money to keep them all happy," he told a forum of military veterans that summer. If the state cannot find ways to support them, he added, "they'll come and carry us out feetfirst, all the ministers, all the politicians, the whole government."

❖

The day after Zelensky returned from the southern front, I went to see the First Lady at her office a couple of floors below his. It was a Monday in June, and the compound felt quiet, much more subdued than it had been a month or two earlier. A lot of the presidential staff had begun to take time off to rest as the weather improved. The main thing on the president's agenda for the day was a meeting with Ben Stiller, one of several Hollywood stars to make the pilgrimage to Bankova Street that summer. At the checkpoint to get inside, the soldiers seemed relaxed, though their faces stiffened when I mentioned my appointment with Olena. A senior officer of the state security service came down to question me about it. The guards searched my bag with particular care, and none of my electronics were allowed near the First Lady.

On the second floor, her bodyguard, the enormous Yaroslav, glared at me from the doorway with a dagger affixed to the front of his belt. Were it not for him and the other soldiers, Olena's suite in the presidential compound would have resembled an upscale design firm, with muted gray walls and violet carpets, a set of ferns in vases of poured concrete. From a table near the entrance, her face looked up at me from the covers of several magazines, one French, another Polish, and the Ukrainian edition of *Vogue*. A photographer had come with me to take her portrait for the cover of *Time*, and when she entered the room, Olena was surprised to find herself inside his studio lights. Several aides fluttered around, adjusting the First Lady's outfit, fixing her hair and makeup. A stylist had dressed her upper body for the cameras in a sharp yellow blazer. But, from the waist down, she was dressed like the old Olena, the screenwriter, in baggy jeans and clunky loafers.

Since the start of the invasion, she had given up working on scripts for her old movie studio. "Before the war I could do both," she told me.

"Not anymore." It felt frivolous when she tried, and now she was eager to talk about her new line of work, the projects she had undertaken to help Ukrainians cope with their trauma and, whenever possible, to support her husband. A few times they had discussed her ideas for offering psychological help to victims of the war, and the president encouraged Olena to do her best. But the distance between them made it difficult to keep him engaged. Their meetings were too brief and infrequent to update Zelensky about the children and other private matters, let alone her public ambitions as First Lady. "He does not give opinions of my work," she told me flatly. "He doesn't get involved."

So Olena set her own agenda and used the power of her office, such as it was, to push her projects through the state bureaucracy. Like many Ukrainians, Olena found relief in doing what little she could to help her country win the war and alleviate the suffering of its victims. Despair set in most easily among the onlookers and the doom-scrollers, while those who found a form of service, whether by filling sandbags or cooking meals for soldiers at a checkpoint, could use it as a way to stabilize the mind and fend off the pull of madness and depression. By early summer, Olena's days were packed with speeches, meetings, panel discussions, and interviews. She set up training programs for Ukrainian trauma counselors and hotlines to make their services widely available. Convincing Ukrainians to seek psychological support turned out to be a major challenge. When we talked about it, Olena borrowed the English phrase "mental health" because the concept is hard to describe in Ukrainian. "We have a particular distrust for terms that include the word *psycho*," she said. The term *psychotherapy* often evokes images of state-run asylums in Ukraine, places that are designed to isolate the ill from society. A lot of that stigma, Zelenska told me, has its roots in the Soviet Union, where generations of Ukrainians were raised to deal with trauma by hiding it away. The attitude, she said, was: "Deal with it, get over it, and if you complain, you're weak."

In cooperation with the Ministry of Health, she began to develop a network of psychologists and therapists who could offer trauma counseling both to soldiers and civilians. The Ministry estimated that, overall, about a third of the population, or fifteen million people, would require some form of mental health care. Olena and her husband were no exception. "You absorb it," she said of the war. "Each of us, including

myself, have felt that our psychological state is not what it should be."
Four months into the invasion, she said, "None of us are okay."

❖

The week after Zelensky returned from his trip to the south, he turned
his focus back to his political agenda in the capital, where he continued
to cull the opposition. The Ministry of Justice imposed an outright ban
on Medvedchuk's political party. The activities of ten other parties were
suspended for the duration of the war due to their alleged ties to Russia. Zelensky also settled a score with his former patron, the media and
banking mogul Ihor Kolomoysky, whose Ukrainian citizenship the state
summarily revoked in July. The same thing happened to Gennady Korban, a major power broker from the Dnipro region. When Korban tried
to enter the country, border guards revoked his passport and refused to
let him pass. The president responded with a smirk when asked to explain this decision. "We grant citizenship and we take it away," he said.
"It's an ongoing process."

By the middle of summer, the leading political clans in Ukraine
were getting sick of Zelensky's high-handedness. Many lawmakers had
begun to wonder whether he could handle the powers entrusted to him
under martial law, and whether he would ever be able to part with
them. "These powers should be used with care," said Serhiy Taruta,
a prominent industrialist and member of parliament from Mariupol.
"They should unite us, not manipulate us. And they should not be used
to fight your political opponents."

On the eve of the invasion, Taruta was among the wealthy businessmen who went to see Zelensky at his office. They had agreed
that night to call a political truce, and most of them had stuck to it.
Public criticism of the administration was muted in the first weeks
of all-out war. The politicians who stayed in Ukraine, regardless of
their prior loyalties, focused their efforts on national defense. Now that
truce had broken down, Taruta told me, and the president's team was
to blame. "They're busy destroying their political rivals," he said. "It's
insane." Under martial law, the parliament did not have much power to
challenge the presidency. It continued to operate behind closed doors,
rubber-stamping the initiatives sent down from Bankova Street. Journalists were not allowed to observe the plenary sessions or even enter

the building. But in their private meetings and deliberations, Taruta told me, the lawmakers had begun to grumble about Zelensky's failures in the lead-up to the invasion. "They could have avoided panic while also getting prepared," he said. "These things are not mutually exclusive."

The fate of Mariupol, his hometown, troubled Taruta most of all. At the start of the war in 2014, he served as the governor of the Donetsk region, which includes Mariupol, and he was familiar with the military's plans for defending the city. To stop the advance of Russian forces from Crimea, the Ukrainians had mined the narrow isthmus that connects Crimea to the mainland. They had also planted explosives around a bridge that leads north from Crimea over the Chonhar Strait. Yet on the morning of February 24, when the invasion began, none of these bombs were detonated. The bridge remained standing, and the armored Russian columns were able to pass right over it, sweeping north into the region of Kherson, and on toward Mariupol. "The Chonhar pass was mined all the way back in 2014," Taruta told me. "Why didn't they blow it up? Why did they allow them to cross?"

No one in the military or the presidential administration had come forward to explain this catastrophic blunder. It was not discussed in detail on the Telemarathon. When Oleksiy Arestovych was asked about it in early May, he gave an honest if unsatisfying answer: "We fucked up." The president and his aides pledged to investigate the failures and punish any officials who assisted the Russian advance through negligence or treason. In the first few months of the war, such promises were enough to deflect demands for accountability. But their opponents lost patience by the middle of summer, and the public was less inclined to give Zelensky the benefit of the doubt. "Everyone was sitting quietly while our survival was an open question," Arestovych told me. "As soon as it was clear that we survived, this whole story started crawling out." It reminded him of an earlier phase of the war, in 2014 and 2015, when the comfortable elites in Kyiv were able to continue their squabbles while the Donbas burned. "Again we're losing the sense of national unity," Arestovych said. "Politics is back."

Journalists, too, had returned to questioning the powerful. Under martial law, which the parliament had prolonged at the end of April, the state had the right to censor the press and control the airwaves. But by summer, reporters began pushing back on these restrictions. At a briefing with Zelensky in June, held in honor of National Journalist's Day, the first question came from a reporter for *Ukrainska Pravda*, who asked the president for his views on wartime censorship. His reply made clear it would remain in effect as long as necessary to win the war. "The weapon of information," he said, "is very important. You see it in my actions and your actions as journalists. It's also important to point this weapon not at one's own head, but in the direction of the enemy." Zelensky went on for a while, comparing journalists to "soldiers at the front" and lauding the Telemarathon as a "unified weapon of information." If this was his chance to put the press corps in their place, he seemed to relish it. His relationship with the media had always been tense. In one famous rant in 2021, a few months before the invasion, he lashed out at one of Ukraine's leading journalists during a televised briefing. "You are one of the destabilizers of this country," he said. "It's thanks to you that this happens, this constant rocking of the boat in our country. It's thanks to the media!"

Few if any publications got under Zelensky's skin like *Ukrainska Pravda*, which was known for its unflinching investigations of oligarchs and the politicians they controlled. Over the years it had paid dearly for its coverage. The outlet's founding editor, Georgiy Gongadze, was murdered in 2000. His killers then cut the head off his body, covered it in acid, and dumped it in a forest outside Kyiv. Ukraine's president at the time, Leonid Kuchma, was accused of ordering the assassination. His own bodyguard secretly recorded Kuchma in his office on Bankova Street, discussing how and when Gongadze should be silenced. Kuchma denied involvement in the murder, and a judge tossed out an attempt to prosecute him for it in 2011. But the stain on his reputation lingered, and the reporters at *Ukrainska Pravda* carried the weight of Gongadze's legacy through the years.

When I visited their newsroom in early June, it was mostly deserted, with only a few desks occupied by reporters, who looked up and acknowledged me with a quiet nod before turning back to their screens. They had just moved into a new office before the invasion started, and their editor, Sevgil Musaieva, apologized for the mess as she showed me around. One of the first things she hung on the wall was a black-and-white portrait of her colleague Pavel Sheremet, a star columnist who was killed in a car bombing in 2016. In one of the moving boxes, she had come across an old backgammon board that had belonged to Gongadze, its wooden surface warped from age and overuse. In another box, she found some photos of his mutilated body at the morgue. "They were just filed away at our old place," she told me. "Now they'll live with us here."

Musaieva, a native of Crimea, was still in her twenties when she took over *Ukrainska Pravda* in 2014, right after her home region was annexed by the Russians and the war in the Donbas began. A careful listener and reluctant talker, she bore the pressure of her role with an intensity that made her seem aloof, and she avoided the prime-time talk shows where the blood sport of Ukrainian politics played out. When Zelensky decided to run for office, Musaieva regarded the antics of his campaign with the same suspicion she would afford to any pretender to the presidency. She told her reporters to dig, and they dug, taking a close look at Zelensky's finances and his use of offshore bank accounts. After winning the race, the president-elect tried to co-opt Musaieva, offering her a job as his press secretary. Her refusal took the form of a question. If she accepted the offer, she asked Zelensky, "then who would watch over you?"

Three years later, the start of the invasion eased some of the tension in their relationship. *Ukrainska Pravda*, like its main competitors, took a break from political muckraking in the spring of 2022. Musaieva's newsroom wanted to show solidarity and respect for the president at a time of all-out war, and to focus on the far more pressing matters of national defense. But soon they went back to reporting on the squabbles inside the president's administration, and it earned them a lot of enemies on Bankova Street. The most sensitive topics for Zelensky and his team were their failure to anticipate the scale of the invasion and their attempts to suppress the warnings that came from the military. Any reporting on the tensions between the president and his top general also received a furious reaction. "They tell us we're toxic, that we only write lies," said Musaieva. "But their conflict with Zaluzhny does exist. They act like we can only have one hero, and that's Zelensky. No one else."

A few weeks later, when enough of her friends and colleagues had returned to Kyiv, Musaieva decided to throw a birthday party at her apartment in the center of the city, and she invited me to come along. The guests were mostly activists and reporters. Many of them had not seen each other in months, and they took a while to adjust to the festive atmosphere. The gauzy light streaming in through the windows, the clinking glasses and bouquets of flowers, all of it felt like a half-forgotten dream, too serene to exist within the nightmare of the war.

Some of the guests were newfangled military veterans, having signed up to fight when the invasion started. A few of them came to the party in uniform. One novelist carried a sidearm on his belt. He said he had come back from the front the previous week and, after his third or fourth glass of whiskey, he shut his eyes and began to describe how he had nearly been killed under Russian shellfire, how he had wished to dig himself into the ground as it heaved beneath his belly, tossing him up in the air every time a mortar hit nearby. Several of his comrades had been killed. When the barrage subsided, the others stood up and kept running toward the Russian positions. "It's hell there," he said, looking around at the sun-filled room. "And nobody here knows about it. Nobody really knows." He closed his eyes again. "It's very hard to come back from that and see you people, sipping wine. But then I think: 'This is what we're fighting for—for this kind of life to exist.'"

Out on the balcony, two young men stood smoking e-cigarettes and discussing the fine points of Russian artillery systems, using the tone that hipsters in Brooklyn might use to talk about rising rent or parking problems. The blast radius of a Kalibr missile, the fact that hypersonic munitions make no noise before they strike, these things passed for small talk among millennials in Kyiv that summer. The only topic that got more attention was politics, and in this crowd, there was no love lost for Zelensky. Between answering the doorbell and raising toasts, Musaieva introduced me to one of her friends and fellow journalists. It was Myroslava Gongadze, the widow of the founding editor of *Ukrainska Pravda*. For months, she had been pestering the president to grant her an interview and, like hundreds of others, had been ignored. "Don't be too generous to him," Gongadze told me. "You don't know what he will become."

CHAPTER 20

INDEPENDENCE DAY

THE UKRAINIAN PEOPLE DID NOT SEE MUCH OF GENERAL ZALUZHNY IN THE FIRST FEW months of the invasion. He was conspicuously absent from the Telemarathon. When he appeared, it was usually in viral images on social media: the general kneeling beside the casket at a soldier's funeral, officiating the wedding of a serviceman, standing at a checkpoint with his troops. Fan pages devoted to him had hundreds of thousands of followers. Headlines called him the Iron General. People printed his image on T-shirts to sell as souvenirs. During the one interview he gave before the invasion, in September 2021, he did not betray any of the hunger for power that some officials in the president's office suspected him of hiding. On the contrary, he seemed to shrink under the glare of the cameras, as though bashful of his massive frame. So it surprised me, five months into the invasion, to hear that the Iron General wanted to talk.

The invitation came from his close adviser, Oleksiy Noskov, whom I had met during my trip with President Zelensky to the Donbas a year earlier. A colonel with a slight frame and a gloomy disposition, Noskov was not the type for heavy combat. He did the bookish work inside the General Staff, specializing in information warfare and psychological operations. He was also in charge of Zaluzhny's public image, his social media accounts and interviews, and he had been urging his boss to raise his public profile; Noskov believed publicity could serve as a shield from any attempts to sideline or dismiss Zaluzhny. For months, Noskov told me, the office of the president urged the commander to avoid speaking on the record to the press. Only in the summer they relented, and Noskov asked me to come for an interview at a hotel in central Kyiv. The place had no discernible connection to the armed forces, no military vehicles, no uniformed personnel, just a handyman out in the blazing sun when I arrived, fixing something at the edge of the parking lot. The guards looked at me with wide eyes and ran back to their booth when I told them I had come to see Zaluzhny. Was it the wrong address? After a few minutes, Noskov appeared with a gun on his hip and instructed them to let me through. "You really caused a panic in there," he told me. "Nobody is supposed to know Zaluzhny lives here."

Soon the commander appeared at the edge of the parking lot, strutting toward us in a pair of cargo shorts and sneakers. His T-shirt looked like the ones available at Kyiv's knickknack stands. It showed the *Moskva*, pride of the Russian Navy, sinking into the waters of the Black Sea, and the immortal line: *Russian warship, go fuck yourself.* On a lanyard around his neck, the general had a badge holder with a picture of a gun inside it, a Sig Sauer M17. Was that a firearms license? Why would a general need a gun permit in the middle of a war? "Oh, that's just to hold my room key," he told me with a smile. "I lost it so many times my wife gave me this to wear around my neck."

His wife? She was living with him? Again Zaluzhny smiled. Near the end of spring, around the time his forces liberated the region of Kyiv, he had moved out of the bunker beneath the Ministry of Defense and reunited with his fairer half. It was too dangerous for them to live at home, so they settled into a hotel commandeered by the military. The place did not have a proper bomb shelter, but the service was good. Waiters brought out a few cans of cola for us and a platter of fruit. Every once in a while, Zaluzhny held a bright yellow vape to his lips and took a drag. It seemed to help him organize his thoughts.

"I'm going to tell you all this once," he said, "and then I'm not going to tell it anymore." Among his more revealing stories went back to the summer of 2020, about a year before the president chose him to lead the military. That August, Zaluzhny organized a series of military drills in the south of Ukraine, and Zelensky flew down to observe them. The drills aimed to showcase Ukraine's ability to fend off a Russian attack from the south, exactly the kind that would unfold about eighteen months later.

The first stop on the tour was Snake Island, an arid fleck of land in the Black Sea where Ukraine had a barracks and a radar station to observe the movements of the Russian Navy. It was an uninspiring sight. Ukraine no longer had much of a navy to showcase. Nearly all its warships had been based in Crimea, and the Russians seized them in 2014 along with the rest of the peninsula. What remained was a creaking fleet of patrol boats and helicopters that Zelensky observed through a set of binoculars, with Zaluzhny by his side. From Snake Island, helicopters took them to a much bigger base in the Mykolaiv region, where the general had prepared a series of tank and infantry maneuvers. They started out well despite the heat, which was punishing that day, especially for the soldiers forced to run around in body armor.

Zaluzhny had decided to test their ability to launch an offensive against the Russians—not just to hold territory but to win it back. He also wanted to show off the reforms underway in the military. Their aim, he explained, was to help Ukrainian forces react to surprises on the battlefield, communicating and supporting each other rather than just waiting for orders from the top. To achieve that, the armed forces needed to uproot the command structure left over from the Red Army, where all decisions of significance had been made in Moscow and handed down. Zaluzhny was passionate about the need to ditch that system. When responding to changes on the battlefield, he argued, officers on the ground need to have the freedom and the confidence to make decisions for themselves. The Americans and other Western allies had spent years advocating for these reforms, which would have brought Ukraine closer to the standards of the NATO alliance. But the resistance from the generals in Kyiv was fierce. All of the older cadres had grown up within the Soviet military, and they saw the changes as a threat to their authority and the discipline within their ranks. "The work could not have been more difficult," Zaluzhny recalled of that period. "The entire Soviet system of control had to be knocked down."

When Zelensky took office he was, at best, vaguely aware of these reforms, and Zaluzhny tried not to overload the president with too much detail. "It's a habit of mine," Zaluzhny said. "My wife often chews me out for it. She says it's like I have three ways of explaining something: one for normal people, another for people with half a clue, and a third for imbeciles." Up on the observation deck, the general could sense that the nuances of the drills were hard for Zelensky to follow through a pair of binoculars. They took time to play out, and the president's office, which had invited a cadre of reporters to cover the exercises, wanted to see a better show. American and European military advisers had also flown down for the occasion and were crowding the deck along with the president's team. To make the event a bit more dramatic, they asked Zaluzhny to introduce a last-minute amendment to the program—a demonstration of the Javelin missile. Reluctantly, he agreed.

The Javelins, an American weapon with a price tag of roughly a quarter million dollars per shot, had come to symbolize U.S. support for Ukraine. The Obama administration refused for years to provide these tank-busters, citing fears of an escalation spiral with the Russians. But in 2017, under President Trump, the U.S. finally shipped some Javelins to Ukraine. They looked like bulky, high-tech bazookas, with a guidance system so advanced that a soldier could, according to the promotional material, "fire and forget." But the slogan was misleading. These were not easy weapons to use, and very few Ukrainians had ever trained with them. Zaluzhny felt nervous about putting them on the stage. "It wasn't my idea," he told me. "And it didn't work." When the marine adjusted the sights and instructed the computer to fire, nothing happened. The observation deck went silent. The rocket was a dud. Or maybe the soldier had not been trained to use it. In any case, Zelensky and the rest of the men in the gallery looked over at Zaluzhny. "Then they bowed their heads, turned around, and walked away." The mishap eclipsed what had been a fine performance from the troops, all of whom had done their best in the punishing heat. When the drills ended that afternoon, the presidential entourage climbed down from the observation deck and went to the mess hall for a lunch of buckwheat and chicken fricassee. Their silence felt worse than any reprimand to Zaluzhny. "To me it meant: you're no good, pack up your stuff and get lost." He was sure he would forever be known in the president's office as "the loser with the faulty Javelins."

The story, which he told with no hard feelings, an amusing anecdote from the distant past, seemed to illustrate a common frustration in his experience as a commander. Zaluzhny made it clear that politicians and generals make awkward partners. They rarely understand each other, and they get along best when they stay out of each other's way. Zaluzhny looked to Zelensky as an embodiment of the state, and he respected the president's courage and leadership once the invasion started. "He is the supreme commander in chief, and for me that's a symbol, a boss." But the military operated best under the command of professionals, and there was no sense in trying to teach the president to run the armed forces. "He doesn't need to understand military affairs any more than he needs to know about medicine or bridge building," Zaluzhny said.

As the invasion drew near, the office of the president got more involved in the military response. They urged Zaluzhny to avoid causing alarm among the public, and he soon stopped asking for permission to take the steps he felt were necessary, such as the movement of forces in the Blizzard exercises. He did not inform the president about the details of his preparations for the war. Apart from the need for secrecy, the general worried that Zelensky and his team would interfere and mess things up, a bit like they had done during those drills back in 2020.

Once the invasion started, their relationship worked best when Zelensky stuck to his specialties—mass communication, foreign affairs, convincing allies to provide the weapons Ukraine needed. But as the initial state of panic in Kyiv wore off and the Russians went into retreat, Zelensky grew more confident. He formed his own military priorities, and they were not always aligned with those of the general. Soon the rift between the two men widened, and they began to clash.

❖

Near the end of June, a couple of weeks after my interview with General Zaluzhny, the United States delivered a powerful new weapon to the forces under his command. The High Mobility Artillery Rocket Systems, known as HIMARS, would vastly expand the range and ambition of the Ukrainian military and shift the balance of forces in the war. Mounted on the back of U.S. army trucks, these rockets had a modest payload but remarkable accuracy. They were capable of hitting a parked car or an outhouse from many miles away.

When combined with fresh intelligence from U.S. military satellites, these weapons could spread panic among the Russian forces, striking their barracks, command centers, fuel depots, and ammunition dumps far behind the front lines. "The satellites allow us to see what the enemy is hiding," Oleksiy Reznikov, the defense minister, told me. "The HIMARS allow us to destroy it." The first reported strike with this weapon in Ukraine killed as many as forty Russian soldiers at the end of June. Typically launched in the dead of night, these attacks soon became routine, and they marked a new level of U.S. involvement in the war. The Americans were now providing both the precise locations of Russian targets and the long-range weapons to destroy them.

For President Joe Biden, the arrangement had been difficult to stomach. He was intent on avoiding an escalation that could pull NATO forces into direct conflict with Russian troops, and it took weeks of debate and wrangling inside the White House to convince him that the value of delivering HIMARS to Ukraine outweighed the risks. General Milley acted as a mediator in these discussions, urging Biden to approve the deliveries as fast as possible while also asking the Ukrainians to be patient. Their wish list of weapons often struck Milley as fanciful, and he told them to keep their demands inside what he called the "reality box." Asking too much of the White House would only strain the relationship.

But Zelensky found it hard to hold back. During a phone call on June 15, about two weeks after the U.S. announced the decision to send HIMARS to Ukraine, Zelensky had barely finished expressing his thanks to Biden before demanding even more, rattling off a list of the weapons the U.S. had yet to provide. Biden reportedly lost his temper at Zelensky. He had just approved another package of military aid to Ukraine worth $1 billion, the biggest since the invasion, and instead of taking a pause to acknowledge American generosity, the Ukrainian leader kept pushing for more. In a meeting with reporters, one U.S. diplomat complained that Zelensky showed less appreciation for Biden than he did for other leaders, such as Boris Johnson, the British prime minister, whose government was providing far less aid.

In the context of the war, such tensions looked petty, and they did not lead to any lasting rupture between Kyiv and Washington. Both sides were committed to defeating the Russians. Throughout July, guided missiles rained down on Russian bases and barracks, command posts and ammunition dumps, seeking to weaken the defenses of the occupiers across southern and eastern Ukraine. The leadership in Kyiv celebrated these strikes with taunts on social media. When night fell in Kyiv, the Ministry of Defense would often release a statement: "It's HIMARS o'clock." Andriy Yermak preferred to announce the attacks by posting an emoji of a rocket on his Twitter feed.

The rockets flew in both directions, and as Russian losses mounted in the east, their commanders took their anger out on innocent civilians.

On July 14, a cruise missile fired from a Russian submarine in the Black Sea struck the center of Vinnytsia, a regional capital in central Ukraine, killing at least twenty-eight people and wounding more than two hundred others. Among the victims was a four-year-old girl named Liza Dmitrieva, who was killed as her mother pushed her along the sidewalk in a stroller. Images of her body spread on social media that day, and by evening, they reached the office of Olena Zelenska on the second floor of the presidential compound. She was busy preparing that day for a visit to Washington, and she decided to take Liza's story with her.

As long as her husband could not travel abroad, Olena realized her most valuable role in the administration would be that of an advocate on the world stage, not only for Zelensky but for all Ukrainian victims of the invasion. She still worried that some false move could embarrass the country and hurt its standing in the world, but the fear of embarrassing herself had passed. "The war broke it," she told me. "I'm not afraid for myself anymore." For security reasons, she and her team took a commercial flight to Washington, hoping to blend in among with the crowds of regular travelers. But, during their layover, the airline announced that the flight was overbooked, and they would be forced to take another one the following day. "We couldn't go making a ruckus," she recalled. "We had not announced the visit ahead of time. It wasn't allowed." Olena's security detail permitted her assistant to inform the airline workers that their passenger was the First Lady of Ukraine, a country at war, and that she was on her way to visit President Biden. Three additional passengers were then allowed to board the flight: Olena, her bodyguard, and one of her assistants. From that point, everything went smoothly, she said, "like the pieces of a puzzle fitting together."

When she arrived at the White House, Jill Biden cut through the pomp with a series of gestures—a hug, an encouraging touch—that made Olena feel like she was visiting friends. It was the first time in memory that any president of the United States received the First Lady of another country in the Oval Office. Later that day, she was invited to address a joint session of Congress, another first for a foreign First Lady. The speech had taken hours to write in consultation with Zelensky and Ukraine's most senior diplomats, who encouraged her to break through the tropes expected of a First Lady's speech and make full use of the opportunity. "I might have wanted to talk about flowers and babies," she joked. "But no."

She had spent half her life writing her husband's scripts. Now she would need to deliver a speech while channeling his new persona, a speech about the war and all its horrors, the Russian attempt to annihilate their country, and the weapons they needed to stay alive. As she read it over on the plane and in her hotel room in Washington, various sections made her choke back tears, especially the point when she told Liza's story. But her delivery was flawless when the moment came to speak. With images projected on a screen behind her, Olena talked about the children who had been killed or lost limbs under Russian bombs, about a family shot dead in their car by Russian soldiers while trying to evacuate. Then she began to ask for help with all the bluntness the world had come to expect from her husband. "I'm asking for weapons," she said. "I'm asking for air defense systems in order for rockets not to kill children in their strollers."

The bright lights on the stage made it difficult for her to see the audience, but she could make out the reaction of the lawmakers in the front rows as they stood to applaud and came up to shake her hand. "I saw tears in the eyes of those respectable men in their expensive ties and jackets," she told me. "And they weren't faking it." When she got back to Kyiv, her friends and colleagues on Bankova Street told her the speech was a triumph. Only Zelensky held back, as though the time had not yet come to assess the value of her trip to Washington. "He thanked me in fairly dry terms," Olena said. "As in, 'Well, it seems everything went fine.'"

His reaction had nothing to do with her delivery in Washington. Olena's speech hit every one of the notes and messages they had worked on together. But the president and his team had decided by the middle of summer that their diplomatic strategy was running out of steam. Their appeals to common values with the West, to the outrage of the world at Russian atrocities, had gone about as far as they would go in securing weapons and financial assistance.

Some European leaders, such as Prime Minister Viktor Orban of Hungary, argued that military aid to Ukraine was fueling the conflict rather than resolving it. "The Ukrainians will not come out victorious," Orban said in a speech at the end of July. The Russians, he added, had an "asymmetrical dominance" that no infusion of Western arms could overcome. With such views catching on among members of NATO, Zelensky realized the best way to counter them would be to show Ukraine's ability to win, to push back the Russians and reclaim the territory they had occupied. "Cynical as it sounds," the president told me, "everyone wants to be on the side of the winner. Of course it's true that America supports Ukraine because of our shared values, but that support starts to weaken when they don't see results."

And the results could only take one form: a counterstrike. Working with their closest allies in NATO, General Zaluzhny and his fellow commanders weighed a range of options with varying degrees of payoff and risk. In a series of virtual war games, they modeled how different lines of attack would play out on the battlefield, and what weapons Ukraine would need to break through Russia's defensive lines. By early July, as the HIMARS began to hammer Russian command posts and ammunition dumps, Zelensky and his team became confident enough with the balance of forces to announce an offensive. Its aim, they said, would be to liberate southern Ukraine, and they urged civilians to evacuate the area.

General Zaluzhny, who was in charge of the operation, wanted to take his time, stockpile weapons, and prepare forces for a southward push that would break the back of the Russian occupation. He wanted to liberate the cities of Kherson and Melitopol before launching a deeper thrust all the way to the edge of Crimea. The mission, he argued, would require secrecy and careful planning, but the president's office wanted to move fast. Data from U.S. satellites showed that the Russian positions were weakest on the opposite end of the front, in the northeast, around the city of Kharkiv. The Russians had shifted a lot of their forces away from that area after Zelensky began warning of an imminent offensive in the south. But Zaluzhny resisted the temptation to strike the Kharkiv region. Though it made for an easier target, the general said its strategic value paled in comparison with what he wanted the offensive to achieve. He also worried about the difficulty of holding the northeastern regions, which touch the Russian border. "The problem with Kharkiv is that we push right up to the border, and then what do we do? We are exposed," said Colonel Noskov. "They can shoot at us from right across the border."

How would the Ukrainians respond? Would they shoot back? Would they proceed with an incursion into Russia itself? In this regard, their hands were tied. As a condition of providing advanced arms to Ukraine, the U.S. insisted those systems should not be used to fire into Russian territory. Around Kharkiv, General Zaluzhny would not be able to repeat the winning tactics from the Battle of Kyiv, as the invaders would not need to stretch their supply lines and leave them exposed. They could pummel Ukrainian positions from the Russian side of the border, making it difficult for Ukraine to hold any territory they might liberate in the northeast.

Zaluzhny therefore continued to focus on the operation in the south, and he appeared to have the backing of Ukraine's Western allies. Instead of sending a phony strategy to the Americans, as he had done before the invasion in February, Zaluzhny and his team shared their plans for a counteroffensive with General Milley and other senior commanders in the U.S. and Europe. "The partners expressed a desire to participate in this successful campaign," said Oleksiy Reznikov, the defense minister. "They said: Give us an understanding of how you want to attack, and we will tell you what help we can provide, what weapons could be effective."

The HIMARS systems, with their ability to hit Russian bases and ammunition dumps far behind enemy lines, proved critical in preparing for the counteroffensive. One of their main targets was the Antonovsky Bridge, a vital supply line for the Russian forces in the south. By the end of July, precision strikes had punched enough holes through the bridge to make it impassable, forcing the Russians to rely on floating pontoon bridges and ferries to deliver food and ammunition to their troops in occupied Kherson. Reznikov told me these strikes were meant to isolate the Russian forces along the southern front and set the stage for their encirclement. But even then, the Ukrainians had not yet settled on a plan of attack. "We were weighing our options," Reznikov said. "Will we manage it? Will we have enough time to build up the resources?"

The debate intensified as the Russian advance crept forward in the Donbas, forcing the Ukrainians to cede more territory. In early July, the invaders gained complete control of the eastern region of Luhansk. The Kremlin hailed it as a major victory, and Vladimir Putin awarded medals to the commanders involved in the offensive. He told them to get some rest and prepare for further advances in the Donbas. These setbacks worried General Zaluzhny, and his demands for weapons became more desperate in his daily phone calls with the president. "He asks the questions," said Noskov, who participated in these calls. "'When will we get the ammo? I have people dying every day. They can't shoot back, so they withdraw. And we end up losing territory. Where are the cannons? Where are the shells? Where's the ammo?'"

Though the supply of HIMARS and other advanced weapons from the West had improved Ukraine's position, they arrived at the front too slowly, and their numbers were too few to answer the relentless waves of incoming fire. The Russians continued to launch up to sixty thousand shells every day. Along a front line that stretched for over two thousand kilometers, they had enough cannons to place one every few hundred paces, while Ukraine could place one every few miles. General Zaluzhny tried everything to fill the gaps. He urged the president and the Ministry of Defense to purchase more stockpiles of Soviet-era weapons rather than waiting for the fancier kit from NATO. In the spring, Zaluzhny even created his own charitable foundation to help pay for these weapons. "The needs of the army in fighting this war are colossal," the general wrote in his public appeal for donations to the fund.

The office of the president looked askance at the initiative. Zelensky and his team had made it their mission to solicit money and arms from foreign donors. Why would the chief of the armed forces decide to start fundraising himself? Didn't he have enough to do? To some officials on Bankova Street, it looked like a sign of Zaluzhny's political ambitions, and the general agreed to distance himself from these efforts after Zelensky created a separate foundation, United 24, to help raise funds for the military. Apart from this incident, the public saw no sign of the mounting tensions between their president and their top military commander. Both men continued to insist on the strength of their relationship. But in private, the general faced increasing pressure to show results with the resources he had. When Zelensky and his aides tried to rush the start of the counteroffensive, Zaluzhny answered: With what? "We've got a hundred cannons out of service, getting repairs," Noskov told me over dinner in the middle of August. "What is he supposed to attack with? What if he goes on the offensive and ends up losing somewhere? They'll say he couldn't cut it."

But they were running out of time. As the Russians relocated forces to defend the south, Ukraine needed to concentrate more and more troops and weapons for its push in that direction, delaying the attack even further. By the end of summer, the president refused to wait any longer. If the conditions were not right for a breakthrough in the south, Zelensky wanted to strike the northeast, where Ukraine could demonstrate its ability to push the Russians back. In a series of strategy sessions, he urged his top generals to launch the attack in the Kharkiv direction. Zaluzhny refused. "He wanted to attack not where we could," Noskov told me, "but where we should."

❖

As the debate dragged on, the president reached for more aggressive ways to showcase Ukraine's ability to strike. The results played out far from the war zone, on a clandestine front where Ukraine could inflict substantial damage on the Russians using the modest weapons it had available. The man put in charge of this strategy was Ukraine's youngest general, Kyrylo Budanov, the thirty-seven-year-old commander of the military intelligence service known as GUR. A special forces commando turned spymaster, Budanov cut a dramatic figure, appearing frequently on television to issue vague threats and dark hints of his plans. "We've been killing Russians," he once bragged, "and we will keep killing Russians anywhere on the face of this world until the complete victory of Ukraine." Budanov, whose confidence verged on the messianic, was not the type to contradict the president or warn him away from a dangerous move. As he put it in another interview, "There are no limits. There is nothing we cannot achieve." He promised to hunt down and "physically exterminate" the perpetrators of the Bucha massacre, and he said it gave him pleasure to hear Russian propaganda refer to him as a terrorist. His deputy later declared in an interview with a German newspaper that GUR agents were plotting to assassinate Putin and a long list of his lieutenants, including the heads of the Russian military-industrial complex.

GUR's handiwork soon became the subject of fervent speculation, which earned Budanov a kind of cult following in Ukraine. In the early months of the invasion, explosions and fires often ripped through Russian military sites and fuel depots in the regions closest to Ukraine, and Russian officials blamed these incidents on Ukrainian drone strikes or saboteurs. At least twice in April, low-flying helicopters swept across the border and struck targets in the Russian region of Belgorod. Ukraine denied responsibility for these attacks, and the Kremlin tended to downplay them to avoid embarrassment. At the end of summer, as President Zelensky and his team grew impatient for the start of a major counteroffensive, these covert strikes became more daring and dramatic. They reached deeper into Russian territory, while official denials of responsibility from Kyiv became halfhearted, routinely accompanied by a wink and a mischievous smile.

Oleksiy Arestovych, a former officer of the GUR and an adviser to Zelensky at the start of the invasion, mentioned some of these attacks when we met in early August. Then he leaned back in his chair, looked at my audio recorder, and silently mouthed the words: *That was us.* We were sitting in our usual spot in the lobby of the Intercontinental, just up the street from Independence Square. A few months earlier, the place had been packed with foreigners. Global news networks booked entire floors that spring to beam their broadcasts live from the balconies. Now most of them were gone. The lobby was empty, and Arestovych sat at a table in the half-light, his bodyguard perched on a sofa nearby. The only other person at the bar, a young woman, approached his table and asked to take a picture with him. "I'm trying to get some authority over my teenage son," the woman said. "He watches you all the time."

The regular briefings Arestovych gave from the presidential podium and through his social media channels made him a household name in the spring, unable to walk down the streets of Kyiv without being hounded by hecklers and fans. His rambling lectures about conditions at the front and the mood on Bankova Street routinely attracted millions of viewers. But his access to the president had been curtailed by the end of summer. What remained of Zelensky's shrinking inner circle criticized Arestovych for being a showboat, as though that were not the reason they invited him onto their team in the first place. "We rarely see each other now," he said of Zelensky.

Like many of the bunker's former denizens, Arestovych often found himself craving those nights underground. He missed the camaraderie, the proximity to the president. "All that time," Arestovych said wistfully, "I lived with him in neighboring rooms. We talked like roommates, brushed our teeth next to each other, ate meals together." He was still a close observer of Zelensky's character, and the changes in him astonished Arestovych. "There used to be this lightweight quality to him. Quick movements, quick decisions, lots of talking, jokes.

Now it's all armor," Arestovych said, giving me his best impression of a bruiser—jaw forward, eyes narrow. To make the point, he picked up his phone and tapped on a fresh news alert. It featured footage of an explosion in the distance. "Crimea," he said. "Just now." Far behind enemy lines, the Ukrainians had blown up a Russian air base crowded with fighter jets. At least eight of them had been destroyed. Vast fireballs and clouds of smoke filled the sky over Crimea as Russian tourists fled the beaches. For Putin, it was a humiliation. Crimea symbolized his claim to empire, and now it was under assault. "That's the new Zelensky," Arestovych said. "He's not fucking around."

We paid our bill and walked out to the edge of St. Michael's Square, where the statue of Princess Olga stood shrouded in sandbags amid a display of wrecked Russian vehicles, trophies of battle covered in graffiti: *Putin is a dickhead! Glory to the Armed Forces of Ukraine!* At the curb, Arestovych offered to give me a ride. My place was on his way, and his chauffeur was waiting in a white Mercedes, the back seat stocked with Arestovych-themed key chains and bottle openers. He gave me a few of the souvenirs, printed with famous lines from his live streams. One said simply, *2–3 weeks*, his notorious prediction for how long Ukraine's victory would take to arrive. In the back of the car, Arestovych returned to the images of Crimea on his phone: the fleeing tourists, the billowing smoke. "They're going to hit Kyiv now," he said under his breath. "Putin won't just let this stand."

The remark lingered in my mind, and for days it felt like the air-raid sirens howled with renewed persistence at my windows. In fact the prediction was off. Ukraine continued hammering Russian military targets far from the front, and the Russians gave no clear response, nothing to match the spectacle of these new strikes. One of them took out a massive stockpile of Russian ammunition and an electrical substation in Crimea, damaging the railway line that Russia used to supply its forces in the south. Zelensky made clear these attacks were only the beginning. In his nightly address after the first attack inside Crimea, he said the war would only end after Ukraine takes back the whole peninsula. "We will never give it up," he said. In the office of the president, his aides watched footage of the explosions and slapped each other on the back in delight. About a week later, a Russian military base in Belgorod went up in flames. Then a drone hit the headquarters of the Black Sea Fleet in occupied Crimea, sending another tower of smoke into the sky. With each attack, the elation in Kyiv was followed by a pang of dread. The Russian response seemed inevitable.

On August 20, four days before Ukraine was set to celebrate its Independence Day, a car bomb struck closer to Putin's imperial court than any attack since the invasion began. The victim was Darya Dugina, a far-right activist and cheerleader for the war who had been a fixture on the Kremlin's propaganda channels. Her father, the neo-imperialist ideologue Alexander Dugin, was credited with building the intellectual framework for Russia's attempts to conquer Ukraine. He had called on the Russian military to smite Ukraine with all its force. "Kill, kill, kill!" he shouted in one video address to his followers in 2014. The bomb that killed his daughter changed the mood among Moscow's elites, at least for a while. The war in Ukraine now felt closer to home. At the time of the explosion, Dugin was supposed to be in the car, driving home from a summit of Russian nationalists that he had attended with his daughter. Instead she was driving into the city alone, and the explosion killed her instantly. In footage shown on Russian state TV, Dugin stood near the wreckage, clutching his head as firefighters arrived to extinguish the flames around his daughter's body. "Our hearts are not simply thirsting for revenge," Dugin wrote soon after the attack. "All we need is victory. My daughter has sacrificed her young life on the altar of victory."

The Kremlin treated the young propagandist as a martyr, and Putin gave her a posthumous honor, the Order of Courage. The Russian security services claimed she was murdered on orders from Kyiv, and U.S. intelligence sources later confirmed to the *New York Times* that it was true. But Zelensky and his government denied any involvement. They realized Russia could use the incident to justify further attacks. "We should be aware that this week, Russia may try to do something particularly nasty, something particularly cruel," Zelensky said after the bombing. "Such is our enemy." He noted that the missile attacks on Ukrainian civilians had never let up, not once, since the start of the invasion. Indeed, the previous week, a rocket struck a home for the elderly in Kharkiv, killing seven people and wounding another sixteen, including a child. But, even by the gruesome standards of these bombings, the threat of a Russian attack on Independence Day made many of Zelensky's allies nervous.

On August 22, two days before the holiday, the U.S. Department of State urged Americans to evacuate Ukraine by any means available, citing an increased risk of Russian attacks against civilian targets. On Bankova Street, the presidential guard issued a temporary ban on non-essential visitors to the compound, including myself. "They don't want anybody in the building right now," one staffer told me, asking to move our meeting to a nearby cafe that afternoon. The warnings had come from U.S. intelligence, he said, and there was "a ninety percent chance" of a missile attack in Kyiv the next day. The primary target was expected to be the office of the president. "When the Americans give us warnings, we don't ignore them anymore," said the staffer. "We learned our lesson."

But the president brushed the precautions aside. While his guards urged the staff at Bankova Street to leave the building that morning, Zelensky filled up his schedule with public events. His spokeswoman invited me to an open-air briefing about a block away from the presidential compound, on the square outside parliament, well within the blast radius of the expected missile strike. Waiting for him in the sun, the only comfort came from a trench that soldiers had dug at the start of the invasion in the lawn beside the parliament. It was about five or six feet deep, reinforced with sandbags, and long enough for all the reporters and presidential aides to squeeze inside if the bombs started falling. Would that be necessary? Was this briefing necessary?

The setting, at least, seemed designed to signal that Zelensky was unafraid. But did he really need to prove that anymore? No one could accuse him of hiding or cowering before the Russian threat. He had shown the world his tolerance for danger. His need to look fearless now resembled an end in itself. Why else would he come out here on the day when the risk was so obvious, the intelligence warnings so specific? It wasn't only his life on the line. The president of Poland, Andrzej Duda, joined Zelensky for the briefing in the sun. A dozen journalists and at least as many soldiers gathered there with the president's entourage. One of the reporters raised a hand and asked about the threat of a missile strike at the place where we were standing. "I think everyone fears death," Zelensky said with nonchalance. "No one wants to die. But no one is afraid of Russia, and that is the most important signal."

CHAPTER 21

COUNTERSTRIKE

Aꜰᴛᴇʀ ᴍᴏɴᴛʜs ᴏꜰ ᴅᴇʙᴀᴛᴇ, ᴘʀᴇᴘᴀʀᴀᴛɪᴏɴ, ᴀɴᴅ ᴘʟᴀɴɴɪɴɢ, ᴛʜᴇ ᴜᴋʀᴀɪɴɪᴀɴ ᴄᴏᴜɴ-
teroffensive began in early September, not in the south, as General Zaluzhny had insisted, but in the northeast, around Kharkiv. The president
got his way. Having let the military brass handle the fighting only a few
months earlier, he now felt sure enough in his own abilities as commander in chief to pull rank on a critical question of military strategy.
Zelensky decided, in the end, to overrule the head of the armed forces
and order the operation to proceed. In doing so, he entrusted Ukraine's
second highest-ranking officer, Colonel General Oleksandr Syrsky, to
lead the northeastern assault.

A slim and stoic man with a high forehead and a stiffness that made
him seem perpetually on guard, Syrsky had been instrumental in the
defense of Kyiv in March. Before the invasion, the president considered
him a candidate to lead Ukraine's armed forces but chose the younger
and more charismatic Zaluzhny instead. Now, at the age of fifty-seven,
Syrsky got his chance to command the biggest counteroffensive of the
war, and he did not disappoint. On September 6, ground forces under
his command smashed through the Russian lines around Kharkiv and,
in the next few days, retook hundreds of towns and villages. In some
of them, locals reported Russian soldiers abandoning their weapons,
changing into civilian clothes, and trying to flee in stolen cars and on
bicycles. The rout ripped another gaping hole in Russia's image as a
military powerhouse. The Ministry of Defense in Moscow was forced
to announce "an organized effort to transfer troops" away from the
battlefield near Kharkiv, a rhetorical fig leaf that barely covered the
shame of their retreat.

Hardly a week into the Kharkiv offensive, while Syrsky and his
troops were still pushing the Russians eastward and trying to encircle

those who remained, President Zelensky paid a visit to the liberated city of Izyum, which had been a critical base for enemy logistics. His security detail organized the most dangerous parts of the trip in total secrecy. Explosions continued to echo in the distance as Zelensky called for a minute of silence on the central square in Izyum, honoring the soldiers killed in the counteroffensive. Throughout the ceremony and most of the visit, General Syrsky remained by his side, and rumors spread through the ranks that he would soon be promoted to the nation's top military post.

General Zaluzhny was nowhere to be seen in the footage shown on the Telemarathon from liberated towns around Kharkiv. He was back in his command center, coordinating the assault along the southern front, which progressed at an excruciating pace and with enormous losses. Some of his aides and allies would long continue to grumble that the northeastern offensive led by General Syrsky, despite its unquestionable value in territory and morale, had been premature. Some argued that it sapped too much strength from the simultaneous push along the southern front, edging the more important prize of Crimea further out of reach. But on Bankova Street, no one doubted that the president had been right to order the strike in the Kharkiv direction, and that Zaluzhny had been wrong to resist it.

Upon returning to Kyiv in the middle of September, Zelensky and his team began to capitalize on their battlefield success with a renewed push for military aid. "The pace is very important now," the president said in one of his nightly addresses at the time. "The pace of providing aid to Ukraine should correspond to the pace of our movement." Oleksiy Reznikov, the defense minister, now found it easier to secure advanced weapons from the West. Two days after the start of the Kharkiv offensive, the White House notified Congress of its intent to make an additional $2.2 billion in "long-term investments" in defense against Russia, bringing the total for U.S. military assistance to Ukraine during the Biden administration to more than $15 billion. Over the next six months, that number would double, as Zelensky's allies saw that foreign assistance did not merely prolong the war by allowing Ukraine to hold on a bit longer. It quickened the approach of Russia's defeat, which now began to seem like the war's most likely outcome. "On a psychological level, it's in our model of survival to side with the victor," Reznikov told me a few days after Zelensky raised the flag over Izyum. "Today we are demonstrating to the world the answer to the main question: Can the Russians be beat? Well, they can be. And I would add, they must be!"

The success of the counteroffensive shocked and scandalized the commentariat in Moscow. The official line on Russian state TV, which had maintained that Putin's "special military operation" was proceeding as planned toward Russian victory, began to seem untenable even to the Kremlin's loyal propagandists. "In the last several days we've been dealt a very painful psychological blow," one of them admitted on a TV talk show during the Ukrainian advance. President Putin tried at first to ignore the disaster. While his troops abandoned their weapons and fled, he celebrated Moscow's birthday on September 10 at the unveiling of a giant Ferris wheel in a city park. That same weekend, the wheel's engine broke down, leaving a few dozen riders dangling in the air—a pitch-perfect image of Russian dysfunction.

Even before the Ukrainian counteroffensive, Russian generals and military hawks pleaded with Putin to start conscripting able-bodied men into the military. His invading force of around two hundred thousand troops had been so badly mangled since February that it stood no chance of holding the territory Russia had occupied, let alone advancing farther. For months the Kremlin downplayed the need for a military draft. At the start of the invasion, Putin promised in a televised address that no conscripts would be sent to fight in Ukraine. But on September 21, within two weeks of the Russian defenses collapsing around Kharkiv, he broke that promise by calling up three hundred thousand additional troops in Russia's first mobilization of military forces since World War II. Putin's speech that day included another threat to use nuclear weapons. Only this time he felt the need to add: "It's not a bluff."

A few days later, Putin announced his intention to annex four regions of eastern and southern Ukraine. "I want the Kyiv authorities and their real masters in the West to hear me, for everyone to remember," he said in a speech at the Kremlin. "People living in Luhansk and Donetsk, Kherson and Zaporizhzhia, are becoming our citizens. Forever." The statement was ridiculous on its face. Russian troops did not fully control the regions Putin now claimed as his own. In the areas they had occupied, officials loyal to the Kremlin were getting picked off left and right. One of them had a nerve agent slipped into his dinner and required medical evacuation to Russia. Another was shot dead in the streets of Kherson. The body of a third was reportedly found on the floor of his home in that city, his girlfriend beside him, barely alive and gushing blood from a stab wound to her neck. In total, Ukrainian agents carried out more than a dozen attacks on Russian-backed officials in these regions, with car bombings among the favored methods used.

When Putin announced the annexation of these regions, Zelensky fired back on the diplomatic front. He penned an official application that day for Ukraine to join the NATO alliance. The document had no immediate effect; NATO still had no intention of accepting Ukraine as a member anytime soon. But the gesture made clear that Zelensky would no longer accept Ukrainian neutrality as a concession to the Russians in exchange for peace. That same day, he drove the message home with presidential decree number 679, which ruled out any further negotiations with Putin. "For our country today, he is the unified image of a terrorist," Zelensky said. "What is there to talk to him about?"

Still, whatever rage Zelensky felt toward Putin in those moments, he was not blinded by it. In the strategic outpost of Lyman, thousands of Russian troops were surrounded at the time by Ukrainian forces. The siege resembled one of the bloodiest episodes of the war, the Cauldron of Ilovaisk, when hundreds of Ukrainian troops were massacred in the summer of 2014 as they tried to retreat from a Russian encirclement. Eight years later, the roles were reversed, and the Armed Forces of Ukraine had a chance to pay the Russians back for that act of barbarism. Zelensky felt the temptation. "I'm not saying there's no desire to take revenge. We all feel it, the hatred for those soldiers. I won't lie to you. We hate them all," he later told me of that moment. "War forces you to make these most difficult decisions, and the Russians made a shameful choice when they mowed those boys down without mercy. This time we were the winners, and we didn't shoot the Russians in the back. We told them to surrender, and many of them did, a decent number."

If the Kremlin saw that as a sign of weak resolve in Kyiv, Zelensky soon corrected them. Shortly before sunrise on the morning of October 8—the day after Putin's seventieth birthday—a delivery truck packed with explosives drove onto the Crimean Bridge, the main path for trains and traffic to reach Crimea from the Russian mainland. The blast it produced at 6:07 a.m. caused catastrophic damage. Two spans of the bridge collapsed into the water below, and the shock wave was powerful enough to rupture and ignite the fuel inside the railway tanker wagons that happened to cross the bridge at that moment. The resulting fire raged through the morning as horrified residents of Crimea lined up on the other side of the bridge, trying to flee. Throughout the invasion, the bridge had served as a vital supply line for Russian forces involved in the invasion of Ukraine, which made it a prime target for Ukrainian special operations forces. The symbolic value of the bridge made the attack still more dramatic. At its unveiling ceremony in 2018, Putin had called the construction of the bridge a "miracle." It stood as a crowning achievement for his imperial project in Ukraine. Now, before the eyes of the world, the Ukrainians blew it up.

The attack infuriated Putin, and his tactics grew more savage as the colder days of autumn arrived. On the day of the explosion, he appointed a new commander to lead the Russian forces in Ukraine, General Sergei Surovikin, a war criminal who had advanced through the ranks under Putin for over two decades with a mix of doltish loyalty and boundless cruelty. The darkest page in his military career played out in Syria, where Surovikin commanded the Russian air campaign in 2017. On his orders, bombers and fighter jets systematically attacked civilian areas in order to break their resistance to the Kremlin's allied regime in Damascus. In appreciation, Putin pinned the coveted Hero of Russia medal on Surovikin's chest that December, while the Russian state media began referring to him admiringly as "General Armageddon."

Five years later in Ukraine, he unleashed the Russian tactics he had honed over Idlib and Aleppo. Once again, in blatant violation of the laws of war, Russian planes began launching missiles at civilian infrastructure, targeting power plants, electrical substations, and utilities that provide heating to urban homes. The apparent aim was to freeze and terrify Ukrainians into submission, creating another wave of refugees that would reach the borders of the European Union in the early days of winter. On Bankova Street, the initial response was a tense foreboding as the lights inside the presidential offices began to flicker, the radiators turned cold, and the taps in the bathrooms ran dry.

Zelensky did not appear to flinch. At the end of October, he recorded a speech in the courtyard outside his office, the windows and street-lights behind him blacked out. At least forty cruise missiles had struck

Ukraine's biggest cities in the previous week, along with sixteen attack drones. The strikes, mostly targeting the electrical grid, had left over a million Ukrainian homes without power and forced the government to start rationing utilities as winter set in. But the president called for more defiance. On the ground beside him lay the remains of an Iranian combat drone, a Shahed-136, the type Russia used to carry out its latest wave of strikes. The distinctive sound they made, like a motor scooter revving its engine as it falls out of the sky, soon became a symbol for a new phase of the war—a banshee's cry that made Ukrainians wake up in the dark and wonder whether their homes were about to get hit. Standing next to one of these machines, Zelensky noted that its form of violence was not fundamentally new. Russia had carried out forty-five hundred missile strikes and eight thousand bombing raids since the start of the invasion. "We will not be broken by shelling," he said. "For us the sound of enemy rockets in our skies is not as scary as hearing the enemy's anthem on our land. We are not afraid of the dark. The darkest times for us are not without light, but without freedom."

By the start of September, only one channel of negotiations remained active and productive between Zelensky's office and the Russians—the one related to prisoners of war. Nearly a thousand of them had returned to Ukraine by then, and the efforts to bring more of them home continued quietly through the ugliest days of the war, through revelations of atrocities and the bombing of civilians. "The president has set a goal of returning everyone as soon as possible," said Andriy Yermak, who oversaw these negotiations. Even if it meant trading away Russians suspected of war crimes, Zelensky insisted they proceed. The task could be agonizing, as the warring sides squabbled over lists of names and the relative value of each captive. The final sign-off on the Russian side sometimes went all the way up to Putin, who could decide to scuttle an exchange that had been months in the making. "These swaps were always on the edge," Yermak told me. "Always hanging by a thread."

The most ambitious one happened to coincide with the counteroffensive, and nearly fell apart because of it. The Ukrainians, even while pushing through enemy defenses and leaving the roads and fields around Kharkiv littered with the bodies of Russian troops, continued maneuvering for the release of Russia's most valuable prisoners. Their list included hundreds of the last defenders of Mariupol, who had surrendered in the middle of May. For months the Russians threatened to stage a show trial of the officers captured at Azovstal, and Zelensky feared it would end with their public execution. Instead the prisoners were kept through the summer, systematically beaten, starved, and tortured in a series of overcrowded camps. In late July, an explosion at the Russian camp in Olenivka, an occupied town in the Donbas, killed fifty-three prisoners of war, wounded at least seventy-five others, and added a desperate sense of urgency to Ukrainian efforts to bring the rest of them home.

Zelensky's most precious bargaining chip turned out to be his former rival, Viktor Medvedchuk, whom the Ukrainians kept hidden away in a secret location for around five months after his capture. He had no obvious strategic value to the Russians. Any realistic hope of installing Medvedchuk in place of Zelensky had been abandoned in March along with the mission to capture Kyiv. His political party had been banned, his TV channels shuttered. But Putin still treated Medvedchuk as a personal friend, and the Russians were willing to trade just about anyone for his freedom. By early September, they even agreed to release the commanders of the Azov Regiment, whose capture at the steel plant in Mariupol had been one of Moscow's few demonstrable victories in this war, and the most valuable in terms of propaganda. On Russian state TV, the Azov Regiment was depicted as a band of satanists and neo-Nazis. When Putin talked about the "de-Nazification" of Ukraine, he meant, first and foremost, the annihilation of the Azov Regiment. But he was willing to send them home in exchange for Medvedchuk.

Around dawn on the morning of September 21, Yermak received a message from the GUR, Ukraine's military intelligence service, informing him that the swap had commenced. They had taken Medvedchuk across the border to Poland, where he waited at an airfield to be released. Five of Russia's most valuable hostages, including Denys Prokopenko, the commander of the Azov Regiment, soon landed in Ankara, the Turkish capital. Throughout the morning, Yermak watched his phone, waiting for updates. He knew the Ukrainian assault around Kharkiv had infuriated Putin, as had the encirclement of Russian forces near Lyman. Putin's speech announcing the mobilization of three hundred thousand Russian conscripts went on air while the prisoner exchange was in motion, and Yermak feared the Kremlin could pull the plug at any moment. Hours passed as Ukrainian envoys—Kyrylo Budanov, the GUR chief, and Denys Monastyrsky, the minister of internal affairs—demanded to see the prisoners aboard the plane that brought them to Ankara. In the picture they sent back to Bankova Street, the prisoners looked wretched, the uniforms hanging off their emaciated bodies, their mouths gagged with tape. But they were alive, and Yermak soon broke the news to the world on social media: "Our heroes are free." In total, the Russians released 215 prisoners, including 108 members of the Azov Regiment, in exchange for 55 captives held in Ukraine, Medvedchuk among them.

The news sparked another wave of outrage among the Russia pundit class and military bloggers. In the days that followed, protests against the military draft broke out across Russia, while Russian commentators fumed over the release of the Azov commanders. Coming so soon after the loss of the Kharkiv region and the encirclement of Russian forces in Lyman, this latest debacle seemed almost too much for the war dogs in Moscow to bear. Igor Girkin, the former intelligence officer who led Russia's incursion in the Donbas in 2014, called the prisoner swap an act of "unbridled stupidity" and sabotage. "You know how this looks?" he wrote. "It looks like they went out and called on the people to 'stand up for Russian lands,' and then they took a shit on the heads of those who answered the call."

Across Ukraine, people celebrated the prisoner swap as a triumph that would help sustain morale through the darkest days of winter. Inside Russia, it made Putin look weak, dishonest about his motives, and indifferent to the sacrifices of the Russian military, while Zelensky had shown a dedication to his troops and an ability to outmaneuver the Russians at the negotiating table. It felt like the war had turned another corner. For months the facade of Kyiv's City Hall had been covered with a sign that read: "Free Mariupol Defenders." Thousands of them were still in Russian captivity. But Zelensky had delivered on his pledge to save the lives of their commanders, and hundreds of others would soon come home in prisoner swaps that Yermak oversaw. Even the president's critics applauded the achievement, and when the dust settled over the battlefields in Kharkiv, his decision to push ahead with that offensive began to look sound. Ukraine's early victory in the battle of Kyiv still struck many observers as a military miracle. But the battle of Kharkiv demonstrated that Ukraine, equipped with weapons and intelligence from the West, could hold its own against the Russian Armed Forces and potentially defeat them.

Still, within the military's upper ranks, the applause was not universal. Senior officers continued to complain that Zelensky and his team had diverted resources away from the southern front, delaying the all-important push toward Crimea. Some saw General Syrsky's role in leading the offensive around Kharkiv as an act of careerism and insubordination. The president's office appeared to be grooming Syrsky to take full command of the armed forces, organizing interviews for him and giving him ample airtime on the Telemarathon. General Zaluzhny, by contrast, was kept out of sight, prohibited from traveling to the front lines or freely interacting with his troops in public. His aide, Colonel Noskov, also came under pressure. The president's office urged Zaluzhny to fire him, and Ukraine's counterintelligence service subjected Noskov to an interrogation and a polygraph test. The agents asked the colonel about his ties to Zelensky's political opponents and the Russian intelligence agencies. No charges were filed, but all the scrutiny forced him to keep a lower profile. Noskov no longer appeared beside Zaluzhny during the general's meetings or video calls with the president. "I've stepped aside, outside the frame," he told me.

When asked about his relationship with Zaluzhny, the president continued to deny having any intention to fire his top commander. But the conflict between them was an open secret within the military and among Zelensky's close associates. Yuriy Tyra, the president's old friend, heard about it from the troops he met while delivering supplies and staging concerts at the front. He was on his way to stage another comedy show in the Donbas when I stopped by his house one night in November. From the latest wave of Russian missile strikes around the capital, the electricity and the cell phone service were out across Tyra's neighborhood in Kyiv, and the noise of his diesel generator drowned out the sound of my banging on his gate for about twenty minutes before he finally appeared in the driveway and invited me into his cluttered garage. The place was piled high with crates of aid and equipment, boxes of tools, ashtrays overflowing with cigarette butts. A busted ambulance stood there, awaiting repairs, and certificates of gratitude and commendation from various military units covered the walls. The oldest ones dated back to the comedy shows Tyra helped organize for Zelensky in the war zone in 2014, the ones that helped convince him to run for president. It felt like a lifetime ago, Tyra said. Back then, the troops ran up to embrace Zelensky and tried to carry him around on their shoulders. Now the rank and file respected his decision to stay and lead the country into war. But the rumors of his conflict with General Zaluzhny made a lot of the officer corps doubt the president's intentions, and that put Tyra in an awkward spot. "People out there keep asking me: Are you with the president or with Zaluzhny?" he said. "It's one or the other."

In that popularity contest, Zelensky did not have the upper hand, at least not among the men and women fighting in the war zone. Out there, Tyra said, the general enjoyed a level of admiration that no politician could hope to achieve. For the image makers on Bankova Street, "the scariest thing is that the young people are for Zaluzhny. The best and brightest are for him." There was little the president's office could do about that. Trying to fire the general or otherwise clip his wings would not be a clever strategy, Tyra said, because the military would rise up to defend their commander. "The worst could come when the war is behind us," Tyra told me. "Mark my words. There will be a massive shitstorm over whether the war could have been prevented, whether we lost too many men." Such debates would remain under the surface while the battles raged around Ukraine. But eventually people would start demanding answers. "The lights will come on," Tyra said. "And the dogs will start barking."

CHAPTER 22

LIBERATION

I N EARLY NOVEMBER, JAKE SULLIVAN, THE NATIONAL SECURITY ADVISER AT THE WHITE House, arrived at the central train station in Kyiv and made his way in an armored convoy to visit President Zelensky on Bankova Street. He did not come empty-handed. A consignment of drones, surface-to-air missiles, and fixed-up Soviet tanks were all part of the $400 million aid package announced during Sullivan's visit, bringing the estimated value of American assistance to more than $25 billion since the start of the invasion. But, back in Washington, the Biden administration felt unsure how long they could keep the supplies flowing at such a pace. The midterm elections were due to take place in the U.S. the following week, and the Republicans were on track to win back control of Congress. Their leader in the House, Kevin McCarthy, had warned Ukraine that it would not get a "blank check" to wage its war forever. Not only in the U.S. but across much of Europe, political leaders had begun to wonder when the fighting would stop, how Zelensky could be persuaded to negotiate with Putin, and whether his confidence in Ukraine's ability to win had blinded him to the limits of the West's ability to help him.

The decree he'd issued a month earlier, number 679, worried some of his Western allies. In response to the Kremlin's proclaimed annexation of four Ukrainian regions, Zelensky had declared a formal ban on any talks with Vladimir Putin. "He does not know what dignity and honesty are," Zelensky said. "Therefore, we are ready for a dialogue with Russia, but with another president of Russia." The statement, reinforced by an order of the National Security and Defense Council, shut off the diplomatic avenues that many of Ukraine's allies still wanted to pursue. By the middle of fall, they began urging Zelensky to leave more room in his rhetoric for the possibility of a negotiated end to the war. On the day of Sullivan's arrival, the foreign ministers of the world's seven wealthiest democracies issued a joint statement that reminded Zelensky to maintain a "readiness for a just peace." Sullivan used this same phrase—"a just peace"—at his meeting with the president and his aides in Kyiv, and he pressed them to consider what such a peace would require.

But Zelensky had little desire to talk about that question. For the first few months of the invasion, even after the atrocities in Bucha, he believed that Putin could be reasoned with, that the crimes of Russian troops had perhaps been hidden from him. Those illusions were gone. After his battlefield success in the Kharkiv region, the president intended to continue using the military to drive the Russians back. He understood that his idea of a "just peace" would not be acceptable to Russia's current rulers. To stop the war, they would need to pull their troops out of all the territory they had occupied in Ukraine, including Crimea. They would need to assist in the punishment of those responsible for crimes of war against Ukraine. Putin and his generals would never accept those terms, so Zelensky saw no basis for conducting any peace talks. He also knew the Russians could not be trusted to keep any promises made at the negotiating table. Even as they claimed to be interested in a cease-fire, their missiles rained down on peaceful cities and their draft offices filled up with new recruits.

"They continue to collect people to send them to death," Zelensky said in a televised address on the night of his meeting with Sullivan. In an apparent concession to his guest, the president included the phrase "a just peace" in his remarks that evening. But he ended with a reminder of the kind of peace that he envisioned. "We remember every corner of our country," Zelensky said. "We will liberate all our cities and villages, no matter how the occupiers plan to prolong their stay on Ukrainian soil. Ukraine will be free. And our entire border will be restored."

❖

A few days later, the Armed Forces of Ukraine took a major step toward that objective. Their counteroffensive on the southern front advanced in fits and starts through the summer and early fall, following the road map that General Zaluzhny drew in consultation with his allies in the West. At enormous cost in soldiers' lives, the Ukrainians clawed back control of towns and villages at the northern edge of the region of Kherson. All the while, they used their advanced artillery systems to hammer Russian supply lines across the Dnipro River. Zelensky celebrated these attacks with a kind of impish glee. "Our little enemies will die," he said with a smile after one successful strike in early November, "just like the dew dries in the sunshine, just like the Russian river crossings under the strikes of our HIMARS."

By then, the Russian positions around Kherson had begun to seem indefensible even to their commanders in Moscow. They soon decided to withdraw. In a video shown on Russian state TV, Sergei Surovikin, better known as General Armageddon, made the announcement while standing stiffly at a map of the battlefield with a pointer in his hand. He explained that Russian forces in the city of Kherson were at risk of being "fully isolated" and needed to pull back. "I understand this is a very difficult decision," Surovikin said. "At the same time, we'll save what's most important—the lives of our troops."

The statement sounded too good to be true. Zelensky and his advisers assumed it was a trap, most likely meant to draw Ukrainian forces away from the southern front or lure them into an ambush. Kherson was the only regional capital the Russians had managed to seize since the start of the invasion. Hardly more than a month had passed since Putin declared that Kherson would be a part of Russia forever. He had threatened to use all military means, including nuclear weapons, to defend this part of Ukraine as his own. Now Zelensky had called the Russian bluff before the eyes of the world, and this was Putin's answer? He would fold up his forces and let them slink away? No one on Bankova Street could believe it. "The enemy does not give us any gifts," Zelensky said that night, urging his people to keep their emotions in check.

But two days later, when the Armed Forces of Ukraine moved into Kherson and raised the national flag over the city center, celebrations broke out across the country. If the Russian withdrawal from Kyiv filled Ukrainians with relief and resilience, and the liberation of the Kharkiv region gave them a realistic sense of hope, this was something new—plain proof that Ukraine could bring the Russians to their knees. The center of Kyiv erupted that night, with car horns blaring in celebration and people waving the national flag in the streets. An unwritten rule against public revelry held through the first months of war in Kyiv. It felt indecent to party while other cities burned. But that taboo was broken with the liberation of Kherson. One of Zelensky's advisers invited me to a nightclub that evening not far from Bankova Street. Down in its dungeon bar, we found a pair of drag queens singing karaoke to warm up the crowd. Slowly at first, then more with every drink, they shed the weights of war and started dancing and belting out songs, no longer afraid to jinx the luck of their survival.

For some, without question, the gloom proved harder to shake than for others, and fears of winter hung over the chatter of the smokers in the street outside. One rumor claimed that Iran had delivered more powerful drones and ballistic missiles to the Russians. People wondered how many would freeze from the attacks on the power grid and central heating systems. Already the residents of tall apartment towers had begun placing supplies of food and water in the elevators for anyone trapped inside during a blackout. Still, the Russian strategy was failing. No great wave of refugees had fled the cities as winter approached. Instead they continued returning from exile, eager not to miss the sense of triumph in the air. Down in the bar, it was palpable. "Ukraine is me!" sang the crowd packed into the karaoke room. "We are Ukraine!"

❖

The invitation from the president's office arrived the next day: *Get ready for a trip*, his aide wrote in a text message, *and pack a toothbrush.* He gave no details about the destination or how we would get there, but it wasn't difficult to guess. From everything Zelensky had revealed of himself since the invasion, it was obvious he would want to reach Kherson as soon as possible. Right up until our departure the following night, his bodyguards urged him to wait. The Russians had destroyed the city's infrastructure, leaving it with no water, power, or heat. Its outskirts were still littered with land mines. Government buildings were rigged with trip wires. On the highway to Kherson, an explosion had collapsed a bridge, rendering it impassable. As they fled, Russians were also suspected of leaving behind agents and saboteurs who could try to attack the presidential convoy, assassinate Zelensky, or take him hostage. There would be no way to ensure his safety on the central square, where crowds had gathered to celebrate their liberation. It was within easy range of Russian artillery, and a hypersonic missile fired from the Black Sea would take a few minutes at most to arrive. "My security was one hundred percent against it," the president told me of the trip. "It's a big risk, and, on my part, a bit reckless."

Then why do it? The Russian goal at the start of the invasion had been to kill or capture Zelensky and decapitate his government. Why give them such an easy chance to strike at the moment when the Russians were at their angriest and most humiliated? The obvious reason had to do with the information war. By rolling right into the city that Putin still claimed as his own, the leader of Ukraine would blow a hole right through the narratives of conquest and imperial glory that Russian propaganda had been using for months to justify the war. Zelensky's visit would deepen the embarrassment of the Russian retreat and strengthen the Ukrainian will to carry on through the winter. It would also degrade the credibility of Putin's nuclear threats, thus weakening the last claim Russia has to being a global superpower.

But these were not the reasons he gave me for the trip. "It's the people," Zelensky told me. "Nine months they've been under occupation, without light, without anything. Yes, they've had two days of euphoria over their return to Ukraine. But those two days are over." Soon the long road to recovery would come into view, and many of them would want a return to normalcy much faster than the state could deliver it. "They are going to fall into a depression now, and it will be very hard," Zelensky said. "As I see it, it's my duty to go there and show them that Ukraine has returned, that it supports them. Maybe it will give them enough of a boost to last a few more days. But I'm not sure. I don't lull myself with such illusions."

❖

Our rendezvous point on that Sunday night was in the usual spot outside the firehouse, a part of central Kyiv that was blacked out by the time the photographer and I arrived. Candles flickered in apartment windows, and people out walking their dogs used their phones to light the sidewalks. Even the central bazaar was in darkness, though the vendors inside still sold fresh fruit and cheese, pickles and pork belly by the glow of electric lanterns. When we passed them, lugging our bulletproof vests and helmets, we made sure to grab some food for the road. *Bring snacks,* one of Zelensky's aides warned in a text message. *These trips tend to be very disorganized.*

You wouldn't know it from the black van that arrived to pick us up— punctually, as agreed, at seven thirty p.m.—and brought us through the military checkpoints. The guards looked familiar, as did the buildings of the presidential compound, though the blackout gave them a haunted look. Soldiers peered out of pillboxes hidden among the trees, and flashlight beams flickered in the windows of Zelensky's office on the fourth floor. "Do you have documents on you?" asked one of the guards as he looked me over. "Good, then we'll know how to mark your grave if you fall behind the convoy." The joke made his comrades double over with laughter.

By the time our convoy left the compound, the streets had emptied out, allowing us to coast through the city center. The military curfew would not take effect for another two hours, but only the brave risked driving in downtown when many of the traffic lights went dark during the blackouts. Near the train station, we turned onto some rutted back roads and crept along until a group of soldiers appeared in the headlights. Behind them, among mounds of construction material, a few train wagons idled at the edge of an industrial lot. The only light came from the open doors of a sleeper car, where an attendant stood smiling, dressed in the uniform of the state railway company. Zelensky's aides and staffers had never seen reporters on the presidential train before, and the novelty amused them. Their only request was that we not take photos or publish details that could allow someone to identify Zelensky's private car. "It's our only mode of transport," one of them explained. "If the Russians find it, that's a bull's-eye."

The train took nine hours that night to travel the length of Ukraine from north to south. Early in the morning, as we approached the city of Mykolaiv, the fog in the eastward-facing windows enveloped the trees like gauze. On the opposite side of the train, the sun rose, sending pink streaks across the sky above the moist black earth, the neat tiles of Ukrainian farmland, much of it pocked and gashed at random by exploding shells. The first image of war appeared at a rural junction, where a few dozen soldiers worked on the tracks, loading a handful of tanks onto platforms. The machines looked ancient, like relics from World War II, while the troops resembled earnest boys clambering around the turrets.

The train soon stopped in a dusty lot full of squat garages and bungalows. A few dozen commandos stood by as we jumped off and ran over to a convoy of vans. "Good morning," I said to one of the soldiers.

"Move faster," came his reply. The liberated city, inaccessible to railway traffic, took about an hour for the convoy to reach even as our drivers raced at full speed, shoving other cars to the shoulder. At one point we encountered a tow truck using a crane to move a military vehicle off the highway, its charred and rusted skeleton dangling in the air. Our driver stopped to let the workers finish, but an impatient voice piped up from his radio: "Resume movement," it said in Russian. "We have no time."

Near the edge of the Kherson region, the collapsed bridge forced us to turn off the highway and into the dried-up riverbed below. Sappers there used metal detectors to scan for land mines and unexploded shells. "Look there," said the voice in the driver's radio. "They destroyed an ambulance." Its husk lay in the wreckage of the bridge, warped and blackened beyond recognition. Every road sign and building for several kilometers was torn up with bullets, shells, and shrapnel, and it soon became obvious why. We were passing the infamous kill zone around Chornobaivka, near the airport that serves Kherson. This was the spot where the enemy advance in the south had been stopped. Dozens of their broken vehicles stood around in the nearby fields, resembling old toys left behind in a sandlot. Several months had passed since the fiercest fighting in the area, but crows still circled over the expanse of wreckage, looking out for meat to pick from human bones.

Nobody informed the people of Kherson that the president was on his way to visit. News of his arrival remained a state secret even among the military officers stationed in the area. Still, halfway through the morning, the security measures around the central square made it obvious that something dramatic was about to happen. For two days, crowds had filled the square to celebrate Kherson's liberation, drawing victory signs on the buildings and taking photos with the Ukrainian troops who wandered around in a daze. Now police had cordoned off the area, allowing only a few dozen onlookers to stand at the square's western edge, near the movie theater. On the opposite side, in front of the regional government headquarters, rows of soldiers stood in loose formation with rifles slung over their shoulders. A few senior officials from Kyiv waited nearby, embracing one another and taking selfies in front of the graffiti scrawled on the buildings: *Glory to the Armed Forces of Ukraine! Glory to the heroes!* One of Zelensky's aides, Dasha Zarivna, grew up in Kherson, and she looked close to tears as she stood there, gazing up at the Ukrainian flags flying over the square. "I was scared I'd never see this place again," she told me. "And here we are."

The first explosion sounded a few minutes later, and everyone froze, looking up at the sky for a shell to come arcing down. Then came another boom. It sounded closer than the first, the sonic wave crashing against the buildings. Someone suggested it was outgoing artillery fire, though this seemed more like an optimistic guess. The Russians had retreated to the left bank of the Dnipro River, which now marked the front line about a mile away. The blasts continued to sound, but Zelensky, standing and waiting next to his Land Cruiser, did not seem bothered by them. He declined as usual to wear a helmet or bulletproof vest. At the edge of the square, the soldiers had installed a Starlink Internet terminal, plugging its satellite dish into a diesel generator. The president took out his phone when he saw it and asked for the Wi-Fi password. Most of the people around him were armed with assault rifles. But this was his weapon, the late-model iPhone Zelensky used to wage the biggest land war of the Information Age.

Soon the media buses arrived, and a few dozen reporters rushed onto the square and set up a line of cameras. Zelensky kept the ceremony brief, not wanting to annoy his guards by spending longer than necessary within range of Russian cannons. They would later inform him that, high above his head on the square, too high for any of us to notice at the time, an enemy reconnaissance drone kept watch, feeding images back to the Russian troops on the other side of the river. It watched Zelensky raise the Ukrainian flag over the square and sing the national anthem, his hand over his heart. It watched him strut to the waiting bank of television cameras to answer a few of the reporters' questions. The first one cut right to the point—Is this the beginning of the end of the war?—and Zelensky repeated it slowly to the cameras, buying himself a few moments to consider his response.

Like previous victories on the battlefield, the one in Kherson made many of Zelensky's allies wonder whether the moment had come for Ukraine to resume the peace process, this time from a position of relative strength. The Russians seemed amenable to sitting down at the negotiating table. Even as their warplanes continued bombing targets across Ukraine and destroying civilian infrastructure, their rhetoric had changed. Putin had stopped calling the authorities in Kyiv "drug addicts" and "neo-Nazis," instead referring to them in late October as his "Ukrainian partners," a phrase he had not used since well before the invasion. That same day, one of Putin's top commanders issued a remarkable statement in praise of Ukraine's leader. "Even though Zelensky is the president of a country hostile to Russia at the moment, he is still a strong, confident, pragmatic, and likable guy," said the Russian warlord Yevgeny Prigozhin, leader of the Wagner mercenary group.

The apparent change in tone did not match Russia's continued acts of barbarism. Prigozhin's mercenary force had begun executing deserters from within their own ranks using a sledgehammer to the head. Across the liberated Kharkiv region, war crimes investigators uncovered evidence of widespread Russian atrocities, including mass graves, filtration camps, and torture chambers. Regardless of the spin on Russian television, the decision to leave Kherson had not been a goodwill gesture from the Russian forces so much as an act of self-preservation. Still, many in the West chose to see it as an opportunity for peace. Even General Mark Milley, one of Ukraine's most influential backers in Washington, began urging Zelensky and his team to resume the peace process. "When there's an opportunity to negotiate, when peace can be achieved, seize it! Seize the moment," Milley said in a speech in New York on November 9, the day the Russians announced their withdrawal from Kherson.

To make his point, Milley raised the example of World War I, when millions died in the trenches of Europe as the front lines shifted back and forth for years. By Milley's estimate, the number of soldiers killed in Ukraine since February had already topped one hundred thousand on each side of the war. European leaders concurred with that figure, even though the Ukrainians continued to hide their real casualty numbers from the public. The last official death toll had come in August from General Zaluzhny, who claimed Ukraine had lost nine thousand of its troops—a gross underestimate. Zaluzhny, in response to Milley's remark about the opportunity for peace, issued an unusually cutting statement on his Facebook page: "Our goal is to liberate all Ukrainian land from Russian occupation," the general wrote. "We will not stop on this path under any circumstances. The Ukrainian military will not accept any negotiations, agreements, or compromise decisions. There is only one condition for negotiations: Russia must leave all captured territories."

Zelensky felt the same way. Why stop when he had the momentum?

The distance to Crimea was about a hundred kilometers from the central square in Kherson. Ukraine's armed forces could reach it within days as long as Zelensky convinced the West to provide enough weapons to break through the Russian defenses. "Is it the beginning of the end of the war?" the president said to the reporters on the square. "You see our strong army. We are step by step coming to our country, to all of the temporarily occupied territories." Then came another question from the scrum: What's next? "Not Moscow," Zelensky said with a smile. "We are not interested in territories of another country. We are interested only in de-occupation of our country, of our territory." Besides, he said, it would make no sense to negotiate with an enemy that talks of peace while bombing civilians. "We don't believe Russia," Zelensky said. "They are tricking all the world. That's why we are going forward."

At that moment a cheer broke out to the left of the president—"Glory to Ukraine!"—and the response was a chorus, mostly of women's voices: "Glory to the heroes!" Zelensky looked over and, to the frustration of his guards, went to greet the crowd of several hundred locals, who surged forward as he approached. The reporters rushed up from behind, locking the president in a crush that his security guards could not control. One of them had terror in his eyes as he scanned the faces in the crowd for threats. Zelensky smiled and waved. "How are you?" he said to his supporters. "You alright?"

❖

From Kherson's central square, the convoy took us to an underground command post, where Zelensky was due to meet the officers in charge of the southern front. The facility was hidden beneath an old machine works littered with debris and broken glass. To reach the entrance, Zelensky climbed down to a heavy metal door, much like the one he used each day in Kyiv to access his wartime accommodations. Otherwise the place did not resemble his well-appointed hideaway. At the end of the stairs, a dark corridor brought us through a laundry room to a space packed tight with the bunk beds of the troops. No one stood at attention or saluted the visiting commander in chief, and no one had spent the morning tidying up the communal head, where spiderwebs full of little flies covered the walls behind the toilets. The officers mostly stayed in their rooms when we arrived, staring at their screens and clacking at keyboards. One of the soldiers continued napping for a while, then he sat up in bed, pulled his uniform over his long johns, and went back to work. Passing by him, Zelensky went to the mess hall, where lunch was served in plastic bowls and paper cups: rice with ragu, sausage soup with day-old bread. Given the choice, Zelensky later told me, he would always prefer to be welcomed as the equal of his soldiers, not their potentate, and the lack of pageantry did not strike him as a sign of disrespect. It encouraged the troops to speak freely about the horrors they had seen and the struggles Kherson had yet to face.

The city had been liberated, but it remained a target for the Russians. Many of their agents had stayed behind, and they had plenty of allies among the local population. Ukrainian security forces now needed to track down and interrogate those who had agreed to work for the occupying forces. Many utility workers, policemen, and bureaucrats had stayed at their posts to keep the city functioning under Russian control. Some local teachers and administrators kept the schools open during the occupation. In the first month of the invasion, Zelensky had signed a law imposing strict punishment for aiding the occupiers, with the worst offenders facing life imprisonment for treason, and the president was not inclined to show mercy to those he perceived as traitors. "They live among us," he told me. "In apartments, in basements, among the civilians, and we have to expose them, because that's a major risk."

As the generals focused on the task of pushing the Russians back, Zelensky reckoned with another dimension of the war. For months he had been promising to liberate every square mile of Ukraine, including all of the Donbas and Crimea. But as a politician, he sensed that the military victory in these regions would mark the start of a much tougher fight. It would be his job to govern the lands Ukraine took back from the invaders, and that would require winning over the people who lived there. In Kherson, it might not be that difficult. The occupation had lasted about nine months, not long enough for the Russians to break the popular resistance. The locals continued to defy the occupiers through civil disobedience, public protests, and, in some cases, violent attacks and assassinations. When the Ukrainian forces returned to Kherson, the people welcomed them, in some cases throwing themselves at the soldiers and weeping with joy. But Zelensky did not expect the same welcome in all the regions he promised to liberate, least of all in the occupied parts of eastern Ukraine. "I would need to speak to them," he said, "and that's assuming those people are ready to listen."

Early in his tenure, the president tried to reach across the front lines and appeal to them, offering pension payments and government services, opening roads for them to leave the occupied parts of the Donbas and visit the rest of Ukraine. Now he feared it would be too late. The children in those regions had been taught to see Kyiv as the enemy, and the men had been conscripted to fight alongside the Russians. The youngest soldiers in the Donbas were only ten years old when the Russian occupation started in 2014, and they had since watched Ukrainian forces lob bombs in their direction, killing their friends and destroying their cities. "They are also dying," Zelensky said. "And when their bodies come home, they are told, 'Look what the Ukrainians have done!'" Getting them to embrace Ukraine as their homeland would require an effort Zelensky could scarcely imagine. "We would need to change those people, to show them that we are meeting them halfway," he said. "We would have to leave our own comfort zone, in which we stand here and say, 'Donbas, can you hear us?' They might not hear us. And it's not enough merely to ask. We have to act, to move closer to them."

If some of them refused in the end to accept the return of Ukrainian authority, or to believe the good intentions of the leadership in Kyiv, he felt it would be wrong to blame or punish them. "I wouldn't consider that treason," he said. "It's passivity. Ukraine needs to be as active as possible in breaking through the channels of information." He wanted to cut off the flow of Russian propaganda to these regions and beam in his own. "But experience shows that as long as we're not there, we can't break through. We can't reach them."

After Ukraine's latest advances in the south, the front lines were not expected to move much before the onset of winter, but the president did not want them to freeze in place. In the chow hall, he cleared his plate and walked to the other side of the bunker, where several officers had prepared a briefing on conditions at the front. Everyone had to leave their phones at the door of the conference room. Inside, a fresh battle map hung on the wall, showing how the invaders had positioned themselves behind two dangerous obstacles, which they now intended to use as shields. To advance from the west, the Ukrainians would need to ford the waters of the Dnipro under a likely hail of artillery and machine-gun fire. In advancing from the north, they would run into Ukraine's largest nuclear power plant, which the Russians had occupied in early March. Its reactors now stood on the front lines, and Zelensky understood that pushing forward around that area would risk a nuclear catastrophe. He had to consider what the Russians, in retreat, might do with those reactors. Had they been rigged to explode? In case of a meltdown at the power plant, how far would the fallout spread?

Such questions were no longer foreign to Zelensky. They had been on his mind for months, and he had developed ways to structure his thoughts around dilemmas that might, in normal times, have overwhelmed him. His first question usually related to human lives: How many would be lost if we take this path? With the decision to advance against Kherson, it was the same. "We could have pushed into Kherson earlier, with greater force," he said. "But we understood how many people would have fallen. That's why a different tactic was chosen, and thank God it worked. I don't think it was some genius move on our part. It was reason winning out, wisdom winning out against speed and ambition."

❖

The sun was close to setting by the time we got back to the president's train. Its locomotive idled at a distance from the nearest station, the carriages warm and ready to depart. The road back to Kyiv would take another nine hours at least. After a full day of meetings, briefings, and ceremonies, the president had plenty of time to start the journey with a break to clear his head. But he preferred not to leave idle moments in his schedule. As soon as the train started moving, his aide came to bring me to his private car, leading me through several wagons of security guards and staffers. In one compartment, Andriy Yermak sat on a cot and yelled into his phone, the reception cutting in and out as he tried to make some urgent point to the Secretary General of the United Nations. At the entrance to Zelensky's chambers, a security guard patted me down and stuck blue tape over the camera lenses on my phone. The room behind him had the generic luxury of an upscale hotel—wood panels, soft light, and golden fixtures that made the tiny space feel even tighter, nearly airless. My expectations of a high-tech command center on wheels were disappointed. The president, dressed in his usual green fleece, sat at a small conference table with a cup of coffee, a swirl of documents in front of him, the blinds closed in all the windows, and a narrow sofa pressed against the wall to his left.

As I sat down across from Zelensky, he picked up a paperback book and looked it over. It was about the lives of Hitler and Stalin during World War II, a comparative study of the two tyrants who had tormented Ukraine the most. Zelensky had not had time to read it yet. "The volume of documents in my profession shoves all literature to the side," he said. But such books of history and biography had long been among his travel companions. Since the invasion started, he had read about the life of Winston Churchill, the historical figure to whom he had most often been compared since the start of the invasion, but he did not appreciate the suggestion that they have anything in common.

"People say different things about him," Zelensky noted dryly, making clear he has no admiration for Churchill when it comes to his record as an imperialist. He would prefer to be associated with other figures from Churchill's era, like George Orwell, one of Zelensky's favorite writers, or with the great comedian who lampooned Hitler in the middle of the Holocaust. "I've raised the example of Charlie Chaplin," Zelensky said, "how he used the weapon of information during the Second World War to fight against fascism. There were these people, these artists, who helped society," he said. "And their influence was often stronger than artillery." That is the type of influence Zelensky wanted to emulate, the pantheon he wanted to join.

As the train moved out of the frontline regions and picked up a bit of speed, it became clear that the aims he had for his wartime leadership went well beyond any victory on the battlefield. He wanted to change the way Ukrainians understood their role in the world, their future, and the traumas of their past. For most of his life, he said, "I didn't have any hate inside me at all." He believed in the human ability to self-correct, to punish the wicked and protect the good. Even when it came to his assessments of history, Zelensky grew up believing that the Soviet Union deserved respect and admiration. It had brought dozens of disparate cultures and nations together, drawing on their diversity and nurturing their talents to produce some of history's greatest achievements in science and the arts. None of these sentiments survived the war, Zelensky told me. "Now I feel revulsion toward everything linked to the past."

More than once in our conversations, he brought up the funeral rites of Joseph Stalin, whose death in 1953 sent the Soviet Union into paroxysms of mourning. During the public procession through Red Square with Stalin's corpse, "people trampled each other, crushed the elderly and children in their path, just to get a look at the ruler who had left them," Zelensky told me in April, when we spoke in his office. Six months later, on the way back from Kherson, these scenes came back to his mind. "They crushed each other," he told me on the train, "just to see him, just to touch this piece of scum who had trampled all over Ukraine."

What drew Zelensky back to those images—the waxen face and withered arm of the generalissimo in his casket, the throngs wailing for him at the Kremlin walls—was the spell the Soviet Union had cast over its people, the way its propaganda had convinced them that the devil was a saint. In the present war, Ukraine was fighting a similar set of delusions, and Zelensky understood the Russians would be hard to defeat not only because of their arsenal but because of the force of Putin's lies. "It shocks me to see the power of this information, the sickness of it," he said. "The scariest thing is that his people can't see through it. Based on the reactions we have seen, they wish us death, they want our children to die." By this point in the war, polls had consistently shown that a majority of Russians supported it, and Zelensky saw it as his mission to break that spell, to subvert the narratives people consumed through Russian television. It helped explain why he had been so fixated on shutting down Russia's propaganda channels in Ukraine before the invasion started—and why Putin had reacted with such fury.

Wars are fought in the minds of men and women long before the shooting starts, and Zelensky, the showman turned president, operated on that plane. He knew the power and the danger of persuasion, and he knew that long before the Russian tanks crossed the borders of Ukraine, the Kremlin had waged its war through propaganda, seeking to convince anyone who speaks the Russian language that Ukraine does not exist, that its leaders are resurrected Nazis in disguise, serving the treacherous aims of the West against Russia. The madness of these notions did not stop them from taking hold. When the invasion started, the state's control over information in Russia allowed Putin to keep sending young men to kill and die in Ukraine by the many thousands without causing any backlash of note from their families, from Russia's citizens.

With Stalin, it had been the same, Zelensky said. Through Soviet censorship and propaganda, the Kremlin got away with the murder of millions of Ukrainians during the forced confiscation of their harvests in the 1930s, the genocide known as the Holodomor. For generations afterward, the Soviet people remained ignorant of these crimes. All the evidence was buried, the witnesses repressed. Zelensky only learned about the details of the famine when he was in high school in the 1990s, years after the Soviet Union collapsed. Only later, during his presidency, he recognized it as part of a pattern. First the Holodomor, then the Holocaust and World War II, then two generations of Soviet oppression. "These tragedies came one after the other," he said. "One tremendous blow followed the next."

I asked whether this history had in some ways hardened Ukraine as a nation, contributing to their resolve in fighting the present war. The question earned me a piercing look. "Some people might say it hardened us. But I think it took away so much of Ukraine's ability to develop. It was one blow after another, the hardest kind. How does that harden us? People barely survived. Hunger broke them. It broke their psyches, and of course that leaves a trace." Now it was his generation's turn to face the next blow from a foreign invader. Instead of Stalin and Hitler, now it was Putin trying to break their will by depriving them of heat and light, destroying their ability to harvest food or to think about much besides survival. The next generation of Ukrainians, including Zelensky's own son, would grow up learning about the tools of war instead of working toward their prosperity. During a recent visit, Zelensky saw the boy going around in a uniform, opining at the age of nine on the types of weapons the military needs.

The aim of his presidency, Zelensky said, would be to end that cycle, to end the pattern of oppression he had failed to recognize as a younger man, and his plan relied on more than weapons. "I don't want to weigh who has more tanks and armies," he said. Russia is a nuclear superpower. No matter how many times its forces are made to retreat from Ukrainian cities, they can still regroup, retrench, and try again. "We are dealing with a powerful state that is pathologically unwilling to let Ukraine go,"

Zelensky said. "They see the democracy and freedom of Ukraine as a question of their own survival." The only way to defeat an enemy like that—not just to win a temporary truce, but to win the war—is to make Ukrainians believe their freedom is worth the sacrifices of the war, and to convince the rest of the democratic world to pull Ukraine in the other direction, toward sovereignty, independence, and peace. That would be Zelensky's contribution. He had already convinced the U.S. and Europe to provide Ukraine with enough weapons to seize the momentum in this war. But his deeper appeal called on his allies to provide more than material support for incremental victories. He warned them again and again in his speeches that the loss of freedom in one nation erodes the freedom in all the rest. "If they devour us," he told me on the train, "the sun in your sky will get dimmer."

We were nearly halfway to Kyiv by then, and the president had only a few hours to rest and prepare for the next item on his schedule. At around three in the morning, Kyiv time, he was due to give a speech at the G20 summit in Bali, where the leaders of the wealthiest nations in the world had gathered to discuss a list of crises. The war in Ukraine topped the agenda. Russia, despite its status as a founding member of the group and one of the most influential, saw its delegation ostracized in Bali. Its foreign minister, Sergei Lavrov, decided to go home early, a retreat that signaled the success of Zelensky's strategy against the Russians. Ukraine was not even a member of the G20, but its president could expect the rapt attention of its leaders when he dialed in from his capital. "The Russians need to understand," he told me as we said goodbye. "They will have no forgiveness. They will have no acceptance in the world."

It was approaching midnight when the lights of Kyiv appeared in the windows. Near the central station, the president's train stopped next to a gap in a concrete wall. Behind it another convoy of cars waited to take him back to his office. His speech was ready. He had written most of it himself, laboring over the message he wanted to send. It would be a call for the smaller nations of the world, those who lack nuclear weapons or colossal armies, to work together in ending the violence they face from their colonizers. A few hours before dawn, Zelensky took his seat in the Situation Room, the trident hanging on the wall behind him, and looked into the camera on the opposite side of the room.

"Greetings," he said, "to the world's majority, which is with us."

THE NEXT TIME I SAW ZELENSKY WAS ON THE OTHER SIDE OF THE WORLD. A FEW DAYS before Christmas, he made a surprise appearance in Washington, his first foreign trip since the start of the invasion. One of his aides, in a text message that morning, gave me half a day's notice to get there from Brooklyn before their plane touched down. Unlike the First Lady, the president did not fly commercial. The White House sent a U.S. Air Force jet to pick Zelensky up in eastern Poland and, with an escort from a NATO spy plane and an F-15 Eagle fighter, delivered him to Joint Base Andrews. From there he followed the footsteps of his wife rather precisely, appearing first in the Oval Office with Joe and Jill Biden before delivering a speech to a joint session of Congress. We saw each other briefly, just long enough for a nod, as he rushed through the halls of the Capitol.

Maybe somewhere, most likely around the eyes, the young Zelensky from the comedy circuit in Kryvyi Rih continued to animate his features that day. But I couldn't see much trace of him as he walked down the aisle of the House Chamber. The easy swing of his body on those early stages of his youth did not survive the impact of the invasion. His gait looked leaden now, fixed in the shoulders, like a bulldog headed for a fight. Dressed in his usual army-green sweatshirt, he declared from the podium in Congress that Ukraine had won the part of the war that matters most. "We defeated Russia in the battle of minds," he said. Not only the minds of Ukrainians, but those of all nations who once feared Russia and lived under the sway of its propaganda. "The Russian tyranny has lost control over us, and it will never influence our minds again."

Still, in Ukraine, the war for lives and land was far from over. The epicenter of the battle for the Donbas had moved to the town of Bakhmut, which Zelensky visited the day before coming to Washington. "Every inch of that land is soaked in blood," he told the members of Congress. (One Russian commander, Yevgeny Prigozhin of the Wagner mercenary group, would later admit to losing some twenty thousand of his fighters in the battle for that one town, whose entire prewar population was only around seventy thousand people.) To defend Bakhmut, Zelensky needed more artillery, as well as tanks, fighter jets, and anti-aircraft missiles, all of which the U.S. and its allies refused to provide. They had not yet conquered their own fear of Russian escalation. To help them do that, he offered the gift of a battle flag from the troops in Bakhmut, its fabric covered in their messages of hope and resilience. "Let this flag stay with you, ladies and gentlemen," he said to the hall. "This flag is a symbol of our victory in this war."

Watching from the balcony, I counted thirteen standing ovations before their frequency forced me to give up counting. One senator told me afterward he could not remember a time in his three decades on Capitol Hill when a foreign leader received such an admiring reception. A few right-wing Republicans and devotees of Donald Trump refused to stand or applaud for Zelensky, but the votes to support him had been bipartisan and overwhelming throughout the year. Congress approved a total of $113 billion in aid to Ukraine in 2022, including $67 billion in defense spending. (For a measure of scale, the average size of Ukraine's entire economy was less than $200 billion in the preceding years.) The single biggest American aid package, worth $40 billion, passed in the House with a vote of 368 to 57 and in the Senate 86 to 11. It granted Ukraine some $7 billion more than the White House had even requested. "Is it enough?" Zelensky asked during his speech to Congress. "Honestly, not really."

From some in the hall, that line earned a chuckle. Others rolled their eyes at Zelensky's chutzpah. For a few more minutes he carried on, ending with a flourish that had become a kind of oratory calling card. He invoked an episode from the history of his audience. In 1777, during the Battle of Saratoga, the Americans won a crucial victory against the British during their war for independence. Soon Ukraine would do the same in Bakhmut, Zelensky said, but it needed help. "We stand, we fight, and we will win because we are united—Ukraine, America and the entire free world." The chamber once again erupted in applause, with members hooting and hollering between shouts of *Slava Ukrainy!—Glory to Ukraine!*

❖

When the speech was finished, the president did not stick around for long in Washington. He rushed back to the plane with his team that night. I stayed behind. It was time to stop gathering material for this book and focus on writing it. The war had not ended, not even close. Nor had some point of clarity or resolution appeared in the distance. But the man at the center of it had, to my mind, finished his transformation into the wartime leader he would continue to be. He had proved his skills as a showman to be at least as valuable in this war as the tactical ingenuity of his generals. They needed each other, and Zelensky delivered for them through the force of his appeals on all the world's political stages; in the way he coaxed and inspired his peers in the West, convincing them to see this war as their own; and, in a diplomatic marathon that went on for hundreds of days without end, by wearing down the reluctance of those who still felt too afraid of Russia. Zelensky gave no hint of being afraid, even though he and his family had a lot to fear.

My time with him, starting on the campaign trail in 2019 and continuing through the first year of all-out war, did not bring into focus every aspect of his character. Some things remained indistinct, and others worried me, especially when I imagined what Ukraine would look like under his leadership after the war. One of the most important tests for him and his administration could come after a few more dramatic victories on the battlefield, or a prolonged stalemate along the front lines, when a critical mass of Ukrainians may decide that the war has stabilized enough for the authorities to lift all curfews, to give adult men back the right to travel freely, to allow parliament to resume its normal functions and, what I suspect will be particularly difficult for Zelensky, to end the Telemarathon and unmuzzle the media. Conditions at the front will no doubt guide these decisions, but there will likely be disagreement between the president's office and the parliament, between the state and the people, when it comes to the timing of their return to life in a constitutional democracy, with regular elections and freedom of the press. I don't know how Zelensky will handle that fraught transition, whether he will have the wisdom and restraint to part with the extraordinary powers granted to him under martial law, or whether he will, like so many leaders through history, find that power too addictive.

When we talked about such questions, his answers helped assuage my fear that, after the war, the next chapter in Ukraine's history might be one of autocracy. He was conscious of the judgement of history and wary of the lofty accolades he received from various international organizations. Once, at the end of the war's first summer, the postmaster general of Ukraine brought a mock-up for a new postage stamp to Zelensky's office on the fourth floor and offered to release it in time for Independence Day in August. It showed a blue-and-yellow rendering of the president's face, gallant and monumental, with weapons of war depicted in the background. Zelensky cringed and closed the folder when he saw it. "It's not the time," he said, "to start a cult of personality."

Modesty, to be sure, has never been his strong suit, but he had enough sense to avoid such acts of self-aggrandizement. He and his team also had enough respect for the work of independent journalists to let me do my job on Bankova Street with no preconditions. When I finished a draft of this book in the summer of 2023, the war continued, and no one could tell what Ukraine's victory, if it came to pass, would look like. Some, like General Zaluzhny, warned me that the war would never really end. "Knowing what I know firsthand about the Russians, our victory will not be final," he said. "Our victory will be an opportunity to take a breath and prepare for the next war."

Eight years of fighting in the Donbas had convinced Zaluzhny that Russia would never cease to be a threat, and he wanted all Ukrainians to face this reality, to prepare for a permanent state of vigilance and an unending cycle of conflict with the nuclear power next door. The armed forces under his command had already come to that understanding, and the rest of society was catching up fast, especially after the atrocities they had witnessed in Bucha and other liberated towns. "Now we see that if we retreat by one kilometer, that kilometer will be covered in blood," Zaluzhny told me. With an enemy like that, he added, "It's not enough to die for your country. You also have to kill."

Some talked of the general as the kind of leader the next Ukraine would need. And Zelensky had considered firing his chosen commander. But by the start of 2023, Zaluzhny appeared to settle his differences with the president. He agreed to dismiss two of the aides who had been grooming his image for politics. After the breakthroughs around Kharkiv and Kherson, he and the president both turned their attention to the broader counteroffensive Zaluzhny had envisioned, a multi-stage assault designed to cut off Crimea from the Russian supply lines that stretched across the Donbas through Mariupol. The president did not appear to rush the preparations for that attack, which began in early June 2023. When it failed through the summer to deliver a breakthrough, Zelensky and Zaluzhny united around a plan to take the war to the enemy's soil, using drone strikes to hit Moscow and other targets far from the front. On some matters they disagreed, as with the question of when to withdraw from the death trap of Bakhmut. The general, realizing the city could no longer be defended, wanted to pull troops out a few weeks sooner than the president, who insisted they continue fighting, mostly to wear down the Russian forces and draw them away from other sections of the front. For Zelensky, Bakhmut was also a symbol of determination, and he won the argument over the need to keep defending its ruins despite the horrifying cost. Overall, he continued to play a far greater role in strategic decisions than he had at the start of the invasion. But the president still kept his focus on what he did best: rallying support, raising morale, keeping Ukraine in the spotlight, and securing supplies of weapons and financial aid.

The persistence he showed in these efforts would inevitably irritate his allies, even the most devoted ones. Ben Wallace, the British defense minister, chastised Zelensky during a NATO summit in July 2023. "People want to see gratitude," he said. "We're not Amazon." The U.K. had already transferred so many mine-clearing vehicles to Ukraine that "I think there's none left," said Wallace. Such admonishments did little to change Zelensky's tone. In the end, it was Wallace who felt the need to apologize for stepping out of line with his remarks, not Zelensky, while the money and materiel continued flowing to Ukraine from the West. Despite nearly a year of delays and refusals, the U.S. began in the second year of all-out war to give Zelensky what he needed most, vastly expanding the range of weapons available to Ukraine's armed forces.

The official announcement about the provision of American and German tanks happened to fall on Zelensky's forty-fifth birthday on January 25, 2023. That evening, his wife posted an unusual message to him on social media. "I am often asked about how you have changed this year," she wrote. "And I always answer: He hasn't changed. 'He is the same. The same guy I met when we were seventeen.'" But that wasn't true, she admitted. "Something has changed: you smile much less now." She wished him more reasons to smile and asked for something in return. "I want to smile with you forever. Give me the opportunity!"

It was not the first time she made such a public plea for his attention, and this time he seemed to hear her. As the war entered its second year, the president and his wife began to appear more often together and to show more affection for each other when they did. Tragedies often brought them closer, united in mourning, as on that awful day when they heard the news of their friend's death. Denys Monastyrsky, the minister of internal affairs, was killed in a helicopter crash in a suburb of Kyiv on January 18, 2023, along with six of his senior aides and members of his staff. Monastyrsky was by Zelensky's side before dawn on the morning of the invasion, and he was among the bravest men I came to know while working on this book. Neither the president nor the First Lady could hold back their tears as they tried to comfort Monastyrsky's loved ones at his funeral. "I want all of us to feel this today," Zelensky said in a video address that night, "to feel how many brilliant people we lose at a time of war."

Years from now, when Ukraine looks back on the horrors of this war, its true toll may come into focus, assuming the state will one day agree to release its casualty figures to the public. Eighteen months into the full-scale invasion, the estimated loss of life stood in the hundreds of thousands, among them the legions of men and women, doctors and DJs, schoolteachers and shopkeepers, people from every corner of society who volunteered to help in the defense of the country they love. Zelensky, in our conversations, never spoke about their sacrifice in jingoistic terms. He never reduced them to a monumental mass who had died for a purpose greater than them. He spoke of them as individuals, and the grief showed on his face.

Once, when we talked about the ways he thinks about the costs of this war, he asked me to imagine a father sitting at a desk, with a framed photo of a son who didn't return from the front, or a daughter killed in a missile strike. "That doesn't inspire the father," he said. "For him it's a great tragedy. . . . That's the price." He paused for a moment, trying to find some sense or purpose in the image he had drawn. Finally, he said, "I think Ukraine has a big chance to get the respect of the world, autonomy from Russian influence." To honor the memory of those who had died, he was determined not to miss that chance, no matter how long it takes or how difficult the struggle. "That's what motivates me," he said. Not the applause and admiration, the fame that came with his position nor even the respect and adoration of millions in Ukraine. He had those things in his former life as a showman. Now he was after something different. He had set out to break a cycle of imperial oppression that began generations before he was born. That was his goal now, and he had long overcome his fear on the road to attaining it. "Later we will be judged," he told me. "I haven't finished this great, important action for our country. Not yet."

| ACKNOWLEDGMENTS |

Hᴵˢᵀᴼᴿʸ ISN'T WRITTEN BY THE VICTORS. IT'S WRITTEN BY THE WITNESSES, AND THEY deserve more credit for this book than I do. Hundreds of them agreed to speak to me over the course of my reporting in Ukraine, some on multiple occasions and for many hours, and I am deeply grateful to all of them for entrusting me with the stories that form the basis of this book. Many of their interviews are cited throughout these pages. But it would take a volume larger than this one to list the names and contributions of all the courageous Ukrainians who inspired me, kept me going, and shared with me their indomitable faith in a free, peaceful, and prosperous Ukraine. To all of them, I offer my enduring thanks and admiration.

In the months after the Russian invasion, my ability to visit the presidential compound in Kyiv did not rely only on President Zelensky's invitation. There was no all-access pass that allowed me to come and go as I wanted. Every day inside the government quarter required a member of the presidential staff to arrange my visit and bring me through the security cordons. For such efforts, and for all their patience and generosity in helping me with my reporting, I want to thank Andriy Yermak, Dasha Zarivna, Serhiy Nikiforov, Mykhailo Podolyak, Serhiy Leshchenko, Iryna Pobedonostseva, Andriy Smyrnov, Kyrylo Tymoshenko, Tetiana Gayduchenko, Oleh Gavrysh, and the many members of the presidential administration and security team who welcomed me on Bankova Street. Lesia Chervinska at the ministry of internal affairs, Iryna Zolotar at the defense ministry, and Oleksiy Noskov at the general staff also did a great deal to facilitate my conversations with key members of the president's wartime cabinet and other important sources. My thanks, also, to Sergiy Kyslytsya, Ukraine's ambassador to the United Nations, who generously invited me around to talk while I was in New York and deepened my understanding of Ukraine's wartime diplomacy.

In the first two years of Zelensky's tenure, Iuliia Mendel helped arrange briefings, trips, and interviews with him in her role as presidential spokesperson, and I thank her for that and for the candor and warmth of our conversations. On the campaign trail in 2019, Olha Rudenko served as my main point of contact to Zelensky, and I am indebted to her for introducing me to him and his team that spring.

At William Morrow, I was privileged to work with Mauro DiPreta, who believed in this book and oversaw its development from start to finish. I am also grateful to William Morrow's publisher, Liate Stehlik, and the rest of the team at Morrow Group and HarperCollins for treating this project with such care and professionalism. For additional editing, I relied on Mark Morrow, whose valuable insights and reflections guided the book from its first draft to the last. My literary agent Todd Shuster (no relation, at least that we know of) did a brilliant job shepherding this project from its inception to its publication. My gratitude to him and the team at Aevitas, especially Vanessa Kerr, Allison Warren, Lauren Liebow, Erin Files, and Jack Haug, for their support.

My heartfelt thanks also to my editors, colleagues, and everyone at *Time* who raised me up and gave me the support and encouragement I needed to write this book, most of all Massimo Calabresi, but also Marc and Lynne Benioff, Edward Felsenthal, Sam Jacobs, Alex Altman, Karl Vick, Vera Bergengruen, W. J. Hennigan, Brian Bennett, Lucas Wittmann, and many others at the magazine who contributed to our coverage of Ukraine and Russia over the years.

While working on the book, I relied on research assistance from Natalia Goncharova and Yuliia Tkach, who also helped with fact-checking, as did Barbara Maddux. My gratitude to all of them.

My thanks and respect to the photographers who traveled and worked with me in Ukraine, particularly Maxim Dondyuk, whom I have been proud to call a friend since we first met on the Maidan in 2014, Anastasia Taylor-Lind, who accompanied me backstage with Zelensky in 2019, and Alexander Chekmenev, who took some of the most iconic portraits of the president in 2022.

As for my deepest debts of gratitude, I owe them to my family—to my grandmother, my parents, my brother, and my wife, Marie, who met me during the awful days in 2014 when the war in Ukraine began and has stayed with me ever since. This book belongs by right to her and to our daughter. Together they sustained me during my absences from home in 2022, and through many long days at the writing table. Thank you.

Mᵧ MAIN SOURCES IN REPORTING THIS BOOK WERE INTERVIEWS WITH PARTICIPANTS in the events described, in particular the five interviews I conducted with Volodymyr Zelensky between the spring of 2019 and autumn of 2022. Most of the interviews are cited directly in the text. In such cases, I have not noted them again in the notes that follow.

Throughout my research for this book, I have relied on the intrepid work of my colleagues in the field, especially Sevgil Musaieva and her team at *Ukrainska Pravda*; the newsrooms of RBC-Ukraine, the *Kyiv Post*, and the *Kyiv Independent*; the Ukrainian services of the BBC and Radio Free Europe/Radio Liberty; and many others. I learned an enormous amount from the international media's coverage of the war by the Associated Press, the *Washington Post*, the *Wall Street Journal*, the *New York Times*, *The Guardian*, CNN, *Bild*, *Der Spiegel*, and others. A number of books have deepened my understanding of Ukraine's history and its war with Russia, particularly those authored by Catherine Belton, Iuliia Mendel, Christopher Miller, Serhii Plokhy, Serhii Rudenko, Shaun Walker, Joshua Yaffa, and Mikhail Zygar.

The following notes point to my sources for specific quotes and other material, especially in cases where my sources may not be evident in the text.

PROLOGUE

Olha Rudenko informed me about the bomb threat backstage at the Palace of Ukraine on March 13, 2019. Roman Nedzelsky, who was general director of the venue at the time, described these events to me in an interview on June 28, 2022, including the police response and the decision made in consultation with Zelensky not to call off the show. A few Ukrainian outlets reported on the bomb threat the following day, including Strana.ua, which cited police sources.

"Going onstage gives me two emotions . . .": Zelensky made this statement in an episode of a documentary series about him and his company, Studio Kvartal 95, that the company produced and posted on YouTube on October 12, 2014, with the title, *Квартал и его команда* (*Kvartal and Its Team*).

CHAPTER 1

The descriptions of the presidential residence at Koncha-Zaspa are based on photographs sent to me by the office of First Lady Olena Zelenska, as well as older images published by the Unian news agency and other Ukrainian outlets that visited the estate.

The investigative journalist Mykhailo Tkach, then working for Radio Free Europe/Radio Liberty, was the first to report in July 2020 that President Zelensky had moved to Koncha-Zaspa with his family.

"Guys, how about we let some kids live in these residences . . . ": Zelensky interview with RBC-Ukraine, April 18, 2019.

"For me it's like a hotel . . .": Zelensky interview with Politico Europe, October 6, 2020, a transcript of which was published on the presidential website.

"These motherfuckers come to power . . .": Zelensky's character in the series premiere of *Servant of the People*.

The descriptions of the first family on the eve of the invasion and their initial reactions to it are drawn from my interviews with Olena Zelenska.

The descriptions of Zelensky's drive to work on the first day of the invasion are based on my visits to Koncha-Zaspa and to the compound on Bankova Street, as well as my interviews with the president and members of his government, especially Denys Monastyrsky.

Oleksiy Danilov, secretary of the National Security and Defense Council of Ukraine, provided details of the scale of the invasion and his response to it.

The estimated number of troops and military vehicles involved in Russia's initial attempt to attack Kyiv from the north comes from RBC-Ukraine's interview with Lieutenant General Oleksandr Pavlyuk, the first deputy minister of defense, published on April 11, 2023.

"At the time we thought these were threats . . .": Zelensky interview with the BBC's John Simpson, aired on the first anniversary of the invasion.

"Whoever tries to hinder us . . .": Vladimir Putin's declaration of war, as published on the Kremlin's website on February 24, 2022.

"We will fight, Boris! . . .": Oleksiy Danilov's interview with *Ukrainska Pravda*, published on September 5, 2022, as part of the outlet's reconstruction of the invasion's first hours and the days leading up to it.

Estimated size of forces on both sides of the invasion are drawn from a report by the European Parliament, published in March 2022, under the title, "Russia's War on Ukraine: Military Balance of Power."

"I was tired of this . . .": Zelensky interview with the *Washington Post*, published on August 16, 2022.

The account of Zelensky's phone call with President Emmanuel Macron on the morning of the invasion is drawn from footage of the call shown in the 2022 documentary film, *Un président, l'Europe et la guerre,* directed by Guy Lagache.

The account of Andriy Yermak's phone call with Dmitry Kozak is drawn from Yermak's interview with the *Washington Post*, published on August 24, 2022, as part of the paper's reconstruction of the invasion.

Details of the first family's evacuation from Kyiv by train are drawn from my interviews with three officials involved in the evacuation, who agreed to discuss it on condition of anonymity.

CHAPTER 2

The account of the president's evacuation to the bunker is drawn from my interviews with five members of his team who were with him that day. Some additional details of the amenities inside the bunker come from officials who helped prepare it or who went there to live with Zelensky later in the invasion.

"She answered me very clearly . . .": Davyd Arakhamia's interview with the *Washington Post*, published on February 24, 2023, as part of the paper's oral history of the invasion.

Efforts to secure the presidential compound were described to me by numerous officials who witnessed these events or participated in them.

Andriy Smyrnov, in describing his destruction of the courthouse servers, showed me pictures of the damage to confirm his account.

The burning of sensitive documents in the courtyard of the Ministry of Defense was described to me by two officials of the General Staff who witnessed it; one of them showed me photos of the burn pits. These officials and others also described the shots fired at the Ministry of the Defense complex from the Manhattan City towers. During a visit to the scene, I observed damage consistent with their accounts, including at the nearby Ministry of Infrastructure.

Details of CIA director William Burns's trip to Kyiv in January 2022 were widely reported in the U.S. media, notably by the *Washington Post*, the *Wall Street Journal*, and CNN.

"How can you believe this?": Zelensky interview with the *Washington Post*, published on August 16, 2022.

Details of the battle for the airport in Hostomel are drawn in part from RBC-Ukraine's reconstruction of these events, published on April 3, 2023.

The president's reactions to these events were recounted to me by Mykhailo Podolyak, Denys Monastyrsky, and other participants.

Details of Zelensky's participation in the E.U. summit on February 24, 2022, are drawn in part from coverage of the event by Politico Europe and the *Washington Post*.

"This may be the last time you see me alive": Zelensky's statement to E.U. leaders at the summit was initially reported by the *Financial Times* and Axios. It was later confirmed to me, along with additional details, by Andriy Sybiha and other aides to Zelensky.

"We are left alone . . .": Zelensky statement in the briefing room as published on the presidential website on February 25, 2022.

"My rays of sunshine . . .": Monastyrsky's message to his family was recovered from his phone after he was killed in a helicopter crash near Kyiv about eleven months later, on January 18, 2023. His wife, Zhanna Monastyrska, shared the recording with me, and I quote from it here with her blessing.

"We're all here . . .": Video of Zelensky and his aides was published on the president's social media accounts on February 25, 2022.

CHAPTER 3

The account of First Lady Olena Zelenska's time on the run with her children is based on my conversations with her, with additional details from her interviews with other journalists, notably Shaun Walker of *The Guardian*.

"My big soul . . .": Zelensky interview with Ukrainian journalist Dmitry Gordon, for his program *Visiting Dmitry Gordon*, first aired in December 2018.

Details of the gang culture in Kryvyi Rih in the 1980s and 1990s are drawn from my interviews with Olena Zelenska and from a report on the topic by the Ukrainian journalist Samuil Proskuryakov, published on Zaborona on September 15, 2020.

The account of Zelensky's family history and childhood are drawn from my interviews with him, with additional details from his interviews with Dmitry Gordon in December 2018 and the *Times of Israel* in January 2020.

"My parents gave me no free time" and other quotes about Zelensky's childhood in this paragraph are from his interview with Dmitry Gordon, aired in December 2018.

"He had issues with arithmetic . . .": Oleksandr Zelensky's interview with Ukraine's TSN network, featured in a documentary about Zelensky that aired on TSN on his Inauguration Day, May 20, 2019.

Oleksandr Pikalov recalled his first meeting with Zelensky in an interview for the documentary program *Pozaochi*, which aired on Ukraine's Inter TV in 2011.

Zelensky's account of his father's refusal to let him travel to Israel appeared in his interview on *Visiting Dmitry Gordon*, aired in December 2018.

"We had a couple shots . . .": Zelensky's interview for the *Pozaochi* documentary, aired in 2011.

"like the Montagues and the Capulets": Olena Zelenska's interview with Shaun Walker of *The Guardian*, published on June 18, 2022.

"Losing is worse than death": Zelensky's remark appears in the same episode cited above from the documentary series *Kvartal and Its Team*.

"turned out to be a decent guy": In his book *War and Punishment*, published in 2023, Mikhail Zygar cites the sketch that Zelensky's troupe performed on October 20, 2002, during a KVN competition against a team from Moscow (p. 213).

"not only of my fate, but that of all Ukraine": A Ukrainian character played by Zelensky delivered this line as part of a KVN all-star show that aired on November 11, 2001, according to a video of the full two-hour performance posted on the KVN fan page KVNbest.ru.

CHAPTER 4

Zelensky recalled his departure from the KVN major league in Moscow during his interview on *Visiting Dmitry Gordon* in 2018.

"Without a doubt, we advised him . . .": Oleksandr Zelensky described his attitude toward his son's professional ambitions in an interview for the documentary program *Pozaochi*, which aired on Ukraine's Inter TV in 2011.

"our 9/11": Gleb Pavlovsky, who served as a political adviser to the Kremlin in the early 2000s, is quoted describing the Orange Revolution this way in Serhiy Plokhy's book, *The Russo-Ukrainian War* (p. 83).

Zelensky stated that his parents voted for Yanukovych's party during his interview with *Visiting Dmitry Gordon* in 2018.

"I can't live without you, Putin . . .": Zelensky and his fellow comedians performed this satirical song in the first episode of *Evening Kvartal,* aired in 2005.

"It was scary, really scary . . .": Zelensky's mother, Rymma, recalled her reaction to her son's political satire in an interview for the documentary series about Studio Kvartal 95, *Kvartal and Its Team,* that the studio produced in 2014.

Details of Zelensky's wealth and his use of offshore accounts were widely reported in the Ukrainian and international media, notably by RBC-Ukraine and *Ukrainska Pravda*, and in the consortium of news outlets that published the Pandora Papers leak of financial records in 2021.

"I don't talk about my income . . .": Zelensky's comments on his personal wealth in this paragraph come from his 2018 interview with *Visiting Dmitry Gordon*.

"All the networks had companies offshore . . .": Zelensky's response to the publication of his financial records as part of the Pandora Papers leak appeared in his interview with Ukraine's ICTV news channel on October 17, 2021.

"I always had conflicts with the news side . . .": Zelensky's account of his tensions with the leadership of Inter TV and Yanukovych's alleged attempts to pay him off with $100 million appear in his 2018 interview on *Visiting Dmitry Gordon*.

Details of the 2010 elections in Ukraine are drawn from my coverage of that presidential race for the Associated Press in Kyiv.

The allegation that Yanukovych and his allies siphoned $100 billion out of Ukraine during his presidential tenure appeared in a Reuters interview with the acting prosecutor general of Ukraine, Oleh Makhnitsky, published on April 30, 2014.

My interview with Yanukovych and related coverage of his presidency were published in *Time* in June 2012.

CHAPTER 5

The account of the Revolution of Dignity and its aftermath is based on my reporting from the scene of those events, published in a series of articles in *Time* in 2014.

The total casualty count during the revolution appears in Serhii Plokhy's book, *The Russo-Ukrainian War* (p. 97).

"We're with the people . . .": Zelensky's press conference in December 2013, promoting the release of *Love in the Big City 3*.

In his book, *Zelensky: A Biography*, published in 2022, Serhii Rudenko describes the controversy surrounding the joke about police batons being used to generate electricity (p. 83).

"We didn't do it for the photos . . .": Yevhen Koshovy described the troupe's attitudes toward the revolution during our interview in Kyiv in June 2022.

"None of us imagined that our neighbors . . .": Oleksandr Polishchuk described the Russian occupation of Crimea during our interview in Kyiv in June 2022, when he was serving as Ukraine's deputy minister of defense.

The account of my interview with Sergei Aksyonov at his headquarters in Crimea first appeared in a feature in *Time* in March 2014.

"They came to believe in their own exceptionalism . . .": Putin's speech as published on the Kremlin website on March 18, 2014.

"No jokes this time" and other quotes in this section are from Zelensky's appearance on the newscast of TSN on March 1, 2014.

"I have a perfect sense of the mentality . . .": Zelensky's press conference at the presidential compound in Kyiv on March 3, 2022.

CHAPTER 6

The account of Zelensky's early days in the bunker are based on my interviews with him and members of his staff, as well as my own observations inside the presidential compound during the invasion.

The account of the military command post where General Valery Zaluzhny lived and worked in the early days of the invasion are based on interviews with him and members of his staff, as well as photos they showed me of the facility.

Serhii Plokhy details the occupation of the Chernobyl plant in *The Russo-Ukrainian War* (p. 158–159).

The Eurobarometer survey of public opinion in Europe was published on May 5, 2022, in a press release from the European Commission titled, "Eurobarometer: Europeans Approve EU's Response to the War in Ukraine."

The Reuters/Ipsos poll of U.S. public opinion about the invasion was published by Reuters on March 4, 2022.

"We have entered a new era . . .": German Chancellor Olaf Scholz's speech as published on the website of the chancellery on February 27, 2022.

"We are not afraid to talk to Russia . . .": Zelensky's address to the nation as published on the presidential website on February 25, 2022.

"I don't really believe this meeting will bring results . . .": Zelensky's address to the nation as published on the presidential website on February 27, 2022.

The account of the first negotiating round in Belarus is based on my interviews with Arakhamia and other Ukrainian negotiators.

A copy of the Ukrainian proposals in the peace talks were leaked to the independent Russian journalist Farida Rustamova, who published them in her newsletter *Faridaily* on March 22, 2022, under the headline "Ukraine's 10-point Plan."

Details of the battle for the airport in Hostomel are drawn in part from RBC-Ukraine's reconstruction of these events, published on April 3, 2023.

"There was the expectation . . .": General Vladimir Shamanov in an interview with the Russian journalist Oksana Kravtsova, posted on YouTube on May 22, 2022.

"We had grandmas making Molotov cocktails . . .": Oleksiy Reznikov's interview with Ukrainian journalist Dmytro Komarov for an episode of his documentary series, *Year. Off-screen*, about the invasion, posted on YouTube on May 5, 2023.

Independent estimates of Russian losses in the opening weeks of the invasion came from various sources, ranging from U.S. intelligence agencies to Western think tanks. I have relied on a thorough analysis of these figures from *The*

Guardian's Andrew Roth, published on March 22, 2022, under the headline "How Many Russian Soldiers Have Died in the War in Ukraine?"

Paul Ronzheimer of Germany's *Bild* newspaper attended Zelensky's televised press conference on March 3, 2022 and later described it to me in detail. The *New York Times* published an account of the event that day by Andrew Kramer under the headline "Behind Sandbags, Ukraine's Leader Meets the Media."

CHAPTER 7

The account of the response on Bankova Street to the Russian occupation of the nuclear power plant in Enerhodar on March 4, 2022, is based on my interviews with several of Zelensky's senior aides and advisers, including Andriy Yermak, Kyrylo Tymoshenko, and Serhiy Leshchenko.

"That's a disgrace . . .": Zelensky's interview with Dmytro Komarov for the first episode of the documentary series, *Year. Off-screen,* released April 28, 2023.

The state's investment in Telekanal Rada was described to me by one of its correspondents, Maxim Zborowsky, who later became a leading anchor on the "United News" Telemarathon.

The influence exerted on the Telemarathon by the office of the president was described to me by Zelensky's senior aide Kyrylo Tymoshenko, who oversaw the Telemarathon.

Isobel Koshiw reported for *The Guardian* about the origins and programming of the Telemarathon in a report published on May 25, 2022, under the headline "'Death to the Enemy': Ukraine's News Channels Unite to Cover War."

The consumption of alcohol in the presidential bunker was described to me by several of its inhabitants. Mykhailo Podolyak, a senior aide to the president, also discussed this topic during a public event I attended in Kyiv on August 11, 2022.

"*Look how our people . . .*": The war ballad, titled "Ukrainian Fury," was written and performed by the singer Khrystyna Soloviy and posted on March 7, 2022, to her YouTube account, where it attracted millions of views. The translation of this stanza from Ukrainian to English is mine.

The detail about female lawmakers receiving handguns on the day of the invasion was reported by Roman Kravets and Roman Romaniuk of *Ukrainska Pravda* in their reconstruction of the day's events, published on September 5, 2022.

Images from the boy's diary were posted on the Facebook account of Mariupol resident Evgeny Sosnovsky on May 3, 2022. They were widely shared online and reported in Ukrainian and international news outlets, including Radio Free Europe/Radio Liberty, which tracked the boy down and identified him as eight-year-old Yegor Kravtsov in a report published on June 22, 2022.

CHAPTER 8

"Some things in life you remember . . .": Zelensky's TV interview on *Snidanok*, a morning show that aired on the 1+1 network in August 2014. His story of meeting a soldier in the Donbas who found it difficult to speak also appeared in that interview.

Putin made the remarks about *Novorossiya* during his annual call-in show on April 17, 2014. A video and transcript appears on the Kremlin website.

"We are essentially one people . . .": Putin's speech at the Kremlin on March 18, 2014, as published on the Kremlin website.

Polls taken in February 2014 by the Kyiv International Institute of Sociology and the Kucheriv Democratic Initiatives Foundation, as cited by the Pew Research Center, found little enthusiasm in Ukraine for the idea of uniting with Russia. Even in eastern Ukraine, only around 26 percent of those surveyed supported it.

The clashes in Odesa, including the fire at the House of Trade Unions that killed at least forty-two people, were covered in a BBC report published on May 6, 2014, under the headline "How Did Odessa's Fire Happen?"

My coverage of the spread of Russian separatism and the ensuing war in eastern Ukraine appeared in a series of dispatches in *Time* in the spring and summer of 2014.

"I'm reporting here from the heart of Russia . . .": Zelensky filmed news parodies at the edge of Red Square in Moscow for the long-running show *Chisto News* in May 2014.

"The feelings were mutual . . .": Zelensky described his departure from Russia in 2014, as well as the severing of his personal and professional relationships in Moscow, during his 2018 interview on *Visiting Dmitry Gordon*, where he also discussed the financial impact on his businesses of losing the Russian market and his refusal to accept invitations to perform in Russia after the annexation of Crimea.

Zelensky's first concerts in the war zone were widely covered in the Ukrainian media in August 2014, including a report that aired on the TSN network at the time.

"We've told Russia to get fucked.": Zelensky performed the song, titled "I Love My Motherland," during his trips to the war zone in 2014, and it became a staple of the Studio Kvartal 95 repertoire in the years that followed.

"Go, just go and touch them . . .": Zelensky's interview on the morning show *Snidanok*, which invited him on to talk about his trip to the front in August 2014.

The scene in which Zelensky's character daydreams of mowing down the Ukrainian parliament appears in Season 2, Episode 8, of *Servant of the People*.

"The process of raising them . . .": Zelensky's press conference in December 2013, promoting the release of *Love in the Big City 3*.

The registration of a new political party called Servant of the People was reported by *Ukrainska Pravda* on December 4, 2017.

A video of Ihor Kolomoysky's rant appeared on Radio Free Europe/Radio Liberty's Ukrainian YouTube channel on March 19, 2015.

Details of Zelensky's relationship with Kolomoysky appeared in my report for *Time* on the Ukrainian presidential elections, published on March 28, 2019.

A nationwide survey published by the Rating Group, a leading Ukrainian pollster, on September 25, 2018, put Zelensky in second place among potential candidates for president, with 7.8 percent support, compared to 6.8 percent for the incumbent and 13.2 percent for Yulia Tymoshenko.

CHAPTER 9

The corruption scandal involving the alleged smuggling and sale of Russian military hardware into Ukraine emerged from an investigative report by Bihus.info, a Ukrainian outlet, published on February 25, 2019, under the headline "Army. Friends. Dough."

The Ukrainian service of the BBC covered the scandal involving recordings of a senior anti-corruption prosecutor, Nazar Kholodnitsky, in a detailed report published on April 4, 2018.

"I am the one who warned you . . .": Petro Poroshenko's speech to the Munich Security Conference on February 16, 2018.

In a social media post from the Munich Security Conference on February 17, 2018, Ukraine's foreign minister, Pavlo Klimkin, appeared to blame the cancellation of that day's peace talks with Russia on "the German delegation," after German foreign minister Sigmar Gabriel, a key mediator in the talks, went back to Berlin to hold a press conference on the release of German journalist Deniz Yücel from a Turkish prison.

The next round of peace negotiations in the so-called Normandy Format, involving the foreign ministers of Russia, Ukraine, Germany, and France, were held in Berlin on June 11, 2018.

Zelensky announced in a social media post on March 13, 2019, more than three months into his presidential campaign, that filming for the third and final season of *Servant of the People* had concluded.

Ukraine's parliament, the Verkhovna Rada, passed amendments on an anticorruption law on October 17, 2019, making good on Zelensky's campaign promise by allowing for the payment of rewards to people who turn in corrupt officials.

Gallup published the results of its international survey on public faith in government on March 21, 2019, under the headline "World-Low 9% of Ukrainians Confident in Government."

My interview with Yulia Tymoshenko first appeared in a feature published in *Time* on March 28, 2019, under the headline "She Was Next in Line to Be the President. He Plays One on TV. Who Will Win Ukraine's Election?"

The third season of *Servant of the People* premiered on March 27, 2019, as reported by the BBC's Ukrainian service. The first round of the presidential elections was held four days later, on Sunday, March 31.

According to the results published by the Central Election Commission of Ukraine, Zelensky received 89 percent of the vote in Luhansk and 87 percent in Donetsk. He only lost the second round in the western region of Lviv, where Poroshenko got 63 percent of the vote.

CHAPTER 10

Seventy-nine percent of respondents expressed trust in Zelensky in a survey published in September 2019 by the Razumkov Center, a leading pollster in Ukraine.

Sixty-five percent of respondents said the first thing the president should do to increase their trust in him was to "end the war in the Donbas," according to a survey conducted in June 2019 by the Rating Group.

"It's impossible to be here . . .": Zelensky made the remark while showing his office to a group of journalists. The Russian-language service of Deutsche Welle posted a video of the tour on its YouTube channel on June 21, 2019.

Interfax-Ukraine was among many Ukrainian outlets to report on Zelensky's income declaration on May 20, 2019, the day of his inauguration.

Reuters reported on the below-market price the Zelensky family paid for its property in Crimea on May 1, 2019, under the headline "Exclusive: Wife of Ukraine President-elect Got Penthouse Bargain from Tycoon."

"Better for me not to criticize him . . .": Olena Zelenska interview with the *Snidanok* morning show on 1+1, posted on the TV network's website on November 25, 2019.

"Let these investigations go forward . . .": The contents of Rudy Giuliani's phone call with Yermak first appeared in my report for *Time* on February 9, 2021. *CNN* later broadcast a partial recording of the call.

"There's a lot of talk about Biden's son . . .": The White House released a transcript of the Trump-Zelensky call on September 24, 2019.

"The entire time you've been talking about this . . .": My interview with Yermak first appeared in *Time* on December 10, 2019.

"like in a fortress . . .": Zelensky's interview appeared in *Time* on December 2, 2019. Apart from me, the president invited three journalists from some of Europe's leading publications: *Le Monde* of France, *Der Spiegel* of Germany, and *Gazeta Wyborcza* of Poland.

CHAPTER 11

My reporting from Bucha first appeared in *Time* on April 13, 2022.

A short video of the mass burial in the churchyard appeared on the Facebook page of Bucha resident Mykola Krivenok, on March 12, 2022. Father Andriy Halavin confirmed the authenticity of the video.

Numerous investigations of the Russian atrocities in Bucha appeared in the international media in the months that followed. On November 3, 2022, the

Associated Press published a report under the headline "Crime Scene: Bucha. How Russian Soldiers Ran a 'Cleansing' Operation in the Ukrainian City." On December 22, 2022, the *New York Times* published a report under the headline "Caught on Camera, Traced by Phone: The Russian Military Unit That Killed Dozens in Bucha."

The casualty figures that the Russia newspaper *Komsomolskaya Pravda* published and quickly deleted were covered by *The Guardian* in a piece published on March 22, 2022, under the headline "How Many Russian Soldiers Have Died in the War in Ukraine?"

The Associated Press published the number of bodies found in the area of Bucha in a report on August 11, 2022, citing municipal authorities.

"He's here on this earth.": Zelensky made the remark about the devil at his press conference on February 24, 2023, marking the first anniversary of the invasion.

The Institute for the Study of War, a U.S. think tank, estimated in its battlefield assessment on August 24, 2022, that the Russians had lost roughly 45,000 square kilometers of territory in Ukraine since March 21, an area larger than Denmark.

"who were shot in the back of the head . . .": Zelensky's speech to the U.N. Security Council, as published on the presidential website on April 5, 2022.

"Golgotha of the twenty-first century.": Tomasz Grodzki, the speaker of Poland's upper house, made the biblical comparison to Bucha and other suburbs of Kyiv in a social media post on April 14, 2022.

"Security guarantees and neutrality . . .": Zelensky spoke at length about the peace negotiations during an interview with a group of independent Russian journalists on March 27, 2022, as reported on the presidential website.

"in order to increase mutual trust . . .": Alexander Fomin, the Russian negotiator, made this statement to reporters in Istanbul on March 29, 2022, as reported by Russia's Interfax news agency.

Oleksiy Danilov, speaking to the *Washington Post* for a report published on February 22, 2023, recalled the details of Zelensky's dinner with his aides in the Situation Room the day after the president visited Bucha for the first time.

"Every such tragedy, every such Bucha . . .": Zelensky made this statement on April 5, 2022, to Ukrainian journalists, as published on the presidential website.

My account of Ursula von der Leyen's visit to Ukraine first appeared in *Time* on April 28, 2022, under the headline "Inside Volodymyr Zelensky's World."

"I don't cry anymore . . .": Zelensky's interview with Paul Ronzheimer of Germany's *Bild* newspaper appeared on April 8, 2022.

CHAPTER 12

"It's one thing to play somebody . . .": Putin's remark at the plenary session of the St. Petersburg International Economic Forum on June 7, 2019, as reported on the Kremlin website.

Data from the International Monetary Fund showed that Ukraine's economy shrank in half from 2013 to 2015, and was far from recovering in 2019.

Hromadske reported on the withdrawal of troops at the start of Zelensky's tenure in a piece published on June 27, 2019, under the headline "Ukraine's War-Torn Stanytsia Luhanska Sees Historic Separation of Forces."

The Organization for Security and Co-operation in Europe confirmed the withdrawal as part of its monitoring mission in eastern Ukraine in a spot report published on June 30, 2019.

"Don't get sucked in.": U.S. ambassador William Taylor told me that he gave this advice to Zelensky in 2019. David Ignatius, in a *Washington Post* column published on November 30, 2021, also cites Taylor giving this advice to Zelensky.

"Everybody tried to scare me . . .": Zelensky made this remark in one of his video blogs, posted to YouTube on July 17, 2019.

The Unian news agency covered the death of four Ukrainian marines and the subsequent phone call between Putin and Zelensky in a report published on August 7, 2019.

The *New York Times*, in a story published on September 7, 2019, was among many outlets that covered the prisoner exchange.

Deutsche Welle reported on Russia's release of the three Ukrainian naval vessels in a story published on November 18, 2019.

"I am absolutely certain of one thing . . .": Poroshenko described his peace plans in our interview for an article published in *Time* on June 12, 2014, under the headline "Petro Poroshenko: Man in the Middle," which also includes my reporting on the clashes in the Donbas that spring.

"This issue of federalism . . .": Biden's speech to the Ukrainian parliament on December 9, 2015, is available in the archives of the Obama White House.

Surveys of public opinion in the occupied parts of the Donbas were conducted in 2019 by the Centre for East European and International Studies in Berlin, whose director, Gwendolyn Sasse, described the results and methodology in a report published on October 14, 2019, in *The Conversation*.

"People should cross over and see . . .": Zelensky's interview with me and three European journalists on November 30, 2019.

"There will be no elections under the barrel of a machine gun . . .": Zelensky's press conference, announcing his plans for the implementation of the Minsk agreements, took place in Kyiv on October 1, 2019.

"I will not agree to go to war in the Donbas . . .": Zelensky's interview with me and three European journalists on November 30, 2019.

The *New York Times* report about Zelensky holding his own in Paris appeared on December 9, 2019, under the headline "In First Meeting With Putin, Zelensky Plays to a Draw Despite a Bad Hand."

Ukraine's parliament, the Verkhovna Rada, passed a law on December 12, 2019, extending the terms of temporary "local autonomy" in the occupied parts of the Donbas for one year, and Zelensky signed it the following week in order to "advance the peaceful resolution of the situation" in those regions, according to a statement published on the presidential website on December 18, 2019.

Deutsche Welle reported on the resolution of Ukraine's financial dispute with Russia in an article published on December 21, 2019, under the headline "Gazprom to Pay $2.9 Billion in New Ukraine Gas Deal."

Reuters reported on the new five-year gas contract on December 30, 2019, under the headline "Russia, Ukraine Clinch Final Gas Deal on Gas Transit to Europe."

Hromadske reported on February 5, 2022, about the parliament shelving a bill that would allow pension payments in the occupied parts of the Donbas.

The parliamentary vote related to elections in the Donbas was reported on the website of the Verkhovna Rada on July 15, 2020, and a full video of that plenary session was posted on the YouTube channel of Telekanal Rada. The full text of the law, registered as No. 795-IX and signed by speaker Dmytro Razumkov, was also posted on the parliamentary website.

"The people of the Donbas have been brainwashed . . .": Zelensky told me about his failure in 2019 and 2020 to engineer a lasting peace in the Donbas during our interview on November 14, 2022.

CHAPTER 13

Among the many outlets to report on Viktor Medvedchuk's role in the state campaign against Soviet dissidents was the *New York Times,* which wrote in a 2015 profile that, "His role in a Soviet crackdown on dissidents ahead of the 1980 Olympics is widely believed to have contributed to the death of a Ukrainian poet and human rights activist, Vasyl Stus." Medvedchuk, who served as Stus's state-appointed lawyer, has long denied aiding the authorities in persecuting Stus.

My report on the relationship between Putin and Medvedchuk and its role in the invasion of Ukraine first appeared in *Time* on February 2, 2022, under the headline "The Untold Story of the Ukraine Crisis."

The Russian outlet LifeNews published a video of Putin's visit to the Medvedchuk family's villa in Crimea in July 2012 that was then broadcast on numerous Ukrainian TV channels.

The Ukrainian service of Radio Free Europe/Radio Liberty published a detailed investigation of Medvedchuk's role in the energy trade on February 21, 2017.

The journalist and author Mikhail Zygar reported on Putin's isolation at Valdai in a piece for the *New York Times* published on March 10, 2022, under the headline "How Vladimir Putin Lost Interest in the Present."

The floor plans and other details of Putin's estate at Valdai were published on April 15, 2021, by the Anti-Corruption Foundation, an activist group run by the dissident Alexei Navalny.

"The European Union confirmed that it will help Ukraine . . .": Zelensky made this comment in a post on his official Telegram channel on October 7, 2020.

In a survey published on October 20, 2020, the Rating Group found that 16.7 percent of those planning to vote in the elections intended to cast their ballots for Zelensky's Servant of the People party.

According to statistics published by Worldometer, the death toll from COVID-19 in Ukraine reached 15,000 in mid-December 2020. The U.N. Office of the High Commissioner for Human Rights estimated that the total death toll from the war in the Donbas from 2014 through 2021 was between 14,200 and 14,400 people, according to a report published in January 2022.

Pfizer and BioNTech, a Germany company, announced on November 9, 2020, that their vaccine candidate was effective against COVID-19.

"With COVID it was like this . . .": Zelensky made the statement in a TV interview with German broadcaster ZDF on October 13, 2022.

In a video posted on its YouTube channel on June 5, 2020, the Ukrainian outlet Censor.net reported in detail on the way Kolomoysky's TV channel had begun criticizing Zelensky.

The Rating Group survey published on December 23, 2020, found the president's approval numbers falling steadily since that spring, with 65 percent of respondents saying at year's end that they disapprove of his administration.

Interfax-Ukraine reported on December 28, 2020, that Medvedchuk's party had overtaken Zelensky's party in the polls, citing two independent surveys conducted around that time.

"This is an illegal mechanism . . .": Razumkov met me for an interview in his office at the Verkhovna Rada on October 6, 2021, the day before Zelensky's majority in parliament voted to strip him of his position as speaker.

"We are very liberal people . . .": Zelensky told me about his legal assault on Medvedchuk during our interview on April 9, 2021.

"come at the expense of freedom of media.": The E.U. Spokesperson for Foreign Affairs and Security Policy, Peter Stano, made this statement to Interfax-Ukraine on February 3, 2021, the day after the sanctions were imposed against Medvedchuk's TV channels.

"We support Ukraine's efforts . . .": The U.S. embassy in Kyiv's statement in response to the sanctions against Medvedchuk's assets was posted on Twitter on February 20, 2021.

"He turned out to be a doer . . .": Briefing with senior State Department officials in the spring of 2021.

"In Ukraine, they just went and shut down . . .": Putin's statement in response to the sanctions was reported by TASS and other Russian state news outlets on February 17, 2021.

The sanctions against Medvedchuk and his wife were imposed via Decree No. 64/2021, posted on the presidential website on February 19, 2021, and signed by Oleksiy Danilov, the secretary of the National Security and Defense Council of Ukraine.

"large scale exercises": The statement announcing the snap Russian military exercises appeared on at least two Ministry of Defense websites on the morning of February 21, 2021, structure.mil.ru and function.mil.ru, and was carried by several outlets and blogs in Russia and Belarus. Among the few Ukrainian news sites to pick up the announcement was NV.ua, which published a report about it that evening, citing the Russian Defense Ministry press service.

CHAPTER 14

The motto of Demining Center 2641, "Mistake is not an option," appeared in English in a banner on its Facebook page (www.facebook.com/deminingcenter 2641) around the time of the battle near Shumy.

The account of the firefight at Shumy is based on my visit to the scene and interviews with military officers involved in the official investigation of the incident, including General Ruslan Khomchak, who oversaw it. A shorter version of the account first appeared in *Time* on April 12, 2021.

"For war you need courage . . .": Zelensky's statement appeared on his official Telegram account on March 26, 2021, and was cited in reports by Interfax-Ukraine and other outlets.

General Khomchak's speech before an extraordinary session of parliament and the ensuing debate appeared on the website of the Verkhovna Rada on March 30, 2021.

Sixty-three percent of respondents expressed distrust in Zelensky in a survey published on March 16, 2021, by the Razumkov Center.

Zelensky's phone call with Biden took place on April 2, 2021, according to a readout on the White House website.

"NATO is the only way . . .": Zelensky's remarks during the call with Jens Stoltenberg were reported by Reuters on April 6, 2021, citing a presidential statement.

"only make the situation worse": Kremlin spokesman Dmitry Peskov's statement to reporters appeared in a *Guardian* article on April 6, 2021.

RBC-Ukraine reported on March 16, 2021, that Zelensky's support in the polls had risen by a few points to 25 percent, citing the Razumkov Center's survey.

An account of my trip with Zelensky to the Donbas first appeared in *Time* on April 12, 2021.

Igor Bezler, the separatist commander known as the Demon, bragged about executions in an interview with Shaun Walker of *The Guardian* published on July 29, 2014.

An account of my meeting with the Russian fighter known as Babay first appeared in a dispatch in *Time* on April 23, 2014.

CHAPTER 15

The account of General Zaluzhny's appointment first appeared in my profile of him for *Time* on September 26, 2022, written in collaboration with my colleague Vera Bergengruen.

"The Armed Forces must develop . . .": General Zaluzhny gave his first public speech as commander-in-chief of the armed forces on August 22, 2021, at a military forum, "Ukraine 30. Defenders." It was live-streamed on YouTube.

"is very pompous and definitely not cheap . . .": Zelensky's remark about the tradition of military parades appeared in a short video on his Facebook page on July 9, 2019.

"What is a powerful country?": Zelensky's speech at the Independence Day parade appeared on the presidential website, along with a video of the parade, on August 24, 2021.

"It is possible and necessary . . .": Zaluzhny's remarks at the closed-door briefing appeared in the published accounts of the participants, including a Facebook post from Defense Ministry spokesman Oleksiy Hodzenko on September 28, 2021.

"We have been waiting . . .": Zelensky's remarks during the signing ceremony with Turkish engineer Haluk Bayraktar appeared on the presidential website on September 29, 2021.

Eado Hecht, "Drones in the Nagorno-Karabakh War: Analyzing the Data," *Military Strategy Magazine*, Volume 7, Issue 4, winter 2022, p. 31–37.

The *Kyiv Post* reported on Ukraine's first use of the Bayraktar TB2 in combat over the Donbas in a story published on October 27, 2021, featuring aerial video of the attack from the General Staff of the Armed Forces of Ukraine.

"Our fears are unfortunately being realized . . .": Kremlin spokesman Dmitry Peskov's comments about the drone strike were reported by Reuters on October 27, 2021.

"It is in this format that Ukraine . . .": Zelensky's comment on the drone strike appeared on the presidential website on October 29, 2021.

U.S. Secretary of State Antony Blinken met Zelensky on November 2, 2021, at a climate summit in Glasgow, Scotland, and warned him about the likelihood of an invasion, according to Blinken's comments to the *Washington Post*, published on August 16, 2022. Ukrainian officials who received these warnings at the time told me the Americans put the chance of an invasion at 75 to 80 percent.

"NATO needs to pack up its stuff . . .": Russian deputy foreign minister Sergei Ryabkov made this statement in an interview with state news agency TASS published on January 9, 2022.

"The gradualism of the past is out . . .": This remark from a senior Biden administration official first appeared in the *Time* cover story published on February 2, 2022, and reported with assistance from my colleagues in Washington, Brian Bennett, W.J. Hennigan, and Nik Popli.

Reuters reported on February 14, 2022, that oil prices had reached a seven-year high of nearly $100 per barrel on fears of a Russian invasion of Ukraine.

In early December, 20 percent of respondents in a nationwide survey said they were ready to vote for Zelensky for president, down from 23 percent in June, according to polling published by the Kyiv International Institute of Sociology.

Nearly half of respondents (49.5 percent) said the case against Poroshenko was an act of political persecution in a survey conducted on January 20 and 21 by the Kyiv International Institute of Sociology and published on its website.

"We see all this . . .": Zelensky commented on the charges against Poroshenko during a press briefing on December 21, 2021, a video of which was posted on the YouTube channel of NV.ua.

Carl Bildt, the former prime minister of Sweden, condemned the charges against Poroshenko as "clearly political" and "hugely damaging" to Ukraine's cohesion, according to his social media post on January 17, 2022.

"This ain't the *Titanic* . . .": This statement was made at Zelensky's press conference with foreign media on January 28, 2022, as reported by Reuters and on the presidential website.

CHAPTER 16

The General Staff announced the official start of the Blizzard-2022 exercises on February 8, 2022, in a statement on its social media accounts.

Minister of Defense Oleksiy Reznikov announced the arrival of 1,300 tons of U.S. military aid in a statement on social media on February 11, 2022.

Sky News reported the "quiet but notable build-up" of British military aid to Ukraine on January 20, 2022, including the 2,000 anti-tank missiles.

"Don't worry, sleep well . . .": Reznikov's comments in parliament made headlines around the world, including by the Associated Press, on January 25, 2022.

"Take a breath, calm down . . .": Zelensky's video message on the presidential website was ridiculed on January 24, 2022, in a scathing report on Ukraine's Channel 5, the network owned by Petro Poroshenko.

The "Keep calm and visit Ukraine" slogan appeared on January 27, 2022, on the website of the state tourism board.

"NATO has put its frontline forces . . .": Putin's famous speech to the Munich conference took place on February 10, 2007, and was published on the Kremlin website.

"It was here, fifteen years ago . . .": Zelensky's full speech can be found in a video on the presidential website from February 19, 2022.

"Just as there are no minor casualties . . .": Zelensky responded to Biden's remark about a "minor incursion" in a statement posted on social media on January 20, 2022.

"[NATO] completely ignore our protests . . .": Putin's speech appeared on the Kremlin website on February 21, 2022.

"There is no reason for you to have a sleepless night . . .": Zelensky's speech appeared on the presidential website shortly before three a.m. on February 22, 2022.

"If we sow chaos among people . . .": Zelensky made this statement in an interview with the *Washington Post* published on August 16, 2022.

"These are preventative measures . . .": Danilov's announcement of a state of emergency was streamed live from the presidential briefing room on February 23, 2022.

"Between us, there are more than two thousand kilometers . . .": Zelensky's speech to the Russian nation appeared on the presidential website on the eve of the invasion.

CHAPTER 17

The Associated Press investigation of the Russian airstrike on the theater in Mariupol, published on May 4, 2022, estimated that it killed 600 people inside and outside the building.

"to smoke the moles out of their holes": Eduard Basurin, a defense spokesman for the pro-Russian separatist fighters in Donetsk, appeared to call for the use of chemical weapons at Azovstal during an interview on Russian state television, according to a report published on April 12, 2022, in the *Kyiv Post*.

"a fly cannot get through.": Putin gave the order to seal off Azovstal during a meeting with his defense minister, a video of which was published on the Kremlin website on April 21, 2022.

"I didn't have the strength to do it.": General Zaluzhny recalled his conversation with the dead pilot's mother in an interview with the journalist Dmytro Komarov as part of the documentary series *Year. Off-screen,* which aired on May 12, 2023.

"Russian troops have begun . . .": Zelensky announced the start of the battle for Donbas in a speech on April 18, 2022, a video of which was posted on the presidential website.

"It is unfair that Ukraine is still forced . . .": Zelensky's address was posted on the presidential website on April 19, 2022.

The Institute for the Study of War reported in a battlefield assessment published on its website on May 14, 2022, that 485 Russian troops may have been killed and 80 pieces of military equipment destroyed under Ukrainian fire while trying to cross the Siversky Donets bridge a few days earlier.

Zelensky's casualty estimate for the battle of the Donbas—sixty to one hundred Ukrainian soldiers killed per day, and around five hundred wounded—appeared in his interview with Newsmax on May 31, 2022.

CHAPTER 18

"We want to see Russia weakened . . .": Lloyd Austin spoke on April 25, 2022, to a group of journalists, who were reportedly asked not to disclose their exact location in eastern Poland.

"Russia is failing . . .": Antony Blinken made the remark at the same televised briefing on April 25, 2022, standing beside Secretary Austin.

"We have opened up the pipes.": General Mark Milley made the remark on May 3, 2022, during testimony to the U.S. Senate Appropriations Committee's Subcommittee on Defense.

"I had to tell them to stop . . .": Zelensky described his wardrobe to Dmytro Komarov during a tour of his quarters on the fourth floor of the presidential compound that appeared in an episode of his documentary series *Year. Offscreen,* on February 24, 2023.

"We are resisting . . .": Ilya Yashin's letter appeared in *Time* on February 10, 2023, under the headline "A Message to the World from Inside a Russian Prison."

Reporters for the Ukrainian outlet Slidstvo.info got inside Medvedchuk's mansion and posted a video report about it on March 13, 2022.

"instinctively, we embraced": Jill Biden's recollection of meeting the First Lady of Ukraine appeared in a piece published in *Time* on April 13, 2023.

A profile of Olena Zelenska published in *The Guardian* on June 18, 2022, featured a photo of one of her passing encounters with her husband in the corridors of the presidential compound.

"Thank you for this TV date . . .": Olena Zelenska and the president granted a joint interview to *Piers Morgan Uncensored* that was posted on the program's YouTube channel on July 27, 2022.

CHAPTER 19

The account of Zelensky's train journey to southern Ukraine is based on my interviews with several of the participants and my experience traveling with the president a few months later on the same train to the southern front.

"We've been left on our own.": Denys Prokopenko's interview with *Ukrainska Pravda* was published on May 8, 2022.

Ukrainska Pravda reported on the secret survey commissioned by the office of the president in an article published on April 21, 2022, under the headline "Politics in a Time of War: How Zelensky Destroys Competitors."

Zelensky's approval ratings stood at 93 percent as of March 1, 2022, according to polls by the Rating Group.

At least three television channels, Espresso, Pryamiy and Channel 5, were taken off the air in April 2022, according to open letters of complaint the channels sent to the president's office at the time.

"We will not have enough money . . .": Arakhamia made the remark on August 22, 2022, during a forum for military veterans called "Defenders. Roll Call," which I attended in the auditorium beneath the Motherland Monument that day. A full video of the forum was later posted on the YouTube channel of the Ministry of Veterans Affairs.

An account of my interview with Olena Zelenska first appeared in *Time* on July 7, 2022.

"We grant citizenship and we take it away . . .": Zelensky made the remark about the revocation of Kolomoysky and Gennady Korban's passports during a public ceremony I attended on July 28, 2022, at the Mariyinsky Palace in Kyiv.

"We fucked up.": Oleksiy Arestovych made the remark about the failure to blow up the Chonhar bridge in a live-streamed interview on May 9, 2022, as reported by the Unian news agency and others.

"You are one of the destabilizers . . .": Zelensky's delivered his criticism of Savik Shuster, one of Ukraine's leading journalists, during a televised briefing on November 26, 2021, as reported by Unian and others.

CHAPTER 20

An account of my interview with General Zaluzhny appeared in a feature in *Time* on September 26, 2022, written in collaboration with Vera Bergengruen.

NBC News reported on October 31, 2022, that Biden had lost his temper with Zelensky during their June phone call, citing four people familiar with the call.

"The Ukrainians will not come out victorious . . .": Viktor Orban delivered this speech on July 23, during a visit to Romania, as reported by Radio Free Europe/Radio Liberty and others.

"We've been killing Russians . . .": Kyrylo Budanov made the remark in an interview with Yahoo News published on May 6, 2023.

"There are no limits . . .": Budanov in a televised interview with Dmytro Komarov for an episode of the documentary series *Year. Off-screen,* aired on May 19, 2023.

Vadym Skibitsky, the deputy head of the GUR, told Germany's *Welt* newspaper about the agency's assassination plans in an interview published May 25, 2023.

The *New York Times,* citing unnamed U.S. officials, reported on October 5, 2022, that U.S. intelligence agencies believe "parts of the Ukrainian government" ordered Darya Dugina's assassination.

"We should be aware that this week . . .": Zelensky issued this warning in his nightly video address on August 21, 2022, three days before Independence Day.

CHAPTER 21

"an organized effort to . . .": Russia's Defense Ministry announced the retreat from the Kharkiv region in a statement on September 10, 2022, as reported by Interfax and others.

"The pace is very important now . . .": Zelensky's call for more military aid amid the Kharkiv offensive appeared in a video address posted on the presidential website on September 19, 2022.

"long-term investments": The Biden administration announced the additional military aid to Ukraine in a statement posted on the State Department's website on September 8, 2022.

"In the last several days we've been dealt . . .": Russian pundit and political consultant Alexander Kazakov made the remark during a talk show on Russia's NTV channel posted on its website on September 9, 2022.

"I want the Kyiv authorities and their real masters . . .": Putin's annexation speech as published on the Kremlin website on September 30, 2022.

The *Moscow Times* reported on the assassinations of Russian-backed officials in the occupied territories in an article published on September 1, 2022.

Decree number 679 was posted on the presidential website on September 30, 2022.

"For our country today . . .": Zelensky rejected the idea of negotiations with Putin in an interview with German broadcaster ZDF aired on October 12, 2022.

Mykhailo Podolyak compared the encirclement of Russian troops at Lyman to the encirclement, eight years earlier, of Ukrainian forces at Ilovaisk, in a social media post on September 30, 2022, noting of the massacre at Ilovaisk: "Russia broke its word. The column was shot. Today [Russia] will have to ask for an exit from Lyman."

The *New York Times* on November 17, 2022, published a detailed reconstruction of the bombing of the Crimean bridge the previous month.

"We will not be broken by shelling . . .": Zelensky's speech beside the Iranian drone appeared in a video posted on the president's YouTube channel on October 27, 2022.

"unbridled stupidity": Igor Girkin issued his criticism of the prisoner swap in a post on his Telegram channel on September 22, 2022.

CHAPTER 22

The U.S. embassy in Kyiv announced the additional military aid package in a statement on its website on November 4, 2022, during Jake Sullivan's visit.

"He does not know what dignity and honesty are.": Zelensky's remarks about Putin appeared in a Reuters report published on October 4, 2022, the day Zelensky's ban on negotiations with Putin went into force.

"readiness for a just peace . . .": The Group of Seven statement appeared on the U.S. State Department's website on November 4, 2022.

"They continue to collect people . . .": Zelensky's speech after his meeting with Sullivan appeared on the presidential YouTube channel on the evening of November 4, 2022.

"Our little enemies will die . . .": Zelensky's remarks appeared in a video address on the presidential YouTube channel on November 9, 2022.

"I understand this is a very difficult decision . . .": Sergei Surovikin's statement on the withdrawal from Kherson appeared on various Russian propaganda outlets on November 9, 2022.

"The enemy does not give us any gifts.": Zelensky's cautious response to the withdrawal appeared in a video address on the presidential YouTube channel on November 9, 2022.

An account of my trip with Zelensky to Kherson appeared in *Time* on December 7, 2022.

"Ukrainian partners": Putin made the remark in a briefing with Russian media in Sochi on October 31, 2022, as reported on the Kremlin website.

"Even though Zelensky is the president . . .": Yevgeny Prigozhin made his comments in praise of Zelensky in a statement to reporters posted on the Vkontakte social media page of his catering company, Concord, on October 31, 2022, as reported by Moskovsky Komsomolets and other Russian media.

"When there's an opportunity to negotiate . . .": General Milley called for negotiations during an appearance at the Economic Club of New York on November 9, 2022, as reported by NPR and published on the ECNY's YouTube channel.

"Our goal is to liberate all Ukrainian land . . .": General Zaluzhny's response to calls for negotiations with Russia appeared in a readout of his phone call with General Milley posted on the official Facebook page of the Ukrainian General Staff on November 14, 2022.

EPILOGUE

The BBC reported on Zelensky's method of travel to the U.S. in an article published December 23, 2022, under the headline "How Did President Zelensky Get to Washington?"

"It's not the time to start a cult of personality.": Ihor Smelyansky, the postmaster general of Ukraine, recounted this incident to me in an interview.

Bild reported on the disagreement between Zelensky and Zaluzhny regarding the strategy in Bakhmut in an article published on March 6, 2023, under the headline "Selenskyj streitet mit wichtigstem General!" ("Zelensky Quarrels with Most Important General!")

"People want to see gratitude . . .": Ben Wallace's remarks were reported by the New York Times on July 12, 2023.